# THE ONE SHOW

# THE ONE SHOW

Judged To Be Advertising's Best Print, Radio, T.V. Volume 13
A Presentation of The One Club for Art & Copy

# THE ONE CLUB
# FOR ART & COPY

**ROBERT REITZFELD**
PRESIDENT

**MARY WARLICK**
DIRECTOR

**WENDY BECKER**
ONE SHOW MANAGER

**ALLAN BEAVER**
DESIGNER

**RYUICHI MINAKAWA**
ART DIRECTOR

**NAOMI MINAKAWA**
LAYOUT & PRODUCTION

**MARY WARLICK**
EDITOR

**MARK ATHERLAY**
**JOHN L. MIMS**
ASSISTANT EDITORS

**CAILOR/RESNICK**
COVER, DIVIDER PAGES
PHOTOGRAPHER

PUBLISHED AND DISTRIBUTED BY
RotoVision S.A.
Route Suisse 9
CH-1295 Mies
Switzerland
Telephone: 22-755-30-55
Fax: 22-755-40-72
IN ASSOCIATION WITH
The One Club for Art & Copy, Inc.
3 West 18th Street
New York, NY 10011
Telephone: (212) 255-7070
Fax: (212) 633-6950

Printed and Bound in Singapore.

# CONTENTS

# PRESIDENT'S MESSAGE

*ROBERT REITZFELD*

**T**he judging of this year's One Show took place in Phoenix, Arizona. At the Arizona Biltmore to be exact. Just what conspires to make an event like this perfect is beyond me. Certainly, we've been in more exotic locations (London, St. Maarten) and, certainly, world conditions have been more favorable (the on-going recession and the just-ended desert war). And yet this year's judging was, for me, as perfect as these often tedious events can get.

Perhaps it was the hotel itself, (a venerable landmark of the Frank Lloyd Wright school), primping like a fine show dog about to win Westminster. Perhaps it was the weather, 97 perfect degrees. Everyday. Perhaps it was the pool, stunningly beautiful, coolly inviting. Or the sunrises. Or the sunsets. Or the mountains outside our rooms.

Well, it was all of those things, but in the end it was the people. Twenty-five of the most talented people our industry has to offer sorting through 14,000 entries, to shape this year's One Show.

We worked hard. We laughed at some ads, groaned at others. We had a picnic in the desert, played trivia games, (Topper was Hopalong Cassidy's Horse), and sang songs around a campfire. We ate food with names we'd never heard before.

We got to know each other. We got to like each other. When the judging was over all of us had to leave, but most of us didn't want to. Sound silly? Sound like college? Well, I'm sorry you couldn't have been there.

# ONE SHOW JUDGES

**DAVID ABBOTT**
Abbott Mead Vickers. BBDO

**DAVID ALTSCHILLER**
Altschiller Reitzfeld/Tracy-Locke

**BILL BERENTER**
Berenter Greenhouse & Webster

**BILL BORDERS**
Borders Perrin & Norrander

**SIMON BOWDEN**
McCabe & Company

**BRYAN BUCKLEY**
Buckley DeCerchio Cavalier

**DIANE COOK-TENCH**
The Martin Agency

**TOM DeCERCHIO**
Buckley DeCerchio Cavalier

**NEIL DROSSMAN**
Campbell-Mithun-Esty

**JOY GOLDEN**
Joy Radio

**JEFFREY GOODBY**
Goodby Berlin & Silverstein

**DEAN HANSON**
Fallon McElligott

**NEIL LEINWOHL**
Korey Kay & Partners

**DAVID LUBARS**
Leonard Monahan Lubars & Partners

**TOM McELLIGOTT**
McElligott Wright Morrison White

**JARL OLSEN**
Fallon McElligott

**PETER RAUCH**
Ammirati & Puris

**ROBERT REITZFELD**
Altschiller Reitzfeld/Tracy-Locke

**SAM SCALI**
Scali McCabe Sloves

**JAMIE SELTZER**
Korey Kay & Partners

**MIKE TESCH**
Ally & Gargano

**BILL WESTBROOK**
Earle Palmer Brown

**DAN WIEDEN**
Wieden & Kennedy

# ONE CLUB MEMBERS

Mike Abadi
Jeffrey Abbott
David Abir
Dory Albert
Joe Alexander
Sabrina J. Alfin
Christine Aliferis
Jordan Allen
Peggy Allen
Carl Ally
Julie Almquist
Lauren Alpert
David Altschiller
Kevin Amter
Ron Anderson
Anthony Angotti
Sharon Appleman
Ricardo Archer
Arnold Arlow
Stephanie Arnold
Abigail Aron
Eric Aronin
Lorraine Arroll
Sharilyn Asbahr
Craig Astler
Mark Atherlay
John Athorn
Judith Atwood
Thomas Baginski
David Baldwin
Jeanine Barone
Linda Barone
Jamie Barrett
Bob Barrie
Clifford Beach
Judy Bean
Rhonda Beaudette-
  Lubow
Allan Beaver
Wendy Beck
Lisa Becker
I. Beery
Frank Bele
Ellen Bellamy deRosset
Gregg D. Benedikt
Mark Benzkofer
Danielle Berger
Sandra Berger
David Bernstein
George Betsis
Bruce Bildsten
Ann Billook

Margarite Birnbaum
Dawn Blaine
Richard Bloom
Ilan Blum
Heath Blumberg
Chris Bodden
William Borders
Michael Borst
Diana Bosniack
Simon Bowden
Doreen Bowens
Christine Boyer
Eric Bradley
Robert Braen
George Brianka
Eden Brody
Bill Brokaw
David Bromberg
Charles Bromley
Stephen Brophy
Nancy Brown Vecilla
Bryan Buckley
Carolyn Buonocore
Ron Burkhardt
Ed Butler
Larry Cadman
Neil Calet
Michael Callela
Elizabeth Callela
Roger Camp
Cathie Campbell
Bob Carducci
David Carlin
Barbara Carmack-
  Zammarchi
Susan Carroll
Janet Casey
Sonya Cashner
Stephanie Cassas
Javier Castillo
Carlos Castro
Koby Cauly
Gregory Cerny
Ronald Cesark
Alan Chalfin
William Champion
Cheryl Chapman
Larry Chase
Vincent Chieco
Marcia Christ
Tom Christmann
Richard Chung

Lisa Ciocci
Veta Ciolello
Perry Cirigliano
Eric Claussen
Cindy Cohen
Robert Cohen
Theodore Cohn
Kay Colmar Pullen
John Colquhoun
D.M. Conboy
Howard Conyack
Paul Cornacchini
David L. Corr
Colin Costello
Ed Cousineau
Jac Coverdale
Robert Cox
Josephine Craig
Lourdes Crespo
Joseph A. Crowley
Bob Culver
Roz Cundell
Greg Curran
Mary Lou Currier
Joanna D'Avanzo
Kim Dahlstrom
James Dale
Boris Damast
Patricia Darcey
Crystal Davenport
Jenny Davidson
Jean Davis
Rena De-Levie
Spencer Deadrick
Scott Decelles
Tom DeCerchio
Jay Deegan
Beth DeFuria
Peter Del Gandio
Jerry Della Femina
Frances DeLong
Dana DeLucia
Paula Dempsey
Salvatore DeStefano
Sal DeVito
Tad DeWree
Michael Dinitz
Angelo Dinoto
Greg DiNoto
Angela Dominguez
Winifred R. Donoghue
William Doody

Titiana Dordik
Penny Dorrance
Daniel J. Drexler
Claudia Dudley
Lorraine Duffy
Peggy Dunn
Laurence Dunst
Jim Durfee
Jackie DuSault
Charles Eaton
Phoebe Eaton
Abbe Eckstein
Stephen Edelman
Shannon Edwards
Arthur Einstein
Todd Eizikowitz
Daanish Ellias
Catherine Elliot
Andy Ellis
Lee Epstein
Brian Evans
Ann Farrell
Peter Fasth
Gene Federico
Doug Feinstein
Neil Feinstein
Barry Feldman
Jeremy Feldman
Roger Feldman
Bernadette Ferrara
Peggy Fields
Scott Finkelstein
Sylvia Finzi
Susan Fitzgerald
Paul Flaherty
Emily Fletcher
John Follis
Dawn Forrest
Susan Olivia Fowler
Michelle Frank
Katherine Frith
Ann Marie Funigiello
Jerry Fury
Tom Gabriel
Cristy Gaffney
Todd P. Gaffney
Bob Gage
Gary Gale
Andrea Gall
Alison Gardner
Amil Gargano
Lisa Garrone

John Gellos
Maria Germano
Robyn Gershberg
Randi Getz-Tessitore
Maria Giacchino
Gary Gianakis
Thomas Gianfagna
Dona Gibbs
Ed Giddens
Frank Ginsberg
Mark A. Girand
Susan Girolami
Robert Gloddy
Charles Goldman
Bruce Scott Goldstein
Mark Goldstein
Susan Golkin
Edward Gori
Milt Gossett
Bob Gouveia
Stella Grafakos
Emily Graff
Kerry Graham
Glenn S. Gray
John Greenberg
Sandy Greenberg
Debra Greene
Audrey Greenfield
Howard C. Greenstein
Tom Greenwald
Robin E. Greif
Dick Grider
Jeff Griffith
Steven Grimes
Brian Gross
Meg Learson Grosso
Roland Grybauskas
Bob Guy
Linda Haas
Carrie Haberman
Perry Hack
David Hackett
Matthew Hallock
Jim Hallowes
Ari Halper
Bryan J. Hammond
Dean Hanson
Sally Harley
Ronald Harper
Cabell Harris
Jay Harris
Karen E. Hawkins

Timothy Hayes
Suzanne Heckt
Barry Hedge
Brent Heindl
Bill Heinrich
John Heinsma
Kathleen Hennicke
Garnet Heraman
Roy Herbert
Madelyn Herschorn
Jennifer Hertslet
Rony Herz
Steve Herz
Ron Herzig
Allyson Heuwetter
Dawn Hibbard
Joan Hillman
Peter Hirsch
David Anthony
  Hoffman
Sally Hogshead
Leslie Hohnstreiter
Bill Hornstein
Laurence Horvitz
Tanya Hotton
Hugh Hough
David Hubbert
Mike Hughes
Stephen Hughes
Neal Hughlett
Lisa Hurwitz
Samantha Hurwitz
Kathy Ann Husten
Jon Iafeliece
David Incantalupo
Raffaella Isidori
George Jaccoma
Jennifer S.Jackman
Dick Jackson
Harry M. Jacobs, Jr.
Corrin Jacobsen
Dino Jalandoni
Stephan Jamilla
John Jarvis
Giulia Javorsky
Mickey Jenkins
Parker John
Amy Johnson
Anthony Johnson
Raymond Johnson
Senguella Johnson
Angelo Juliano

Phil Jungman
Karen Just
Sharla Kahan
Barbara Ann Kaplan
Diana Kaplan
Elissa A. Karp
Peter Katz
Woody Kay
Phillip L. Kellogg
Susan Kelly
Douglas Kim
Richard Kirshenbaum
Richard Klauber
Christopher Klein
Joe Knezic
Ronni Korn
Paula Korpalski
Renee Korus
Kimberly Sue Krause
Helmut Krone
Stuart Krull
Isabelle Kuriata
Galina Lachman
Larry Laiken
Mike LaMonica
Christopher J. Landi
Frank Landi
Robin G. Landis
Andy Langer
Anthony LaPetri
Mary Wells Lawrence
Diane Lazarus
Bruce Lee
Michael Lee
Ruth Lee
Joyce Lempel
Mitch Lemus
Dany Lee Lennon
Kevin Leonard
Margaret M. Leonard
Stanford Lerner
Mike Lescarbeau
James Lesser
Sharon Lesser
Diane Letulle
Robert Levenson
Susan Levine
Peter Leviten
David Levoy
Alexander Lezhen
Susan Lieber
Chris Lindau

David Lindberg
Katherine H. Lipsitz
Peter Lish
Wallace Littman
Margaret Livingston
Roger Livingston
George Lois
Brad Londy
Eric J. Lontok
Margaret Lubalin
Peter Lubalin
David Lubars
Steve A. Lubin
Lisa Lurie
Chuck Lustig
Tony Macchia
Louis Macino
Robert Mackall
Laurie Magee
David E. Mahoney
Jamie Mambro
Michael Mangano
Bradley Manier
Howard Margulies
John Mariucci
Amy Marks
Rodd Martin
Genevieve Martineau
Jim Marvy
D. Alex Matuszeski
Elizabeth Mauldin
Courtney Mayer
Scott McAfee
Ed McCabe
Kevin McCabe
Clem McCarthy
Ruth McCarthy
Kevin McCaul
Christopher McCormack
Tom McDonnell
Tom McElligott
Laura McFarland-
  Taylor
Alex McIntosh
Robin McIver
William B. McKenna
Paul McKittrick
Gordon McNenney
Rob McPherson
Suzanne P. McRoberts
Deborah Meier
Frank Merriam

Mario G. Messina
Tom Messner
David Metcalf
Lyle Metzdorf
Terri Meyer
Karen Micciantuono
Scott Michelson
Rick Midler
Don Miller
Jessica Miller
Josh Miller
Lawrence Miller
Thomas Miller
John Lane Mims
Jonathan L. Mindell
P. Todd Mitchell
Thomas J. Monahan
Steve Montgomery
Deborah Morrison
Regina Morrone
Dina Morrongiello
Jim Mountjoy
Stan Moy
Norman Muchnick
William Munch, Jr.
Edoardo Mungiello
Lynette Munich
Thomas Muratore, Jr.
Michael Musachio
Thomas Nathan
Ted Nelson
Thomas Nelson
Gary Neuwirth
Steve Nicholas
Jeff Nicosia
Angela Nitkin
Jennifer Noble
Dick O'Brien
Theresia O'Connor
Kevin O'Neill
Mark Oakley
David Oakley
Sharon L. Occhipinti
Rip Odell
Rafe Offer
David Ogilvy
Vicky Oliver
Peter Oravetz
Seymon Ostilly
Cele Otnes
Maxine Paetro
Joan Palmer

Kerri Palumbo
Azita Panahpour
Jeff Pappalardo
Elaine Paque
Anne M. Patanella
Joanne Pateman
Michael Pavone
Dante Pawels
Michael Paxton
Andrew Payton
Ron Pellegrino
Steven Penchina
John Perls
Susan Pettorino
David Piatkowski
Dallene Pierce
Christopher Pierro
Donna Pilch
Betsy Plevritis
Chris Pollock
Dean Polsky
Shirley Polykoff
Nandita Prakash
Jennifer Pretzeus
Tony Pucca
James Pyle
Elissa Querze
Brian Quinn
Rick Rabe
Lynda Raihofer
David Rakowiecki
Red Dog Films, Inc.
Edilsa Reilly
Robert Reitzfeld
Bill Replogle
Susan M. Resnick
David Reuss
Nancy Rice
Hope Rich
Bill Ringler
Tim Roan
Nancy Robbins
Phyllis Robinson
Jonathan Rodgers
Manny Rodriguez
Danielle Rogers
Courtney Rohan
Richard Rosenberg
Ron Rosenfeld
Robert G. Rosenthal
Stuart Rosenwasser
Tom Rost

Ippolita Rostagno
Mark Rothenberg
Carolyn A. Rothseid
Natan Rotmensz
Renee Rottenbucher
Steve Rotterdam
John Russo
Steve Russo
Mel Rustom
Mike Rylander
Norbert C. Saez
Paul Safsel
Steve Sage
Tracy Sage
Nelson Salis
Jonathan Saltzberg
Kenneth Sandbank
Jon Sandhaus
Bret Sanford-Chung
Jon Saunders
Joanne Scannello
Michael Scheiner
Glenn Scheuer
Scott Schindler
Agnes Schlenke
Robert Schnapp
Sy Schreckinger
Ruth Schubert
Jay Schulberg
Michael Schwabenland
Robert B. Schwartz
Paul Scolaro
Adam Seifer
Tod Seisser
Peter Sereny
Ted Shaine
Sherrie Shamoon
David Shane
Gary A. Shaw
Regina Sheahan
Steve Shearin
Joseph Sherlock
Michael Shetler
Brett Shevack
Edward Shieh
Bob Shiffrar
Harry M. Shilling
Kelvin L. Shiver
Constantine Shoukas
Dean Shoukas
Virgil Shutze
Tim Siedell

Fred Siegel
Larry Silberfein
Mark Silveira
Kate Silverberg
Anthony Siminerio
Leonard Sirowitz
Carolyn Slapikas
Mike Slosberg
Robert Slosberg
Dennis Smith
Hilary Smith
Linda Leigh Smith
Greg Sokil
Andrew Sokol
Richard Solomon
Dennis Soohoo
John A. Sowinski
Hazel Spector
Larry Spector
Mark Spector
Bill Speidell
Paul Spencer
Tracy Spinney
Helayne Spivak
Paige Elizabeth
   St. John
Pamela A. Stansel
Todd Stanton
Lynne Stark
Joe Stauppi
Scott Stefan
Dean Stefanides
Karl H. Steinbrenner
Michael Stocker
Bevin Stone
Lisette Sucari
Shunsaku Sugiura
Bob Sullivan
Christine Sullivan
E. Ski Sullivan
Luke Sullivan
Pamela Sullivan
James Robert
   Sullivan, Jr.
Jeffrey Supper
Robert Swartz
Joe Sweet
Leslie Sweet
John Sweney
Noriko Takabishi
Gary Tam
Arty Tan

Geraldine Tancredi
Norman Tanen
Craig Tanimoto
Ellen Tao
Thomas Tarulli
Jay Taub
Charlie Tercek
Mike Tesch
Alfred Tessier
Tom Thomas
Tommy Thompson
Elsebeth Thomsen
Sean Tierney
Muneharu Tokura
Garrett Tom
Guy Tom
Bill Tomlinson
Lori Travis
Wendy W. Tripp
Lynn Troncone
Michael Tubis
Rebecca Tudor-Foley
Vinny Tulley
Dion Tulloch
Anne Tum Suden
Carol Turturro
Rodney Underwood
Gerard Vaglio
Paul Venables
Paul Villacis
Michael Vitiello
Thomas Vogel
Ronald Wachino
Nina Wachsman
Elaine Wagner
Deena Wald
Judy Wald
Marvin Waldman
Matt Warhaftig
Alan Washa
Karen Wasserman
Peter Watson
Mary Webb
Les Weiner
Bill Westbrook
Tom White
Anne V. Whitney
Connie Whittington
Richard Wilde
Steve Williams
Claire Willms
Emil Wilson

Michael Wilson
Jennifer Winn
Greer Winston
Tom Witt
David Wojdyla
Stefen Wojnarowski
Lloyd Wolfe
David Wong
Adrienne T. Wright
H. Scott Wyatt
Elizabeth Wynn
Richard Yelland
Sue Yoder
John Young
Timi Young
Scott Zacaroli
Michelle Zadlock
Lisa Zaslow
Rainer Zierer

# RALPH AMMIRATI

**I**n a day and age when good enough passes for great, and passable is more than sufficient, Ralph Ammirati has based his career on a very simple philosophy; no second class anything, any time, any place.

How he maintains this quality is really quite simple. No detail escapes him. Even though he has enough laurels to rest on quite comfortably, he still looks at every director's reel, listens to every new music tape and tracks down new photographers with an unquenchable enthusiasm in his pursuit of perfection. I will admit as someone who worked for him and in some cases with him for over three years, perfection is not an easy thing for lesser mortals to achieve on a consistent basis. But for Ralph, we made the extra effort. "Will Ralph like it?" was the question, and "Ralph liked it!" was the ultimate goal. However, he isn't any harder or more demanding of any of his writers and art directors than he is of himself.

Over the years Ralph has fought valiantly, sometimes violently, but always successfully to maintain the standard of excellence and attention to detail that few people today have the persistence or the patience to carry on. And it shows in every facet of his life, personal as well as professional.

While usually used to describe Waterford Crystal (an Ammirati & Puris client), there is one line that best describes Ralph Ammirati's style: steadfast in a world of wavering standards.

*HELAYNE SPIVAK*
New York 1991

Traveling for a living is no way to live.

HERTZ 1967

AFTER 209 YEARS OF MAKING FINE VERMOUTH, AMERICANS HAVE COME TO KNOW AND LOVE US FOR OUR ASHTRAYS.

CINZANO 1967

MR. FERRARI DRIVES A FIAT.

FIAT 1971

NEW YORK RACING ASSOCIATION 1963

HERTZ "POOR SOUL" 1967

HERTZ "WE TRY HARDER" 1966

FIAT "STUNT DRIVER" 1973

SCHWEPPES "UNCOMPROMISING" 1990

BMW "CROSSWINDS" 1990

# TOM McELLIGOTT

**I**t must feel great to be elected to the Creative Hall of Fame.

I guess the next best thing would be to work with one who was.

I did, and it was. Great, I mean.

It was 1971 when a young Tom McElligott came in to see me with a book fresh out of Dayton's department store. The ads were expected retail stuff with the exception of several ads for an Episcopalian summer camp.

The kid showed promise. I took a chance. It was a chance that paid off in spades.

I like to say I taught Tom everything he knows, but not everything I know. The truth, however, is that I learned more from him than he possibly could learn from me.

Tom McElligott was and is a driven man. A man with a passion for excellence. A man whose uncompromising dedication to his craft has brought him to the pinnacle of our business.

I saw in him a rare combination of insight, instinct and intelligence. Over the ten years at Bozell, he refined and honed his skills to the point where he was ready for his first entrepreneurial challenge.

In 1981, he left with Nancy Rice to join Pat Fallon in a venture which was to make advertising history and make Tom McElligott one of the most talked about and emulated writers in history.

In 1988, he left Fallon McElligott and one year later joined Chiat Day.

But, the incredible draw of entrepreneurship brought him back to Minneapolis and the beginning of a new agency, McElligott Wright Morrison White.

Where he continues to write history.

*RON ANDERSON*
New York 1991

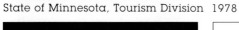

We admit that
there are times in Minnesota
when our lakes become
overcrowded.

Every spring it happens.
Flocks of geese and ducks, weary from winging their way north, stop to rest awhile in the splendid solitude of Minnesota's lakes and rivers and ponds.

And some, each year, decide to fly no further north, but to remain in this enchanted land of rolling woods and peaceful waters.

So it is, too, with the visitors who come each year. They find not only the stunning scenery for which Minnesota has long been known, but also a people who are as warm and open as the Minnesota summer itself.

They find not just the abundant fishing and camping and swimming they expected to find, but also a rich array of superb theater, fine restaurants, elegant shopping,

and major league sports that they perhaps hadn't expected to find.

As the days pass, they find the cares and worries they brought with them disappear, replaced with a renewed spirit and energy.

And for some, each year, the temptation to remain proves too strong. But even those who must leave promise themselves that they will return again next year.

Just as the geese and ducks.

Yes, I'm interested in discovering more about what's in a Minnesota vacation for me. Please send me your free Vacation Guide.

Name
Address
City
State          Zip

Write to: State of Minnesota
Division of Tourism, Box 837
Minneapolis, MN 55440

## Minnesota
Lakes. And a whole lot more.

State of Minnesota, Tourism Division  1978

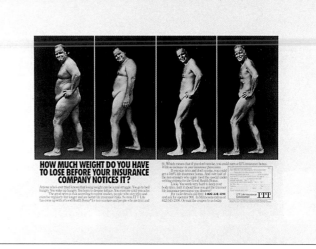

**HOW MUCH WEIGHT DO YOU HAVE TO LOSE BEFORE YOUR INSURANCE COMPANY NOTICES IT?**

ITT Life  1983

In the church
started by a man
who had six wives,
forgiveness goes
without saying.

The Episcopal Church

The Episcopal Church  1985

"This rug is beautiful.
Where can I find more?" I said.
"Have you ever
ridden a camel?" He replied.

bloomingdale's

Bloomingdale's  1987

Mr. Coffee 1982

You put it on with your hands,   now take it off with your hands.

AMF  1984

## Compromise is for politicians.

Porsche  1988

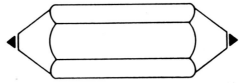

GOLD, SILVER & BRONZE AWARDS

# IN ONE AMERICAN STATE, THE PENALTY FOR EXPOSING YOURSELF IS DEATH.

In the winter of 1968, Mount Washington in New Hampshire was the unlucky recipient of 566 inches of snowfall. Or to put it another way, that's just a little over forty-seven feet.

Snowstorms with winds in excess of a hundred miles an hour are not uncommon. Which makes the wind-chill factor too cold to measure with existing instruments.

The weatherman simply warns that at times like these, exposed flesh freezes instantly.

Some of the old folks in the state can recall the time in '34, when the Mountain was the site of the strongest wind gust ever recorded on earth: 231 mph.

They can recite articles from the local paper, The Littleton Courier, about hikers freezing to death up there in the middle of summer.

And they'll tell you, in no uncertain terms, that it's less important to dress according to the latest fashion than it is to dress according to the latest weather report.

It is this almost inbred respect for nature's wrath that compels the people at Timberland in Hampton, New Hampshire to design their outdoor clothing the way they do.

This clothing is ideal for people who venture outdoors regardless of the forecast and who pride themselves on being ready for the worst.

Take, for example, our Timberland leather coats. The leather is the best you can find, because it's the best we can find.

To get hides that meet our standards, we travel the world looking for sources of supply. A search made more difficult by our insistence on hides from animals raised on the open range. While that may sound pernickety, you'll never see scarring from barbed wire on a Timberland coat.

But we're not just concerned about how our hides are treated while they're raised. We also give them special treatment once we get them back to our workshops.

All the leathers used by Timberland get a dunking in chemical agents for water repellency. Then, to keep them looking new in any kind of weather, we give them special finishes that will never wear off.

When we use Split Suede, for instance, we give it a light-resistant finish to avoid fading. So it's not only rainproof, but sunproof, as well.

As for our Weatherguard Newbuck leather, it's given a unique chrome-tan finish so it stays supple throughout its life.

Partial as Timberland is to leathers like Newbuck and Split Suede, we realise that man cannot live by leather alone.

Which is why in some Timberland outerwear we use Gore-Tex, a man-made fabric with over nine billion pores per square inch. These microscopic openings are too small to let water in, yet large enough for perspiration molecules to get out.

Once we have the right materials in place, we start sewing coats that will last year after year after year.

On the coat you see here, we double stitch the seams that will be exposed to the heaviest wear. We run a pull cord through the waist of the coat to keep cold air from creeping up underneath. And we fit zippers of solid brass, so they'll never rust.

Since people who wear Timberland coats often venture off the beaten path, we've also taken special care that the pockets won't get torn in heavy brush. Each one is closed up with a thick leather cover and secured by buttons made from brass and bone.

And to make sure you never end up looking for those buttons in the woods (worse than looking for a needle in a haystack), we use heavy cord thread and reinforce each one on the backside with quarter-inch guards.

The finished product is a coat that will protect you from cold, wet and, on one of its more hospitable days, perhaps even the Mountain itself.

But it's not just outerwear that Timberland makes to last. Our clothing range also includes the kind of things you might wear when the temperature soars to above freezing.

Starting with stalwarts like wool, denim, canvas and cotton, Timberland makes a range that's always at home in the wild. Sweaters, trousers, jackets and shirts, even the duffle bags to carry them in.

Each item designed to withstand the twin tests of weather and time.

Of course, if you own a pair of our boots or shoes, you're already familiar with the unique way Timberlands hold together.

What you may not know is why they do.

We tape seal the seams of some of our boots with latex to make sure water can't get through to your feet.

We impregnate our shoe and boot leather with silicone, to give it a longer life. We sew in doubleknot pearl stitching that won't come undone even if it's accidentally cut. We use self oiling laces that won't rot, and solid brass eyelets that won't rust.

The list, like the winters up on Mount Washington, goes on and on.

Suffice to say that at Timberland, making outdoor clothing and boots is not just a way of life. It's a way of living.

Timberland (UK) Limited, Unit Four, St. Anthony's Way, Feltham, Middlesex. TW14 0NH. Telephone 081 890 6116.

**1 GOLD**

# FROM THE DAYS WHEN MEN WERE MEN. AND SO WERE THE WOMEN.

The old West was definitely no place for wimps and faint hearts.

Those foolhardy enough to go in search of Eldorado were hard-bitten, unfeeling brutes who often had to wrestle with wild animals for their food, build entire cabins with the most rudimentary of tools and had to dispatch Apaches with their bare hands on a daily basis.

The men were pretty tough too.

Yes, as the history books show, it was women who were America's true pioneers.

While the menfolk went buffalo hunting and killing, gold-mining and killing or sometimes just shooting and wounding, the girls were left to fend for themselves in the wilderness for months on end.

And exactly what kind of fending was involved?

Well, they made almost everything they stood up in except, ironically, their boots.

This particular item of clothing proved beyond even their resourcefulness. Which is totally understandable.

In these circumstances, footwear needed to be tough and long-lasting, though not so heavy that it could be thought unlady-like. Most important of all, their boots had to keep out the rain and snow of the appalling prairie winters.

A tall order. One that even today would be hard to fill.

And while those intrepid womenfolk had to trek for days to their local trading post to obtain such a pair of boots, their descendants are more fortunate. All they have to do is buy a pair of boots made by Timberland.

For enshrined in all our boots are the very same qualities that helped those brave women slog gamely across America.

Naturally, the materials we use today are a little less, shall we say, rustic than in those days.

You only have to compare the leathers we have at our disposal today with the rather limited choice they had.

Their rawhide was often just that, with an odour which was not at all helpful to relationships with menfolk.

Our hides, on the other hand, are hand-picked from tanneries across the country who pride themselves on making strong, durable leathers soft and supple.

Understandably, a woman abandoned in uncharted Indian territory would not have been overly concerned about the colour scuffing or flaking off her boots.

Or whether, indeed, the degree of water repellency was all it was cracked up to be.

(When women were out pioneering, such things were not exactly top of the agenda.)

Way up in the wilds of Hampton, New Hampshire, however, this is precisely the kind of thing our craftsmen worry about constantly.

Which is why immediately the leathers are brought to the workshops, we dye them right through, then impregnate them with silicone oils.

Not only does this preserve the colour of the boot after years of wear, it also acts as a seal against the elements.

Looking back, it is difficult to understand why the early settlers didn't stop a passing Red Indian and enquire as to the precise method employed in the making of their footwear.

Certainly, it is now acknowledged that the original moccasin design was uniquely comfortable.

Which is exactly the reason we utilise the wraparound construction, using one piece of leather, for all our boots and shoes.

Of course, however warm and comfortable we make the actual boot, if water gets in all our painstaking handiwork counts for nothing.

Let us put your mind (and feet) at ease.

Unlike the womenfolk who blazed the Oregon Trail, you won't have to worry about the occasional deluge or ten foot snowdrift.

The boot in our picture is, for example, guaranteed 100% waterproof.

First, we sew each boot with a high strength nylon yarn, using a double knot, pearl stitch. Then, we seal each seam with not one but two coats of latex. Add a Gore-Tex inner bootie, glove leather lining and a soft padded collar and the boot becomes positively luxurious.

Although just to make absolutely certain your feet never have to encounter the kind of hardship that caused many a pioneer woman to die with her boots on, we didn't stop there.

The midsole is stitched to a lightweight polyurethane mini-lug outsole after which it is bonded to the upper.

No doubt all those hardy travel-weary females who opened up the West could have done with a pair or two of our boots. Or some clothes from our new womens' Weathergear outdoor collection.

Even one of our bags or a belt would have come in handy.

But then they might have looked like women, the men would have stayed home and the wild West would still be wild to this day.

Timberland (UK) Limited, Unit Five, St. Anthony's Way, Feltham, Middlesex. TW14 0NH.

THE NEW 'DAW' WOMENS' BOOT

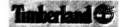

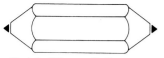

Gold, Silver, & Bronze
Awards

**CONSUMER NEWSPAPER
OVER 600 LINES: SINGLE**

**3 SILVER**
**ART DIRECTOR**
Bill Schwab
**WRITER**
Dean Buckhorn
**PHOTOGRAPHERS**
Michael Pohuski,
National Archives
**CLIENT**
Bunker Hill PX
**AGENCY**
Earle Palmer Brown/
Bethesda

**4 BRONZE**
**ART DIRECTOR**
Ron Brown
**WRITER**
David Abbott
**TYPOGRAPHER**
Joe Hoza
**CLIENT**
The Economist
**AGENCY**
Abbott Mead Vickers
BBDO/London

**5 BRONZE**
**ART DIRECTOR**
Gary Marshall
**WRITER**
Paul Marshall
**PHOTOGRAPHER**
John Claridge
**CLIENT**
Nationwide
**AGENCY**
Leagas Delaney/London

Ahhh, those were the days. Roosevelt was in the White House. Rita Hayworth was in the movies. And Detroit was actually building something that worried the Japanese.

They were called Sherman Tanks. And with turret-mounted machine guns and 75-mm cannons, these babies could blow the doors (and

# Relive the days when the Japanese actually worried about what rolled out of Detroit.

everything else) off a Nissan Sentra. It was an exciting time in America. And now it's possible to recapture some of that excitement. At Bunker Hill surplus.

Every shelf is piled high with the spoils of war. You'll find stack after stack of authentic military clothing.

From the tiger-stripe camouflage of Nam to the olive-drab fatigues of the Second World War.

And that's just the beginning. We've got plenty of accessories. Boots, hats, canteens, mess kits, camping gear. And, for you die-hard soldiers, we've

even got a dog tag machine right here in the store.

You won't find a military clothing collection like this anywhere else. So stop by

Bunker Hill soon. To shop. Or just to browse around.

And relive the days when American technology wasn't just beating the rest of the world. It was blowing them away.

**Bunker Hill PX**
*1711 Laurel Bowie Road, Laurel, MD (301) 776-7870*

3 SILVER

# It's lonely at the top, but at least there's something to read.

**The Economist**

# There's only one problem with introducing tax free savings. Rod Stewart will come home.

It's enough to make any tax exile book their passage home.

From January 1st 1991, you can open a new five year tax free savings account called TESSA.

At Nationwide, unlike most other building societies, we are offering a choice of TESSAs: A Flexible Savings Plan or a Bond Account.

The Flexible Savings Plan lets you invest as much as you want, when you want. You can save from £25 up to £3,000 in the first year and up to £1,800 in each of the following four years, provided your total investment doesn't exceed £9,000.

Whereas with the Bond, you invest a lump sum of between £3,000 and £9,000 and we automatically feed the maximum permitted amount into your TESSA each year.

In return, the Bond pays a remarkable 14.00% pa tax free. Whilst the Flexible Savings Plan has five tiered rates ranging from 13.50% to 14.00% pa tax free. (Now don't you think that's sexy).

And with the special bonuses we're offering, it is possible to earn even higher rates.

For further information call into your nearest branch of Nationwide. After all, TESSA is excellent news for taxpayers. Even if it's not such good news for mothers with beautiful blonde daughters.

**Nationwide**
The Nation's Building Society.

# IN ONE AMERICAN STATE, THE PENALTY FOR EXPOSING YOURSELF IS DEATH.

In the winter of 1968, Mount Washington in New Hampshire was the unlucky recipient of 566 inches of snowfall. Or to put it another way, that's just a little over forty-seven feet.

Snowstorms with winds in excess of a hundred miles an hour are not uncommon. Which makes the wind-chill factor too cold to measure with existing instruments.

The weatherman simply warns that at times like these, exposed flesh freezes instantly.

Some of the old folks in the state can recall the time in '34, when the Mountain was the site of the strongest wind gust ever recorded on earth: 231 mph.

They can recite articles from the local paper, The Littleton Courier, about hikers freezing to death up there in the middle of summer.

And they'll tell you, in no uncertain terms, that it's less important to dress according to the latest fashion than it is to dress according to the latest weather report.

It is this almost inbred respect for nature's wrath that compels the people at Timberland in Hampton, New Hampshire to design their outdoor clothing the way they do.

This clothing is ideal for people who venture outdoors regardless of the forecast and who pride themselves on being ready for the worst.

Take, for example, our Timberland leather coats. The leather is the best you can find, because it's the best we can find.

To get hides that meet our standards, we travel the world looking for sources of supply. A search made more difficult by our insistence on hides from animals raised on the open range. While that may sound pernickety, you'll never see scarring from barbed wire on a Timberland coat.

But we're not just concerned about how our hides are treated while they're raised. We also give them special treatment once we get them back to our workshops.

All the leathers used by Timberland get a dunking in chemical agents for water repellency. Then, to keep them looking new in any kind of weather, we give them special finishes that will never wear off.

When we use Split Suede, for instance, we give it a light-resistant finish to avoid fading. So it's not only rainproof, but sunproof, as well.

As for our Weatherguard Newbuck leather, it's given a unique chrome-tan finish so it stays supple throughout its life.

Partial as Timberland is to leathers like Newbuck and Split Suede, we realise that man cannot live by leather alone.

Which is why in some Timberland outerwear we use Gore-Tex, a man-made fabric with over nine billion pores per square inch. These microscopic openings are too small to let water in, yet large enough for perspiration molecules to get out.

Once we have the right materials in place, we start sewing coats that will last year after year after year.

On the coat you see here, we double stitch the seams that will be exposed to the heaviest wear. We run a pull cord through the waist of the coat to keep cold air from creeping up underneath. And we fit zippers of solid brass, so they'll never rust.

Since people who wear Timberland coats often venture off the beaten path, we've also taken special care that the pockets won't get torn in heavy brush. Each one is closed up with a thick leather cover and secured by buttons made from brass and bone.

And to make sure you never end up looking for those buttons in the woods (worse than looking for a needle in a haystack), we use heavy cord thread and reinforce each one on the backside with quarter-inch guards.

The finished product is a coat that will protect you from cold, wet and, on one of its more hospitable days, perhaps even the Mountain itself.

But it's not just outerwear that Timberland makes to last. Our clothing range also includes the kind of things you might wear when the temperature soars to above freezing.

Starting with stalwarts like wool, denim, canvas and cotton, Timberland makes a range that's always at home in the wild. Sweaters, trousers, jackets and shirts, even the duffle bags to carry them in.

Each item designed to withstand the twin tests of weather and time.

Of course, if you own a pair of our boots or shoes, you're already familiar with the unique way Timberlands hold together.

What you may not know is why they do.

We tape seal the seams of some of our boots with latex to make sure water can't get through to your feet.

We impregnate our shoe and boot leather with silicone, to give it a longer life. We sew in doubleknot pearl stitching that won't come undone even if it's accidentally cut. We use self oiling laces that won't rot, and solid brass eyelets that won't rust.

The list, like the winters up on Mount Washington, goes on and on.

Suffice to say that at Timberland, making outdoor clothing and boots is not just a way of life. It's a way of living.

Timberland (UK) Limited, Unit Four, St. Anthony's Way, Feltham, Middlesex. TW14 0NH. Telephone 081 890 6116.

**Timberland**

# THE PENTAGON. AMERICA'S LAST DEFENCE AGAINST COMMUNISM, TYRANNY AND BUNIONS.

Left, right. Left, right. Left, right.

Multiply this simple leg exercise a few thousand times and you can begin to imagine what square-bashing in a new pair of US army boots does to a young man's feet.

Or can you?

Contrary to the myth, the army boot is not an instrument of torture used to initiate raw recruits.

In fact, such is the concern for the feet of men under their command that the US military issues standards for their standard issue boots.

Very high standards they are too.

The boots have to be tough and durable, naturally. They also have to be waterproof and the leather has to be flexible. In other words, the US army boot has to be an efficient part of the soldier's equipment.

Out in civvy street, few boot makers even try to match the exacting standards laid down by the Pentagon.

Up in the small town of Hampton, New Hampshire, however, there's a company that believes their boots are every bit as good as the army's.

And what's more they'll fight any man who says different.

The company is called Timberland.

To make their point, all leathers destined to become Timberland boots are subjected to a machine known as a MaserFlex.

It's designed to test just how long leathers remain waterproof in extreme circumstances.

Only if hides can withstand a minimum of 15,000 flexes can they be passed as equal to the highest standards demanded (and we mean demanded), by the US military.

Naturally, all our boots pass muster.

Only by testing the leathers in this way can we be sure that your feet won't suffer ailments caused by less well made boots.

(No less an authority than Blake's Medical Dictionary blames bunions on ill-fitting footwear in general and short or cramped boots in particular. We couldn't agree more.)

Of course, our concern for the well-being of your feet isn't left solely in the hands of a machine.

Even though we might not have quite the same budget as the Pentagon (theirs was two hundred and sixty nine thousand, nine hundred and eighty one million dollars in the fiscal year October 1989 to October 1990) we probably spend more on our hides than they do on theirs.

How come?

Remember, army boots are free. Whereas

we expect our customers to invest a small fortune for a pair of Timberlands.

So we're just plain picky on their behalf.

We trek all round the country in search of tanneries that can meet our ridiculously high standards.

When we find one, we simply pay what it takes to bring every hide in the place back to Hampton.

(When the comfort of your feet is at stake, we never argue over nickels and dimes.)

We insist on premium, full grain leathers and nothing less. A rare oxhide leather called Norwegian Krymp is a particular favourite.

Back in the workshops, we dye the leathers right through. This ensures that the colour will not scuff off or crack up even under the strain of the longest march.

We could paint the colour on like other manufacturers do but pretty soon it would get a bit flaky, not unlike the manufacturers themselves.

It's at this stage of the process that we soak the leathers in silicone oil.

Impregnating them in this way keeps them supple. It also ensures that water can't seep through and give your feet a real soaking.

Rest assured, the only way you are going to get soaked with our boots is when you fork out the money for a pair.

Now you may be asking yourself if the Army can afford to give their boots away free, why on earth are ours so darned expensive?

Blame the gnarled hands and nimble fingers of the old boys who put our uppers together.

The kind of craftsmanship that can mould one piece of leather on a special geometric last doesn't come cheap.

And we'd always contend that fingers that can sew better than a machine are certainly

worth shelling out a little extra for.

Mind you, while your wallet may be taking a pounding, you can take some comfort from the fact that, unlike the army, we have a policy of pampering your feet.

To make absolutely sure snow and rain can't get in, the midsoles are injection moulded to the base, creating a waterproof seal with the rubber lug sole.

A cushioned inner sole is then inserted to keep your feet snug and warm.

This is made from soft glove leather or high performance Cambrelle. Likewise those collars you get on most of our boots.

Aside from providing extra comfort, these padded collars follow the form of your ankle to help to stop the elements sneaking in.

Meanwhile, inside the boot we usually insulate the tongue, shaft and quarter with Thinsulate and the toe with Ensolite.

And we invariably add a Gore-Tex lining for good measure.

This remarkable man-made fabric has 9 billion pores per square inch, each one 20,000 times smaller than a raindrop but 700 times larger than a molecule of perspiration. As a result, your feet can actually breathe.

But just in case your feet get too cosy in there, most of our boots are fitted with a special removable polypropylene insole to absorb any excess perspiration.

What of the good old army boot? Haven't there been any concessions to the warmth and comfort to be found in a pair of Timberlands?

No sir. None at all, sir.

The US military may have finally defeated the bunion but a soldier's boot still has to live in pretty spartan surroundings.

And that, soldier, is an order.

THE TAN BUCK BOOT

**Timberland** ®

---

# FROM THE DAYS WHEN MEN WERE MEN. AND SO WERE THE WOMEN.

The old West was definitely no place for wimps and faint hearts.

Those foolhardy enough to go in search of Eldorado were hard-bitten, unfeeling brutes who often had to wrestle with wild animals for their food, build entire cabins with the most rudimentary of tools and had to dispatch Apaches with their bare hands on a daily basis.

The men were pretty tough too.

Yes, as the history books show, it was women who were America's true pioneers.

While the menfolk went buffalo hunting and killing gold-mining and killing or sometimes just shooting and wounding, the girls were left to fend for themselves in the wilderness for months on end.

And exactly what kind of fending was involved?

Well, they made almost everything they stood up in except, ironically, their boots.

This particular item of clothing proved beyond even their resourcefulness. Which is totally understandable.

In these circumstances, footwear needed to be tough and long-lasting, though not so heavy that it could be thought unlady-like. Most important of all, their boots had to keep out the rain and snow of the appalling prairie winters.

A tall order. One that even today would be hard to fill.

And while those intrepid womenfolk had to trek for days to their local trading post to obtain such a pair of boots, their descendants are more fortunate. All they have to do is buy a pair of boots made by Timberland.

For enshrined in all our boots are the very same qualities that helped those brave women slog gamely across America.

Naturally, the materials we use today are a little less, shall we say, rustic than in those days.

You only have to compare the leathers we have at our disposal today with the rather limited choice they had.

Their rawhide was often just that, with an odour which was not at all helpful to relationships with menfolk.

Our hides, on the other hand, are handpicked from tanneries across the country who

pride themselves on making strong, durable leathers soft and supple.

Understandably, a woman abandoned in uncharted Indian territory would not have been overly concerned about the colour scuffing or flaking off her boots.

Or whether, indeed, the degree of water repellency was all it was cracked up to be.

(When women were out pioneering, such things were not exactly top of the agenda.)

Way up in the wilds of Hampton, New Hampshire, however, this is precisely the kind of thing our craftsmen worry about constantly.

Which is why immediately the leathers are brought to the workshops, we dye them right through, then impregnate them with silicone oils.

Not only does this preserve the colour of the boot after years of wear, it also acts as a seal against the elements.

Looking back, it is difficult to understand why the early settlers didn't stop a passing Red Indian and enquire as to the precise method employed in the making of their footwear.

Certainly, it is now acknowledged that the original moccasin design was uniquely comfortable.

Which is exactly the reason we utilise the wraparound construction, using one piece of leather, for all our boots and shoes.

Of course, however warm and comfortable we make the actual boot, if water gets in all our painstaking handiwork counts for nothing.

Let us put your mind (and feet) at ease.

Unlike the womenfolk who blazed the Oregon Trail, you won't have to worry about the occasional deluge or ten foot snowdrift.

The boot in our picture is, for example, guaranteed 100% waterproof.

First, we sew each boot with a high strength nylon yarn, using a double knot, pearl stitch. Then, we seal each seam with not one but two coats of latex. Add a Gore-Tex inner bootie, glove leather lining and a soft padded collar and the boot becomes positively luxurious.

Although just to make absolutely certain your feet never have to encounter the kind of hardship that caused many a pioneer woman to die with her boots on, we didn't stop there.

The midsole is stitched to a lightweight polyurethane mini-lug outsole after which it is bonded to the upper.

No doubt all those hardy travel-weary females who opened up the West could

THE NEW 'DAM' WOMENS' BOOT

have done with a pair or two of our boots.

Or some clothes from our new womens' Weathergear outdoor collection.

Even one of our bags or a belt would have come in handy.

But then they might have looked like women, the men would have stayed home and the wild West would still be wild to this day.

Timberland (UK) Limited, Unit Five, St. Anthony's Way, Feltham, Middlesex. TW14 0NH.

**Timberland** ®

# Develop a nose for business. Bury it in The Economist.

# You can tell an Economist reader by the company he owns.

# It's lonely at the top, but at least there's something to read.

The Economist

# TIMBERLAND GIVES YOU BACK THE COAT FOUR MILLION YEARS OF EVOLUTION TOOK AWAY.

There was a time when Man could venture into the wilderness clad in nothing but the coat God gave him.

But that was quite a while ago.

Sometime during the Lower Paleolithic Era, Homo Erectus became a creature of the great indoors. The thick hair that once covered his entire body was gone, and in its place came a man-made imitation.

Hampered by a brain the size of a walnut, man's earliest attempts at outdoor clothing were, needless to say, somewhat primitive.

Fortunately, however, our species has continued to evolve, and today can produce coats that protect us when the need for food, recreation and a disposable income forces us outside our central heated caves.

At a company called Timberland, in Hampton, New Hampshire, we design outerwear whose natural practicality rivals the coats our animal relatives were born with. Coats that provide shelter from howling wind, pelting rain and mornings as cold as an ice age.

Witness our Timberland leather coats.

They're made from the best hides we can find, and believe us, we spend a lot of time looking.

We insist upon cowhides from the open range, to avoid ugly nicks from barbed wire fences. Which means we often have to travel as far as other continents in order to find a supply that meets our standards.

We use two styles of leather on our outerwear at Timberland, Split Suede, and in the coat you see here, Weatherguard Newbuck.

Each is given a thorough dunking in waterproofing agents before getting a special finish to protect its suppleness and colour.

But we make more than leather coats that will help to keep you dry in the rain.

In other Timberland outerwear, we use a material that keeps you free of perspiration.

To let these coats 'breathe' (just like the ones Mother Nature used to make) we include a layer of Gore-Tex. This man-made fabric, with over nine billion pores per square inch, allows moisture to escape from your body, but remains waterproof.

Of course, we wouldn't take all this trouble finding perfect materials only to turn around and make a coat that doesn't last.

To make doubly certain a Timberland Trenchcoat holds together, we double stitch the seams that will be exposed to the heaviest

wear, a practice that's all but extinct today.

On other Timberland coats, we overstitch many seams to prevent wind and rain from penetrating the tiny holes left behind by our sewing needles.

The result is outerwear that leaves Man as well adapted to the outdoors as he's been in millions of years.

Our sturdy coats are just one example of the Timberland Clothing range, albeit a good one, since everything we make is built to last you for aeons.

Using workhorses like canvas, cotton, wool and denim, Timberland puts together sweaters, shirts and trousers, even the duffle bags to carry them in. And since practical clothing doesn't ever seem to go out of fashion, you'll be able to wear them season after season.

Naturally, if you own a pair of Timberland boots or shoes, you're already familiar with the way we do things.

You may know, for example, that we impregnate the leather of all Timberland footwear with silicone to give it a longer life and to keep your feet dry no matter what.

That we pre-stretch our leathers on a special geometric last to keep them from cracking with time.

And that seams on many Timberland boots are sealed twice with latex, because that's the only method sure to keep the water out.

The truth is, here at Timberland, we wouldn't really know how to go about things any other way.

We've even gone as far as to find a machine that can test our waterproof leathers better than we ever could by hand. It's called a Maser Flex, and it helps us make sure that our leathers will withstand 15,000 flexes. Which, by the way, is equal to the highest standard demanded by the U.S. Military.

But while we admit that our practices may seem a little obsessive, there is method to our madness.

We use solid brass eyelets in our boots, not because they look better, but because they don't rust when they get wet.

We use self oiling raw-hide laces for the simple reason that they don't get soaked with water and rot.

And we certainly don't construct our footwear using double knot pearl stitching because we think it's fun. (Even in Hampton, New Hampshire, there are more entertaining things to do).

We do it so that the seams won't unravel, even if they're accidentally cut open on the sharp rocks and thick brush that Timberland wearers often find themselves in.

As you might suspect, all of these time consuming steps in constructing them don't serve to make Timberland boots or clothing any cheaper.

In fact, the chances are very good you'll pay more for a Timberland coat than you would most others.

But like everything Timberland makes, you'll be wearing it long after you've forgotten the price you paid.

Which even someone with a shelf-like forehead and one continuous eyebrow can tell you is a very good thing.

In fact, even mankind's most distant ancestors would certainly have preferred a Timberland coat to their own hairy variety.

Ours, after all, have pockets.

Timberland (UK) Limited, Unit Four, St. Anthony's Way, Feltham, Middlesex. TW14 0NH. Telephone enquiries, please ring 081 890 6116.

# IN HAMPTON NEW HAMPSHIRE, EVEN THE SHOES CAN HOLD THEIR LIQUOR.

Tucked inside every box of Timberland Weatherbuck shoes is a card. On it is written a polite warning to the owner.

It reads as follows.

'Please Note: At Timberland, we use only premium grade, full grain natural leather. Natural leathers with high fat-liquor content sometimes develop a white surface haze. This natural occurrence is known as 'blooming'.

This white residue, more noticeable on darker colours, can be easily wiped off with a damp cloth. These natural leathers may also tend to bleed their colour onto light coloured socks the first few times they are worn.'

Of course, we don't have to tell you about these small inconveniences. We could just figure that once you've bought a pair of our boots or shoes, you're on your own.

But up in New Hampshire, folks aren't like that.

Maybe it's the Puritan blood still coursing through our veins. Or you could put it down to plain good manners.

Either way, we reckon if you're prepared to stump up the extra for a pair of Timberlands, the least we can do is prepare you for ownership.

Truth is, we wouldn't have to issue warnings if we weren't so darned pernickety about the leathers we use.

We trek all across the United States searching for tanneries that will meet the ridiculously high standards we demand.

Tanneries that know a thing or two about turning tough hides into soft leathers.

When we find hides we like, we happily pay through the nose for them.

(Leathers that hold their liquor content don't come cheap. But we believe that when it comes to your feet, money's no object.)

After we get the leathers back to New Hampshire, we dye them all the way through. It's the reason the colours sometimes 'bleed' when you first wear a pair of Weatherbucks.

Since it's also why the colour won't scuff or flake off even after years of regular wear, we reckon a pair of dirty socks is a small price to pay.

It's at this stage that we impregnate all our leathers with silicone oils.

This provides a seal against the elements while at the same time preserving the natural qualities that keep the leather supple.

Ironically, the hall mark of every pair of Timberland shoes is something you can't see.

We're referring, of course, to the famous wraparound construction of the uppers.

Unfortunately, we can't claim credit for this ingenious piece of shoe design, that must go to the Red Indians and their famous moccasin.

No matter. For the sake of your feet (and our business) we've shamelessly snaffled the idea.

This entails a single piece of leather being stretched and moulded on a special last. Pre-stretching them in this way stops the leather cracking with time and also has the effect of breaking them in

THE WEATHERBUCK.

before you wear them.

Your comfort isn't the only thing that concerns the old boys in our workshops.

Perhaps because New Hampshire gets its fair share of rain (average annual rainfall 36.2 inches) they have a fixation about making sure your feet stay dry.

In fact, the Weatherbuck is just one of the shoes we guarantee 100% waterproof.

Every place water tries to get in, we put something in its path.

Where other manufacturers are content to use one row of nylon stitching, we insist on four.

The seams are sealed with not one but two coats of latex to stop water sneaking in through the tiniest needle hole.

And then we call on one of our many patents to permanently bond the dual-density polyurethane sole to the upper to produce a watertight seal. Even the glove leather lining has been given a special waterproofing treatment.

We're equally protective about the cold.

(Hardly surprising when you consider that Mount Washington, a few miles up the road from us, regularly has over forty five feet of snow dumped on it in winter).

To keep your feet snug, we put Thinsulate in the tongue, shaft and quarter of our boots.

While shoes like the Weatherbuck have added insulation in the form of Ensolite in the lining of the sole.

And in our new clothing range, you'll find a liberal use of Gore-Tex, the man-made fabric that was specially developed to perform in extreme temperatures.

Even down to the knapsack on your back.

And each item displays the same legendary obsession with detail you've come to expect from us.

Our Weathergear clothing and accessories range has button holes that are bound with calfskin and stitched both sides for longer wear.

The cotton used in shirts and jackets isn't just cotton. It's coated with a resin finish for water repellency.

More often than not, this new outerwear has two piece under arm gussets to give arms the freedom they need when you're mountaineering or trekking.

The overnight bags and duffles are leather lined, the stresspoints are reinforced with brass studs and the buckles and zips are either brass or nickel. Even the belts have nickel-plated brass buckles.

Yes sir, we've come a long way since the days when we only made working boots.

But when you're stuck up in the wilds of New Hampshire, the importance of simple values and basic needs is hard to forget.

Course, nowadays we know that folks in Rome, Paris and London have taken a fancy to the things we make. Some of them probably even think they're fashionable.

But in Hampton, we don't worry about all that highfalutin stuff. We just know how to keep the cold and rain out.

And it looks like there's still enough of that to keep us in business for a few years yet.

Timberland (UK) Limited, Unit Five, St. Anthony's Way, Feltham, Middlesex. TW14 0NH. Telephone enquiries, please ring 081-890 6116.

Timberland

# THE ALL-AMERICAN SHOE MADE IN AMERICA VERSUS THE ALL-AMERICAN SHOE MADE IN CYPRUS.

Isn't it strange how many things which are considered typically American don't seem to be made in America anymore?

Denim jeans are more often made in Hong Kong, Italy or France.

Flat bed trucks, convertibles, motor-bikes, you'd think the Japanese had invented them. Even an American icon like the T-shirt is no longer able to claim sole US citizenship.

There are, of course, exceptions.

There's one small shoe company holed up in the north eastern corner of the United States that still believes in the good old American way.

It's called Timberland.

Yet even as you read this, shoe companies in places that are better known for growing fruit are busily trying to fool the public into thinking that their all-American shoes are the ones we make in the small town of Hampton, New Hampshire.

Timberland's classic hand sewn, for instance, must be about the most imitated shoe in the whole world.

That's if you discount our famous Tan Buck boot. And equally renowned boat shoe.

While we search the length and breadth of the country for tanneries who know how to turn out tough yet supple leathers, they simply search the length and breadth of their local wholesaler and buy what's in stock.

Naturally, they pay less for hides than we do. But we reckon that if you buy cheap, your customers feet end up paying the price.

Our imitators engage in other decidedly un-American activities.

Like painting the colour on their shoes. This pretty well ensures that after a little wear the colour will scuff or flake off.

At Timberland, we don't brush colours on, we dye them right through. But only after we've impregnated the leathers with silicone to make them completely water repellent.

As you'd expect, when the manufacturers that copy our shoes begin the labour-intensive business of constructing the upper, they begin by saving on labour. The opposite is true at Timberland.

The old boys in our workshops may not be as fast as machines, or as cheap. But we believe that if you're paying top dollar for a hand-sewn, some hands should be involved in making it. Preferably experienced ones.

So each leather we use is moulded by hand on a special geometric last.

Then, a set of gnarled but nimble fingers goes to work making the uppers along the lines of the moccasin.

In all our years of turning out shoes, we haven't been able to improve on the original Red Indian design. A quick study of our two pictures and you'll see why.

That one-piece upper is a good example of their ingenuity and our workmanship. It's smooth, tidily finished off, with no unnecessary seams. You can make your own judgement about the copy.

Of course, the real test of a hand-sewn is how long the upper stays joined to the sole. Other manufacturers glue them together, sew them, then cross their fingers. Not us.

We created a permanent bonding process that's unique to us. With a patent to prove it.

What's more, each shoe is sewn with high strength nylon yarn using a double knot, pearl stitch. Then all the seams are sealed with not one but two coats of latex.

More than can be said of the people who copy us.

If they had any pride they'd use the same solid brass eyelets and self-oiling raw-hide laces we do.

When they 'knocked-off' our Tan Buck boots, they'd put Thinsulate in the tongue, the shaft and the quarter just like us.

And if they were really worried about your feet being warm, they'd use the Gore-Tex linings we insist on in Hampton.

Truth is, the people who copy Timberland boots and shoes don't do any of these things.

Which, when you consider how little they charge for their handiwork, is hardly surprising.

But we figure it this way.

It costs a lot of money to make an item that lasts.

It isn't cheap to check out those new materials, like the Vibram EVA we now use on our new Ultra Light shoe range.

And it's pretty darned expensive to make a collection of bags and accessories to the same standard as our boots and shoes.

Thankfully, we have loyal customers who understand that you get what you pay for.

And what could be more all-American than that?

Timberland Shoes (UK) Limited, Unit Five, St. Anthony's Way, Feltham, Middlesex. TW14 0NH. Or, for any telephone enquiries, you can call us anytime on 081-890 6116.

THE CLASSIC HAND SEWN.

Timberland

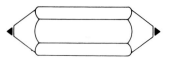

Gold, Silver, & Bronze
Awards

**9 BRONZE**
**ART DIRECTOR**
Neil French
**WRITER**
Neil French
**PHOTOGRAPHER**
Willie Tang
**CLIENT**
Pacific Beauty Care
**AGENCY**
The Ball Partnership/
Singapore

(Be careful with the Kaminomoto)

(Be careful with the Kaminomoto)

(Be careful with the Kaminomoto)

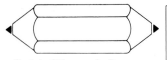
# SO, YOU'RE FEELING A BIT GLOOMY THIS MORNING? READ ON. BY LUNCHTIME YOU CAN BE SUICIDAL.

1. Concentrate. How miserable *are* you exactly? A little 'down'? Depressed? Or on the verge of crying, stamping, and generally behaving like John McEnroe on one of his better days?

Is there a glimmer of hope on your personal horizon? Count your blessings. After all, the Straits Times has arrived without any evident signs of charring, so you can assume that the country's still in good hands. And, judging by the low growl not unadjacent to your left ear, you're still married.

Feeling worse, yet? Fine. Now we're getting somewhere.

2. Have you noticed that the lounges aren't open yet? This is obviously an oversight. Have these people no idea of how much hooch they could sell to those of us with a teeny-weeny little headache of a morning?

3. Outside the sun is shining.

4. This is no cause for merriment and joy. Sooner or later, you have to go out in it, and there's no brand of shades known to science or Michael Jackson that can protect a retina used only to the delicate pastels of neon, and the soothing glow of disco-strobes. This sunlight business is a killer.

5. Have you ever considered, in the light (is it too early for bad puns? It's always too early... OK) of the above, that you may be a vampire? Look in the mirror; are you there? Are you sure? If not, send out for a mallet, a stake, and someone who doesn't like you very much. Then brace yourself.

On the other hand, which blood-group do you prefer? It has to be cheaper than drinking Beck's, which is some consolation, I guess.

6. Beck's Beer is outrageously, unfairly, expensive. Ordinary beer isn't.

7. Life itself is unfair. (See above).

8. It is, you'll agree, the rich what gets the pleasure, and the poor what gets the blame. The poor also gets the sticky end of every other deal going: Viz and to whit, no Beck's. If you are poor, you'll agree that this, too, is very unfair indeed. If you are rich, get on with your Beck's. And I hope you drown in it.

9. One red traffic-light is always followed by another red traffic-light.

10. Especially when you're in a hurry.

11. More especially when you're late for an appointment you wish you hadn't made in the first place.

12. And when you get there, wringing wet, with anxiety and exertion, your appointment is always later still.

13. When he arrives, he is always calm, composed, and dry as a pawnbroker's eye.

14. You are not allowed to kill him. It is apparently frowned upon in polite circles. Unwarranted pickiness, in our view.

15. When you're young, fit, and attractive, you haven't got any money, so the girls ignore you.

16. When you get older, and richer, you also get fat, ugly, and bald. The girls suddenly show a bizarre preference for younger, poorer men.

17. If you have a full head of hair, girls tell you that bald men are sexy.

18. If you are bald, this previously immutable fact seems to escape them.

19. Life's a bitch. Then you marry one.

20. On the other hand, there's always Bangkok. Or Manila.

21. Or Aids.

22. Becks is a lot more expensive than ordinary beers. Have we mentioned the fact before? It's preying on our minds. With some justification.

23. Buttered toast, when dropped, always lands butter-side down. This well-known law of physics could be the answer to life, the Universe, and everything. The answer previously having been believed to be 48.

24. Lawyers are allowed to wear curly wigs, and long black frocks.

25. Gentlemen who are *not* lawyers, but wear long black frocks and curly wigs, are likely to be sent to jail. By lawyers wearing long black frocks & curly wigs. Or, if they're top-gun type lawmen, in *long* curly wigs, and long *red* frocks. (Black stockings, suspenders, and frilly underwear are apparently purely optional, in either case).

26. Lawyers are allowed to drink Beck's and they can afford it, too. This is very, very irritating indeed.

27. Ben Hunt cannot afford Beck's but still drinks it. Mind you, he'll drink *anything*.

28. The bad guys frequently win.

29. Unless you happen to *be* a bad guy, in which case, welcome to Changi; this is your bucket. Enjoy.

30. The makers and sellers of Beck's are allowed to roam the streets, despite the fact that they are horrid, larcenous, greedy, and totally devoid of humanity.

31. A man who trifles with the affections of defenceless young girls should be damn well hung. And usually, is.

32. It is impossible to get a decent hot pastrami sandwich in Singapore. This is especially peeving when you consider how well hot pastrami-on-rye goes down with a nice, cold, Beck's.

33. On the other hand, nearly anything goes down nicely with Beck's, except the price of the Beck's, which gives you raging indigestion. If this is fair, then I'm a Chinaman. Which I'm not, so that proves it.

34. You may well *be* a Chinaman, and if you can afford Beck's, I hate you, and in any case, it's your round.

35. When you get home, late and drunk, the wife is always wide-awake, waiting.

36. When you get home early and sober she's gone to her Mother's for the night. This is occasionally referred-to as Sod's Law. As opposed to Murphy's. (see 23).

37. That delightful seventeen-year-old over there is going to look like her Mother one day.

38. Unless her Mother's beautiful, in which case she'll grow to look like her Dad. Or, alternatively, her goldfish.

39. If you lived in Europe, you could buy a Mercedes for the same price as a mid-range Japanese car costs here. A Rolls-Royce, here, costs the same as a three-bedroom apartment in London. Wherever you live, Beck's is ridiculously expensive, so you may as well stay home.

40. No matter how much money you earn, you spend it.

41. Copywriters get paid absurd amounts of money for writing reams of stuff that nobody bothers to read. This, for instance. They then spend most of it on loose women, fast cars, and Beck's, and just waste the rest. This is absolutely, incredibly unfair, and I don't give a hoot.

42. Is it lunchtime yet? Oddly enough I feel *much* better now. Think I'll go and have a Becks.

43. Hang the expense.

Nobody in their right mind would pay this kind of money for a beer. Now, if someone could just help me out of this strait-jacket...

# How To Survive Six Hours Trapped In A Lift With An Eternal Optimist.

Hell could be like this: Given the choice of demons inserting red hot pokers into one's more squidgy bits for eternity, or an afternoon in close proximity with a die-hard optimist, and most sensible folk will opt for the kindness of demons.

Everyone knows that life isn't fair. And since 'life' encompasses just about everything that happens on the planet, it doesn't leave much room for optimism, does it?

Unless you include a whole lot of really contented rocks.

But no. The eternal optimist will tell you that even at the Heart of Darkness there glows a light so bright that God can't pay the electricity bill; that all people are basically good; and that, yes, there are crabs that can walk in a straight line, and sweet-talk a policeman when they're pulled-over for drunk-driving.

Try telling them otherwise and they'll drown you out with a heart-warming rendition of Louis Armstrong's 'What a Wonderful World', or something equally distressing.

Naturally, you do everything in your power to avoid these people.

But life being what it is, (a bitch, and we'll come to that later), there's a good chance that one fine day you'll be stuck in a lift. There will be one other person in that lift with you. It will not be a sixteen-year-old nymphomaniac for whom claustrophobia brings on waves of desire followed by total amnesia. It will be an eternal optimist.

When that day comes, you owe it to yourself, and to all of us, to destroy him.

FIRST HOUR

Soften him up. A few range-finding jabs. Ask him,. first and foremost, in a world where we spend millions on new and interesting ways to kill each other, *why* is it, .we still haven't invented a lift that never breaks down.

Why is it that his wife will believe him when he says "Sorry I'm late, dear, but I got stuck in a lift for six hours". And yours won't.

Why is it that your mistress won't believe you, either, and that it'll provide them both with the excuse they've been looking for all these years, to take you to the cleaners. Your wife with a divorce, and your mistress with one of those breach-of-promise suits that begin with "He made me do things..."

So far, this is not going well. He is still as happy as a post-lobotomy loony, while you are just about ready for the razor-blades in a warm bath.

Hit him where it hurts.

"Why is Beck's Beer so excruciatingly expensive, then? Tell me *that!*"

SECOND AND THIRD HOURS

Why? Why? Why?! Yes, yell it at him. See if you can shake the poor sap out of the state of Vaseline-hazed euphoria that is best left in the Singapore girl commercials, and nowhere else.

And while you're on the subject of Singapore airlines hostesses, ask, him why, when you've spent more hours in the air than a carrier pigeon with no sense of direction, they *still* politely refuse even your most vulgar advances.

(At this point, he'll probably tell you h married one. And that the reason he did it was that she sent him a glass heart on the first day of every month, for four years. "You know, I felt sorry for her". You will then go into shock for an hour. When you come out of it, you will feel like hitting him).

Do not do so yet. You have more to say.

FOURTH HOUR

YES! MUCH MORE! Calm down, now. Calm down. Be logical.

Where are the firemen, then? It's been three hours already, and although you feel like ripping this grinning poltroon to bits, what you *really* need is a cigarette. Stuff it. Have one. At this point a cigarette is well worth $500. Come to that, you might as well have a wee as well, and go the whole hog. You can practically guarantee they'll have you out of there in five minutes, then.

How much tax do you pay every year? $10,000? $20,000?

Just to fund the childhood fantasies of some delinquent who wants to drive round in a big red truck, and gets off on sliding down poles...

And doesn't GET PEOPLE OUT OF LIFTS! Point this out to your companion. "What about the firemen, then!" Your voice may have a slight quaver in it by now. That's alright. No doubt you intended it.

(At this point he will probably ask you for a cigarette. He has never smoked before. But suddenly he feels like one, all the same).

FIFTH HOUR

Why is he crying?

"Why are you crying, man? Don't you realise there are starving people in Ethiopia who would give their right foot to be trapped in this lift with us, right now? Just so they could eat us."

Yes. He realises. You are making progress.

Sneak one in below the belt: "When we get out of here, I'm going to have a beer with you, pal. In fact, I'm going to have several. And since it's your round, I'm going to have Beck's." That should bring fresh tears to his eyes.

SIXTH HOUR

Tap. Tap. Tap.

The firemen have arrived. They tell you they'll have you out of there in an hour. Unless there's a fire, in which case, it may take a bit longer, and by the way, goodbye. Only joking, ha ha.

Hurry. When you get out, you can take your time garrotting the funny fireman with his own hose. Meanwhile, you've only minutes left in which to convert the optimist to reality.

First, grab that tie off him. After this final assault, you may find it hard to explain why you did nothing to prevent him hanging himself.

You are yelling, now. "Life's a bitch, then you marry one! Are you aware that the biggest band of the '80s was Huey Lewis's lot? Why does my daughter only go out with sailors? Why does my *son* only go out with sailors?"..

And you top it off with a piece of infinite wisdom... "The price of Beck's beer is cruel, vicious, demoralising, inhuman, & above all, absolutely *unfair!* So. What have you got to smile about, eh?"

There's a rousing cheer from the firemen below.

The eternal optimist smiles on, and smiling still, kicks you in the groin. He says that you, like all men, are essentially evil. On the way out, he kicks a fireman.

You've won.



# A Few Encouraging Words For The Totally Incompeten T.

It's perfectly alright to be incompetent for hours on end.

I am. And so is everyone I know.

Of course, being of this persuasion, I shall never be able to afford a bottle of Beck's Beer. Which is why the people who sell Beck's Beer got me to write this ad.

They see it as a sort of public service announcement; as a way of consoling those who moan at the unfairness of it all. A way of making the 'have-nots' feel glad that they 'haven't'.

So here, for the first time, are the great names: The people who were so bad in their chosen sphere of endeavour that they achieved greatness.

People who believed that success is overrated.

And who believed, as G. K. Chesterton once said, that 'If a thing's worth doing, it's worth doing badly."

THE WORST BOXING DEBUT

Ralph Walton was knocked out in 10½ seconds of his first bout, on 29th September, 1946, in Lewison, Maine, USA.

It happened when Al Couture struck him as he was adjusting his gum-shield in his corner. The 10½ seconds includes 10 seconds while he was counted out.

He never fought again.

THE LEAST-SUCCESSFUL WEATHER REPORT

After severe flooding in Jeddah, in January 1979, the Arab News gave the following bulletin: "We regret that we are unable to give you the weather. We rely on weather reports from the airport, which is closed, on account of the weather. Whether or not we are able to bring you the weather tomorrow depends on the weather."

THE WORST SPEECH-WRITER

William Gamaliel Harding wrote his own speeches while President of the USA, in the 1920's.

When Harding died, e. e. cummings said, "the only man, woman or child who wrote a simple, declarative sentence with seven grammatical errors, is dead".

Here is a rewarding sample of the man's style. "I would like the government to do all it can to mitigate, then, in understanding, in mutuality of interest, in concern for the common good, our tasks will be solved."

THE MOST UNSUCCESSFUL ATTEMPT AT DYING FOR LOVE

When his fiancee broke off their engagement, Senor Abel Ruiz, of Madrid, decided to kill himself for love.

Reviewing the possibilities available on such occasions, he decided to park himself in front of the Gerona to Madrid express. However, jumping in its path, he landed between the rails and watched, gloomily, as the train passed over him.

He suffered only minor injuries, and promptly received First Aid at Gerona Hospital.

Later that day, he tried again. This time he jumped in front of a passing lorry, again only acquiring some more bruises. His rapid return to the hospital led doctors to call a priest, who made Sr. Ruiz see the folly of his ways. Eventually, he decided to carry on living, and to seek a new girlfriend.

Glad to be alive, he left the hospital and was immediately knocked down by a runaway horse; he was taken back to Gerona Hospital, this time quite seriously injured, for the third time that day.

THE WORST JUROR

There was a rape case at a Crown Court in Northern England in the late 1970's at which a juror fell fast asleep, during which time the victim was asked to repeat what her attacker had said prior to the incident.

To save her embarrassment, the girl was allowed to write it on paper, instead. This was then folded, and passed along the jury. Each member read the words which, in effect, said "Nothing, in the history of sexual congress, equals the comprehensive going-over which I am about to visit upon your good self."

Sitting next to the dozing juror was an attractive blonde. After reading the note, she refolded it, and nudged her neighbour, who awoke with a start.

He read the note, and looked at the blonde in astonishment. To the delight of the entire court, he then read the note again, slowly. Then he winked at the blonde, and put the note in his pocket.

When the judge asked him for the piece of paper, the recently dormant juror refused, saying that 'it was a personal matter'.

This is what the label on a bottle of Beck's Beer looks like. Since its the closest you'll probably ever get to one, we've given you a dotted line, so you can cut it out, and put it on your wall as a kind of ikon. When you've finished cutting it out, plasters can be bought from any pharmacy.

THE LEAST-SUCCESSFUL WEAPON

The prize for the most useless weapon of all time goes to the Russians, who invented the dog-mine. The rather ingenious plan was to train the dogs to associate food with the underside of tanks, in the hope that they would run hungrily beneath the advancing Panzer divisions. Bombs would be strapped to their backs, which endangered the dogs to a point where no insurance company would look at them.

Unfortunately, they associated food solely with *Russian* tanks, and totally destroyed half a Soviet division on their first outing.

The plan was quickly abandoned.

THE WORST BUS SERVICE

Can any bus-service rival the fine Hanley to Bagnall route, in Staffordshire, England? In 1976 it was reported that the buses no longer stopped to pick up passengers.

This came to light when one of them, Mr Bill Hancock, complained that buses on the outward journey regularly sailed past queues of elderly people; up to thirty of them sometimes waiting in line.

Councillor Arthur Cholerton then made transport history by stating that if the buses stopped to pick up passengers, it would disrupt the timetable.

THE LAST WORD

"They couldn't hit an elephant at this dist..." The last words of General John Sedgwick, spoken while looking over the parapet at enemy lines during the Battle of Spotsylvania, in 1864.

OH, ALRIGHT, THEN; HERE ARE SOME MORE

Typography has never been our strong point, so here are a few more determined losers, to fill out the column: The Welsh choir who were the sole entrants in a competition, and came second; the Swiss pornographer who was heavily fined because his wares were insufficiently pornographic; the writer of this ad, who, unable to master the art of précis, copied the entire thing, word for word, from Stephen Pile's 'Book of Heroic Failures', thereby incurring almost certain legal action.

There, feel better now, don't you? After all, the price of a bottle of Beck's Beer may well be so high as to be audible only to highly-trained bats but at least you're not the only one who'll never be able to afford it.

(Oh, no. Three more lines. How abou a jingle? Beck's diddly-dee-de-dah, Beck's, tiddly-pom. The end).

Gold, Silver, & Bronze
Awards

**CONSUMER NEWSPAPER
600 LINES OR LESS: SINGLE**

**11 GOLD**
**ART DIRECTOR**
Doug Trapp
**WRITER**
Jean Rhode
**CLIENT**
Li'l Red Grocery
**AGENCY**
Ads Infinitum/
Minneapolis

**12 SILVER**
**ART DIRECTOR**
Doug Chapman
**WRITER**
Joey Baron
**ILLUSTRATOR**
Tony DeLuz
**CLIENT**
Gold's Gym
**AGENCY**
DoJo Advertising/
Brookline

**13 BRONZE**
**ART DIRECTOR**
Woody Kay
**WRITER**
Al Lowe
**CLIENT**
Providence Country Day
**AGENCY**
Pagano Schenck & Kay/
Providence

# Tear this out and use it for toilet paper.

## 50¢ off bathroom tissue

This coupon is valid for 50¢ off the regular price of any four pack of in-stock bathroom tissue. Limit one coupon per purchase per customer. Offer expires 10/31/91. Redeemable only at Eden Prairie Grocery, 7447 County Road No. 4, Eden Prairie, Minnesota 55344, 937-8892.

### "Lil-Red" Eden Prairie Grocery
7447 County Road No. 4, 937-8892

**11 GOLD**

# They laughed when I sat down at the piano. They stopped when I picked it up.

Let's not play around. Whether you're into Schwarzenegger or Shostakovich, no one gives you a better workout then Gold's Gym.

## GOLD'S GYM®
### AND FITNESS CENTER

38 Swampscott Road, Salem, MA

**12 SILVER**

# ON THIS TEST, IT'S NOT WHO YOU KNOW. IT'S WHOM.

What you know is also important. And on our scholarship examination, February ninth at 8:30 a.m., you'll get a chance to show us everything you know. Any young woman or man now in the 8th, 9th or 10th grade outside our school is eligible. If you get the top score, you can win a scholarship of at least $1,000 a year. Financial aid may also be awarded to others who score well. To find out about the application process or to learn more about enrolling at Providence Country Day, please call Admission Director Jack Kurty at (401) 438-5170. Of course, PCD encourages applicants of any race, color, creed, gender, national or ethnic origin.

**PROVIDENCE COUNTRY DAY SCHOOL SCHOLARSHIP EXAMINATION**

**13 BRONZE**

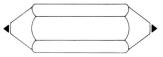

# For those nights when the only thing you want to stick in the oven is your head.

If you've had one of those days, the last thing you want to do is cook at night. So why bother? Just call 941-FOOD and we'll have dinner delivered hot out of the oven and to your house in around 30 minutes. **BRINGER'S**™

# For those nights when you're too tired to burn anything.

Tired of Macaroni Flambe? Then call us at 941-FOOD for delivery of our 10-Layer Lasagna, our Beef & Broccoli Stir Fry, or any one of the other 18 items on our menu. **BRINGER'S**™

# We'll make your dinner, then step on it.

Want to see our Chicken Fajitas or our Beef & Broccoli Stir Fry go 55 mph? Just call in your order at 941-FOOD and we'll be at your place with dinner in around thirty minutes. **BRINGER'S**™

**CONSUMER NEWSPAPER
600 LINES OR LESS:
CAMPAIGN**

15 **BRONZE**
**ART DIRECTORS**
Woody Kay, Rob Rich
**WRITER**
Al Lowe
**CLIENT**
Providence Country Day
**AGENCY**
Pagano Schenck & Kay/
Providence

# HERE'S A CHANCE TO GET INTO A GREAT SCHOOL BY PASSING A TEST. NOT A FOOTBALL.

At PCD it's brain power that counts. That's why our February 10th scholarship examination is the primary factor we use in selecting a 7th or 10th grade boy from outside our school to receive an award of at least $1,000 a year. (Incidentally, financial aid may also be awarded to other boys who score well.) If you're a bright 6th or 9th grader, we hope you'll call Headmaster Porter Caesar at (401) 438-5170 to find out about the application process and all requirements. Of course, Providence Country Day School encourages applications from and admits students of any race, color, creed, national or ethnic origins, and will not discriminate in awarding this scholarship on those bases.)

**PROVIDENCE COUNTRY DAY SCHOOL SCHOLARSHIP EXAMINATION**

# ON THIS TEST, IT'S NOT WHO YOU KNOW. IT'S WHOM.

What you know is also important. And on our scholarship examination, February ninth at 8:30 a.m., you'll get a chance to show us everything you know. Any young woman or man now in the 8th, 9th or 10th grade outside our school is eligible. If you get the top score, you can win a scholarship of at least $1,000 a year. Financial aid may also be awarded to others who score well. To find out about the application process or to learn more about enrolling at Providence Country Day, please call Admission Director Jack Kurty at (401) 438-5170. Of course, PCD encourages applicants of any race, color, creed, gender, national or ethnic origin.

**PROVIDENCE COUNTRY DAY SCHOOL SCHOLARSHIP EXAMINATION**

# A FEW YEARS AGO, WE LET THE BOYS STOP WEARING TIES. NEXT YEAR, WE'RE ALLOWING DRESSES.

This fall, Providence Country Day School is ready to enroll girls in grades 9–12, as well as boys in grades 5-12. If you're a student who would be interested in attending a school which has a friendly, caring environment, small classes, and outstanding teachers, we urge you to call our Director of Admissions Jack Kurty for additional information, at 401-438-5170. And no matter what clothes you wear on the outside, we think you'll find this is one school that will genuinely appreciate you for what you have on the inside.

**PROVIDENCE COUNTRY DAY SCHOOL IS NOW ENROLLING WOMEN.**

Gold, Silver, & Bronze
Awards

**CONSUMER MAGAZINE
B/W: 1 PAGE OR SPREAD**

**16 GOLD**
**ART DIRECTOR**
Ron Rosen
**WRITER**
Richard Kelly
**CLIENT**
Nikon
**AGENCY**
Scali McCabe Sloves/
New York

**17 SILVER**
**ART DIRECTOR**
Steve Dunn
**WRITER**
Tim Delaney
**PHOTOGRAPHER**
John Claridge
**CLIENT**
Sanyo
**AGENCY**
Leagas Delaney/London

**18 BRONZE**
**ART DIRECTOR**
Brian Kelly
**WRITER**
Mike Browne
**PHOTOGRAPHER**
Gail Specht
**CLIENT**
John Nuveen & Company
**AGENCY**
Hal Riney & Partners/
Chicago

A three-year old boy saluting
at his father's funeral.

A woman crying over
the body of a student shot
by the National Guard.

An American President lifting his
pet beagle up by its ears.

A lone student standing
in front of four tanks.

© 1990 Nikon Inc.

If you can picture it in your head,
it was probably taken with a Nikon.

**Nikon**®
We take the world's greatest pictures®

**16 GOLD**

# Buy this compact hi-fi system. And get a cumbersome black thing absolutely free.

the same ear-shattering 35 watts RMS bass effect. (Leave this system with an Iron Maiden fan at your peril.)

The rather terrifying bass sound system augments two sets of Sanyo's highly-innovative 'pod' speakers.

Mounted in two's, they can be swivelled to ensure that no corner of the room escapes the 25 watts RMS per channel.

Of course, this is by no means the only piece of technical wizardry.

The computer programmable CD player can select the playing order of up to 24 tracks, play the tracks in random order or scan the introduction of each track.

A computer is also employed on the twin auto reverse decks, allowing you to 'Backskip Edit' when you're recording from CD.

Ingeniously, when the tape on one side runs out, the deck skips over and starts the track from the beginning on the new side.

There's even a 'Fade Out Edit' so that music doesn't stop abruptly.

And the tuner has no less than 36 pre-sets which you're going to need for all the new radio stations.

Finally, the whole system can be controlled using a 48-key remote.

All in all, we can't think of a good reason why an intelligent person like you wouldn't want an SF-5.

But there's still one little problem to sort out. Where on earth are you going to put that big black thing?

**SANYO**

*For information on all products in Sanyo's hi-fi range, please write to Anne Branton, Consumer Affairs, Dept 101, 6 The Business Village, Wexham Road, Slough, Berks. SL2 5HF.*

Look at that marvellously modern, compact Sanyo hi-fi system over there.

CD. Twin cassette players. FM/AM tuner. The latest 8cm 'pod' speakers.

What, though, is that rather large, decidely uncompact-looking object at the bottom of the page opposite?

That 'thing' is a whole bass sound system in its own right.

Complete with its own discrete amplifier capable of producing sounds below 100 Hz. For non-buffs, 100 Hz is

the point at which the human ear cannot tell which direction the notes are coming from.

This means that rather than having to put this speaker next to the hi-fi system you can put it absolutely anywhere in a room and still enjoy

**17 SILVER**

---

THE GUPPY HAS a rather unique way of handling the problems of parenthood.

And while we would never adopt this method, there are times when we can't help admiring its simplicity. Like when we're faced with the prospect of planning for a child's education.

For as young as your little one may be, it won't be long before the little beezer is off to college, enrolling in Rhetoric 101, buying books and paying lab fees. (Not to mention making a request or two for spending money.)

Of course, there are a number of ways to handle this impending financial dilemma, but none, perhaps, more comforting than the College Investment Program from John Nuveen & Company.

Nuveen deals exclusively in tax-free* municipal bonds. So we can offer investors the relative security of a conservative portfolio (particularly relevant for something as important as your child's future), as well as tax-free income (so more of the money you earn goes towards your child's education).

Yet, it isn't just the tax-free nature

of the bonds that makes Nuveen investments so ideally suited to college funding. It has more to do with the way we select them.

## NOW we know *why* GUPPIES *eat their young.*

We start by reviewing billions of dollars worth of municipal bonds each year. Only then do we finally invest in a select few (including some that other investment firms have overlooked).

The performance of these bonds is then scrupulously monitored over the long-term, with one goal in mind: to provide a high level of tax-free income over time, while still protecting our

client's initial investment.

And should you decide to choose Nuveen for your child's college fund, you'll find your choice isn't limited to a particular University. (What if your child doesn't want to attend your *old alma mater?*) And the money that you invest with Nuveen is always yours to do with as you wish. In fact, you don't even have to use it for college.

To find out more about the ways you can finance your child's future without mortgaging your own, ask your personal banker, broker or financial adviser about the Nuveen Tax-Free College Investment Program.

*For more complete information on Nuveen tax-free open end mutual funds or unit trusts, including charges and expenses, call for a prospectus. Read it carefully before you invest or send money.*

*\*Income may be subject to state and local taxes. Capital gains, if any, will be subject to capital gains taxes.*

*A FREE OPPORTUNITY FOR PARENTS TO BECOME COLLEGE EDUCATED.*
Have you wondered what tuition fees will be like 5, 10 or even 50 years from now? Then call us toll-free at 1-800-524-6500. We'll prepare a personalized tuition projection that will illustrate the cost of sending your child to any four year college in the country. And we'll send it to you free of charge.

**NUVEEN**

Specialists In Tax-Free Investments Since 1898.

**18 BRONZE**

TREAD LIGHTLY—DRIVE RESPONSIBLY OFF-ROAD.    PLEASE BUCKLE UP FOR SECURITY. © 1990 RANGE ROVER OF NORTH AMERICA, INC.

# The British have always driven on the wrong side of the road.

It's not that we can't get it right. We simply have our own way of doing things.

While other automobiles are either unusually rugged, or extravagantly civilized, we've made the one luxury car that isn't dependent on the luxury of a road.

Short of going across endangered terrain, there are very few places you won't see it.

With its massive chassis, and permanent 4-wheel drive, a Range Rover can go through anything from a desert to a snowstorm. In fact, it can even go through time, gracefully.

Range Rovers in their third decade are still performing automotive impossibilities from the Serengeti to the Himalayas.

LAND-ROVER **RANGE ROVER**

Lest we remain complacent, though, we always manage to make improvements that improve even a Range Rover.

The 1991, for example, has a quieter ride, along with a larger fuel tank for increased touring range.

Why not call 1-800-FINE 4WD for a dealer near you? Obviously, at around $42,400, a Range Rover isn't inexpensive.

But it's an investment you'll feel quite comfortable with.

Whichever side of the road you're on.

19 GOLD

# Is it any wonder the prisons are full?

In the mid 1950's, researchers at the University of Pennsylvania began conducting what has become a landmark study.

Its purpose: to determine the effect violent toys have on our children.

What they found was rather disturbing. The researchers stated that violent toys cause children to become more violent. That they actually may, in fact, teach children to become violent.

At Dakin, we've always tried to produce toys that teach children some other things.

Toys that, rather than teach a child how to maim, would teach a child how to love.

That, rather than teach a child how to hurt, would teach a child how to care for something.

Toys that, rather than being designed to be played with in only one way, would challenge the child's imagination to use them in a variety of ways. From playing house. To playing veterinarian. To playing Mr. Big Shot Hollywood movie director.

Naturally, researchers and child psychologists have had something to say about toys like the Dakin stuffed animal you see on the left: That they can play a very important role in helping children develop into secure, well-adjusted individuals.

You see, as parents ourselves, we at Dakin don't design toys solely on the basis of whether or not they'll make money.

We design them on the basis of whether we'd want our children playing with them.

## Gifts you can feel good about.™

DAKIN®

Gold, Silver, & Bronze
Awards

**CONSUMER MAGAZINE**
**COLOR: 1 PAGE OR SPREAD**

**21 BRONZE**
**ART DIRECTOR**
Martin Galton
**WRITER**
Will Awdry
**PHOTOGRAPHER**
Richard Avedon
**CLIENT**
Levi Strauss
**AGENCY**
Bartle Bogle Hegarty/
London

**22 BRONZE**
**ART DIRECTOR**
Martin Galton
**WRITER**
Will Awdry
**PHOTOGRAPHER**
Richard Avedon
**CLIENT**
Levi Strauss
**AGENCY**
Bartle Bogle Hegarty/
London

**23 BRONZE**
**ART DIRECTOR**
Tracy Wong
**WRITER**
Rob Bagot
**ILLUSTRATOR**
Gwenne Wilcox
**PHOTOGRAPHERS**
Jay Maisel, Stock
**CLIENT**
Royal Viking Line
**AGENCY**
Goodby Berlin &
Silverstein/San Francisco

*I get around to liking them after two, maybe three years.*

Erik Rodenbeck, welder.
Midtown Manhattan, New York, 29/3/90.

**21 BRONZE**

*I like them best just before they fall apart.*

Peter Ivan, plumber.
Brooklyn, New York, 10/3/90.

Levi's

BRITTANY HAIFA LAHAINA WATERFORD BALI NICE SYDNEY TANGIER JUNEAU LENINGRAD NAWILIWILI LISBON VANCOUVER LIVORNO PERTH MYKONOS KUALA LUMPUR NEW YORK OSLO PIRAEUS LONDON PAPEETE BORDEAUX SYRACUSE WHITTIER HAMBURG BANGKOK QUEBEC

as brief a time as five days, or for as long as fifteen, she will be nothing less than your own private island.

At your disposal are the services of 33 European chefs, six sommeliers, and a concierge. Fresh lobster? A '58 Bordeaux? Golf reservations? Of course, of course, of course.

Would you like to hear a little music? Perhaps take in a show? These, too, can be arranged, as quickly and effortlessly as 24-hour room service appears at your door. After all, this is a five-star-plus ship. Should you expect anything less?

**ROYAL VIKING LINE**
THE WORLD'S FINEST

From October to April, this little island stands ready to sail to your rescue. If this sounds like your type of getaway, contact your friendly travel agent, or telephone Royal Viking for a complimentary brochure at (800) 426-0821.

As always, we look forward to seeing you on board.

QUITE MAGICALLY, THE MOST ALLURING ISLAND
IN THE CARIBBEAN COMES AND GOES AS IT PLEASES.

A few moments ago it was here, off Martinique. Tomorrow it will be just north of Barbados. The next day, you will find it exactly ten miles due south of St. Lucia.

She is the Royal Viking Star. And for

Bahamian Registry.

PLAYA DEL CARMEN NAPLES MANILA KETCHIKAN LAS PALMAS OCHO RIOS MELBOURNE PUERTO VALLARTA SHANGHAI CARTAGENA BRISBANE ST NAZAIRE CALDERA SOUTHAMPTON MAUI PICTON FORT-DE-FRANCE SANTAREM CAPRI SAN BLAS ISLANDS BOMBAY SINGAPORE ROME

© Royal Viking Line 1990

Gold, Silver, & Bronze
Awards

**24 GOLD**
**ART DIRECTOR**
Tracy Wong
**WRITER**
Rob Bagot
**ILLUSTRATOR**
Gwenne Wilcox
**PHOTOGRAPHERS**
Randy Miller, Jay Maisel,
Stock
**CLIENT**
Royal Viking Line
**AGENCY**
Goodby Berlin &
Silverstein/San Francisco

Gold, Silver, & Bronze
Awards

**CONSUMER MAGAZINE
COLOR: 1 PAGE OR SPREAD/
CAMPAIGN**

**25 SILVER**
**ART DIRECTORS**
Frank Todaro, Kirk Mosel
**WRITERS**
Larry Cadman, Debbie
Kasher
**PHOTOGRAPHERS**
Lynn Sugarman,
Robert Ammirati,
Steve Krongard
**CLIENT**
Pella Windows and Doors
**AGENCY**
Scali McCabe Sloves/
New York

Pella windows are one of the great classified secrets of all times.

Mention in the

That in addition to being a comfortable place to live, it's probably a good long-term investment.

So if you're building or renovating a

## PELLA SELLS WINDOWS. APPARENTLY, WE SELL HOUSES, TOO.

classifieds that a house has Pella windows, and it somehow seems to sell better.

It's amazing.

Then again, maybe not so amazing. Because Pella windows speak volumes about any house they're in. They tell people that a house is top of the line. That whoever built

it probably didn't cut corners.

house, be sure to choose Pella windows.

Because a Pella window is the handiest tool of all. A selling tool.

For a free copy of our Window-scaping Idea Book, and the location of The Pella Window Store nearest you, please call 1-800-524-3700.

**BUILT TO IMPOSSIBLY HIGH STANDARDS. OUR OWN.**

It took man 1,930 years to figure out how to bend wood. And the engineers at Pella another 40 to learn how to keep it straight.

So while other door companies offer you the warmth and natural beauty of polyurethane foam, extruded alumi-

num or honeycomb substrate, only Pella can give you real wood doors which are just that. Real wood.

Using eleven crossbanded layers of wood, we have virtually eliminated warping,

*Paimio Scroll Chair by Alvar Aalto, c. 1931*

Besides being more beautiful on the outside, you'll also appreciate wood from the inside because it's a natural insulator.

So visit a Pella Window Store℠ and you'll see an array of magnificent genu- ine wood entryways

© 1990 Rolscreen Company

*Hawthorne wood door by Pella, c. 1989*

## BENDING WOOD WAS A PRETTY NEAT TRICK. KEEPING IT PERFECTLY STRAIGHT IS POSITIVELY AMAZING.

sticking, splitting and other problems associated with ordinary wood doors.

And our exclusive Woodsaver™ system not only protects, seals and preserves the fine wood, it also doubles the life of the finish.

**Pella**

**BUILT TO IMPOSSIBLY HIGH STANDARDS. OUR OWN.™**

with doors, sidelights and transoms. All built to the same impossibly high standards as our windows.

Because at Pella, we have this theory that bent wood is something you should sit on. Not knock on.

For more information on The Pella Wood Door Entry Systems,™ or the address of The Pella Window Store® nearest you please call 1-800-524-3700.

The Pella Window Store

---

*Colonial window, 1822.*

*Mission window, 1793.*

*Prairie window, 1909.*

*Palladian window, 1761.*

## INTRODUCING THE ARCHITECT SERIES.™ TO COME ALONG SINCE THE DRAFTY,

## THE MOST BEAUTIFUL LINE OF WINDOWS INEFFICIENT ORIGINALS.

All the truly great classic windows, it seems, were designed before the age of insulating glass.

Back then, no one worried about R Values or heating bills or energy conservation. What people cared about were aesthetics. Elegant and grace-

ful lines. Beauty for beauty's sake. With the advent of double pane insulating glass, however, things changed.

Window glass became much heavier, so the cross pieces that held the panes had to become thicker, less elegant. Then, instead of windows with small individual panes of glass (true divided light), manufacturers began offering single large sheets of insulat- ing glass with fake "snap-in" crosspieces to simulate the look of true divided light.

But now Pella® has come up with a radically new manufacturing technology that eliminates both those compromises. It's called Integral Light Technology.™

**INTRODUCING THE ARCHITECT SERIES FROM PELLA.**

It allows us to pro- duce windows that combine the energy- efficiency of insulating glass with the grace and elegance of classic older designs.

It also permits an extraordinary poten-

© 1990 Rolscreen Company

tial for custom window design that has never existed before.

This new series of windows is called, appropriately enough, The Architect Series.™ To believe it, you have to see it. And to see it, you have to visit The Pella Window Store.®

That trip has always been important for anyone building or renovating a home. Now, however, it's essential.

For more information on The Architect Series and the location of The Pella Window Store nearest you, call 1-800-524-3700.

**BUILT TO IMPOSSIBLY HIGH STANDARDS. OUR OWN.™** **Pella**

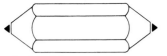

Gold, Silver, & Bronze
Awards

**CONSUMER MAGAZINE
COLOR: 1 PAGE OR SPREAD/
CAMPAIGN**

**26 SILVER**
**ART DIRECTORS**
Nick Parton, John Bayley
**WRITERS**
Nick Parton, John Bayley
**PHOTOGRAPHER**
Peter Rauter
**CLIENT**
Lever Bros.
**AGENCY**
Ogilvy & Mather/London

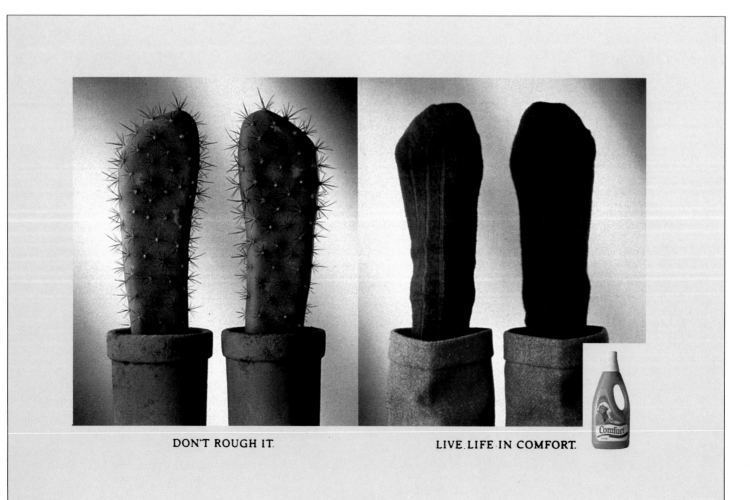

DON'T ROUGH IT.                    LIVE. LIFE. IN COMFORT.

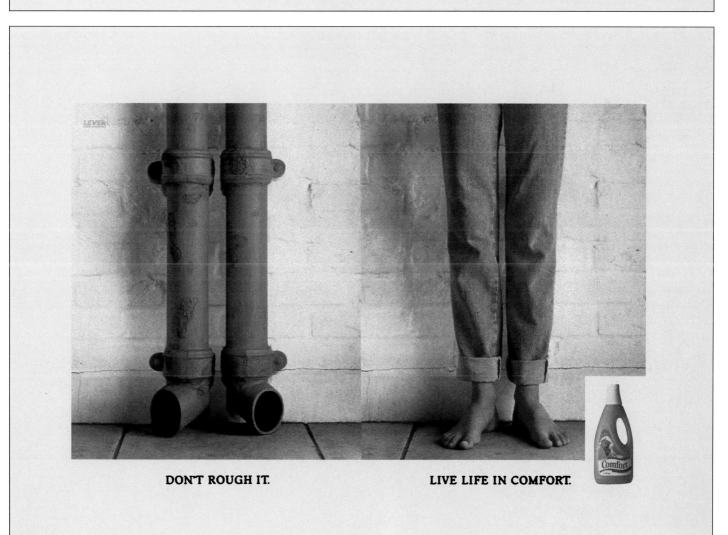

**CONSUMER MAGAZINE
COLOR: 1 PAGE OR SPREAD/
CAMPAIGN**

**27 BRONZE**
**ART DIRECTOR**
Amy Watt
**WRITER**
Edward Boches
**ILLUSTRATOR**
Amy Watt
**PHOTOGRAPHERS**
John Huet, Cheryl Clegg,
Stock
**CLIENT**
Smartfoods
**AGENCY**
Mullen/Wenham

Gold, Silver, & Bronze
Awards

**CONSUMER MAGAZINE
LESS THAN A PAGE
B/W OR COLOR: SINGLE**

**28 SILVER**
**ART DIRECTOR**
Barton Landsman
**WRITER**
Amy Krouse Rosenthal
**CLIENT**
Riverside Chocolate
Factory
**AGENCY**
Boy & Girl Advertising/
Chicago

**29 BRONZE**
**ART DIRECTOR**
Amy Watt
**WRITER**
Edward Boches
**ILLUSTRATOR**
Amy Watt
**PHOTOGRAPHERS**
Cheryl Clegg, Stock
**CLIENT**
Smartfoods
**AGENCY**
Mullen/Wenham

**30 BRONZE**
**ART DIRECTOR**
Brian Burke
**WRITER**
Chris Wigert
**PHOTOGRAPHER**
Steve Umland
**CLIENT**
Fred Arbogast
**AGENCY**
TBWA Kerlick Switzer/
St. Louis

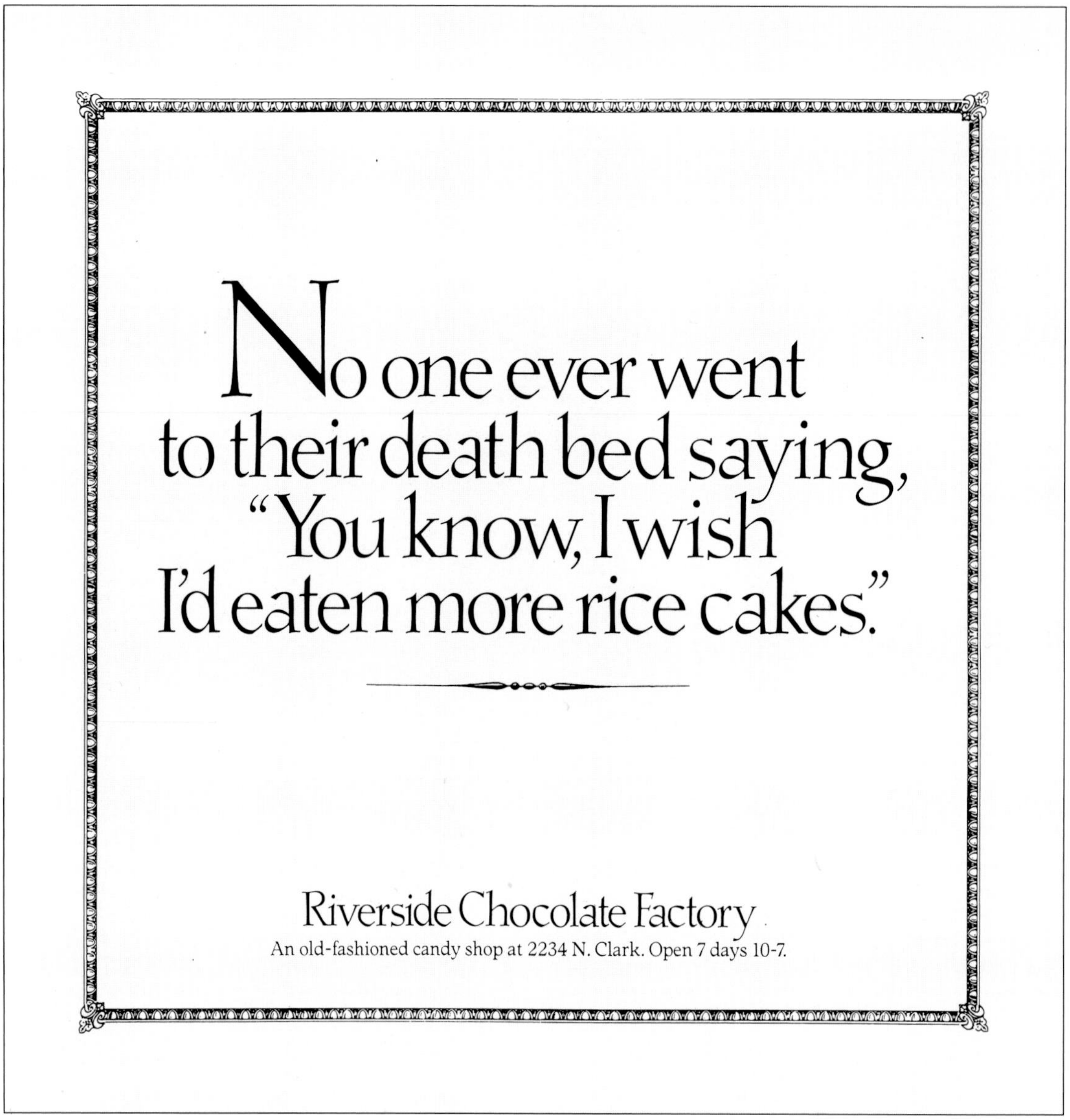

No one ever went
to their death bed saying,
"You know, I wish
I'd eaten more rice cakes."

Riverside Chocolate Factory
An old-fashioned candy shop at 2234 N. Clark. Open 7 days 10-7.

**28 SILVER**

*YOU CAN'T GET IT OFF YOUR MIND*

Totally natural SMARTFOOD®. Air-popped popcorn smothered in white cheddar cheese.

*JITTERBUG®, The Legendary Bass Lure We Introduced In 1938.*     *HULA POPPER®, Another Surface Classic From Fred Arbogast. Since 1941.*     *MUD-BUG®, Deep-Diving Winner In Scores Of Bass Tournaments Since 1968.*

## For Over 50 Years, They've Been The Most Popular Lures In America. Particularly Among Fish.

More hawgs have been landed by the classic Fred Arbogast lures above than anything else designed for that purpose. So it's no wonder that they're still standard equipment for successful anglers today. Because modern fish are no smarter than the ones of thirty or forty years ago. Which is why our classic lures continue to bring home the big ones. On your next fishing trip, why not see for yourself? Chances are, you've already got our lures somewhere in your tackle box. (FRED ARBOGAST®)

The configurations of the Hula Popper lure and Jitterbug lure are both federally registered trademarks and represent nearly 20 million lures sold.

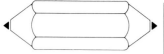

**CONSUMER MAGAZINE
LESS THAN A PAGE
B/W OR COLOR: CAMPAIGN**

**31 GOLD**
**ART DIRECTOR**
Barton Landsman
**WRITER**
Amy Krouse Rosenthal
**CLIENT**
Riverside Chocolate
Factory
**AGENCY**
Boy & Girl Advertising/
Chicago

No one ever went
to their death bed saying,
"You know, I wish
I'd eaten more rice cakes."

Riverside Chocolate Factory
An old-fashioned candy shop at 2234 N. Clark. Open 7 days 10-7.

Not until you've
tried one of our homemade
ice cream bars will you
fully understand the purpose
of having a mouth.

Riverside Chocolate Factory
An old-fashioned candy shop at 2234 N. Clark. Open 7 days 10-7.

Remember, aside
from Shirley MacLaine,
we only live once.

Riverside Chocolate Factory
An old-fashioned candy shop at 2234 N. Clark. Open 7 days 10-7.

**CONSUMER MAGAZINE
LESS THAN A PAGE
B/W OR COLOR: CAMPAIGN**

**32 SILVER**
**ART DIRECTOR**
Amy Watt
**WRITER**
Edward Boches
**ILLUSTRATOR**
Amy Watt
**PHOTOGRAPHERS**
Cheryl Clegg, Stock
**CLIENT**
Smartfoods
**AGENCY**
Mullen/Wenham

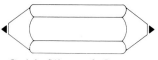

KENTUCKY STRAIGHT BOURBON WHISKEY. ALC. BY VOL. 50.5%. AUSTIN NICHOLS DISTILLING CO., LAWRENCEBURG, KY © 1990.

# A bird in the hand is a very good idea, indeed.

**WILD TURKEY**

8 years old, 101 proof, pure Kentucky.

KENTUCKY STRAIGHT BOURBON WHISKEY ALC. BY VOL. 50.5%. AUSTIN NICHOLS DISTILLING CO. LAWRENCEBURG, KY © 1990.

# Too good to keep cooped up.

**WILD TURKEY**

8 years old, 101 proof, pure Kentucky.

KENTUCKY STRAIGHT BOURBON WHISKEY ALC. BY VOL. 50.5%. AUSTIN NICHOLS DISTILLING CO. LAWRENCEBURG, KY © 1990.

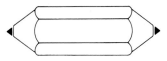

Gold, Silver, & Bronze
Awards

## OUTDOOR: SINGLE

**34 GOLD**
**ART DIRECTOR**
Matt Myers
**WRITER**
Rick Rosenberg
**CLIENT**
Museum of Flight
**AGENCY**
Livingston & Company/
Seattle

**35 SILVER**
**ART DIRECTOR**
David Page
**WRITER**
Dave O'Hare
**PHOTOGRAPHER**
Alan Krosnick
**CLIENT**
Jose Cuervo Tequila
**AGENCY**
Goodby Berlin &
Silverstein/San Francisco

**36 BRONZE**
**ART DIRECTOR**
Matt Myers
**WRITER**
Rick Rosenberg
**CLIENT**
Museum of Flight
**AGENCY**
Livingston & Company/
Seattle

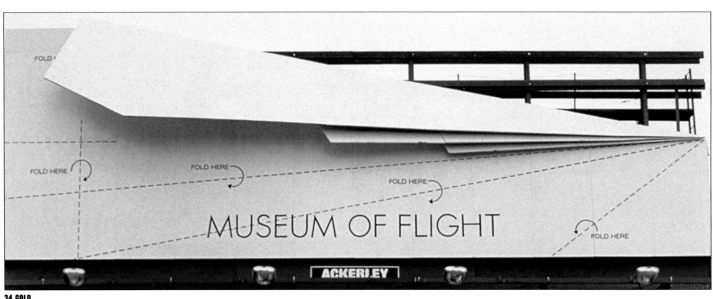

**34 GOLD**

# MISTLETOE? YOU DON'T NEED NO STINKING MISTLETOE.

MUSEUM OF FLIGHT

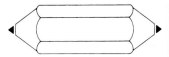

**OUTDOOR: CAMPAIGN**

**37 GOLD**
**ART DIRECTOR**
Steve Dunn
**WRITER**
Tim Delaney
**CLIENT**
Courtauld Institute
**AGENCY**
Leagas Delaney/London

## Madonna tickets.
## 071 872 0220.

The Madonna with Child and Angels
Quentin Matsys

The Courtauld Institute Galleries' priceless collections of paintings can finally be seen in their entirety at Somerset House, the Strand. 10am-6pm Monday to Saturday and 2pm-6pm Sunday. Also 6pm-8pm on Tuesdays, July to September. Admission £2.50. Concessions £1.

**Courtauld Institute Galleries**

## Another carpenter who promised to come back one day and finish the job.

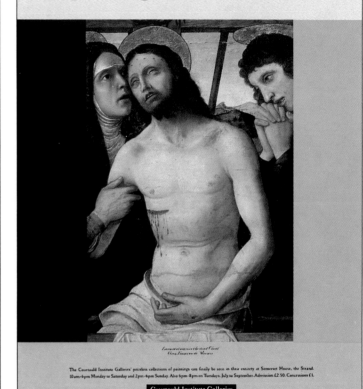

Lamentation over the dead Christ
Gian Francesco de Maineri

The Courtauld Institute Galleries' priceless collections of paintings can finally be seen in their entirety at Somerset House, the Strand. 10am-6pm Monday to Saturday and 2pm-6pm Sunday. Also 6pm-8pm on Tuesdays, July to September. Admission £2.50. Concessions £1.

**Courtauld Institute Galleries**

**37 GOLD**

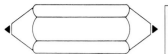

Gold, Silver, & Bronze
Awards

**OUTDOOR: CAMPAIGN**

**38 SILVER**
**ART DIRECTOR**
Amy Watt
**WRITER**
Edward Boches
**PHOTOGRAPHERS**
Cheryl Clegg, Stock
**CLIENT**
Smartfoods
**AGENCY**
Mullen/Wenham

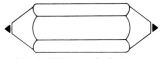

Gold, Silver, & Bronze
Awards

**OUTDOOR: CAMPAIGN**

**39 BRONZE**
**ART DIRECTOR**
Bill Oberlander
**WRITER**
David Buckingham
**ILLUSTRATOR**
Tom Hart
**CLIENT**
New York Post
**AGENCY**
Kirshenbaum & Bond/
New York

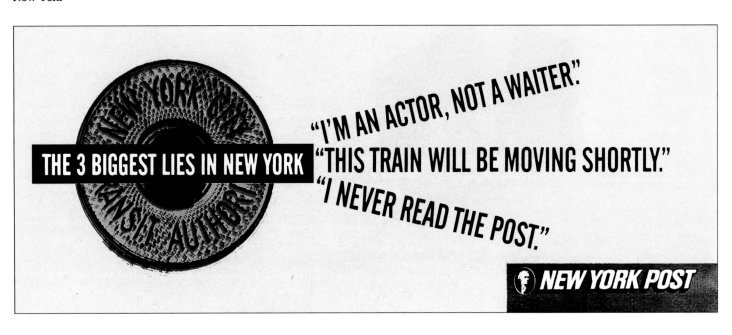

**THE 3 BIGGEST LIES IN NEW YORK**

"I ONLY WATCH CHANNEL 13."
"I WAS WORKING LATE, HONEY. HONEST."
"I NEVER READ THE POST."

 **NEW YORK POST**

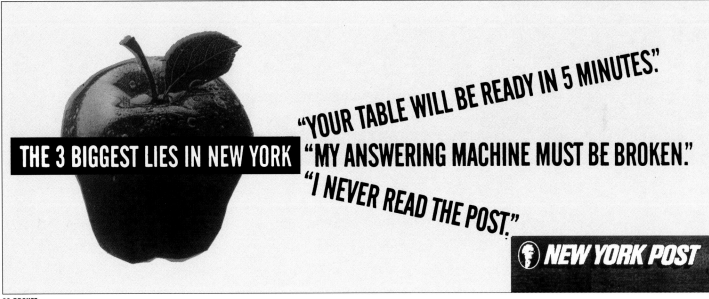

**THE 3 BIGGEST LIES IN NEW YORK**

"YOUR TABLE WILL BE READY IN 5 MINUTES."
"MY ANSWERING MACHINE MUST BE BROKEN."
"I NEVER READ THE POST."

**NEW YORK POST**

39 BRONZE

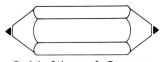

Gold, Silver, & Bronze
Awards

**OUTDOOR: CAMPAIGN**

**40 BRONZE**
**ART DIRECTOR**
Tom Lichtenheld
**WRITERS**
Luke Sullivan,
Doug deGrood
**CLIENT**
General Mills/Bringer's
**AGENCY**
Fallon McElligott/
Minneapolis

# Hungry? Tired? Divorced?
## BRINGER'S
### CALL 941-FOOD

Too fried to cook?
BRINGER'S
CALL 941-FOOD

Now serving couch potatoes. BRINGER'S
CALL 941-FOOD

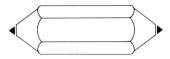

Gold, Silver, & Bronze
Awards

**TRADE B/W 1 PAGE
OR SPREAD: SINGLE**

**41 GOLD**
**ART DIRECTOR**
Tracy Wong
**WRITER**
Clay Williams
**ILLUSTRATOR**
Greg Dearth
**CLIENT**
Clarks of England
**AGENCY**
Goodby Berlin &
Silverstein/San Francisco

**42 SILVER**
**ART DIRECTOR**
Nick Cohen
**WRITER**
Ty Montague
**CLIENT**
The Creative Register
**AGENCY**
Mad Dogs & Englishmen/
New York

**43 BRONZE**
**ART DIRECTOR**
Ron Rosen
**WRITER**
Richard Kelly
**CLIENT**
Nikon
**AGENCY**
Scali McCabe Sloves/
New York

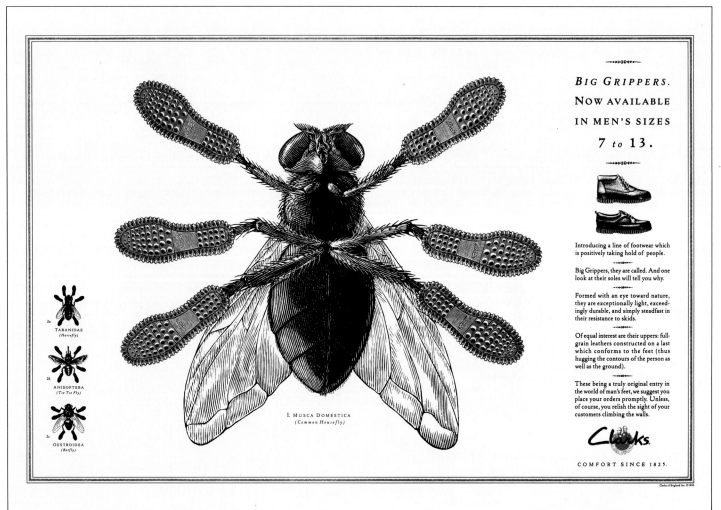

41 GOLD

*Fig I. Ca Ca.*

DON'T HATE ME because I'm beautiful.

I'm not a doctor, but I play one on TV. Did

somebody say deal? A double pleasure is

waiting for you, tra la la la. I liked it so

much I bought the company. Colt 45, works

every time. He loves my mind <u>and</u> he

drinks Johnny Walker. If any of this reminds

you of your portfolio, please get on your

Pontiac and ride. THE CREATIVE REGISTER.

Advertising Talent Scouts. (212) 533 3676.

**42 SILVER**

If you can picture it in your head,
it was probably taken with a Nikon.

**43 BRONZE**

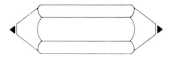

Gold, Silver, & Bronze
Awards

**TRADE COLOR 1 PAGE
OR SPREAD: SINGLE**

**44 GOLD**
**ART DIRECTOR**
Tracy Wong
**WRITER**
Rob Bagot
**ILLUSTRATOR**
Gwenne Wilcox
**PHOTOGRAPHERS**
Jay Maisel, Stock
**CLIENT**
Royal Viking Line
**AGENCY**
Goodby Berlin &
Silverstein/San Francisco

**45 GOLD**
**ART DIRECTOR**
Ed Evangelista
**WRITER**
Paul Wolfe
**CLIENT**
LIFE Magazine
**AGENCY**
Messner Vetere Berger
Carey Schmetterer/
New York

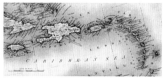

QUITE MAGICALLY, THE MOST ALLURING ISLAND
IN THE CARIBBEAN COMES AND GOES AS IT PLEASES.

Beginning in October, the Royal Viking Star will be gracing the deep blue seas of the Southern Caribbean.

Included in her itineraries are such Caribbean hot spots as St. Thomas, St. John, Barbados, Antigua and Martinique. Along the way, jazz musicians will be featured and nightly shows will light up the ship's lounge.

These five-, six-, ten- and eleven-day voyages include all the five-star-plus service for which we are renowned: the Scandinavian stewardesses, the penthouse butler, the white-gloved waiters, the six sommeliers – in short, the countless many who make Royal Viking Line the most lauded fleet of cruise vessels on earth.

If you have clients who insist they just don't have time for a cruise, inform them of our five- and six-day offerings, then casually mention the complimentary two-day land packages included therein. This has proven to be an irresistible combination.

For all particulars regarding these Barbados Series cruises, departing from Ft. Lauderdale and Barbados, call sales assistance at (800) 346-8000, or reservations at (800) 422-8000. In Canada, the number is (800) 448-4785.

As always, we look forward to your call.

ROYAL VIKING LINE
THE WORLD'S FINEST

# HI. MY NAME'S JACK. I'M HERE TO SEE YOUR DAUGHTER.

He's an actor's actor and a studio executive's entry to paradise. He's also a rake, a charmer, a genius and a rogue. All these terms apply. To a reporter for LIFE, he sums it up with the internationally patented grin: "How I do love to play!"

LIFE was granted intimate access to Jack and his latest creations: Two Jakes and one baby, the latter an unexpected daughter with an actress in the film.

In the current tidal wave of Nicholson coverage, why does the most powerful actor in Hollywood feel comfortable offering LIFE his revelations? Maybe he sees his work as substantive and enduring, and thinks of LIFE the same way.

Photo: Harry Benson

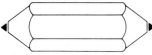

Gold, Silver, & Bronze
Awards

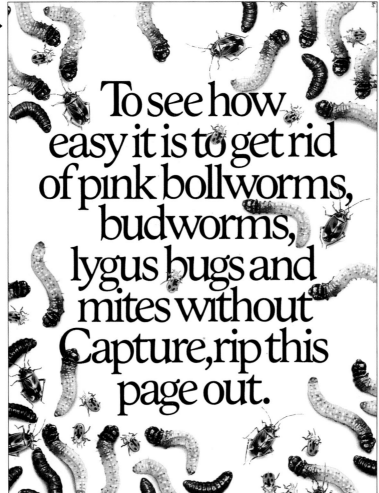

To see how easy it is to get rid of pink bollworms, budworms, lygus bugs and mites without Capture, rip this page out.

Had enough?

If you thought getting rid of pests here was a pain, imagine when they're in your cotton field. Luckily though, there's Capture® insecticide/miticide.* It's the single easiest way to control mites, aphids, worms and whitefly. So get some Capture. And leave the hard work to magazine readers. **FMC**

**46 SILVER**

# A FACE ONLY FOUR PRESIDENTS COULD LOVE.

They carried on a love affair for twenty years: the C.I.A. and General Manuel Noriega.

It was a clandestine love, flourishing under four U.S. presidents despite full knowledge of the General's role in drug trafficking, Cuban espionage and assassinations of the presidents of both Panama and Ecuador.

The affair is exclusively chronicled now for LIFE by Pulitzer-Prize winning journalist Seymour Hersh.

How powerful is the story? Ecuador's government re-opened its investigation the morning LIFE hit the stands.

Photo: Wesley Boxce/Sipa Press

# THIS SHOULD HAVE RUN LAST WEEK.

We're looking for a media buyer with at least
1½ years experience in television and print buying.
If you're interested in placing ads
rather than reading them,
call David Cairns at 585-9992.

## CHIAT/DAY

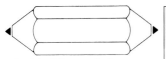

Gold, Silver, & Bronze
Awards

**TRADE ANY SIZE
B/W OR COLOR: CAMPAIGN**

**49 GOLD**
**ART DIRECTOR**
Neil French
**WRITERS**
Ben Hunt, Neil French,
Ernest Shackleton
**PHOTOGRAPHER**
Alex KaiKeong
**CLIENT**
The Ball Partnership
**AGENCY**
The Ball Partnership/
Singapore

## There are plenty of excellent reasons for leaving the country.

### Frankly, 'The chance to do better ads' isn't usually regarded as one of them.

For most advertising people, England, and London in particular, has become a sort of benign prison. And not always that benign.

"If I'm not here," you hear them say, "I won't be able to do great ads." As if the air itself, polluted and carcinogenic as it is, in some way contributes to the creative process.

But in all seriousness, how many great ads have you seen lately?

More importantly, how many have you done, yourself? Honestly, now.

(Of course, it may be that you're basically inept, in which case, you're probably no longer reading this, and good riddance).

Some of those still with us may, however, have a nagging suspicion that we have a point. Or may eventually get round to making one.

So. Why do people flock, Whittington-like, to London, when, these days, the entire world is their mollusc? Fear is the key.

Not just the fear of 'not being at the heart of things'. It's the greater fear... of the unknown. That, once you leave, you can never return.

Nonsense, of course. If you're good, you can go anywhere. For instance, Paul Leeves worked in Singapore for a while, and it didn't slow him down.

But in any case, is it so crucially important that you should return? Why would you want to? Is London really that special?

Today, take a look around you.

Is it the weather that keeps you here? (This is, quite clearly, a joke. There are few major cities in the world with as unattractive a climate as ours. Minsk, perhaps. Or possibly Melbourne).

Is it the absence of crime? If it is, you must live in Gwent. Or Downing Street.

The freedom of the individual? The justice and sanity of having your car clamped for hours in the very position in which it was, presumably, causing an obstruction in the first place?

Perhaps you're just proud of being British? Haven't been abroad lately, have you? Not where they play football, anyway.

You believe, possibly, that despite it all, this is still a great place to bring up a family. That must be it. There are no drink problems, no drugs and no violence: The education system and sickness service are in splendid shape: And for the young, these days, buying a home is so easy. Right?

Seriously, now. What are you doing here?

The Option.

You could live somewhere else.

Give yourself a moment to get over the shock of the concept, and then get the world map out of your Filofax. First time you've ever needed it, yes?

Over on the right is the Pacific. It's the large blue bit. All the land in and around it is called the Pacific Rim. And for the next few decades, that is where the action's going to be.

Japan, of course, and Australia. And some day, China. But right now, Hong Kong, Thailand, Taiwan, Malaysia, Indonesia, South Korea. And Singapore.

All the major agency groups are already in position there. They have to be. But only one was actually 'born' there, and predictably, it is quickly becoming the most successful. The name can wait for now, because first let's talk about just one of those countries.

Singapore is a small island, with ambitions to become the Switzerland of Asia. Its population of 2.5 million is swollen by a constant invasion of visitors. Singapore has more First-Class Hotels per square mile than anywhere else on earth. And they include the tallest, and one of the oldest, in the world.

It is practically free of street-crime. Burglary is rare. Corporal punishment is mandatory for rape and violence. Drug-pushers are hanged.

It has the most modern subway-system in the world. Parking is easy. Traffic-jams are cause for remark.

The city is clean, green, bursting with life. It is, admittedly, hot and humid. But air-con makes a welcome change from central heating. It rains in stair-rods occasionally. No hurricanes, though, or earthquakes.

The people are Chinese, Malay, Indian and Caucasian. Most speak English. Their commercial history is one of trading and entrepreneurship. Consequently, they tend to be marvellous, brave, clients. (Not all, of course. But a lot).

Finally, the cost of living well is rather lower than in the UK. And tax is a lot lower.

What about this 'better ads' bit? Singapore produces some of the best ads in the world.

Bullshit? Not at all. Every year, some of the world's top admen fly to Singapore to judge their awards (it's known as the Gong Show), and every year they're amazed at the standard.

Ask Steve Grounds, Jeff Stark, Peter Harold, Suzie Henry, or Tony Brignull. Call Helmut Krone, Ed McCabe, Andrew Rutherford, or Ron Mather.

At the moment, one agency in Singapore is very hot indeed. It's called The Ball Partnership. Creatively, we're No.1. (As we are in Malaysia).

But the fact that we won the lion's share of Singapore's Awards may not mean much to you. Even the fact that we walked off with more Asian Awards than any other agency may not impress. A wallfull of Clio finalists? No?

OK, then. How many ads did you get in the D&ADA Annual this year? We got seven.

We're understandably cocky. But we want to do better. We're looking for a Creative Director. Ideally, an art-director who can write. Definitely a thinker. Without doubt, a leader. Possibly not from London at all, but a denizen of the rather more ballsy 'provinces'. (I'm a Brummie, myself).

If you're interested, write to Neil French, at The Ball Partnership, 172 Drury Lane, London WC2, with your C.V. and examples of some of your best work, (stats will do). Don't bother to call in or phone, though; I'll be somewhere in Asia. In the sun.

## The D&ADA jury thought this was a pretty good ad.
## Unfortunately, none of them was looking for a job at the time.

To be brutally honest, this ranks with Jeff Stark's 'Blind Man', as a much-admired bummer. Nice ad, shame about the response.

Mind you, in retrospect, we put every effort into making absolutely sure it would fail.

We bunged it in 'Campaign', in the Christmas issue before last, when everyone thought they had a job for life, and were too pissed to read it anyway.

'Campaign' themselves did their bit, too, insisting on their horrible, clunky, Sits Vac header across the top, thus destroying any semblance of style or balance the ad might have had.

(Good grief, look; they've done it again! Presumably they're afraid that people scanning the back of the rag may be looking for a Lonely Hearts section, and might be confused otherwise. Hopeless).

Anyway, we had a few replies, and filled the position internally, as the unpleasantly anatomical phrase has it.

But, just as a second marriage is said to be the triumph of hope over experience, here we go again.

Now, you can either squint your way through the ad above, or take it from the jury that it's brilliantly written, & settle for the short version:

England's cold, grey, and depressing: Singapore isn't.

A few things have changed since last year: Warren Brown came out to judge our awards, as did Paul Arden, who may not remember. But ask either of them about us, please.

Add Hong Kong to the list of places we're said to be No.1; Add a Gold at Cannes to our list of awards; and we got three ads in D&ADA this year, of which the above is two.

We need a creative director, and a senior team, because we've doubled our size, & the last CD has been promoted, God help him.

Write today, or fax everything to (65)339-1508. By the time this gets in The Book, it'll be too late.

# IS THIS

# THE BEST AD

# EVER WRITTEN?

MEN WANTED for Hazardous Journey. Small wages, bitter cold, long months of complete darkness, constant danger, safe return doubtful. Honour and recognition in case of success — Ernest Shackleton.

When this little advertisement ran, in 1900, Ernest Shackleton was snowed under with replies.

Why? Surely, by all the accepted rules, he shouldn't have been. For a start, the 'promise' is entirely negative. And there's no picture.

So let's rewrite the ad, according to the rules.

"Men wanted for exciting journey. Good money, excellent conditions, certainty of massive royalties from publishing and movie rights. Reply now!"

Brilliant. Run it.

And if they had, you know instinctively that, even though they might have had a bagful of replies, it's very doubtful that they'd have got anywhere near the South Pole.

And certainly, no-one would have returned, to cash in on the deal.

And we wouldn't now be talking about the ad either. Would we?

Isn't the strength of that advertisement, then, in its simplicity? Isn't its sheer power in its honesty?

And is not its most brilliant quality the way it appeals precisely, and absolutely exclusively, to the very specialised section of the market it addresses?

'Wimps need not apply' would be superfluous. It's written large enough between the lines.

No doubt Shackleton wrote the ad straight off the cuff, pausing only to count the words, and the cost. It works because it has passion, and belief, and you can feel the leadership, if not fanaticism, in every phrase.

But *this* advertisement is written for an agency. An advertising agency. We produce ads, every day, for a living.

And frankly, rarely for as romantic a cause, or as inspiring a journey, as Ernest's.

But we do like to think that, at times, our work is as focussed, and as simple, as his: We know for certain that it can be as effective.

To help us, we've evolved systems that *force* us to take a fresh look at every problem; to wring the very last drop of information out of the product and the market; and to avoid at all costs, the trite, the formula-led, and especially the downright boring.

We've even produced an example, to show how, in all likelihood, our system would have led us to the same conclusion to which Shackleton's inspiration led him. (To his ad, that is. Not to the South Pole.)

If you'd be interested in finding out how we work, give us a call. We're in Hong Kong, Malaysia, Thailand, Taiwan, and Singapore.

We're The Ball Partnership.

---

## THERE IS A SPELLING MISTAKE IN THIS ADVERTISEMENT.
## THE FIRST PERSON TO SPOT IT WILL RECIEVE $500.

No, it's not in this line.

Or, you'll have guessed, in this line, either.

You're going to have to read this entire page, with the eyes of a school examiner, to spot it.

Which, when you think, makes it rather a good advertisement, doesn't it? Since ads, like the editorial they sidle up to, are written to be read.

How many of the other ads in this week's 'Media' are going to get this amount of attention?

One, maybe? Two?

It's more than likely that you haven't read *any* of them. Be honest, now:

You've given them the same treatment you give those suspiciously friendly encyclopaedia salesmen, who knock on your door and ask for five minutes of your time.

No, thank you: Slam the door. (Or in this case, turn the page.)

No sale. And we don't blame you. You saw the sell coming. Why waste your time?

The majority of ads are like that, too. Predictable, dull, and not very well presented.

They resolutely ignore the fact that the average consumer sees one thousand, six hundred advertising messages every day, and would be perfectly content not to see any at all.

You see, with the possible exception of seven year old brats with a passion for Teenage Mutant Ninja Turtles, PEOPLE DON'T LIKE ADS. There, we've said it. In a publication dedicated to the creed that advertising is a profession comparable only in its saintliness and altruism with being one of Mother Teresa's little helpers, we've spilt the beans:

We are not universally popular: If spacemen came down and took every person connected with advertising away for dissection, it would be a long time before we were missed. And even then, it would be because people discovered that their newspapers had become more interesting, and their TV programmes more enjoyable, for our absence.

(See? Heresy spoken out loud. And still we write. No thunderbolts from on high. God doesn't like ads, either.)

And yet...

And yet, in the face of reams of irrefutable evidence to the contrary, the majority of advertising agencies (and let's spread the blame a bit, their clients, too), persist in the belief that this just ain't so.

They sincerely believe that buying a space also guarantees readership of whatever they fill it with.

Sadder still, the higher the cost of the space, the more tense and creatively constipated they become, and the more safe and generic is their message: It's a new rule; the bigger the budget, the blander the ads.

Even the relatively enlightened feel that if they find, and mention, some semblance of a benefit in that space, they've *really* done a good job.

That by some miracle, the consumer is going to home in on their ad, shrieking "Just what I've always wanted!"

Sure. If your benefit is "Free Beer".

OK; *definitely*, if your benefit is "Free Beer". But if it's not, you're in big trouble.

You're going to be thrown in there with washing powders that get clothes whiter, toothpastes that taste nicer, tires that grip better ...

In other words, you're going to be ignored.

Don't misunderstand us, please. If your product has a substantial benefit over its competitors, you'd be mad not to tell everyone. The point is, it'd be mad to think that's *all* you had to do.

The public, as we've said, has become immune to everyday advertising.

For an ad to succeed these days, it has to work on many levels. It has to be relevant to the reader: It has to speak to him in language he can relate to: If there *is* a benefit to crow about, it has to be a benefit that's important to the *consumer*, not just to the manufacturer: To revert to the door-to-door salesman analogy, it has to look good ...the sort of person you'd invite into your home; the sort of advertisement you'd welcome into your mind...

But most of all, it has to be 'different'.

It has to jump from the page, or leap off the screen, screaming "Read me! Watch me!"

And it has to do so with a degree of seduction in its voice, rather than the foot-in-the-door brazen insistence, that leads only to the zap, the flip, and the broken toe.

Now. Doubtless there are sceptics out there who may say that this particular advertisement meets none of the criteria that it has been at such pains to expound.

That it is visually dull, dull, dull.

That it's criminally overwritten: That it's also a stupid concept, and that the one and only reason that they're reading it is to find the spelling mistake and qualify for $500 in the currency of their choice.

They may, of course, be right. (Found it yet, by the way? Keep going; concentrate.)

But at the Ball Partnership we'll do anything to get people to read ads.

Ours. Or yours.

This advertisement has cost us $22,336 to run. As you can imagine we're more than happy to give away $500 to make sure that everybody reads it. If you've found the spelling mistake (and if you haven't by now, you've missed it), call The Ball Partnership in Hong Kong, Malaysia, Singapore, Taiwan or Thailand and ask to speak to the Managing Partner. Of course, you're almost certainly too late to get the five hundred bucks, but call anyway. We like to chat about ads.

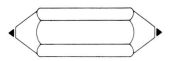

Gold, Silver, & Bronze
Awards

**TRADE ANY SIZE
B/W OR COLOR: CAMPAIGN**

**50 SILVER**
**ART DIRECTOR**
Joe Shands
**WRITER**
Rob Rosenthal
**PHOTOGRAPHER**
Doug Petty
**CLIENT**
The American Advertising
Museum
**AGENCY**
Cole & Weber/Portland

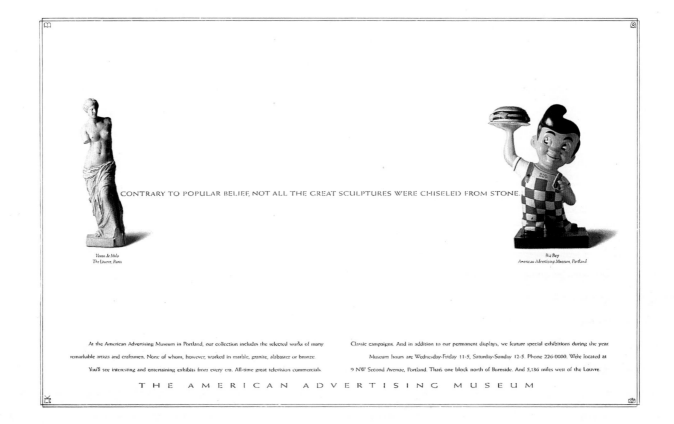

CONTRARY TO POPULAR BELIEF, NOT ALL THE GREAT SCULPTURES WERE CHISELED FROM STONE.

Venus de Milo
The Louvre, Paris

Big Boy
American Advertising Museum, Portland

At the American Advertising Museum in Portland, our collection includes the selected works of many remarkable artists and craftsmen. None of whom, however, worked in marble, granite, alabaster or bronze. You'll see interesting and entertaining exhibits from every era. All-time great television commercials. Classic campaigns. And in addition to our permanent displays, we feature special exhibitions during the year. Museum hours are Wednesday-Friday 11-5, Saturday-Sunday 12-5. Phone 226-0000. We're located at 9 NW Second Avenue, Portland. That's one block north of Burnside. And 5,136 miles west of the Louvre.

THE AMERICAN ADVERTISING MUSEUM

Van Gogh's "Self-Portrait with Bandaged Ear"
Courtauld Collection, London

WE DON'T HAVE ANY VAN GOGHS. BUT THEN AGAIN, THEY DON'T HAVE ANY BERNBACHS.

Doyle Dane Bernbach's "Think Small"
American Advertising Museum, Portland

Only a great master, could take a product like the world's ugliest automobile, and transform it into a remarkable work of art. A craft thats commonly known as "advertising."

At the American Advertising Museum, you'll get a fun and fascinating look at advertising from every era.

The all-time great commercials. The classic campaigns. And the talented individuals who created them.

So come visit us Wednesday-Friday 11-5, Saturday-Sunday 12-5  9 NW Second Avenue, Portland.

Phone 226-0000 And see for yourself that the world's greatest works of art don't all hang in art museums.

### THE AMERICAN ADVERTISING MUSEUM

---

Koufax No-Hitter
Baseball Hall of Fame, Cooperstown

WHILE WE'RE NOT A BASEBALL MUSEUM, WE'VE IMMORTALIZED SOME VERY MEMORABLE PITCHES.

Avis Rent-A-Car Campaign
American Advertising Museum, Portland

They have men in pinstripes. We have men in pinstripes. They have Ruth, DiMaggio, Koufax and Mays. We have Snap, Crackle & Pop, the Jolly Green Giant, Speedy Alka Seltzer and the Tidy Bowl Man.

At the American Advertising Museum, you'll get a fun and fascinating look at advertising from every era.

The all-time great commercials. And classic ad campaigns that gave new meaning to the term "hard ball."

So come visit Wednesday-Friday 11-5, Saturday-Sunday 12-5. We're located at 9 NW Second Avenue, Portland. Phone 226-0000. And see advertising's greatest pitches. Not to mention the biggest hits.

### THE AMERICAN ADVERTISING MUSEUM

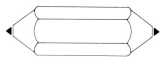

Gold, Silver, & Bronze
Awards

# SHOCKING NEW EVIDENCE REVEALS ELVIS IS DEAD.

He's been spotted everywhere from a flying saucer to aisle three of a Texas supermarket.

But the truth is, the King of Rock 'n Roll still lies, as ever, beneath the grass of Graceland.

The extraordinary news is how he got there. And in the June issue of LIFE, Elvis biographer Albert Goldman discloses a gruesome new set of facts supplied by Presley's step-brother.

The facts reveal that Elvis Presley died neither from the rocking pneumonia nor the boogie woogie flu.

He committed suicide.

# A FACE ONLY FOUR PRESIDENTS COULD LOVE.

They carried on a love affair for twenty years: the C.I.A. and General Manuel Noriega.

It was a clandestine love, flourishing under four U.S. presidents despite full knowledge of the General's role in drug trafficking, Cuban espionage and assassinations of the presidents of both Panama and Ecuador.

The affair is exclusively chronicled now for LIFE by Pulitzer-Prize winning journalist Seymour Hersh.

How powerful is the story? Ecuador's government re-opened its investigation the morning LIFE hit the stands.

Photo: Wesley Boxe/Sipa Press

# HI. MY NAME'S JACK. I'M HERE TO SEE YOUR DAUGHTER.

He's an actor's actor and a studio executive's entry to paradise. He's also a rake, a charmer, a genius and a rogue. All these terms apply. To a reporter for LIFE, he sums it up with the internationally patented grin: "How I do love to play!"

LIFE was granted intimate access to Jack and his latest creations: Two Jakes and one baby, the latter an unexpected daughter with an actress in the film.

In the current tidal wave of Nicholson coverage, why does the most powerful actor in Hollywood feel comfortable offering LIFE his revelations? Maybe he sees his work as substantive and enduring, and thinks of LIFE the same way.

Photo: Harry Benson

Gold, Silver, & Bronze
Awards

**TRADE ANY SIZE
B/W OR COLOR: CAMPAIGN**

**52 BRONZE**
**ART DIRECTOR**
Tracy Wong
**WRITER**
Clay Williams
**ILLUSTRATOR**
Greg Dearth
**CLIENT**
Clarks of England
**AGENCY**
Goodby Berlin &
Silverstein/San Francisco

# AIR CYRUS.

Meet Cyrus Clark, co-founder of Clarks shoes and overall Renaissance man.

Years ago, Cyrus realized that air is a remarkable shock absorber. Which is why it's been a long-standing feature in many of our shoes (besides its reasonable price and easy availability).

Technically speaking, Clarks Air Casuals operate like a sort of pump — exchanging air from cone to cone with every step — thus cushioning the feet, knees and lower back.

This, when paired with our numerous other innovations, makes for shoes which are, in truth, more comfortable than a well-worn pair of sneakers (and oftentimes more appropriate).

Our competitors have only recently begun to get air. We, on the other hand, are just getting our second wind.

## Clarks

COMFORT SINCE 1825.

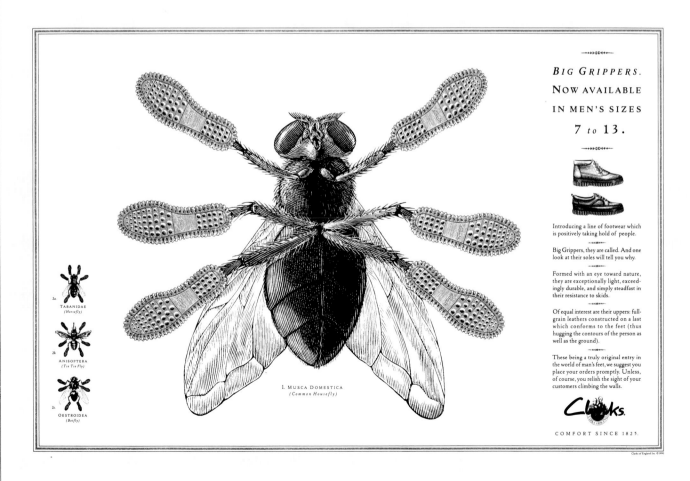

2a. TABANIDAE *(Horsefly)*

2b. ANISOPTERA *(Tie Tie Fly)*

2c. OESTROIDEA *(Botfly)*

I. MUSCA DOMESTICA *(Common Housefly)*

# BIG GRIPPERS.
## NOW AVAILABLE IN MEN'S SIZES 7 *to* 13.

Introducing a line of footwear which is positively taking hold of people.

Big Grippers, they are called. And one look at their soles will tell you why.

Formed with an eye toward nature, they are exceptionally light, exceedingly durable, and simply steadfast in their resistance to skids.

Of equal interest are their uppers: full-grain leathers constructed on a last which conforms to the feet (thus hugging the contours of the person as well as the ground).

These being a truly original entry in the world of man's feet, we suggest you place your orders promptly. Unless, of course, you relish the sight of your customers climbing the walls.

## Clarks

COMFORT SINCE 1825.

Clarks of England Inc. ©1990

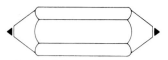

Gold, Silver, & Bronze
Awards

**COLLATERAL BROCHURES
OTHER THAN BY MAIL**

**53 GOLD**
**ART DIRECTOR**
Ben Wong
**WRITER**
Sam Pond
**PHOTOGRAPHER**
Robert Mizono
**CLIENT**
The Mirage
**AGENCY**
Hal Riney & Partners/
San Francisco

**54 SILVER**
**ART DIRECTOR**
Bill Schwab
**WRITER**
Tom Darbyshire
**PHOTOGRAPHER**
Claude Vazquez
**CLIENT**
Earle Palmer Brown
**AGENCY**
Earle Palmer Brown/
Bethesda

**55 BRONZE**
**ART DIRECTORS**
Lynne Scrimgeour,
Chris Overholser
**WRITER**
Connie Whittington
**PHOTOGRAPHER**
Claude Vazquez
**CLIENT**
Earle Palmer Brown
**AGENCY**
Earle Palmer Brown/
Bethesda

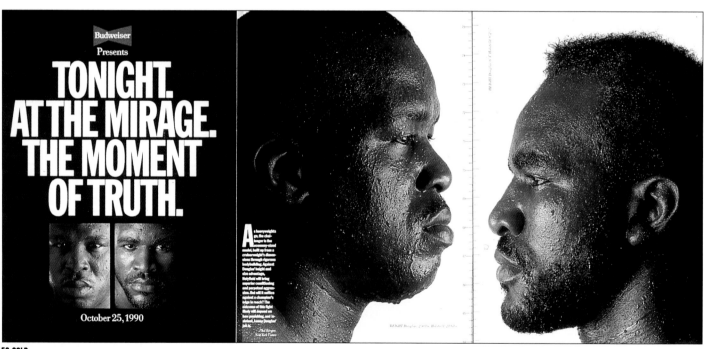

**53 GOLD**

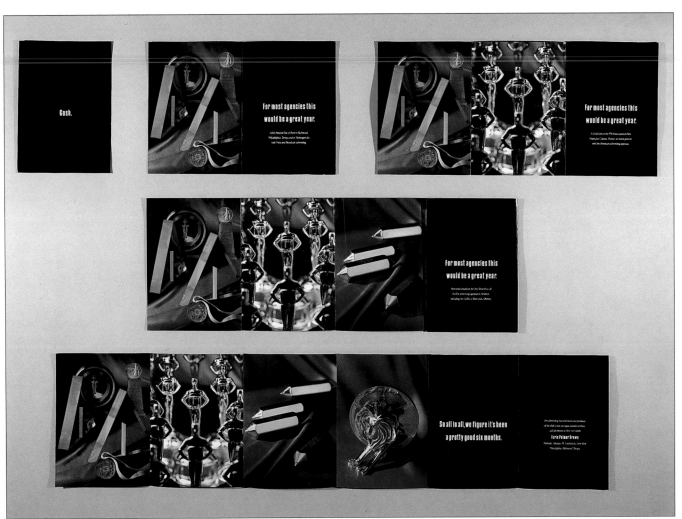

**54 SILVER**

**55 BRONZE**

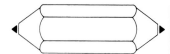

Gold, Silver, & Bronze
Awards

**COLLATERAL DIRECT MAIL:
SINGLE**

**56 GOLD**
**ART DIRECTOR**
Dean Hanson
**WRITER**
Bruce Bildsten
**CLIENT**
Fallon McElligott
**AGENCY**
Fallon McElligott/
Minneapolis

**57 SILVER**
**ART DIRECTOR**
Jelly Helm
**WRITER**
Jelly Helm
**CLIENT**
Jelly Helm
**AGENCY**
Self-Promotion

**58 BRONZE**
**ART DIRECTOR**
Bob Brihn
**WRITER**
John Stingley
**CLIENT**
Fallon McElligott
**AGENCY**
Fallon McElligott/
Minneapolis

# WORDS CANNOT DESCRIBE HOW EXCITED WE ARE TO BE THE NEW AGENCY FOR PURINA DOG FOODS.

# FALLON McELLIGOTT

**56 GOLD**

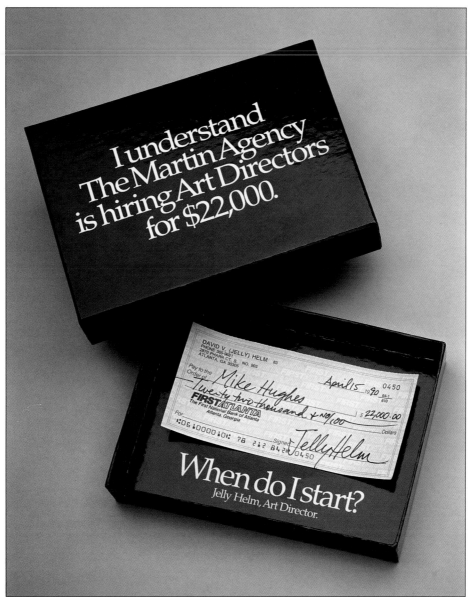

Gold, Silver, & Bronze
Awards

**COLLATERAL DIRECT MAIL:
CAMPAIGN**

**59 SILVER**
**ART DIRECTOR**
Steve Sweitzer
**WRITER**
Todd Tilford
**PHOTOGRAPHER**
Dennis Fagan
**CLIENT**
Tabu Lingerie
**AGENCY**
GSD&M/Austin

**IT'S LIKE WAVING A RED
FLAG IN FRONT OF A BULL.**

*Crossroads Center, 183 & Burnet, Mon.-Sat. 10-8, Sun. 12-6, 452-TABU*  **TABU** *Lingerie*

**THE RECENT SHOPPING SPREES
WERE BEGINNING TO GIVE HER HUSBAND
SOME SLEEPLESS NIGHTS.**

*Crossroads Center, 183 & Burnet, Mon.-Sat. 10-8, Sun. 12-6, 452-TABU* **TABU**
*Lingerie*

**MONDAY NIGHT FOOTBALL
HAS MET ITS MATCH.**

*Crossroads Center, 183 & Burnet, Mon.-Sat. 10-8, Sun. 12-6, 452-TABU* **TABU**
*Lingerie*

Gold, Silver, & Bronze
Awards

**COLLATERAL DIRECT MAIL:
CAMPAIGN**

**60 BRONZE**
**ART DIRECTOR**
Bill Santry
**WRITER**
Daniel Russ
**CLIENT**
Earle Palmer Brown
**AGENCY**
Earle Palmer Brown/
Bethesda

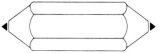

Gold, Silver, & Bronze
Awards

**COLLATERAL P.O.P.**

**61 GOLD**
**ART DIRECTOR**
Jelly Helm
**WRITER**
Raymond McKinney
**PHOTOGRAPHER**
Roy Boy
**CLIENT**
Bernie's Tattooing Parlor
**AGENCY**
The Martin Agency/
Richmond

**62 SILVER**
**ART DIRECTOR**
David Jenkins
**WRITER**
Jerry Cronin
**PHOTOGRAPHER**
Harry DeZitter
**CLIENT**
Nike
**AGENCY**
Wieden & Kennedy/
Portland

**63 BRONZE**
**ART DIRECTOR**
Rob Dalton
**WRITER**
Rod Kilpatrick
**CLIENT**
Spindler Antiques
**AGENCY**
Freelance Project

**61 GOLD**

There are clubs you can't belong to, Neighborhoods you can't live in, Schools you can't get into, But the roads are always open. Just do it.

**62 SILVER**

# OLD!

Announcing the opening of a new antique store.

SPINDLER ANTIQUES AND DESIGN
Harvard at Olive, one block off Broadway. 322-7732

**63 BRONZE**

Gold, Silver, & Bronze
Awards

**PUBLIC SERVICE
NEWSPAPER OR MAGAZINE:
SINGLE**

**64 GOLD**
**ART DIRECTOR**
Bob Barrie
**WRITER**
Luke Sullivan
**CLIENT**
People for the Ethical
Treatment of Animals
**AGENCY**
Fallon McElligott/
Minneapolis

**65 SILVER**
**ART DIRECTOR**
Chris Mitton
**WRITERS**
Jamie Warde-Aldam,
Chris Mitton
**PHOTOGRAPHER**
Neil Barstow
**CLIENT**
Royal National Institute for
the Deaf
**AGENCY**
Ogilvy & Mather/London

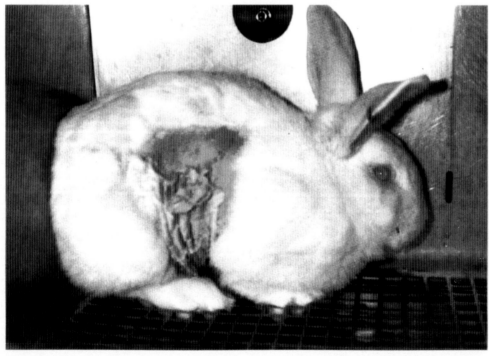

# Call Gillette and ask somebody in public relations to explain this picture.

Dial 617-421-7000.

Ask for Gillette's CEO Colman Mockler. Tell whoever answers you'd like to know why Gillette's still torturing and killing animals. Of course, when they hear this, they'll transfer you to public relations, where "problems" such as you and your questions are quietly dealt with.

Questions like: Is Gillette still pouring Liquid Paper into the eyes of rabbits when such a test doesn't make Liquid Paper any safer for human beings?

Is Gillette still shaving off the skins of rabbits and pouring chemicals directly into their wounds, when scientifically-sophisticated non-animal tests have been developed?

Is Gillette still doing lethal dose tests, wherein groups of animals are force-fed shampoos until many of them die?

And, finally, ask: given that none of these tests result in changes that make any of their products safer, why does Gillette continue to do them?

If you don't get a satisfactory answer, join us. Boycott Gillette.

**NEAVS** New England Anti-Vivisection Society
Research Modernization and Animal Rights
333 Washington St., Suite 850
Boston, MA 02108-5100
Phone (617) 523-6020

☐ Yes, I want to help stop animal testing. Here's $ _____.

Name _____

Address _____

City _____ State _____ Zip _____

*The Boycott Gillette Campaign is organized in coopera-
tion with People For The Ethical Treatment of Animals.* **PeTA**

**64 GOLD**

# "THE NOISE GETS EXTREMELY IRRITATING AFTER ABOUT THIRTY SECONDS. I'VE HAD TO LIVE WITH IT FOR TWELVE YEARS."

This is what tinnitus can sound like. If you don't like it, you can simply close the page.

Lucy Butler can't. She is forced to listen to it night and day.

Like the ten million other tinnitus sufferers in Britain, she's had to learn to cope with it.

No-one knows what causes it, or how to cure it.

But there are ways to help.

The RNID have already helped develop tinnitus maskers which can reduce the suffering.

And with your help we can set up a National Helpline.

To make a donation please phone 081 200 0200 or send a cheque payable to the RNID to Stuart Etherington, Director of Public Affairs, 105 Gower Street, London WC1E 6AH.

You can ignore this appeal. Lucy can't ignore this sound.

## R·N·I·D

THE ROYAL NATIONAL INSTITUTE FOR THE DEAF.

65 SILVER

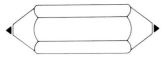

# The saddest part isn't that this photo exists, but that we had 1,500 more to choose from.

It is estimated that there are some 2.5 million homeless people in America. And that over 25% are children. With the United Way

Donor Option Program, you can give to the specific issues, like homelessness, that you care about most. Call 521-9000 to find out how.

UNITED WAY
It brings out the best in all of us.™

**66 SILVER**

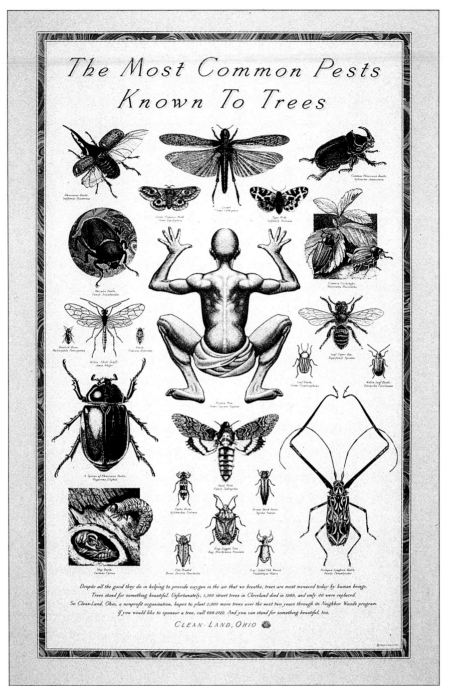

**PUBLIC SERVICE
NEWSPAPER OR MAGAZINE:
CAMPAIGN**

68 **SILVER**
**ART DIRECTOR**
Steve Dunn
**WRITER**
Mike Lescarbeau
**PHOTOGRAPHER**
John Claridge
**CLIENT**
Royal Marsden Hospital
**AGENCY**
Leagas Delaney/London

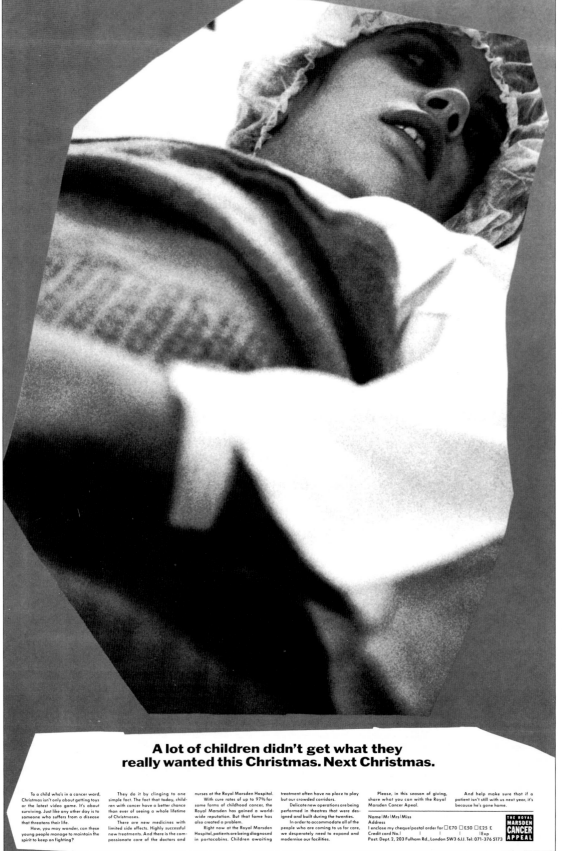

**A lot of children didn't get what they
really wanted this Christmas. Next Christmas.**

To a child who's in a cancer ward, Christmas isn't only about getting toys or the latest video game. It's about surviving. Just like any other day is to someone who suffers from a disease that threatens their life.

How, you may wonder, can these young people manage to maintain the spirit to keep on fighting?

They do it by clinging to one simple fact. The fact that today, children with cancer have a better chance than ever of seeing a whole lifetime of Christmases.

There are new medicines with limited side effects. Highly successful new treatments. And there is the compassionate care of the doctors and nurses at the Royal Marsden Hospital.

With cure rates of up to 97% for some forms of childhood cancer, the Royal Marsden has gained a world-wide reputation. But that fame has also created a problem.

Right now at the Royal Marsden Hospital, patients are being diagnosed in portacabins. Children awaiting treatment often have no place to play but our crowded corridors.

Delicate new operations are being performed in theatres that were designed and built during the twenties.

In order to accommodate all of the people who are coming to us for care, we desperately need to expand and modernise our facilities.

Please, in this season of giving, share what you can with the Royal Marsden Cancer Appeal.

And help make sure that if a patient isn't still with us next year, it's because he's gone home.

Name I Mr I Mrs I Miss
Address
I enclose my cheque I postal order for ☐ £70 ☐ £50 ☐ £25 £
Credit card No. I        I        I        I Exp
Post: Dept. 2, 203 Fulham Rd., London SW3 6JJ. Tel: 071-376 5173

THE ROYAL **MARSDEN CANCER APPEAL**

**If this brings a lump to
your throat, just pray it doesn't stay there.**

When you consider the plight of cancer patients, it's impossible not to be moved. They undergo treatments that make them violently ill. They often lose all their hair and develop painful skin conditions.

Some suffer from severe reactions when their bodies try to reject transplants that are meant to help them.

But, perhaps worst of all, cancer patients must endure these things without ever being certain they will survive the disease.

How can people with cancer possibly manage the strength and the hope to keep on fighting?

By finding things they can be thankful for, in spite of their troubles.

Their families. Their friends. Their faith. And, in many cases, the doctors and nurses at The Royal Marsden Hospital.

But this hospital, so vitally important to so many people, has begun to show its age. Doctors are performing delicate new operations in theatres that were built during the twenties.

Children awaiting treatments often have no place to play but crowded corridors. Patients are being diagnosed in portacabins.

The Royal Marsden desperately needs to expand and modernise its cancer care facilities.

Please consider the sacrifices of cancer patients, and make a sacrifice

of your own to the Royal Marsden Cancer Appeal today.

You can't imagine what a generous donation means to someone with cancer. And, God willing, you'll never have to find out.

Name | Mr | Mrs | Miss
Address
I enclose my cheque/postal order for □ £70 □ £50 □ £25 £
Credit card No.|          |          |          |Exp
Post: Dept. 14, 203 Fulham Rd., London SW3 6JJ. Tel: 071-376 5173

THE ROYAL
MARSDEN
CANCER
APPEAL

**It's easy asking for money once
you've asked a three year old for bone marrow.**

Asking you to donate money isn't something we're accustomed to at the Royal Marsden Hospital.

But there are a lot of difficult tasks we have to undertake in order to help people fight cancer.

We often have to ask our patients and their families to endure countless operations, and the painful side effects

of drug and radiation therapy. Some even give up limbs in the process. And that's just to have a hope of beating this dreadful disease.

Considering the sacrifices these people make, we thought you might welcome the chance to make a small sacrifice of your own.

The problem is simple.

The Royal Marsden has earned a worldwide reputation for cancer care, and that has brought us more patients than we can handle in our antiquated buildings.

Your money will help us expand the hospital, making room for a new diagnostic unit (we're currently doing examinations in portacabins), new

operating theatres to replace the ones built during the twenties, and recreation areas for young children, who are often limited to playing in crowded corridors.

Today, the cure rate for some types of cancer is as high as 97%. It's success rates like this that make any effort against cancer, whether made by a

patient or a donor, so very worthwhile.

Please give what you can.

When we think what some people have to give up in order to overcome this disease, we're glad all we have to ask you for is a cheque.

Name | Mr | Mrs | Miss
Address
I enclose my cheque/postal order for □ £70 □ £50 □ £25 £
Credit card No.|          |          |          |Exp
Post: Dept. 1, 203 Fulham Rd., London SW3 6JJ. Tel: 071-376 5173

THE ROYAL
MARSDEN
CANCER
APPEAL

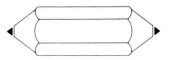

Gold, Silver, & Bronze
Awards

**PUBLIC SERVICE
NEWSPAPER OR MAGAZINE:
CAMPAIGN**

**69 SILVER**
**ART DIRECTOR**
Cabell Harris
**WRITER**
Mike Lescarbeau
**PHOTOGRAPHER**
Jack Richmond
**CLIENT**
Save the World
**AGENCY**
Chiat/Day/Mojo,
New York

We currently throw away enough iron and steel to continuously supply all the nation's automakers.

Carelessly discarding old appliances like refrigerators is a threat to the earth's protective ozone layer, due to the gasses they release.

A seemingly harmless plastic yoke from a six-pack can wreak havoc when discarded into the environment. The non-biodegradable webs often kill wildlife.

Tons of waste are being turned away at landfills because there is simply no more room. Recycling is our only alternative.

Plastic and even paper grocery bags pollute our environment. Bring a tote bag from home when you shop.

The improper disposal of waste is responsible for breeding huge populations of flies and pests that often spread disease.

Wonder products like solvents, aerosols and pesticides are poisoning the planet.

Americans throw away enough glass jars and bottles every two weeks to fill the twin towers of New York's World Trade Center. We not only lose recyclable material, we're running out of places to put it.

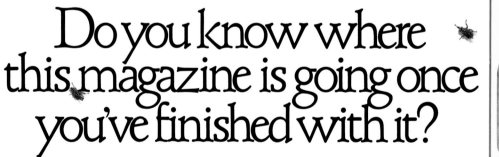

# Do you know where this magazine is going once you've finished with it?

Every three months, American consumers and industry throw away enough aluminum to rebuild our commercial airfleet.

Every Sunday more than half a million trees are used to produce the 88% of America's newspapers that are never recycled.

If only human beings could thrive on waste the way Rattus Norvegicus does. Unfortunately, we don't eat garbage, so we must dispose of it in an ever-decreasing amount of space. Countries all over the world must safeguard against the spread of disease and toxic chemicals into the environment.

**SAVE THE
WORLD**
If we're not all helping,
we're all hurting.

# If you don't think one person can make a difference in the world, consider what you've done already.

Low flow showerheads and dripless faucets save hot water and the fossil fuels it takes to create it. They also save you money.

Paint thinners give off fumes that deplete the ozone layer. Vinegar is a safe alternative.

Carpooling, taking public transportation or even riding your bike to work can reduce the pollution that causes global warming. Try one of these alternatives at least one day a week. You'll save money and you'll also be in a better mood when you get there.

Our landfills are full and highly toxic wastes are leaking into our groundwater, rivers and lakes. Recycle everything you possibly can.

Many household cleaning products can be replaced with homemade non-polluting alternatives.

Aerosols and even some roll-ons deplete the ozone layer. Make sure the products you buy are ozone-friendly. An alternative is equal parts of baking soda and cornstarch.

Each year the amount of energy wasted in the United States is equivalent to the energy produced from all the oil that flows through the Alaska pipeline.

Your baby could be making a bigger mess than you think. Disposable diapers can take up to 500 years to decompose, and their contents can spread disease. Use a diaper service.

The sprays we use to kill bugs in our homes are also harmful to our environment. You can learn to control household pests using good old-fashioned home remedies.

Every regular bulb you replace with a fluorescent one saves a ton of coal over the course of just five years.

Toilet tissue made from recycled paper reduces deforestation, and it doesn't leak harmful dyes into the water supply.

Our environmental problems are so big most of us assume the solutions are big, too. But the long-term solution to things like global warming, overpopulation, extinction and waste disposal is really quite small. The solution is one person at a time deciding he or she is going to help the world, not hurt it. It's you, with all your other obligations in life, realizing that saving our environment isn't just up to people who like whales. Government and corporations aren't going to provide the real answers. Commitments on the part of ordinary people will. To find out how you can get involved in a cause you care about, call 1-800-433-0880.

## SAVE THE WORLD
If we're not all helping, we're all hurting

---

The growing amount of traffic on our roads is accelerating the greenhouse effect and causing dangerous global warming. We have to develop alternatives to commuting in gas powered cars.

When we throw away kids' diapers, we're throwing away their future, too. Disposable diapers are a leading cause of the growing waste disposal problem.

Deforestation now threatens many essential species of plant and animals with extinction.

We are throwing away more trash all the time and have fewer and fewer places to put it. Without a major recycling effort, we're going to be buried in garbage.

According to the EPA, 66 pesticides currently sprayed on fruits and vegetables contain cancer causing agents. Kids are at highest risk.

# Isn't it time you started thinking about what you're going to leave your kids?

When most people think about wills and inheritance, they think in terms of money and earthly possessions. But what about the earth itself? What kind of planet will we be leaving to our children and to theirs? Today we can still do something about global warming, waste disposal, overpopulation and extinction. But unless each of us takes on that responsibility right now, the next generation may not be able to do anything at all. Start by calling 1-800-433-0880 and getting involved in an environmental cause that you care about. Let's leave your children a world for which they can thank us, instead of blame us.

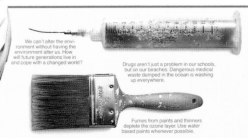

We can't alter the environment without having the environment alter us. How will future generations live in and cope with a changed world?

Drugs aren't just a problem in our schools, but on our beaches. Dangerous medical waste dumped in the ocean is washing up everywhere.

Fumes from paints and thinners deplete the ozone layer. Use water based paints whenever possible.

The burning of trash and forestland contributes to the pollution that causes the greenhouse effect.

Poaching and the destruction of habitats are driving hundreds of plant and animal species to extinction. We must refuse to buy products that threaten the survival of these essential forms of life.

The vinyl containers used for condiments are non-biodegradable, and they can't be recycled. Glass bottles are a good alternative.

## SAVE THE WORLD
If we're not all helping, we're all hurting

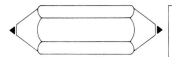

**PUBLIC SERVICE
NEWSPAPER OR MAGAZINE:
CAMPAIGN**

**70 BRONZE**
**ART DIRECTOR**
Peter Cohen
**WRITER**
Jamie Barrett
**PHOTOGRAPHER**
Stock
**CLIENT**
Coalition for the Homeless
**AGENCY**
Chiat/Day/Mojo,
New York

Gold, Silver, & Bronze
Awards

**PUBLIC SERVICE OUTDOOR**

**71 SILVER**
ART DIRECTOR
Wade Koniakowsky
WRITERS
Bob Kerstetter,
Chuck McBride
CLIENT
Constitutional Rights
Foundation
AGENCY
Franklin & Associates/
San Diego

**72 BRONZE**
ART DIRECTOR
David Wojdyla
WRITER
Leland Rosemond
PHOTOGRAPHER
Barry Seidman
CLIENT
NeuroCommunication
Research Laboratories
AGENCY
Bozell/New York

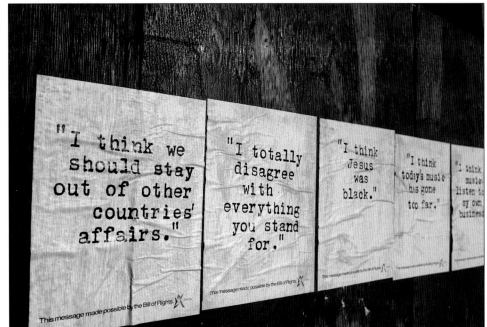

# ADMIT IT.
# A PART OF YOU
# WANTS TO
# PARTICIPATE.

Volunteer for this National Condom Preference Study funded by the U.S. Public Health Service and the data you provide
will be used in a non-profit survey to encourage safe sex. For more information call 1-800-336-1935, Mon-Fri, 9AM-3PM

This confidential mail survey is conducted by NeuroCommunication Research Laboratories, Inc., Danbury, CT. ©1990

## NATIONAL CONDOM PREFERENCE STUDY

72 BRONZE

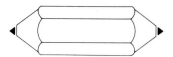

Gold, Silver, & Bronze
Awards

## CONSUMER RADIO: SINGLE

### 73 GOLD
**WRITER**
David Shane
**AGENCY PRODUCER**
Vicki Blucher
**CLIENT**
NYNEX Information
Resources
**AGENCY**
Chiat/Day/Mojo,
New York

### 74 SILVER
**WRITER**
Don Austen
**AGENCY PRODUCER**
Deed Meyer
**PRODUCTION COMPANY**
Clacks Recording
**CLIENT**
Little Caesar's Enterprises
**AGENCY**
Cliff Freeman & Partners/
New York

### 75 BRONZE
**WRITER**
Mike Lescarbeau
**AGENCY PRODUCER**
Eric Jones
**PRODUCTION COMPANY**
Editel
**CLIENT**
Massachusetts State Lottery
**AGENCY**
Hill Holliday Connors
Cosmopulos/Boston

**73**

MIKE: It really is true, you can find anything in the NYNEX Yellow Pages. And, today, I'm talking to Midge . . .

MIDGE: Hi, Mike.

MIKE: . . . whose salon, Midge's Makeovers, is dedicated entirely to the care and maintenance of eyebrows.

MIDGE: Specializing in eyebrow weaves.

MIKE: Midge, why would anyone have their eyebrows woven?

MIDGE: 'Cause not everybody was born with attractive eyebrows. Some of my girls have very thin arching brows which give them that, you know, surprised look. They're always surprised. You could say hello, good morning and they'll look, like, what? They're shocked.

MIKE: So I guess most of your clients are women?

MIDGE: Oh no Michael, we get plenty of guys. They come in and they have the one long eyebrow across their forehead, and you look at them and you just have to wonder what's wrong with this person.

MIKE: I see.

MIDGE: Mike, people don't think about their eyebrows enough. They walk out of the house, they don't even look up. You know, I'd love to do something with your eyebrows.

MIKE: Actually, I'm pretty happy with them . . .

MIDGE: Oh, you have lovely eyebrows Michael, it's just . . .

MIKE: What?

MIDGE: Well, it's just that they're doing kind of a wandering, nomadic thing all over your forehead. It's a little disconcerting, frankly.

MIKE: Well, there you have it. Further proof that if it's out there, it's in the NYNEX Yellow Pages.

MIDGE: We could take care of that for you.

MIKE: Thanks, maybe next time. Why would anyone need another.

MIDGE: You could be cuter.

**74**

ANNCR: And now a reenactment of the ancient discovery of pizza crust.

(SFX: MUSICAL FANFARE)

ROMAN 1: Augustus, tastus das crustus . . .

(SFX: LOUD CRUNCH)

ROMAN 2: Kill him.

ANNCR: Now what would that scene have been like if they'd had Little Caesars new Crazy Crust . . .?

(SFX: MUSICAL FANFARE)

ROMAN 1: Augustus, tastus das Crazy Crustus . . .

(SFX: LOUD CRUNCH)

ROMAN 2: Mmmmm . . . Estus sesame . . . Kill him.

ANNCR: New Crazy Crust! Your choice of four flavored crusts on two medium pizzas with eight toppings for only $8.88. Now at Little Caesars.

**75**

PARISH: My name is Robert Parish. You know, as a young man, I always dreamed of being a professional athlete. More specifically, I always dreamed of being one of the top jockeys in thoroughbred horse racing. But I didn't have the size to be a jockey. So I became the starting center for a professional basketball team. Sure I'm disappointed. But fortunately, I can play Winner's Circle, the new Instant game from The Lottery that's just like a real horse race. I can pretend I'm a jockey with my feet up in the stirrups where they belong, instead of dragging back behind my horse. And if I'm ever feeling big and unwieldly, I just think of Winner's Circle's largest ever collection of over $82 million in cash prizes, and I feel tiny by comparison. What's more, frustrated jockeys like me can win up to five times on a ticket. If you enjoy horse racing, think about playing Winner's Circle. If you enjoy winning, think about playing Winner's Circle. If you just enjoy laughing, think about me wearing a little jockey's cap and sitting on top of a Shetland pony.

ANNCR: Play Winner's Circle. The Lottery's newest instant game with fifteen chances to win on a ticket, and more cash prizes than ever before.

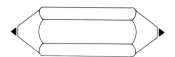

Gold, Silver, & Bronze
Awards

**CONSUMER RADIO: SINGLE**

**76 BRONZE**
**WRITERS**
John DeCerchio, Gail Offen
**AGENCY PRODUCERS**
John DeCerchio, Gail Offen
**CLIENT**
Chiquita Brands
**AGENCY**
W. B. Doner & Company/
Southfield

**CONSUMER RADIO:
CAMPAIGN**

**77 SILVER**
**WRITER**
David Shane
**AGENCY PRODUCER**
Vicki Blucher
**CLIENT**
NYNEX Information
Resources
**AGENCY**
Chiat/Day/Mojo,
New York

**76**

INTERVIEWER: Hello. I'm from Chiquita with an incredible statistic. When asked what's the most perfect food in the world, everyone said Chiquita Bananas. Amazing. Here is an example.

(SFX: OUTDOOR AMBIENCE)

INTERVIEWER: We're here with?

GUY: Randy Samuels.

INTERVIEWER: Randy, let's say you were going to the chair.

GUY: Okay.

INTERVIEWER: What highly nutritious food would you want as your last meal?

GUY: I'm . . . I'm going to the chair? Why am I going to the chair?

INTERVIEWER: C'mon, nobody likes a crybaby . . .

GUY: Well, how about a nice steak.

INTERVIEWER: Okay, that's a bit heavy. How about something full of vitamin C.

GUY: Oh, orange juice, I guess.

INTERVIEWER: Something with more fiber . . .

GUY: A bran muffin?

INTERVIEWER: You're going to the chair and you want a bran muffin? C'mon.

GUY: Uh, it's kinda hard to think with this sentence hanging over my head.

(SFX: PHONE RING)

INTERVIEWER: Excuse me, Randy. Hello. Uh huh . . .

(SFX: PHONE BEING HUNG UP)

INTERVIEWER: Good news . . . Randy, the governor says that if you were to say Chiquita Bananas . . . he might issue a pardon.

GUY: Oh . . . well, Chiquita Bananas.

INTERVIEWER: The Governor said more enthusiasm.

GUY: Chiquita Bananas!

INTERVIEWER: Okay. There you have it. When asked to pick the most nutritious food, 100% said Chiquita Bananas. And we've got many more interviews just as convincing.
Chiquita Bananas, quite possibly the world's perfect food.

MIKE: They say you can find anything in the NYNEX Yellow Pages. Well, today, under entertainers I found Silly Willy, the clown.

SILLY: Hi ho.

MIKE: Hi ho, Silly. Your ad promises a good time will be had by one and all.

SILLY: That's right, Mike. A silly willy good time.

MIKE: Tell me Silly, is it difficult playing to young audiences?

SILLY: Yeah, real difficult. Six-year-olds aren't exactly the most discerning critics, Mike. You poke yourself in the eye with an umbrella, they're in hysterics.

MIKE: I see.

SILLY: Real subtle stuff.

MIKE: Well, can you give us an idea of what you do in your act?

SILLY: I'm a clown Mike. I walk like a duck, I fall on my face. You want a free sample, go to a yogurt stand.

MIKE: Silly, forgive me for saying this, but you seem a little...

SILLY: Bitter, Mike?

MIKE: Uh, yes.

SILLY: Well, let's just say my life hasn't worked out exactly like I thought it would.

MIKE: I see, well thank you very much Silly.

SILLY: As a young man you dream of playing Hamlet at the Old Vic and where do you end up? In someone's living room wearing twenty-inch shoes and a bulbous red nose.

MIKE: Well, there you have it. The bitter-sweet comedy of Silly Willy.

SILLY: Bitter-sweet? Is that a smart crack or something?

MIKE: Further proof that if it's out there . . .

SILLY: Smart guy, huh?

MIKE: . . . it's in the NYNEX Yellow Pages.

SILLY: You're just like my wife. She ran off with Tubby Wubby, the bouncing clown.

MIKE: Why would anyone need another.

SILLY: I'll bounce him if I ever find him.

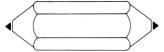

Gold, Silver, & Bronze
Awards

CONSUMER TELEVISION
OVER :30 (:45/:60/:90)
SINGLE

**78 GOLD**
**ART DIRECTORS**
Newy Brothwell,
Phil Rylance
**WRITERS**
Paul Cardwell,
Kim Durdant-Hollamby
**AGENCY PRODUCER**
Joanne Cresser
**PRODUCTION COMPANY**
Aardman Animation
**DIRECTOR**
Nick Park
**CLIENT**
Electricity Association
**AGENCY**
GGK/London

**79 GOLD**
**ART DIRECTORS**
Newy Brothwell,
Phil Rylance
**WRITERS**
Paul Cardwell,
Kim Durdant-Hollamby
**AGENCY PRODUCER**
Joanne Cresser
**PRODUCTION COMPANY**
Aardman Animation
**DIRECTOR**
Nick Park
**CLIENT**
Electricity Association
**AGENCY**
GGK/London

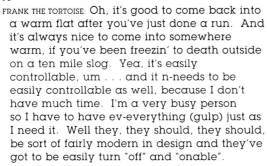

**78**
FRANK THE TORTOISE: Oh, it's good to come back into a warm flat after you've just done a run. And it's always nice to come into somewhere warm, if you've been freezin' to death outside on a ten mile slog. Yea, it's easily controllable, um . . . and it n-needs to be easily controllable as well, because I don't have much time. I'm a very busy person so I have to have ev-everything (gulp) just as I need it. Well they, they should, they should, be sort of fairly modern in design and they've got to be easily turn "off" and "onable".
ANNCR: For all your creature comforts.
Heat Electric.

**79**
PABLO THE PARROT: I am . . . sensitive to the cold weather and, er, therefore I need . . . er . . . you know, it's like, you know, a priority for me when I first arrive in England to have come to a house that had heating. You know I wouldn't be here otherwise. You know it's nice to know that you can go home and you will be a bit warmer and you know it's very agreeable to be, you know, heated up. I mean, I just think for monetary reasons . . . er . . . I just think that it's great . . . er . . . I don't know, I think you just feel warm really.
ANNCR: For all your creature comforts.
Heat Electric.

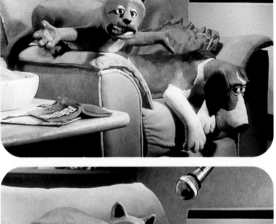

**80 SILVER**
**ART DIRECTORS**
Newy Brothwell,
Phil Rylance
**WRITERS**
Paul Cardwell,
Kim Durdant-Hollamby
**AGENCY PRODUCER**
Joanne Cresser
**PRODUCTION COMPANY**
Aardman Animation
**DIRECTOR**
Nick Park
**CLIENT**
Electricity Association
**AGENCY**
GGK/London

**81 BRONZE**
**ART DIRECTOR**
Don Schneider
**WRITERS**
Lee Garfinkel,
Jonathan Mandell
**AGENCY PRODUCERS**
Regina Ebel, Bob Kirschen
**PRODUCTION COMPANY**
Pytka Productions
**DIRECTOR**
Joe Pytka
**CLIENT**
Pepsi Cola Co.
**AGENCY**
BBDO/New York

**80**

CAROL THE CAT: It's bliss, absolute bliss, you walk in, you get past the dog, he's snoring his head off normally, you go in the lounge, slob around for a bit, I mean the whole house is warm. I had a flat once, it was freezing. And it's just lovely being here, 'cos you never have to worry about being cold, it's just like that all the time . . . And especially like, you know, when you come in and you've been dancing all night, there's still plenty of hot water and the house is still lovely and warm, it's just like unbelievable really. And you get into bed and it's lovely and warm and you wake up in the morning and it's still nice and warm. I mean you just don't wanna go to work in the morning.
ANNCR: For all your creature comforts. Heat Electric.

**81**

(MUSIC: UPBEAT)
OLD WOMAN 1: Rock and roll is okay but I prefer rap.
OLD MAN 1: Hey Joe.
OLD WOMAN 2: Right on.
OLD MAN 2: Hot, hey, hey.
OLD MAN 3: Awesome.
OLD MAN 1: This music is good but nobody can touch Hendrix.
OLD MAN 3: Awesome.
DELIVERY MAN 1: Wait a second. Shady Acres was supposed to get the Coke and the frat house was supposed to get the Pepsi.
DELIVERY MAN 2: Coke, Pepsi, what's the difference?
(MUSIC: CLASSICAL)
FRAT BOY: I-24.
(MUSIC: UPBEAT)
OLD WOMAN 3: Do you like slam dancing?
OLD MAN 1: Love it.
OLD MAN 3: This is radical.
SUPER: PEPSI. THE CHOICE OF A NEW GENERATION.

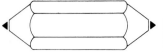

Gold, Silver, & Bronze
Awards

**CONSUMER TELEVISION
OVER :30 (:45/:60/:90)
CAMPAIGN**

**82 GOLD**
**ART DIRECTORS**
Newy Brothwell,
Phil Rylance
**WRITERS**
Paul Cardwell,
Kim Durdant-Hollamby
**AGENCY PRODUCER**
Joanne Cresser
**PRODUCTION COMPANY**
Aardman Animation
**DIRECTOR**
Nick Park
**CLIENT**
Electricity Association
**AGENCY**
GGK/London

**82 I**

FRANK THE TORTOISE: Oh, it's good to come back into
a warm flat after you've just done a run. And
it's always nice to come into somewhere
warm, if you've been freezin' to death outside
on a ten mile slog. Yea, it's easily
controllable, um . . . and it n-needs to be
easily controllable as well, because I don't
have much time. I'm a very busy person
so I have to have ev-everything (gulp) just as
I need it. Well they, they should, they should,
be sort of fairly modern in design and they've
got to be easily turn "off" and "onable".
ANNCR: For all your creature comforts.
Heat Electric.

**82 II**

CAROL THE CAT: It's bliss, absolute bliss, you walk
in, you get past the dog, he's snoring his head
off normally, you go in the lounge, slob
around for a bit, I mean the whole house
is warm. I had a flat once, it was freezing.
And it's just lovely being here, 'cos you never
have to worry about being cold, it's just like
that all the time . . . And especially like, you
know, when you come in and you've been
dancing all night, there's still plenty of hot
water and the house is still lovely and warm,
it's just like unbelievable really. And you get
into bed and it's lovely and warm and you
wake up in the morning and it's still nice and
warm. I mean you just don't wanna go to
work in the morning.
ANNCR: For all your creature comforts.
Heat Electric.

PABLO THE PARROT: I am . . . sensitive to the cold
weather and, er, therefore I need . . . er . . .
you know, it's like, you know, a priority for
me when I first arrive in England to have
come to a house that had heating. You know
I wouldn't be here otherwise. You know it's
nice to know that you can go home and you
will be a bit warmer and you know it's very
agreeable to be, you know, heated up. I
mean, I just think for monetary reasons . . . er
. . . I just think that it's great . . . er . . . I don't
know, I think you just feel warm really.

ANNCR: For all your creature comforts.
Heat Electric.

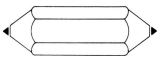

Gold, Silver, & Bronze
Awards

**CONSUMER TELEVISION
:30/:24 SINGLE**

**83 GOLD**
ART DIRECTOR
Ron Rosen
WRITER
Richard Kelly
AGENCY PRODUCER
Daniel Miller
PRODUCTION COMPANY
In House
CLIENT
Nikon
AGENCY
Scali McCabe Sloves/
New York

**84 SILVER**
ART DIRECTOR
Jon Iles
WRITER
Paul Fishlock
AGENCY PRODUCER
Alison Moss
PRODUCTION COMPANY
Ibbetson and Cherry
DIRECTOR
Derek Hughes
CLIENT
DHL International
AGENCY
Saatchi & Saatchi/Sydney

**85 BRONZE**
ART DIRECTOR
Benjamin BenSimon
WRITER
David Innis
AGENCY PRODUCER
Sandy Cole
PRODUCTION COMPANY
Calibre Digital Design
DIRECTOR
Chris Armstrong
CLIENT
Ciba-Geigy
AGENCY
MacLaren:Lintas/Toronto

A three-year old boy saluting
at his father's funeral.

A lone student standing
in front of four tanks.

If you can picture
it in your head,
it was probably taken
with a Nikon.

**83**
(SFX: CAMERA'S SHUTTER)
SUPER: A THREE-YEAR-OLD BOY SALUTING AT HIS
FATHER'S FUNERAL.
SUPER: AMERICAN PRESIDENT LIFTING HIS PET
BEAGLE UP BY ITS EARS.
SUPER: WOMAN CRYING OVER THE BODY OF A
STUDENT SHOT BY THE NATIONAL GUARD.
SUPER: RETURNING P.O.W. BEING GREETED WITH
OPEN ARMS BY HIS DAUGHTER.
SUPER: A LONE STUDENT STANDING IN FRONT   F
FOUR TANKS.
SUPER: IF YOU CAN PICTURE IT IN YOUR HEAD, IT
WAS PROBABLY TAKEN WITH A NIKON.
SUPER: NIKON.  WE TAKE THE WORLD'S GREATEST
PICTURES.

**84**
(SFX: BEEP OF TELEPHONE THROUGHOUT)
ELECTRONIC VOICE: Welcome to DHL.  Please enter
your account number.  Please enter the
service you require.  Please enter the
destination code.  Thank you for calling DHL.
SUPER: NOW YOU CAN ORDER THE WORLD'S
MOST RELIABLE AIR EXPRESS SERVICE.
WITHOUT SPEAKING TO DHL.
DHL MAN: Package for Africa?
(SFX: BUDGIE GIGGLES)
SUPER: DHL WORLDWIDE EXPRESS.

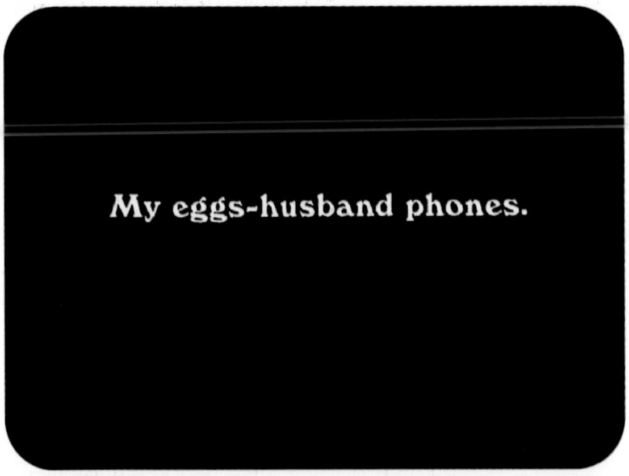

**My eggs-husband phones.**

**Zays he wants me bag.**

The na al spray
ost re ommended by do ors.

**Otrivin** Decongestant

**85**

(SFX: BACKGROUND MUSIC, PHONE RINGS, DOG BARKS)
SUPER: BRIDAY NIGHT. HAB THIS TERRIBLE CODE.
MY EGGS-HUSBAND PHONES. ZAYS HE WANTS
ME BAG. I SAY DOUGH. HE ZAYS HOW MUCH.
MEN.
(SFX: PHONE PLACED BACK ON RECEIVER)
SUPER: I DEED PROFESSIONAL HELB.
SUPER: THE NAZAL SPRAY BOST REGOMMENDED
BY DOGDORS.
(SFX: SQUIRT, SQUIRT)
(SFX: SIGH OF RELIEF)
SUPER: THE NASAL SPRAY MOST RECOMMENDED
BY DOCTORS.
SUPER: OTRIVIN DECONGESTANT NASAL SPRAY.

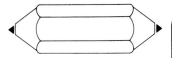

Gold, Silver, & Bronze Awards

**CONSUMER TELEVISION :30/:24 CAMPAIGN**

**86 GOLD**
**ART DIRECTOR**
Benjamin BenSimon
**WRITER**
David Innis
**AGENCY PRODUCER**
Sandy Cole
**PRODUCTION COMPANY**
Calibre Digital Design
**DIRECTOR**
Chris Armstrong
**CLIENT**
Ciba-Geigy
**AGENCY**
MacLaren:Lintas/Toronto

Der I was wid dis lobely lady.

My eggs-husband phones.

Told her I couldn't breed.

Zays he wants me bag.

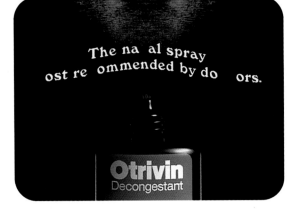

The na al spray
ost re ommended by do ors.

Otrivin
Decongestant

The na al spray
ost re ommended by do ors.

Otrivin
Decongestant

**86 I**

(SFX: QUIET RESTAURANT SOUNDS)

SUPER: DER I WAS WID DIS LOBELY LADY. MY NOSE TOTALLY BLOGGED. SHE LOOKED DEEB INDO MY EYES. I GASPED FOR BREAD. TOLD HER I COULDN'T BREED. SHE SLABBED ME. I DEED PROFESSIONAL HELB.

SUPER: THE NAZAL SPRAY BOST REGOMMENDED BY DOGDORS.

(SFX: SQUIRT, SQUIRT)

(SFX: SIGH OF RELIEF)

SUPER: THE NASAL SPRAY MOST RECOMMENDED BY DOCTORS.

SUPER: OTRIVIN DECONGESTANT NASAL SPRAY.

**86 II**

(SFX: BACKGROUND MUSIC, PHONE RINGS, DOG BARKS)

SUPER: BRIDAY NIGHT. HAB THIS TERRIBLE CODE. MY EGGS-HUSBAND PHONES. ZAYS HE WANTS ME BAG. I SAY DOUGH. HE ZAYS HOW MUCH. MEN.

(SFX: PHONE PLACED BACK ON RECEIVER)

SUPER: I DEED PROFESSIONAL HELB.

SUPER: THE NAZAL SPRAY BOST REGOMMENDED BY DOGDORS.

(SFX: SQUIRT, SQUIRT)

(SFX: SIGH OF RELIEF)

SUPER: THE NASAL SPRAY MOST RECOMMENDED BY DOCTORS.

SUPER: OTRIVIN DECONGESTANT NASAL SPRAY.

He was dall, dark and hadsomb.

I told him I'm stubbed up.

The na al spray
ost re ommended by do ors.

**Otrivin**
Decongestant

**86 III**

(SFX: PARTY SOUNDS NOT VERY LOUD)

SUPER: DEN OUR EYES MET FROM AGROSS DA ROOM. HE WAS DALL, DARK AND HADSOMB. HE WALKED UB TO ME. HE ASD ME TO DANCE. I TOLD HIM I'M STUBBED UP. ZO HE DANCED WID MY FRIEND. I DEED PROFESSIONAL HELB.

SUPER: THE NAZAL SPRAY BOST REGOMMENDED BY DOGDORS.

(SFX: SQUIRT, SQUIRT)

(SFX: SIGH OF RELIEF)

SUPER: THE NASAL SPRAY MOST RECOMMENDED BY DOCTORS.

SUPER: OTRIVIN DECONGESTANT NASAL SPRAY.

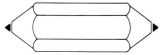
**CONSUMER TELEVISION
:30/:24 CAMPAIGN**

**87 SILVER**
**ART DIRECTOR**
Michael Vitiello
**WRITER**
Rochelle Klein
**AGENCY PRODUCER**
Rachel Novak
**PRODUCTION COMPANIES**
Coppos Films,
Phil Marco Productions
**DIRECTORS**
Mark Coppos, Phil Marco
**CLIENT**
Maidenform
**AGENCY**
Levine Huntley Vick &
Beaver/New York

**88 BRONZE**
**ART DIRECTORS**
Donna Weinheim,
John Colquhoun,
Steve Miller, Jeff Alphin
**WRITERS**
Cliff Freeman, Don Austen,
Jeff Alphin, Jane King
**AGENCY PRODUCERS**
Anne Kurtzman,
Melanie Klein
**PRODUCTION COMPANIES**
Story Piccolo Guliner,
Highlight Commercials
**DIRECTORS**
Mark Story, David Wild
**CLIENT**
Little Caesar's Enterprises
**AGENCY**
Cliff Freeman & Partners/
New York

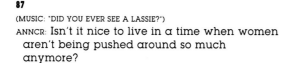

**87**
(MUSIC: "DID YOU EVER SEE A LASSIE?")
ANNCR: Isn't it nice to live in a time when women aren't being pushed around so much anymore?

**88**
DAD: Okay Sal, I want onions and you don't. But we can solve this . . . we'll arm wrestle for it.
SAL: Okay, Daddy.
(SFX: WHOMP)
DAD: Onions it is!!! Onions, onions, onions it is!!! Onions, onions, onions it is!!!
ANNCR: Little Caesars Family Choice gives you one pizza with ten toppings for the adults and one with two toppings for the kids. All for one low price.
LITTLE CAESAR FAMILY: Pizza! Pizza!

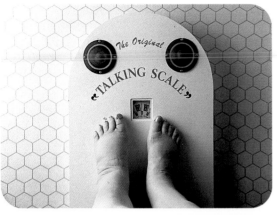

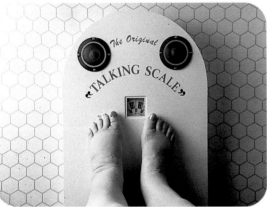

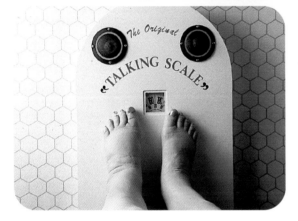

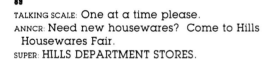

**CONSUMER TELEVISION
UNDER :24 SINGLE**

**89 GOLD**
**ART DIRECTOR**
Donna Weinheim
**WRITER**
Donna Weinheim
**AGENCY PRODUCER**
Anne Kurtzman
**PRODUCTION COMPANY**
Story Piccolo Guliner
**DIRECTOR**
Mark Story
**CLIENT**
Hills Department Stores
**AGENCY**
Cliff Freeman & Partners/
New York

**90 SILVER**
**ART DIRECTOR**
Steve Miller
**WRITER**
Don Austen
**AGENCY PRODUCER**
Melanie Klein
**PRODUCTION COMPANY**
Highlight Commercials
**DIRECTOR**
David Wild
**CLIENT**
Little Caesar's Enterprises
**AGENCY**
Cliff Freeman & Partners/
New York

**89**
TALKING SCALE: One at a time please.
ANNCR: Need new housewares?  Come to Hills Housewares Fair.
SUPER: HILLS DEPARTMENT STORES.

**90**
(SFX: "JAWS" - LIKE MUSIC)
ANNCR: Five different meats piled on two medium pizzas.
  For some it's a dream, for others their worst nightmare.
(SFX: SCREAMING)
ANNCR: New Meatsa! Meatsa!  Five meat toppings only $9.99.
LITTLE CAESAR: Meatsa!  Meatsa!
ANNCR: At Little Caesars.

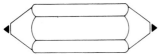

Gold, Silver, & Bronze
Awards

**CONSUMER TELEVISION
UNDER :24  SINGLE**

**91 BRONZE**
ART DIRECTOR
Peter Holmes
WRITER
Donna McCarthy
PRODUCTION COMPANY
Last Minute Films
DIRECTOR
Frank Anzalone
CLIENT
CJCL 1430 Radio
AGENCY
Franklin Dallas Kundinger/
Ontario

**CONSUMER TELEVISION
UNDER :24  CAMPAIGN**

**92 GOLD**
ART DIRECTOR
Tony Davidson
WRITER
Kim Papworth
AGENCY PRODUCER
Sarah Pollitt
PRODUCTION COMPANY
Hutchins Film Co
DIRECTORS
Martin Brierly, Steve Lowe
CLIENT
Crookes Healthcare
AGENCY
BMP DDB Needham/
London

Are your
eyes
trying

to tell
you
something?

**91**
(MUSIC: "UNFORGETTABLE" BY NAT KING COLE)
ANNCR: Isn't it time you listened to music that
annoys the kids?
SUPER: CJCL 1430 AM STEREO.

**92 I**
(SFX: SPLISHING AND SPLASHING)
WALLACE: (SINGING)  *I'm singing in the rain, just
singing in the rain . . .*
DESMOND: Will you hurry up in there.
WALLACE: *What a wonderful feeling . . .*
DESMOND: You weren't the only one out late last
night.
WALLACE: *. . . I'm happ-happ-happy again.*
DESMOND: And don't forget to clean the bath
when you've finished!
WALLACE: *. . . Dum dee da . . .*
ANNCR: Optrex.  Are your eyes trying to tell you
something?

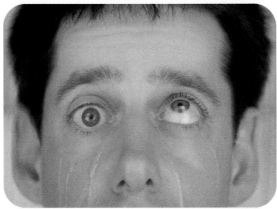 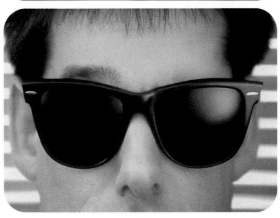

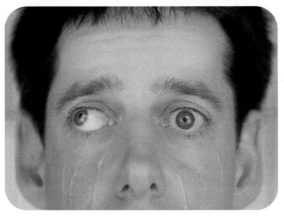 

Are your eyes trying to tell you something?

Optrex EYE LOTION

Optrex EYE DROPS

CROOKES Healthcare

**92 II**

(MUSIC: "I'M WISHING" FROM WALT DISNEY'S SNOW WHITE)

DESMOND: (SINGING) *I'm wishing . . .*

WALLACE: (SINGING) *I'm wishing . . .*

DESMOND: *For the one I love . . . to find me.*

WALLACE: *. . . to find me.*

DESMOND: *Today.*

WALLACE: *Today.*

ANNCR: Optrex. Are your eyes trying to tell you something?

**92 III**

WALLACE: So why are we wearing these then?

DESMOND: Because when you become major television celebs you have to take certain precautions.

WALLACE: Celebs?

DESMOND: Flash bulbs, bright lights.

WALLACE: Sounds very tiring. Will we still get our Optrex?

DESMOND: Magnums of it.

WALLACE: I think I'm going to like being a celebs.

ANNCR: Optrex. Are your eyes trying to tell you something?

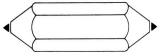

Gold, Silver, & Bronze
Awards

**CONSUMER TELEVISION
UNDER :24 CAMPAIGN**

**93 SILVER**
**ART DIRECTORS**
Donna Weinheim,
Steve Miller
**WRITERS**
Donna Weinheim,
Andy Spade, Cliff Freeman
**AGENCY PRODUCER**
Anne Kurtzman
**PRODUCTION COMPANIES**
Firehouse Films,
Story Piccolo Guliner
**DIRECTOR**
Mark Story, Peter Lauer
**CLIENT**
Hills Department Stores
**AGENCY**
Cliff Freeman & Partners/
New York

**94 BRONZE**
**ART DIRECTORS**
Donna Weinheim,
John Colquhoun,
Steve Miller
**WRITERS**
Cliff Freeman, Don Austen
**AGENCY PRODUCERS**
Anne Kurtzman,
Melanie Klein
**PRODUCTION COMPANIES**
Highlight Commercials,
Story Piccolo Guliner
**DIRECTORS**
Mark Story, David Wild
**CLIENT**
Little Caesar's Enterprises
**AGENCY**
Cliff Freeman & Partners/
New York

**93**
ANNCR: The day after Thanksgiving, anyone who gets to Hills beginning at 8:00 a.m. will receive $254 worth of coupons. Better hurry. Offer good that day and that day only.
SUPER: HILLS DEPARTMENT STORES.

**94**
WOMAN: Two pizzas with ten toppings for $9.99, that's impossible.
MAN: Anything's possible. I taught my dog to say I love you.
DOG: I wuv you. I wuv you.
ANNCR: Little Caesars has done the impossible. Two pizzas with ten toppings for $9.99.
LITTLE CAESAR: Pizza! Pizza!

**PUBLIC SERVICE TELEVISION SINGLE**

**95 GOLD**
ART DIRECTOR
John Colquhoun
WRITERS
Jane King, Jeff Alphin,
Rick LeMoine
AGENCY PRODUCER
Mary Ellen Duggan
PRODUCTION COMPANY
The Partners
DIRECTOR
John Zurik
CLIENT
ASPCA
AGENCY
Cliff Freeman & Partners/
New York

**96 SILVER**
ART DIRECTOR
Lachlan McPherson
WRITER
Sean Cummins
AGENCY PRODUCERS
Kelly Curtain, Tanja Andor
PRODUCTION COMPANY
Leave It To Beaver
DIRECTOR
Igor Auzins
CLIENT
RSPCA
AGENCY
Lachlan McPherson/
Melbourne

RSPCA
De-sex your dog
or cat.

**95**
GILBERT: No . . . don't take that dog. Don't take that dog. Come over here. Here you want me . . . you want me. Here look I'm cute . . . I'm fluffy. Here you can take me. You can feed me dog food or a bone . . . or a bone. I like bones. Okay, here watch me roll over. I'm rolling over. Here watch I can stand on two feet. Ohhh my head. Wait a second, let me try that again. Ahhh I did it again. Wait a second, look outside the cage I'm very good at that . . . I'm real good. I can stand on two feet outside the cage. Oh, good choice, you made an excellent choice . . . an excellent choice.
SUPER: ASPCA.

**96**
ANNCR: De-sexing. What does it really mean? It means that your dog will fight less. It'll be less inclined to wander. It'll be healthier. And happier. There'll be no unwanted litters. And it won't lead to a life of frustration. De-sexing. So that man's best friend will stay, just friends.
SUPER: DE-SEX YOUR DOG OR CAT. RSPCA.

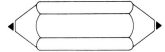

Gold, Silver, & Bronze
Awards

**PUBLIC SERVICE TELEVISION
SINGLE**

**97 BRONZE**
**ART DIRECTOR**
Paul Gay
**WRITER**
Steve Reeves
**DIRECTORS**
Steve Reeves, Paul Gay
**CLIENT**
Health Education Authority
**AGENCY**
BMP DDB Needham/
London

**PUBLIC SERVICE TELEVISION
CAMPAIGN**

**98 SILVER**
**ART DIRECTOR**
Craig Gillespie
**WRITER**
David Canright
**AGENCY PRODUCERS**
Bruce Davidson
**PRODUCTION COMPANY**
Epoch Films
**DIRECTOR**
Jeff Preiss
**CLIENT**
Burger King Corporation
**AGENCY**
D'Arcy Masius Benton &
Bowles/New York

**CINEMA/VIDEO**

**99 SILVER**
**ART DIRECTOR**
Warren Eakins
**WRITER**
Steve Sandoz
**AGENCY PRODUCERS**
Warren Eakins,
Steve Sandoz
**PRODUCTION COMPANY**
Tyee
**DIRECTORS**
Warren Eakins,
Steve Sandoz
**CLIENT**
Northwest Film & Video
Center
**AGENCY**
Steve & Warren's Excellent
Ad Venture/Portland

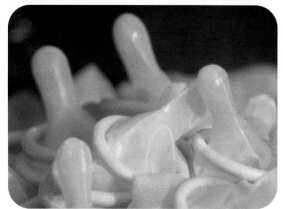

**97**

VERA CONWAY: Of course, working here we're the first to notice a change in peoples behavior. We're making more of these things than ever before. Obviously it's down to AIDS and HIV. Young people can't afford to take chances these days. It seems they've got their heads screwed on though . . . After all I've never been so busy.

SUPER: KEEP MRS. CONWAY BUSY. USE A CONDOM.

SUPER: A CONDOM CAN PROTECT YOU FROM HIV, THE VIRUS THAT CAUSES AIDS. FOR MORE INFORMATION PHONE THE FREE 24 HOUR NATIONAL AIDS HELPLINE 0800 567 123.

**98**

(SFX: CAR NOISES)

VO TINY: I wanna be really rich and live on a farm . . .

(SFX: MUSIC UNDER)

VO TINY: . . . with a bunch of horses which is my main best animal, and have three yachts or more, and diamonds, and jewels, and all that stuff. When I left school I was thirteen. I really didn't like it, and didn't want to go. And so I left home.

(SFX: TV NOISES)

VO MOTHER: She has grown up quite a bit since she's been on the streets. She's fourteen goin' on twenty one. Oh, when I was drinking, her and I used to get in some bad arguments, and I could see in her mind, she's thinking oh no not again.

TINY: Thank you mom.

NURSE: So you don't have any symptoms right now?

TINY: I don't think so.

NURSE: But you do have some concern that you might have a sexually transmitted disease?

TINY: Nothin' serious, but just might be Trichomona, but, I don't know.

NURSE: Uh, huh. You ever had one before?

But American films and

foreign films actually

have many things in common.

TINY: Um hum.

NURSE: What'd you have?

TINY: I've had Chlamydia, Trichomona, and Gonorrhea.

NURSE: That's quite a bit.

VO TINY: I think it is very strange that older men like little girls 'cause they're perverts is what they is. I mean, I like the money but I don't like them. My real dad, I've never known. He could be a guy that's really rich driving a Mercedes you know or he could be one of these bums on the streets. For all I know, you know, he could be one of these dates roaming around, I could have dated him for all I know.

VO MOTHER: My fear is that someday I'm gonna get a phone call or a knock on my door and it's . . . She's not gonna be there anymore.

SUPER: TINY DROPPED OUT OF SCHOOL AT 13.

SUPER: SOMETIMES BREAKING THE RULES MEANS STAYING IN SCHOOL.

**99**

(MUSIC: FRENCH SOUNDING TRACK)

SUBTITLES: MANY PEOPLE WON'T GO TO SEE A FOREIGN FILM. THEY THINK IT WOULD PROBABLY BE TOO, WELL, FOREIGN. BUT AMERICAN FILMS AND FOREIGN FILMS ACTUALLY HAVE MANY THINGS IN COMMON. FOR INSTANCE, BOTH HAVE A FAIR AMOUNT OF FIGHTING. LET'S TAKE A LOOK.

(SFX: TRACK FROM "MAGNIFICENT SEVEN")

SUPER: AMERICAN FILM.

(SFX: TRACK FROM "SEVEN SAMURAI")

SUPER: FOREIGN FILM.

(MUSIC: FRENCH FILM MUSIC)

SUBTITLE: THEY BOTH HAVE SLAPSTICK HUMOR.

(SFX: TRACK FROM "PINK PANTHER")

SUPER: AMERICAN FILM.

(SFX: TRACK FROM "THE GODS MUST BE CRAZY")

SUPER: FOREIGN FILM.

(MUSIC: FRENCH FILM MUSIC)

SUBTITLE: THEY BOTH HAVE CLINT EASTWOOD.

(SFX: TRACK FROM "DIRTY HARRY")

SUPER: AMERICAN FILM.

(SFX: TRACK FROM "THE GOOD, THE BAD AND THE UGLY")

SUPER: FOREIGN FILM.

(MUSIC: FRENCH FILM MUSIC THROUGH END OF SPOT)

SUBTITLES: IN FACT, THERE'S REALLY ONLY ONE DIFFERENCE BETWEEN THE TWO. THESE THINGS AT THE BOTTOM OF THE SCREEN CALLED SUBTITLES. WHICH YOU'VE BEEN READING FOR THE LAST 2 MINUTES AND 6 SECONDS WITHOUT ANY PROBLEM AT ALL. HMMMMMM. SO NOW WHAT'S YOUR EXCUSE? THE PORTLAND INTERNATIONAL FILM FESTIVAL. FEBRUARY 14 TO MARCH 3. PRODUCED BY THE OREGON ART INSTITUTE'S NORTHWEST FILM AND VIDEO CENTER.

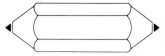

Gold, Silver, & Bronze
Awards

# NOT

# ALL

# ADVERTISING

# BRINGS

# IN

# SALES.

**HAVE YOU SEEN ME?**

NAME MONICA NICOLE
DASILVA
DATE MISSING 09/23/90
DOB 06/12/83
AGE 7
HT 3'0"
EYES Brown
HAIR Blonde
WT 40 lbs.
SEX Female
FROM Reno, Nevada

**CALL 1-800-843-5678**
National Center for Missing and Exploited Children

The most important advertising has nothing to do with buying or selling. It has to do with helping.
From finding a lost child to finding a cure for AIDS, each year advertising helps promote countless worthy causes.

**American Association of Advertising Agencies**

## No matter what advertisers say or do, the choice is still yours.

Despite what some may say, advertising is about choices. While it has the power to move you emotionally, it can not move you physically.

It can, however, inform and educate you about your options, increase your awareness of the world around you and give you the opportunity to experience

different ways of looking at things.

So the next time you're faced with a decision, after having seen or heard an advertisement, just remember that it isn't

what we say that's important, but what you do.

American Association of Advertising Agencies

**101 SILVER**

RAY CEDARS WAS A GROCER WITH A GREAT MANY DIVERSE TALENTS AND SKILLS. HE WAS KNOWN AROUND THE COUNTRY FOR HIS

# R A Y

UNCANNY ABILITY TO GROW FRUITS, VEGETABLES AND ESPECIALLY PISTACHIO NUTS. RAY'S GROWING SKILLS BY FAR EXCEEDED HIS

# P A I N T E D

ABILITY TO SELL WHATEVER HE PRODUCED, AND AFTER A PERIOD OF TIME THIS IMBALANCE LEFT RAY WITH A GREAT SURPLUS OF

PERISHABLE FOOD, PARTICULARLY PISTACHIOS. NO MATTER HOW MANY PEOPLE FROM AROUND THE COUNTRY CAME AND BOUGHT

# H I S

NUTS FROM RAY, HE ALWAYS SEEMED TO HAVE PLENTY LEFT ON THE SHELF AT CLOSING TIME. HAVING USED UP ALL THE OTHER

OPTIONS TO INCREASE SALES AVAILABLE TO HIM RAY DECIDED TO ADVERTISE HIS PISTACHIOS IN A LOCAL NEWSPAPER. IN ORDER TO

MAKE IT EASIER FOR ALL HIS NEW CUSTOMERS TO FIND HIS NUTS, RAY TOOK TO PAINTING THEM BRIGHT RED AND PROUDLY

# N U T S

DISPLAYING THEM IN THE FRONT OF HIS STORE FOR EVERYONE TO SEE. RAY'S ADVERTISING TECHNIQUE BECAME SO POPULAR, AND

HIS PISTACHIOS SOLD SO WELL THAT ALL THE OTHER FARMERS AROUND HIM IN LOWER WHIP A WILLOW CREEK ALSO STARTED TO PAINT THEIR NUTS

# R E D

BRIGHT RED. THIS FAD BECAME A TREND THAT OVERTOOK THE NATION AND IS STILL POPULAR IN AMERICA TODAY. ADVERTISING. ENOUGH SAID.

(BASED ON A TRUE STORY)

**102 BRONZE**

FRANK THE TORTOISE: Oh, it's good to come back into a warm flat after you've just done a run. And it's always nice to come into somewhere warm, if you've been freezin' to death outside on a ten mile slog. Yea, it's easily controllable, um . . . and it n-needs to be easily controllable as well, because I don't have much time. I'm a very busy person so I have to have ev-everything (gulp) just asI need it. Well they, they should, they should, be sort of fairly modern in design and they've got to be easily turn "off" and "onable".
ANNCR: For all your creature comforts. Heat Electric.

PABLO THE PARROT: I am . . . sensitive to the cold weather and, er, therefore I need . . . er . . . you know, it's like, you know, a priority for me when I first arrive in England to have come to a house that had heating. You know I wouldn't be here otherwise. You know it's nice to know that you can go home and you will be a bit warmer and you know it's very agreeable to be, you know, heated up. I mean, I just think for monetary reasons . . . er . . . I just think that it's great . . . er . . . I don't know, I think you just feel warm really.
ANNCR: For all your creature comforts. Heat Electric.

CAROL THE CAT: It's bliss, absolute bliss, you walk in, you get past the dog, he's snoring his head off normally, you go in the lounge, slob around for a bit, I mean the whole house is warm. I had a flat once, it was freezing. And it's just lovely being here, 'cos you never have to worry about being cold, it's just like that all the time . . . And especially like, you know, when you come in and you've been dancing all night, there's still plenty of hot water and the house is still lovely and warm, it's just like unbelievable really. And you get into bed and it's lovely and warm and you wake up in the morning and it's still nice and warm. I mean you just don't wanna go to work in the morning.
ANNCR: For all your creature comforts. Heat Electric.

## BEST OF SHOW

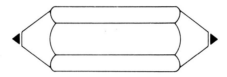

**ART DIRECTORS**
Newy Brothwell, Phil Rylance
**WRITERS**
Paul Cardwell,
Kim Durdant-Hollamby
**AGENCY PRODUCER**
Joanne Cresser
**PRODUCTION COMPANY**
Aardman Animation
**DIRECTOR**
Nick Park
**CLIENT**
Electricity Association
**AGENCY**
GGK/London

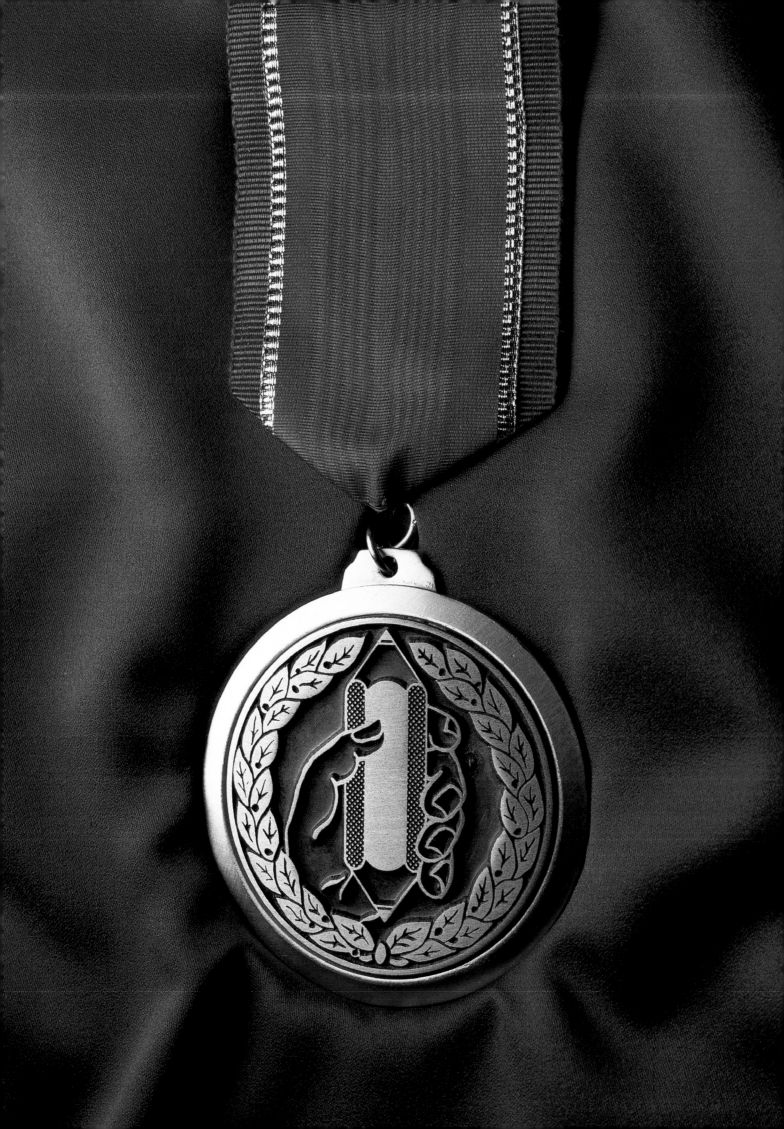

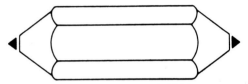

**THE GOLD AWARD WINNERS ON
THE GOLD AWARD WINNERS**

## CONSUMER NEWSPAPER
## OVER 600 LINES: SINGLE

AGENCY: Leagas Delaney/London
CLIENT: Timberland

What do an art director from Newcastle and a
copywriter from Minneapolis have in
common? Nothing.

So when the two of us sat together trying to
come up with this Timberland ad, we didn't
have a lot to talk about.

Except the weather.

*MIKE LESCARBEAU*
*TIM DELANEY*
*STEVE DUNN*

## CONSUMER NEWSPAPER
## OVER 600 LINES: SINGLE

AGENCY: Leagas Delaney/London
CLIENT: Timberland

We wrote this ad to glorify the role that
women undoubtedly played in the
development of the United States. (We'd say
anything to avoid a barrage of feminist hate
mail).

*TIM DELANEY*
*STEVE DUNN*

# IN ONE AMERICAN STATE, THE PENALTY FOR EXPOSING YOURSELF IS DEATH.

In the winter of 1968, Mount Washington in New Hampshire was the unlucky recipient of 566 inches of snowfall. Or to put it another way, that's just a little over forty-seven feet.

Snowstorms with winds in excess of a hundred miles an hour are not uncommon. Which makes the wind-chill factor too cold to measure with existing instruments.

The weatherman simply warns that at times like these, exposed flesh freezes instantly.

Some of the old folks in the state can recall the time in '34, when the Mountain was the site of the strongest wind gust ever recorded on earth: 231 mph.

They can recite articles from the local paper, The Littleton Courier, about hikers freezing to death up there in the middle of summer.

And they'll tell you, in no uncertain terms, that it's less important to dress according to the latest fashion than it is to dress according to the latest weather report.

It is this almost inbred respect for nature's wrath that compels the people at Timberland in Hampton, New Hampshire to design their outdoor clothing the way they do.

This clothing is ideal for people who venture outdoors regardless of the forecast and who pride themselves on being ready for the worst.

Take, for example, our Timberland leather coats. The leather is the best you can find, because it's the best we can find.

To get hides that meet our standards, we travel the world looking for sources of supply. A search made more difficult by our insistence on hides from animals raised on the open range. While that may sound pernickety, you'll never see scarring from barbed wire on a Timberland coat.

But we're not just concerned about how our hides are treated while they're raised. We also give them special treatment once we get them back to our workshops.

All the leathers used by Timberland get a dunking in chemical agents for water repellency. Then, to keep them looking new in any kind of weather, we give them special finishes that will never wear off.

When we use Split Suede, for instance, we give it a light-resistant finish to avoid fading. So it's not only rainproof, but sunproof, as well.

As for our Weatherguard Newbuck leather, it's given a unique chrome-tan finish so it stays supple throughout its life.

*Partial as Timberland is to leathers like* Newbuck and Split Suede, we realise that man cannot live by leather alone.

Which is why in some Timberland outerwear we use Gore-Tex, a man-made fabric with over nine billion pores per square inch. These microscopic openings are too small to let water in, yet large enough for perspiration molecules to get out.

Once we have the right materials in place, we start sewing coats that will last year after year after year.

On the coat you see here, we double stitch the seams that will be exposed to the heaviest wear. We run a pull cord through the waist of the coat to keep cold air from creeping up underneath. And we fit zippers of solid brass, so they'll never rust.

Since people who wear Timberland coats often venture off the beaten path, we've also taken special care that the pockets won't get torn in heavy brush. Each one is closed up with a thick leather cover and secured by buttons made from brass and bone.

And to make sure you never end up looking for those buttons in the woods (worse than looking for a needle in a haystack), we use heavy cord thread and reinforce each one on the backside with quarter-inch guards.

The finished product is a coat that will protect you from cold, wet and, on one of its more hospitable days, perhaps even the Mountain itself.

But it's not just outerwear that Timberland makes to last. Our clothing range also includes the kind of things you might wear when the temperature soars to above freezing.

Starting with stalwarts like wool, denim, canvas and cotton, Timberland makes a range that's always at home in the wild. Sweaters, trousers, jackets and shirts, even the duffle bags to carry them in.

Each item designed to withstand the twin tests of weather and time.

Of course, if you own a pair of our boots or shoes, you're already familiar with the unique way Timberlands hold together.

What you may not know is why they do.

We tape seal the seams of some of our boots with latex to make sure water can't get through to your feet.

We impregnate our shoe and boot leather with silicone, to give it a longer life. We sew in doubleknot pearl stitching that won't come undone even if it's accidentally cut. We use self oiling laces that won't rot, and solid brass eyelets that won't rust.

The list, like the winters up on Mount Washington, goes on and on.

Suffice to say that at Timberland, making outdoor clothing and boots is not just a way of life. It's a way of living.

Timberland (UK) Limited, Unit Four, St. Anthony's Way, Feltham, Middlesex. TW14 0NH. Telephone 081 890 6116.

**Timberland ®**

1

# FROM THE DAYS WHEN MEN WERE MEN. AND SO WERE THE WOMEN.

The old West was definitely no place for wimps and faint hearts.

Those foolhardy enough to go in search of Eldorado were hard-bitten, unfeeling brutes who often had to wrestle with wild animals for their food, build entire cabins with the most rudimentary of tools and had to dispatch Apaches with their bare hands on a daily basis.

The men were pretty tough too.

Yes, as the history books show, it was women who were America's true pioneers.

While the menfolk went buffalo hunting and killing, gold-mining and killing or sometimes just shooting and wounding, the girls were left to fend for themselves in the wilderness for months on end. And exactly what kind of fending was involved?

Well, they made almost everything they stood up in except, ironically, their boots.

This particular item of clothing proved beyond even their resourcefulness. Which is totally understandable.

In these circumstances, footwear needed to be tough and long-lasting, though not so heavy that it could be thought unlady-like. Most important of all, their boots had to keep out the rain and snow of the appalling prairie winters.

A tall order. One that even today would be hard to fill.

And while those intrepid womenfolk had to trek for days to their local trading post to obtain such a pair of boots, their descendants are more fortunate. All they have to do is buy a pair of boots made by Timberland.

For enshrined in all our boots are the very same qualities that helped those brave women slog gamely across America.

Naturally, the materials we use today are a little less, shall we say, rustic than in those days.

You only have to compare the leathers we have at our disposal today with the rather limited choice they had.

Their rawhide was often just that, with an odour which was not at all helpful in relationships with menfolk.

Our hides, on the other hand, are handpicked from tanneries across the country who pride themselves on making strong, durable leathers soft and supple.

Understandably, a woman abandoned in uncharted Indian territory would not have been overly concerned about the colour scuffing or flaking off her boots.

Or whether, indeed, the degree of water repellency was all it was cracked up to be.

(When women were our pioneering, such things were not exactly top of the agenda.)

Why up in the wilds of Hampton, New Hampshire, however, this is precisely the kind of thing our craftsmen worry about constantly.

Which is why immediately the leathers are brought to the workshops, we dye them right through, then impregnate them with silicone oils.

Not only does this preserve the colour of the boot after years of wear, it also acts as a seal against the elements.

Looking back, it is difficult to understand why the early settlers didn't stop a passing Red Indian and enquire as to the precise method employed in the making of their footwear.

Certainly, it is now acknowledged that the original moccasin design was uniquely comfortable.

Which is exactly the reason we utilise the wraparound construction, using one piece of leather, for all our boots and shoes.

Of course, however warm and comfortable we make the actual boot, if water gets in all our painstaking handiwork counts for nothing.

Let us put your mind (and feet) at ease. Unlike the womenfolk who blazed the Oregon Trail, you won't have to worry about the occasional deluge or ten foot snowdrift.

The boot in our picture is, for example, guaranteed 100% waterproof.

First, we sew each boot with a high strength nylon yarn, using a double knot, pearl stitch. Then, we seal each seam with not one but two coats of latex. Add a Gore-Tex inner bootie, glove leather lining and a soft padded collar and the boot becomes positively luxurious.

Although just to make absolutely certain your feet never have to encounter the kind of hardship that caused many a pioneer woman to die with her boots on, we didn't stop there.

The midsole is stitched to a lightweight polyurethane mini-lug outsole after which it is bonded to the upper.

No doubt all those hardy travel-weary females who opened up the West could have done with a pair or two of our boots.

Or some clothes from our new weapons' Weathergear outdoor collection.

Even one of our bags or a belt would have come in handy.

But then they might have looked like women, the men would have stayed home and the wild West would still be wild to this day.

Timberland (UK) Limited, Unit Five, St. Anthony's Way, Feltham, Middlesex. TW14 0NH.

**Timberland ®**

2

# THE PENTAGON. AMERICA'S LAST DEFENCE AGAINST COMMUNISM, TYRANNY AND BUNIONS.

Left, right. Left, right. Left, right.

Multiply this simple leg exercise a few thousand times and you can begin to imagine what square-bashing in a new pair of US army boots does to a young man's feet.

Or can you?

Contrary to the myth, the army boot is not an instrument of torture used to initiate raw recruits.

In fact, such is the concern for the feet of men under their command that the US military issues standards for their standard issue boots.

Very high standards they are too.

The boots have to be tough and durable, naturally. They also have to be waterproof and the leather has to be flexible. In other words, the US army boot has to be an efficient part of the soldier's equipment.

Out in civvy street, few boot makers even try to match the exacting standards laid down by the Pentagon.

Up in the small town of Hampton, New Hampshire, however, there's a company that believes their boots are every bit as good as the army's.

And what's more they'll fight any man who says different.

The company is called Timberland.

To make their point, all leathers destined to become Timberland boots are subjected to a machine known as a MaterFlex.

It's designed to test just how long leathers remain waterproof in extreme circumstances.

Only if hides can withstand a minimum of 15,000 flexes can they be passed as equal to the highest standards demanded (and we mean demanded), by the US military.

Naturally, all our boots pass muster.

Only by testing the leathers in this way can we be sure that your feet won't suffer ailments caused by less well made boots.

(No less an authority than Blake's Medical Dictionary blames bunions on ill-fitting footwear in general and short or cramped boots in particular. We couldn't agree more.)

Of course, our concern for the well-being of your feet isn't left solely in the hands of a machine.

Even though we might not have quite the same budget as the Pentagon (theirs was two hundred and sixty nine thousand, nine hundred and eighty one million dollars in the fiscal year October 1989 to October 1990) we probably spend more on our hides than they do on theirs.

How come?

Remember, army boots are free. Whereas

we expect our customers to invest a small fortune for a pair of Timberlands.

So we're just plain picky on their behalf.

We trek all round the country in search of tanneries that can meet our ridiculously high standards.

When we find one, we simply pay what it takes to bring every hide in the place back to Hampton.

(When the comfort of your feet is at stake, we never argue over nickels and dimes.)

We insist on premium, full grain leathers and nothing less. A rare oxhide leather called Norwegian Krymp is a particular favourite.

Back in the workshops, we dye the leathers right through. This ensures that the colour will not scuff off or crack up even under the strain of the longest march.

We could paint the colour on like other manufacturers do but pretty soon it would get a bit flaky, not unlike the manufacturers themselves.

It's at this stage of the process that we soak the leathers in silicone oil.

Impregnating them in this way keeps them supple. It also ensures that water can't seep through and give your feet a real soaking.

Rest assured, the only way you are going to get soaked with our boots is when you fork out the money for a pair.

Now you may be asking yourself if the Army can afford to give their boots away free, why on earth are ours so darned expensive?

Blame the gnarled hands and nimble fingers of the old boys who put our uppers together.

The kind of craftsmanship that can mould one piece of leather on a special geometric last doesn't come cheap.

And we'd always contend that fingers that can sew better than a machine are certainly

worth shelling out a little extra for.

Mind you, while your wallet may be taking a pounding, you can take some comfort from the fact that, unlike the army, we have a policy of pampering your feet.

To make absolutely sure snow and rain can't get in, the midsoles are injection moulded to the base, creating a waterproof seal with the rubber lug sole.

A cushioned inner sole is then inserted to keep your feet snug and warm.

This is made from soft glove leather or high performance Cambrelle. Likewise those collars you get on most of our boots.

Aside from providing extra comfort, these padded collars follow the form of your ankle to help to stop the elements sneaking in.

Meanwhile, inside the boot we usually insulate the tongue, shaft and quarter with Thinsulate and the toe with Ensolite.

And we invariably add a Gore-Tex lining for good measure.

This remarkable man-made fabric has 9 billion pores per square inch, each one 20,000 times smaller than a raindrop but 700 times larger than a molecule of perspiration. As a result, your feet can actually breathe.

But just in case your feet get too cosy in there, most of our boots are fitted with a special removable polypropylene insole to absorb any excess perspiration.

What of the good old army boot? Haven't there been any concessions to the warmth and comfort to be found in a pair of Timberlands?

No sir. None at all, sir.

The US military may have finally defeated the bunion but a soldier's foot still has to live in pretty spartan surroundings.

And that, soldier, is an order.

Timberland ®

11

6

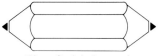
## CONSUMER MAGAZINE B/W:
## 1 PAGE OR SPREAD
## INCLUDING MAGAZINE SUPPLEMENTS

AGENCY: Scali McCabe Sloves/New York
CLIENT: Nikon

It took four photographers to finally get
this ad to look right.

*RON ROSEN*
*RICHARD KELLY*

## CONSUMER MAGAZINE
## COLOR: 1 PAGE OR SPREAD
## INCLUDING MAGAZINE SUPPLEMENTS

AGENCY: Grace & Rothschild/New York
CLIENT: Range Rover of North America

We wanted to show Range Rover's off-
road capability, and at the same time,
communicate its British heritage.

After months and months of digging, we
finally unearthed a little-known fact
about England we thought people might
find interesting.

*DON MILLER*
*GARY COHEN*

16

19

## CONSUMER MAGAZINE
## COLOR: CAMPAIGN
## INCLUDING MAGAZINE SUPPLEMENTS

AGENCY: Goodby Berlin & Silverstein/
San Francisco
CLIENT: Royal Viking Line

We were originally going to photograph
an all-American family playing together.
But when the adorable five-year-old girl
with the one missing tooth got on the
hobby horse, we knew we had the
dream shot. The headline "Happiness
Starts at Home" just sort of came
naturally. The rest is history.

*ROB BAGOT*
*TRACY WONG*

## CONSUMER MAGAZINE
## LESS THAN A PAGE
## B/W OR COLOR: CAMPAIGN

AGENCY: Boy & Girl Advertising
CLIENT: Riverside Chocolate Factory

We were entirely thrilled about the gold
pencil until we were stopped at the
metal detector at JFK Airport. The lady
there said, "Oh, it's those pencil things
again. Somebody just came through
with a whole bunch of them." Must have
been those guys from Goodby.

*AMY KROUSE ROSENTHAL*
*BARTON LANDSMAN*

24

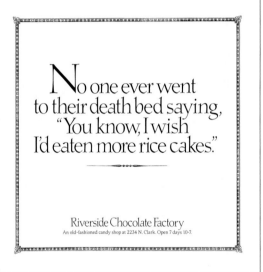

31

## OUTDOOR: SINGLE

AGENCY: Livingston & Company/Seattle
CLIENT: Museum of Flight

They say an outdoor board should be simple enough to be readable from a car traveling 35 m.p.h. We drive a little faster than that.

*MATT MYERS*
*RICK ROSENBERG*

## OUTDOOR: CAMPAIGN

AGENCY: Leagas Delaney/London
CLIENT: Courtauld Institute

Now we've helped to move Samuel Courtauld's Van Goghs, Monets and Renoirs, who knows, we might get the chance to work on a really priceless collection: Jay Chiat's.

*TIM DELANEY*
*STEVE DUNN*

34

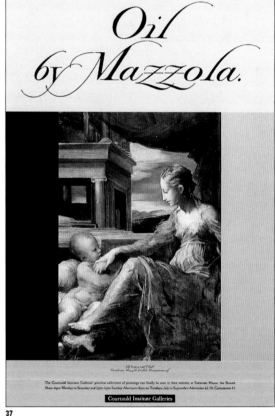

37

## TRADE B/W: 1 PAGE OR SPREAD

AGENCY: Goodby Berlin & Silverstein/
San Francisco
CLIENT: Clarks of England

"So what's with this shoe."
"Little suction cups on the soles."
"How about a fly?"
"Yeah. Wearing the shoes."
"HA HA HA HA HA HA HA HA HA HA
HA HA HA HA HA HA HA HA HA HA HA
HA HA HA HA HA HA HA HA HA HA HA
HA HA HA HA HA HA HA HA HA HA HA
HA HA HA HA HA HA HA HA HA HA HA
HA HA HA HA HA HA HA HA HA HA HA
HA HA HA HA HA HA HA HA HA HA HA."
"Never in a million years."
"Yeah. What else."

*CLAY WILLIAMS*
*TRACY WONG*

## TRADE COLOR: 1 PAGE OR SPREAD

AGENCY: Goodby Berlin & Silverstein/
San Francisco
CLIENT: Royal Viking Line

When you show a big product shot, you win your client's love and respect.

When you don't show one at all, you win a Pencil.

*ROB BAGOT*
*TRACY WONG*

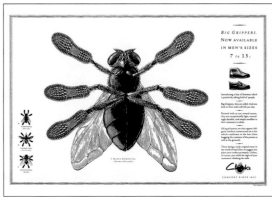

41

44

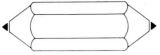

The Gold Award
Winners on
The Gold Award
Winners

## TRADE COLOR: 1 PAGE
## OR SPREAD

AGENCY: Messner Vetere Berger Carey
Schmetterer/New York
CLIENT: LIFE Magazine

We're very grateful for the One Show's
response to this ad.

Jack Nicholson's response was also
overwhelming.
He sued LIFE for $100,000.

*PAUL WOLFE*
*ED EVANGELISTA*

## TRADE ANY SIZE
## B/W OR COLOR: CAMPAIGN

AGENCY: The Ball Partnership/Singapore
CLIENT: The Ball Partnership

Frankly, if you can't write half-way
decent ads when you're your own client,
you should be shot...and not with a
golden bullet. Still, isn't it nice that
Ernest Shackleton finally got a gong for
his ad. Where do I send it?

*NEIL FRENCH*

45

49

## COLLATERAL BROCHURES
## OTHER THAN BY MAIL

AGENCY: Hal Riney & Partners/
San Francisco
CLIENT: The Mirage

Coming from a sadomasochistic business
ourselves, dreaming this thing up was no
problem.

*SAM POND*
*TOM TIECHE*
*BEN WONG*

## COLLATERAL DIRECT MAIL:
## SINGLE

AGENCY: Fallon McElligott/Minneapolis
CLIENT: Fallon McElligott

We'd like to thank our Creative Director,
Pat Burnham, for doing the illustration.

*BRUCE BILDSTEN*
*DEAN HANSON*

53

56

The Gold Award
Winners on
The Gold Award
Winners

## COLLATERAL P.O.P.

AGENCY: The Martin Agency/Richmond
CLIENT: Bernie's Tattooing Parlor

Unfortunately, there is a tragic ending to
this story. The model in our poster really
did surprise his wife and she clocked him
in the head with a skillet.

*JELLY HELM
RAYMOND MCKINNEY*

## PUBLIC SERVICE
## NEWSPAPER OR MAGAZINE:
## SINGLE

AGENCY: Fallon McElligott/Minneapolis
CLIENT: People for the Ethical Treatment of
Animals

It doesn't take any great skill to do these
P.E.T.A. ads.

You simply show whatever medieval
horrors are being visited upon animals
this week, point out the group of
misguided individuals that's doing it,
print their address and phone number,
and get out of the way.

*LUKE SULLIVAN
BOB BARRIE*

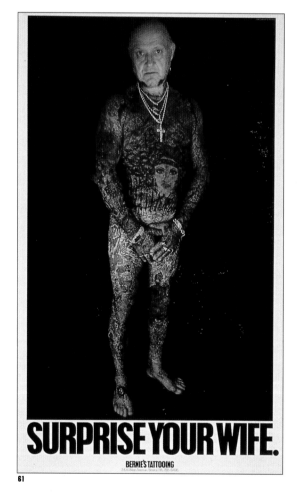

61

64

## CONSUMER RADIO: SINGLE

AGENCY: Chiat/Day/Mojo, New York
CLIENT: NYNEX Information Resources

I was, of course, delighted to win a gold pencil for "Midges Makeovers." Until I learned that some of the judges (thankfully, not all of them) had found the spot amusing. It suddenly occurred to me that they had missed the whole point. "Midges" was never intended to be funny. I was simply trying to call attention to the silent suffering of the literally handfuls of people born each day with...unfortunate eyebrows. I myself am afflicted with a condition called, "Tuftaperipetica," or "Wandering brows." They can turn up anywhere, at any time...on my chin, on the nape of my neck, alongside my ears. (I occasionally try to pass them off as sideburns, with little success.) "Midges Makeovers", then, was intended as a tribute to the heroic stoicism of the eyebrow impaired, in the face of almost constant ridicule. This pencil is for them.

*DAVID SHANE*

## CONSUMER TELEVISION OVER :30 (:45/:60/:90) SINGLE

AGENCY: GGK/London
CLIENT: Electricity Association

Thanks, Nick.

*PAUL CARDWELL*
*NEWY BROTHWELL*
*PHIL RYLANCE*
*KIM DURDANT-HOLLAMBY*

78

79

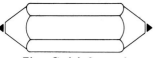

The Gold Award
Winners on
The Gold Award
Winners

## CONSUMER TELEVISION
## OVER :30 (:45/:60/:90)
## CAMPAIGN

AGENCY: GGK/London
CLIENT: Electricity Association

This campaign isn't creative. It isn't
brilliant. It isn't a breakthrough. It isn't
any of that bullshit.

It's human.

People like it.

In the end, that's what matters.

*PAUL CARDWELL*
*NEWY BROTHWELL*
*PHIL RYLANCE*
*KIM DURDANT-HOLLAMBY*

## CONSUMER TELEVISION
## :30 SINGLE

AGENCY: Scali McCabe Sloves/New York
CLIENT: Nikon

Maybe there are some creative teams
who enjoy two week location shoots in
warm, sunny climates, working with top
directors and bikini clad actress/models,
while staying in the finest hotels and
eating in four star restaurants. All
expenses paid.

But we much more prefer producing all
type commercials in two hours, three
blocks away from our office and
enjoying day-old salad from Smiler's
Delicatessen.

*RON ROSEN*
*RICHARD KELLY*

82

A three-year old boy saluting
at his father's funeral.

83

## CONSUMER TELEVISION
## :30 CAMPAIGN

AGENCY: MacLaren: Lintas/Toronto
CLIENT: Ciba-Geigy

Dis honour has left us breadless!

*BENJAMIN BENSIMON*
*DAVID INNIS*

## CONSUMER TELEVISION
## UNDER: 24 SINGLE

AGENCY: Cliff Freeman & Partners/New York
CLIENT: Hills Department Stores

Lorraine was picked, not because she looked good in a towel, (there were some scary moments with towel slippage and left breast exposure), but primarily for her plumped feet. We did apply fake toenails, though, and Lorraine opted for orchid frost nail enamel. I believe this single-minded strategy of casting is what brought us to win a gold in The One Show.

*DONNA WEINHEIM*

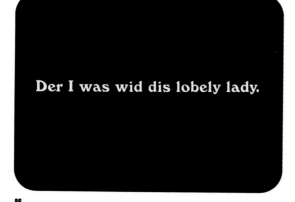

86

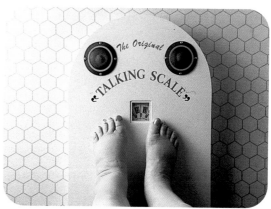

89

The Gold Award
Winners on
The Gold Award
Winners

## CONSUMER TELEVISION
## UNDER :24 CAMPAIGN

AGENCY: BMP DDB Needham/London
CLIENT: Crookes Healthcare

As the great Bill Bernbach once said:

"Has anyone seen the top to my red
magic marker?"

*TONY DAVIDSON*
*KIM PAPWORTH*

## PUBLIC SERVICE TELEVISION
## SINGLE

AGENCY: Cliff Freeman & Partners/New York
CLIENT: ASPCA

It was a dog of a project and we knew it.

*RICK LEMOINE*
*JANE KING*
*JEFF ALPHIN*
*JOHN COLQUHOUN*

92

95

## COLLEGE COMPETITION

SCHOOL: Massachusetts College of Art,
University of Minnesota
ASSIGNMENT: American Association of
Advertising Agencies

What a great topic for a couple of guys
that love advertising. Not yet hardened
by years of work in the business, we
came up with quite a few positives on
which to base the ad. With the art
director in Boston and the writer in
Minneapolis, it was a little difficult to put
it together, but after some preliminary
brainstorming we had the concept. After
that, it was just a matter of hammering it
out over the phone and through the
mail.

So, with this opportunity, we'd like to
thank the U.S. Postal Service and a
couple of other people. From Ed, thanks
to Tom Burke and Marilyn Gabarro at
Mass. Art. From Mark, thanks to Steve
Kahn at the U of M, and Mary Fuller at
Colle & McVoy. And from both of us,
thank God that the Clio's aren't the ones
with the college competition.

*ED PARKS*
*MARK WEGWERTH*

# NOT

# ALL

# ADVERTISING

# BRINGS

# IN

# SALES.

**HAVE YOU SEEN ME?**

NAME: MONICA NICOLE DASILVA
DATE MISSING: 09/03/90
DOB: 06/12/83
AGE: 7
HT: 3'6"
EYES: Brown
HAIR: Blonde
WT: 40 lbs
SEX: Female
FROM: Reno, Nevada

**CALL 1-800-843-5678**
National Center for Missing and Exploited Children

The most important advertising has nothing to do with buying or selling. It has to do with helping.
From finding a lost child to finding a cure for AIDS, each year advertising helps promote countless worthy causes.

**American Association of Advertising Agencies**

**PRINT FINALISTS**

# You can tell an Economist reader by the company he owns.

103

---

The rise and rise of the British chef. Who deserves the compliments?

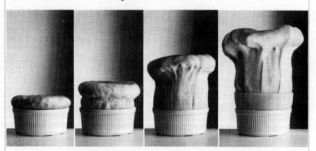

Britain is no longer a wasteland for foodies.

We like our vegetables crisp, our pasta al dente and our lamb pink.

Our hotels have stars in the guide book and still more in the kitchen.

As the leisure and catering industry's leading journal, 'Caterer & Hotelkeeper' can claim credit for many of the changes.

With a weekly readership of 250,000, it is very much the voice of a major industry. (Employing 2·5 million people.)

Owned by Reed International it also makes a tasty contribution to the corporate pot.

104

# THE THRILL OF DRIVING A SAAB. THE JOY OF USING SOMEONE ELSE'S MONEY.

Saab presents a truly exciting plan to preserve your capital.

It's called Saab-Lease, and it does exactly what its name suggests.

First, it gets you into a Saab. Which means you'll be driving a true European touring car whose sheer zeal, roadworthiness and safety are legendary.

Second, it lets you do so while leaving your own finances intact. Instead of withdrawing your money to buy the car, you let it sit in the bank and do what it does best: namely, earn interest, which helps pay for the lease.

And even that is made easier because you'll be dealing directly with Saab. The "someone else" whose money you'll be using is Saab's own financing company, instead of a middleman. So you can expect rates that are quite favorable.

But along with fun and fiscal responsibility, Saab-Lease also gives you flexibility. Because it lets you choose from a variety of lease periods. And whether or not to buy your Saab when the lease period ends.

If you buy it, you can choose the Saab Buy-Back Option, which guarantees you an agreed-upon price, no hidden costs or other surprises.

If you decide not to buy when your lease expires, you can do that, too. In which case you can reexperience the thrill of driving a new Saab, once again using someone else's money.

Finally, no matter what choices you make, you can make them with the convenience of one-stop shopping. Your Saab dealer orchestrates the details, leaving you with almost nothing to do except the most important thing: having fun with your Saab.

For complete details, see your Saab dealer. He'll be happy to show you how to pursue financial well-being and enjoy every mile of the trip.

SAAB

© 1990 Saab-Scania of America, Inc.

105

WITH ALL THE TALK

ABOUT FUSION THESE DAYS,

WE'D LIKE TO REMIND

THE SCIENTIFIC COMMUNITY

THAT WE WERE FIRST

TO PRODUCE ENERGY

IN A COMPLETE VACUUM.

ELECTROLUX

106

# A Few Encouraging Words For The Totally Incompeten T.

It's perfectly alright to be incompetent for hours on end.

I am. And so is everyone I know.

Of course, being of this persuasion, I shall never be able to afford a bottle of Beck's Beer. Which is why the people who sell Beck's Beer got me to write this ad.

They see it as a sort of public service announcement; as a way of consoling those who moan at the unfairness of it all. A way of making the 'have-nots' feel glad that they 'haven't'.

So here, for the first time, are the great names: The people who were so bad in their chosen sphere of endeavour that they achieved greatness.

People who believed that success is overrated.

And who believed, as G. K. Chesterton once said, that 'If a thing's worth doing, it's worth doing badly."

## THE WORST BOXING DEBUT

Ralph Walton was knocked out in 10½ seconds of his first bout, on 29th September, 1946, in Lewison, Maine, USA.

It happened when Al Couture struck him as he was adjusting his gum-shield in his corner. The 10½ seconds includes 10 seconds while he was counted out.

He never fought again.

## THE LEAST-SUCCESSFUL WEATHER REPORT

After severe flooding in Jeddah, in January 1979, the Arab News gave the following bulletin: "We regret that we are unable to give you the weather. We rely on weather reports from the airport, which is closed, on account of the weather. Whether or not we are able to bring you the weather tomorrow depends on the weather."

## THE WORST SPEECH-WRITER

William Gamaliel Harding wrote his own speeches while President of the USA, in the 1920's.

When Harding died, e. e. cummings said, "the only man, woman or child who wrote a simple, declarative sentence with seven grammatical errors, is dead".

Here is a rewarding sample of the man's style. "I would like the government to do all it can to mitigate, then, in understanding, in mutuality of interest, in concern for the common good, our tasks will be solved."

## THE MOST UNSUCCESSFUL ATTEMPT AT DYING FOR LOVE

When his fiancee broke off their engagement, Senor Abel Ruiz, of Madrid, decided to kill himself for love.

Reviewing the possibilities available on such occasions, he decided to park himself in front of the Gerona to Madrid express. However, jumping in its path, he landed between the rails and watched, gloomily, as the train passed over him.

He suffered only minor injuries, and promptly received First Aid at Gerona Hospital.

Later that day, he tried again. This time he jumped in front of a passing lorry, again only acquiring some more bruises. His rapid return to the hospital led doctors to call a priest, who made Sr. Ruiz see the folly of his ways. Eventually, he decided to carry on living, and to seek a new girlfriend.

Glad to be alive, he left the hospital and was immediately knocked down by a runaway horse; he was taken back to Gerona Hospital, this time quite seriously injured, for the third time that day.

## THE WORST JUROR

There was a rape case at a Crown Court in Northern England in the late 1970's at which a juror fell fast asleep, during which time the victim was asked to repeat what her attacker had said prior to the incident.

To save her embarrassment, the girl was allowed to write it on paper, instead. This was then folded, and passed along the jury. Each member read the words which, in effect, said "Nothing, in the history of sexual congress, equals the comprehensive going-over which I am about to visit upon your good self."

Sitting next to the dozing juror was an attractive blonde. After reading the note, she refolded it, and nudged her neighbour, who awoke with a start.

He read the note, and looked at the blonde in astonishment. To the delight of the entire court, he then read the note again, slowly. Then he winked at the blonde, and put the note in his pocket.

When the judge asked him for the piece of paper, the recently dormant juror refused, saying that 'it was a personal matter'.

This is what the label on a bottle of Beck's Beer looks like. Since its the closest you'll probably ever get to one, we've given you a dotted line, so you can cut it out, and put it on your wall as a kind of ikon. When you've finished cutting it out, plasters can be bought from any pharmacy.

## THE LEAST-SUCCESSFUL WEAPON

The prize for the most useless weapon of all time goes to the Russians, who invented the dog-mine. The rather ingenious plan was to train the dogs to associate food with the underside of tanks, in the hope that they would run hungrily beneath the advancing Panzer divisions. Bombs would be strapped to their backs, which endangered the dogs to a point where no insurance company would look at them.

Unfortunately, they associated food solely with *Russian* tanks, and totally destroyed half a Soviet division on their first outing.

The plan was quickly abandoned.

## THE WORST BUS SERVICE

Can any bus-service rival the fine Hanley to Bagnall route, in Staffordshire, England? In 1976 it was reported that the buses no longer stopped to pick up passengers.

This came to light when one of them, Mr Bill Hancock, complained that buses on the outward journey regularly sailed past queues of elderly people; up to thirty of them sometimes waiting in line.

Councillor Arthur Cholerton then made transport history by stating that if the buses stopped to pick up passengers, it would disrupt the timetable.

## THE LAST WORD

"They couldn't hit an elephant at this dist..." The last words of General John Sedgwick, spoken while looking over the parapet at enemy lines during the Battle of Spotsylvania, in 1864.

## OH, ALRIGHT, THEN; HERE ARE SOME MORE

Typography has never been our strong point, so here are a few more determined losers, to fill out the column: The Welsh choir who were the sole entrants in a competition, and came second; the Swiss pornographer who was heavily fined because his wares were insufficiently pornographic; the writer of this ad, who, unable to master the art of précis, copied the entire thing, word for word, from Stephen Pile's 'Book of Heroic Failures', thereby incurring almost certain legal action.

There, feel better now, don't you? After all, the price of a bottle of Beck's Beer may well be so high as to be audible only to highly-trained bats, but at least you're not the only one who'll never be able to afford it.

(Oh, no. Three more lines. How about a jingle? Beck's diddly-dee-de-dah, Beck's, tiddly-pom. The end).

107

# So, You're Feeling A Bit Gloomy This Morning? Read On. By Lunchtime You Can Be Suicidal.

1. Concentrate. How miserable *are* you exactly? A little 'down'? Depressed? Or on the verge of crying, stamping, and generally behaving like John McEnroe on one of his better days?

Is there a glimmer of hope on your personal horizon? Count your blessings. After all, the Straits Times has arrived without any evident signs of charring, so you can assume that the country's still in good hands. And, judging by the low growl not unadjacent to your left ear, you're still married.

Feeling worse, yet? Fine. Now we're getting somewhere.

2. Have you noticed that the lounges aren't open yet? This is obviously an oversight. Have these people no idea of how much hooch they could sell to those of us with a teeny-weeny little headache of a morning?

3. Outside the sun is shining.

4. This is no cause for merriment and joy. Sooner or later, you have to go out in it, and there's no brand of shades known to science or Michael Jackson that can protect a retina used only to the delicate pastels of neon, and the soothing glow of disco-strobes. This sunlight business is a killer.

5. Have you ever considered, in the light (is it too early for bad puns? It's always too early... OK) of the above, that you may be a vampire? Look in the mirror; are you there? Are you sure? If not, send out for a mallet, a stake, and someone who doesn't like you very much. Then brace yourself.

On the other hand, which blood-group do you prefer? It has to be cheaper than drinking Beck's, which is some consolation, I guess.

6. Beck's Beer is outrageously, unfairly, expensive. Ordinary beer isn't.

7. Life itself is unfair. (See above).

8. It is, you'll agree, the rich what gets the pleasure, and the poor what gets the blame. The poor also gets the sticky end of every other deal going: Viz and to whit, no Beck's. If you are poor, you'll agree that this, too, is very unfair indeed. If you are rich, get on with your Beck's. And I hope you drown in it.

9. One red traffic-light is always followed by another red traffic-light.

10. Especially when you're in a hurry.

11. More especially when you're late for an appointment you wish you hadn't made in the first place.

12. And when you get there, wringing wet, with anxiety and exertion, your appointment is always later still.

13. When he arrives, he is always calm, composed, and dry as a pawnbroker's eye.

14. You are not allowed to kill him. It is apparently frowned upon in polite circles. Unwarranted pickiness, in our view.

15. When you're young, fit, and attractive, you haven't got any money, so the girls ignore you.

16. When you get older, and richer, you also get fat, ugly, and bald. The girls suddenly show a bizarre preference for younger, poorer men.

17. If you have a full head of hair, girls tell you that bald men are sexy.

18. If you are bald, this previously immutable fact seems to escape them.

19. Life's a bitch. Then you marry one.

20. On the other hand, there's always Bangkok. Or Manila.

21. Or Aids.

22. Becks is a lot more expensive than ordinary beers. Have we mentioned the fact before? It's preying on our minds. With some justification.

23. Buttered toast, when dropped, always lands butter-side down. This well-known law of physics could be the answer to life, the Universe, and everything. The answer previously having been believed to be 48.

24. Lawyers are allowed to wear curly wigs, and long black frocks.

25. Gentlemen who are *not* lawyers, but wear long black frocks and curly wigs, are likely to be sent to jail. By lawyers wearing long black frocks & curly wigs. Or, if they're top-gun type lawmen, in *long* curly wigs, and long *red* frocks. (Black stockings, suspenders, and frilly underwear are apparently purely optional, in either case).

26. Lawyers are allowed to drink Beck's and they can afford it, too. This is very, very irritating indeed.

27. Ben Hunt cannot afford Beck's but still drinks it. Mind you, he'll drink *anything*.

28. The bad guys frequently win.

29. Unless you happen to *be* a bad guy, in which case, welcome to Changi; this is your bucket. Enjoy.

30. The makers and sellers of Beck's are allowed to roam the streets, despite the fact that they are horrid, larcenous, greedy, and totally devoid of humanity.

31. A man who trifles with the affections of defenceless young girls should be damn well hung. And usually, is.

32. It is impossible to get a decent hot pastrami sandwich in Singapore. This is especially peeving when you consider how well hot pastrami-on-rye goes down with a nice, cold, Beck's.

33. On the other hand, nearly anything goes down nicely with Beck's, except the price of the Beck's, which gives you raging indigestion. If this is fair, then I'm a Chinaman. Which I'm not, so that proves it.

34. You may well *be* a Chinaman, and if you can afford Beck's, I hate you, and in any case, it's your round.

35. When you get home, late and drunk, the wife is always wide-awake, waiting.

36. When you get home early and sober she's gone to her Mother's for the night. This is occasionally referred-to as Sod's Law. As opposed to Murphy's. (see 23).

37. That delightful seventeen-year-old over there is going to look like her Mother one day.

38. Unless her Mother's beautiful, in which case she'll grow to look like her Dad. Or, alternatively, her goldfish.

39. If you lived in Europe, you could buy a Mercedes for the same price as a mid-range Japanese car costs here. A Rolls-Royce, here, costs the same as a three-bedroom apartment in London. Wherever you live, Beck's is ridiculously expensive, so you may as well stay home.

40. No matter how much money you earn, you spend it.

41. Copywriters get paid absurd amounts of money for writing reams of stuff that nobody bothers to read. This, for instance. They then spend most of it on loose women, fast cars, and Beck's, and just waste the rest. This is absolutely, incredibly unfair, and I don't give a hoot.

42. Is it lunchtime yet? Oddly enough I feel *much* better now. Think I'll go and have a Becks.

43. Hang the expense.

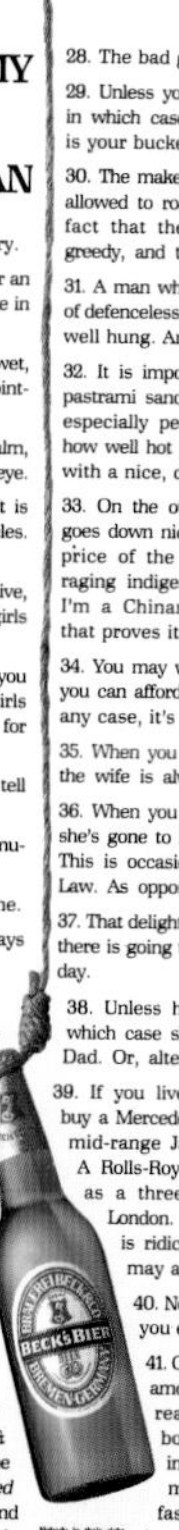


108

CONSUMER NEWSPAPER
OVER 600 LINES: SINGLE

**109**
**ART DIRECTOR**
Neil French
**WRITER**
Neil French
**PHOTOGRAPHER**
Willie Tang
**CLIENT**
Pacific Beauty Care
**AGENCY**
The Ball Partnership/
Singapore

**110**
**ART DIRECTOR**
Neil French
**WRITER**
Neil French
**PHOTOGRAPHER**
Willie Tang
**CLIENT**
Pacific Beauty Care
**AGENCY**
The Ball Partnership/
Singapore

**111**
**ART DIRECTOR**
Neil French
**WRITER**
Neil French
**PHOTOGRAPHER**
Willie Tang
**CLIENT**
Pacific Beauty Care
**AGENCY**
The Ball Partnership/
Singapore

**112**
**ART DIRECTOR**
Rosie Arnold
**WRITER**
Charles Hendley
**PHOTOGRAPHER**
Francois Gillet
**CLIENT**
Shell
**AGENCY**
Bartle Bogle Hegarty/London

(Be careful with the Kaminomoto)

109

(Be careful with the Kaminomoto)

110

(Be careful with the Kaminomoto)

# WHAT THEY DO FOR YOUR INSIDES, SHELL ADVANCED PETROL DOES FOR YOUR ENGINE.

Give your car a better diet. Use Shell Advanced petrol which contains a detergent that actually cleans the engine as you drive.

Which means smoother running and less carbon monoxide in the exhaust. Foods like wholemeal bread, muesli and prunes help keep your body healthy. Now you can do the same for your car by putting Shell petrol on the menu.

**YOU CAN TELL WHEN IT'S SHELL.**

The reason they don't make Coke® the way they used to.

On April 23, 1985, Coca-Cola® tried to imitate the great taste of Pepsi with New Coke® Five years later they're at it again, this time with Coke II® With Pepsi as an inspiration, who knows, maybe one day we'll see a Coke XII.

**Pepsi. The Choice Of A New Generation®**

113

**Bristol to the Monet Exhibition 12 times a day.**

Everyday we run 47* trains from Bristol to London. At least 12 of these
will get you to London in time to see the Monet Exhibition, which runs until 9th December 1990.

MONET EXHIBITION (WEEKDAY OPENING 10AM-6PM.) TICKET OFFICE 071 793 1000.
TRAIN INFORMATION BRISTOL 294255.

*INTERCITY*

*Weekday service*

114

# 1 out of 315 disability cases involves someone falling off a ladder. 1 out of 5 involves someone climbing up.

We don't want to cause you any undue stress, but there are a few things you should know about disability insurance.

For one thing, it's not just about industrial accidents anymore. In fact, according to New York Life statistics, 20% of all disability cases involve mental/nervous disorders.*

To the point where they have now become the leading cause of disability—ahead of back pain, heart disease, high blood pressure and, needless to say, falling off a ladder.

At New York Life, we anticipated this trend. We recognized that there are any number of ways a person can become disabled.

So we designed our products to protect you—whether your disability is due to pressure in your lower back, or simply the pressures of everyday life.

For example, if you work full-time, but have an income loss of 20% or more due to your disability, you can still receive benefits. If you're unfortunate enough to lose 80% of your income or more, we still pay you in full.

And if you're receiving total disability benefits, and are confined to a nursing facility, there are certain New York Life policies under which your benefit payments can actually be increased by 50%.

Let's face it. We live in an all too stressful world. And no one, not even you, is immune to the pressures that are often brought to bear.

So if you'd like to remove one of your worries, contact New York Life at 1-800-331-7622.

We can tell you everything you need to know. Like the difference between long-term disability and the short-term coverage you may be receiving at work. Or how we can design a policy that meets your specific needs.

Once that's taken care of, you can concentrate on reaching the next few rungs.

**NEW YORK LIFE**

The Company You Keep.®

---

# At one time or another everything in your office has broken down. Why should you be any exception?

"It'll never happen to me."
"I don't know anyone who's ever needed it."
"I think I'm covered at work."

It's easy to come up with reasons why you shouldn't have long-term disability insurance. It's even easier to come up with reasons why you should.

After all, disability insurance is not just for people who have lost a limb. The fact is, most cases involve people who suffer from problems far less tangible. Like back pain. High blood pressure. Or heart disease.

And yes, it really could happen to you. If you're not convinced, just sample some of these recent disability statistics.

One out of seven people will be disabled *for more than a year* by the time they're 65.[1]

One out of five New York Life disability claims involves mental/nervous disorders, which are the leading cause of disability.[2]

And to top it all off, less than 20% of employees have group long-term disability coverage.[3]

Of course, we could go on at length about the importance of disability coverage. And we could point out the various financial consequences of having no source of income for what could be an indefinite period of time.

But these kinds of issues, given the fact that they concern your own personal situation, are probably best left to a discussion between you and a New York Life agent.

If you'd like to set up an appointment, simply call us toll-free at 1-800-331-7622. We may not be able to help you when your copier breaks down, but if anything should ever happen to you, we'll be there.

**NEW YORK LIFE**

The Company You Keep.®

---

# Get well cards aren't the only things disabled people receive in the mail.

If you become disabled, and lose your source of income, how long would your money last?

Two years? One year? Six months? Six weeks?

How long, for example, would it take to deplete your savings account? At what point would you have to sell your car? Or worse still, your home?

Many Americans are just a few paychecks away from financial disaster. And yet the majority of us continue to live on the edge, failing to consider the consequences of losing our income through disability.

At New York Life, we're getting more of our customers to think seriously about long-term disability insurance. And notice, by the way, that we said "long-term."

You see, although many of you may receive disability insurance through work, chances are you're covered for just three to six months.

Long-term disability, on the other hand, can cover you for as long as you're unable to work. And rather than duplicate an existing policy, it can pick up wherever your short-term coverage leaves off—which means you won't have to pay any premiums twice.

And what are the chances you'll ever be disabled long-term? Far greater, in fact, than you might suspect.

According to recent statistics, one out of seven people will be disabled for *more than a year* by the time they're 65.[1] And unlikely as it may seem, less than 20% of employees have long-term disability coverage.[2]

If you're one of the uninsured 80%, and you're starting to feel a bit uneasy about it, it's time we talked. Simply call New York Life, toll-free, at 1-800-331-7622.

We can help you feel a lot more secure about what the future—or your mailman—may bring.

**NEW YORK LIFE**

The Company You Keep.®

---

# Finally, Someone In The Oil Business You Can Trust.

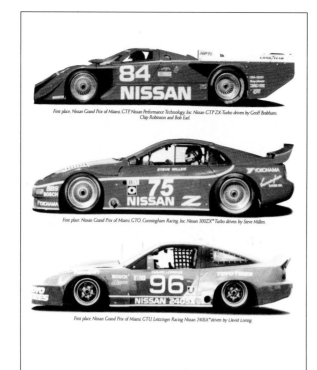

First place, Nissan Grand Prix of Miami, GTP. Nissan Performance Technology, Inc. Nissan GTP ZX-Turbo driven by Geoff Brabham, Chip Robinson and Bob Earl.

First place. Nissan Grand Prix of Miami, GTO. Cunningham Racing, Inc. Nissan 300ZX* Turbo driven by Steve Millen.

First place. Nissan Grand Prix of Miami, GTU. Leitzinger Racing Nissan 240SX* driven by David Loring.

Winning isn't everything. Unless of course you win everything.

Built for the Human Race.

119

---

## IF YOU DON'T THINK EMPLOYEES APPRECIATE THEIR BENEFITS, TRY TAKING SOME OF THEM AWAY.

This thing with rising employee health benefit costs is turning into a real dogfight.

Employees are angry because they don't want to give up the benefits they have. And they sure don't want to pay for something they feel entitled to.

Employers, on the other hand, are upset with the huge bite rising costs are taking out of their budgets and want some cost control.

What to do about it has most health insurance carriers up in the air.

But not NWNL Group. In fact, we're showing companies how they can control costs by using our unique approach to flexible benefits.

You see, using our flex plan you won't be taking any benefits away from your employees. You'll be giving them a budget and the opportunity to create their own plan. So everybody wins.

And don't worry that you'll be giving them something they won't understand. We've developed an entirely new program that explains flex by using simple step-by-step instructions that show your employees how to enroll. And how options are applied to best suit their needs.

Our special booklet— Employees As Partners In Cost Control—will show you how flex can help build employee support for your benefit plan. For a copy call or write Rick Naymark, NWNL Group, Box 20, Minneapolis, MN 55440, (612) 342-7137.

We'll help you avoid fighting like cats and dogs over benefits.

**NORTHWESTERN NATIONAL LIFE INSURANCE COMPANY**

NWNL Group is a division of Northwestern National Life Insurance Company, Minneapolis, MN (not admitted in the state of New York). The North Atlantic Life Insurance Company of America, Jericho, NY is member of The NWNL Companies, Inc.

120

# THE MOST EXPENSIVE GOWNS AREN'T FROM CALVIN KLEIN, BILL BLASS, OR YVES SAINT LAURENT.

Do you believe this?

Last year, the average cost of a designer gown was about $3,000. But the average cost of a hospital gown and stay was about $4,800.

And you thought high fashion was expensive.

Hospitals and doctors aren't solely responsible for driving health care costs up. Utilization, new technology and catastrophic claims all contribute to the rising cost of employee health benefits. Which, incidentally, are expected to increase this year an average of 16.5%.

Is there any way to control these ever-rising costs?

At NWNL Group, our experience shows us the answer is yes. But the solution is not to give you a low rate just to get your business, and a big increase a year later to make up for it. Instead, we ask you to make some tough but fair choices about your benefits program.

We'll help you identify what those choices are and we'll show you how they could affect your plan. For example, our catastrophic case management program could save you thousands of dollars.

Our special booklet—Case Management: What Works, What Doesn't—will tell you more about this approach to cost control. For a copy call or write Rick Naymark, NWNL Group, Box 20, Minneapolis, MN 55440. (612) 342-7137.

Considering what your costs are, you can't afford any gaps in your coverage.

**NORTHWESTERN NATIONAL LIFE INSURANCE COMPANY**

NWNL Group is a division of Northwestern National Life Insurance Company, Minneapolis, MN (not admitted in the state of New York). The North Atlantic Life Insurance Company of America, Jericho, NY is (a member of The NWNL Companies, Inc.)

121

---

# Breathtaking Views 25¢.

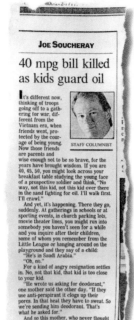

**JOE SOUCHERAY**

## 40 mpg bill killed as kids guard oil

It's different now, thinking of troops going off to a gathering for war, different from the Vietnam era, when friends went, protected by the courage of being young. Now those friends are parents and wise enough not to be so brave, for the years have brought wisdom. If you are 40, 45, 50, you might look across your breakfast table studying the young face of a prospective soldier and think, "No way, not this kid, not this kid over there in the sand fighting for oil. I'll walk first. I'll crawl."

And yet, it's happening. There they go, suddenly. At gatherings in schools or at sporting events, in church parking lots, movie theater lines, you might run into somebody you haven't seen for a while and you inquire after their children, some of whom you remember from the Little League or hanging around on the playground and they say of a child:

"He's in Saudi Arabia."

"Oh, no."

For a kind of angry resignation settles in. No, not that kid, that kid is too close to your kid.

"He wrote us asking for deodorant," one mother said the other day. "If they use anti-perspirant it clogs up their pores. In that heat they have to sweat. So we're sending him deodorant. That's what he asked for."

And so this mother, who never thought it would hap...... includes in her ......

---

**NICK COLEMAN**

## Rudy, Jon, Arne: Yes. Yes. Maybe

A week has come and gone since last Tuesday's primary election left Minnesotans with a choice for governor between Rudy Perpich and What's-his-name. It still stinks.

Papa Perp, the DFL incumbent, has made running for governor a way of life because he can't think of anything else to do. He said again last week that if and when he leaves the governor's mansion (which he refers to as "the house" in the manner you might call the Cathedral of Notre Dame "the chapel"), he'll pack his bags for Europe.

We all know that Perpich vastly prefers Austria to Gopherville. But if the Perp Monster wins another term, he'll be governor 14 years — about seven years for each good idea he has had.

The other choice, What's-his-name, is Jon Grunseth, the Grinch Who Stole Christmas from Arne Carlson by winning the Republican nomination.

Grunseth is described in the newspapers as "an Afton businessman," which makes him sound like a kindly soul who makes his living selling hot dogs to leaf watchers on autumn Sunday afternoons. Not exactly. "Afton businessman" means Grunseth is a pinstripe who lives among the horse ranches of exurbia and commutes to his fancy desk job at the company that owns ChemLawn, the largest weed poisoner in Minnesota.

I'm n.. s.......ting Weed-be-gone Gru..

---

**TOM POWERS**

## Love of Holtz at U hard to understand

Let me ask you something. How come when Lou Holtz led the Golden Gophers to a 6-5 record he was considered a genius, but when John Gutekunst goes 6-5 he is practically accused of strangling the program with his bare hands?

Please, I'm serious. Somebody tell me. Because obviously I haven't grasped the situation. The record book shows that Holtz compiled a 10-12 mark here in two years. It shows that he lost his last two games as coach of the Minnesota Golden Gophers by a composite score of 79-16. That's embarrassing. Yet Holtz's presence still hovers over the program like a neon sign that reads "vacancy."

Maybe you had to be here to catch all the one-liners and to have your back slapped. But since I wasn't, it's hard for me to be mesmerized by a guy who promised loyalty, delivered a losing record, then took off for a bigger payday. Yet there are so many people here who fantasize about his return as if it would mark the real second coming.

Why is that? Why would people want him back? When somebody kicks me in the behind, I do not bend over in their presence again.

"Lou Holtz has proved at other places that he is a great coach," said Rick Bay, the Gophers athletic director. "But here he lost two more than he won."

Currently, the Gophers football program is in the midst of a crisis. Support ...........d to the point wh......

Columnists Joe Soucheray, Nick Coleman, and Tom Powers—their views can take your breath away and leave you gasping for more. So why not start enjoying exciting views from your front door every day. *For home delivery, call 291-1888.*

**PIONEER PRESS**

122

---

You are here.

# Win this contest and pigeons will look at you completely differently.

Once again, the Pioneer Press is doing everything humanly possible to improve your Springtime outlook. It's the second annual Pioneer Press Spring Fever Sweepstakes.

from Sunday, April 15th through Friday, June 29th. And we're giving away a Mazda Miata, a Pontiac Sunbird LE, a Ford Mustang LX, or a Chrysler LeBaron convertible every week.

You can also win hundreds of other fair-weather prizes like windsurfers, sailboats, golf clubs, patio furniture, and much more. Entry forms and rules can be found in today's paper. Enter

as often as you like. Just fill in your Social Security number and drop it in the mail. (Use a homing pigeon if you have to.) But don't delay. With only eleven weeks of prizes, time will fly by.

## Weekly Convertible Winners In The Pioneer Press Spring Fever Sweepstakes.

124

125

126

# 75,000 Germans shooting at him and he's worried about finding his suicide pill.

The Messerschmitts roared in with their machine guns blazing. But if the pilots had known who they were shooting at, they would have held their fire. Two of the scrambling figures on the beach were far more valuable captured than killed.

Colonel David Bruce of Charlotte County, Virginia, had not expected to be at Normandy. As chief of OSS in Europe, his talents lay in the field of espionage. Spying, code breaking, cloak and dagger stuff. Yet here he was, part of the largest amphibious invasion in history, Operation Overlord.

Bruce was there on orders from the man bleeding next to him on the beach, General William "Wild Bill" Donovan. Ironically, the General was not there on orders. In fact, Allied high command had given specific instructions forbidding General Donovan from stepping foot anywhere near the beaches of Normandy. He was, after all, head of the entire OSS organization and privy to some of the most sensitive secrets of the war.

As the General's nickname would imply, however, Wild Bill Donovan was something of an adventurer. So twenty-four hours earlier he put on his Medal of Honor, collected Colonel Bruce and proceeded to talk his way onto the USS *Tuscaloosa*.

If Ike found out, there would be hell to pay.

Meanwhile, Field-Marshal Erwin Rommel intended to make their arrival as unpleasant as possible. Over six million mines were laid along the coastline from Holland to France. Huge concrete bunkers faced the sea with heavy guns that could sink a ship fifteen miles away. Anti-tank obstacles littered every possible landing beach. Stationed in the immediate vicinity between Cherbourg and Le Havre were eight infantry divisions. And three Panzer divisions, including the 12th "*Hitlerjugend*" S.S. Panzer Division with dreaded Tiger tanks, could roll in at the first sign of an invasion.

It was appropriately called the Atlantic Wall. The Allies controlled the skies. But the Messerschmitts slipped through just in time to welcome Bruce and Donovan coming ashore.

Donovan leaped for cover behind their landing craft. Bruce did the same, landing heavily on the General and gashing Donovan's chin with his steel helmet. With blood running down his neck, General Donovan turned to Bruce and happily exclaimed, "Now it will be like this all the time."

They made a run for it.

Shortly after passing through Allied lines the two officers practically ran into a hail of enemy machine gun fire. *Ack ack ack. Ack ack ack.* Between bursts the General reminded Bruce that neither of them could be taken alive, "We know too much." Bruce nodded. The General continued, "Have you your pills with you?" Bruce thought: pills?...pills? Then it dawned on him. OSS officers had been issued suicide pills for just such an occasion.

Not expecting to be in the field, Bruce realized that, indeed, he did not have his pills. Embarrassed, he apologized to the General. Donovan forgave him at once and told the Colonel that he would give him one of his own suicide pills. (Whether or not Bruce thanked the General is unknown.)

As it turned out, Donovan searched his pockets and also came up empty-handed. With alarm, the General realized he left his pills in a hotel room in London. When...*if* they got back to the ship, Bruce was to radio Claridge's and have the General's "medical supplies" gathered up and safely deposited with the hall porter.

They began their retreat.

The next time that David Bruce met the Germans things would be considerably different. Instead of Colonel Bruce, he would be called Ambassador Bruce. In addition to West Germany, David Bruce became ambassador to both Great Britain and France. He was senior U.S. representative to the People's Republic of China. During the Vietnam War, he was America's representative at the Paris peace talks. And in 1976, he ended his remarkable career as Ambassador to NATO.

David K. E. Bruce was one of the most distinguished diplomats in modern American history. But history might have been different had it been for a single bullet. Or a single pill.

In the collections of the Virginia Historical Society, Ambassador Bruce's Presidential Medal of Freedom is standing on display. Many of his official papers and personal diaries are waiting to be read.

The Virginia Historical Society is literally overflowing with history. Virginia's Liberty Bell, Stonewall Jackson's bookcase, rare paintings and maps are just a fraction of what's here.

### Virginia Historical Society
*The Center for Virginia History*

To house these treasures a new wing is being added to the Society's Richmond building. A campaign called the Fifth Century Fund has been started to pay for the expansion. For information on how you can help or to become a Society member please call us in Richmond at (804) 358-4901.

**130**

---

# Dr. James Ambler saved 13 men from freezing to death. Unfortunately, he wasn't one of them.

While awaiting reassignment at Portsmouth, Virginia Naval Hospital, Dr. James Ambler, USN, received a telegram that would change his life. In fact, it would end it.

Lieutenant Commander George W. DeLong, USN, was assembling a crew of 33 brave and talented men for the most ambitious arctic exploration ever attempted. Destination: North Pole.

On July 8, 1879, their ship, the *Jeannette*, set sail from San Francisco Bay.

The *Jeannette* lumbered slowly northward. Too slowly. Forced to stop in Alaska to pick up dog sleds, dog teams and Indian drivers, the *Jeannette* didn't reach the Arctic Ocean until early September. Too late.

She was greeted by ice packs. Surrounded and unable to escape, the expedition had come to a sudden, frozen halt. It was going to be a long winter.

Fortunately, James Ambler was one of the first doctors to understand the importance of preventive medicine. Lime juice was now ordered for each crew member.

(There would be no scurvy on his ship.) He made sure the drinking water was pure. Ambler himself led daily exercise classes on the ice. He also organized games and competitions.

And when Lieutenant John Danenhower, USN, developed snow blindness, Dr. Ambler performed eye surgery by lantern light.

With the arrival of summer the men still had their health and their sanity. But not their freedom. The towering ice floes that gripped the *Jeannette* had refused to melt.

Time passed. Anything was welcomed to break the monotony. Except what happened on June 10, 1881.

Just before midnight shockwaves ripped through the ship. All hands on deck! All hands on deck! The *Jeannette* was being crushed.

The order to abandon ship came at eight the following evening. Each man performed magnificently. Supplies, dogs, sleds and three small boats were all calmly transported to the ice.

In the eerie light of an arctic summer night the *Jeannette* listed slowly to starboard, took on one gallon too many, and sank.

The following day, Dr. Ambler started an "ice diary."

He first noted the condition of the men: Mr. Chipp could not move; Mr. Danenhower was almost blind; Captain DeLong's head was wrapped in bandages from an earlier, almost fatal accident; several of the sailors were now suffering from lead poisoning.

In the hands of a lesser physician they most certainly would have died. Yet Ambler nursed them all to health and for the first time in almost two years the expedition began to move. Progress was painfully slow. Roads had to be cut through the jagged ice. Bridges were built by hand using tons of snow. When the dogs exhausted themselves pulling the heavy sleds, men took their place in the harnesses.

Throughout it all only one of the officers volunteered for manual labor: James Ambler. Ice diary: "I worked hard all day yesterday with a pick...then sleeping in wet clothes in a wet bag on wet ice makes every bone and separate muscle ache in the morning. Today I have not been able to draw a breath without pain."

A month later they reached open water and launched the three small boats. Siberia lay to the southwest.

A heavy gale blew for days. But the boat carrying Ambler and DeLong finally managed to ground itself in shallow water and they waded the last chilling mile to shore.

The others were nowhere in sight.

By this time frostbite had taken its toll on seaman Hans Ericksen. Flesh stripped from his feet until muscle and tendons were exposed to the frigid arctic air. Still Ambler refused to leave the crippled man behind.

With only four days' rations left, seamen William Nindemann and Louis Noros were sent to find help. Ambler, DeLong and nine others waited as long as they could. Then they died.

As it turned out, one of the other boats also made it to shore. Natives came across the half-starved men and brought them to safety in the Siberian village of Bulun.

Later that spring, Dr. Ambler's body was found with the others beneath a foot of snow. In his hand was the captain's pistol. In his pockets were the ice diary and a letter to his brother back home in Virginia.

A single line in it tells all, "I am resigned to bow my head in submission to the divine will."

In 1883, a naval board of inquiry determined that those men who had survived owed their lives in great part to Dr. James Markham Marshall Ambler, USN.

In the vast collections of the Virginia Historical Society, Dr. Ambler's ice diary is sitting on display along with thousands of other precious artifacts relating to this state's long and extremely colorful past.

To house these treasures a new wing is being added to the Society's Richmond building.

### Virginia Historical Society
*The Center for Virginia History*

A campaign called The Fifth Century Fund has been started to pay for the expansion. For information on how you can help or to become a Society member call us in Richmond at (804) 358-4901.

**131**

**135**
ART DIRECTOR
Mark Johnson
WRITER
John Stingley
PHOTOGRAPHER
Jeff Zwart
CLIENT
Porsche Cars North America
AGENCY
Fallon McElligott/Minneapolis

**136**
ART DIRECTOR
Mark Johnson
WRITER
John Stingley
PHOTOGRAPHER
Jeff Zwart
CLIENT
Porsche Cars North America
AGENCY
Fallon McElligott/Minneapolis

**137**
ART DIRECTOR
Mark Johnson
WRITER
John Stingley
PHOTOGRAPHER
Jeff Zwart
CLIENT
Porsche Cars North America
AGENCY
Fallon McElligott/Minneapolis

**138**
ART DIRECTOR
Bob Brihn
WRITER
Bruce Bildsten
PHOTOGRAPHER
Rick Dublin
CLIENT
Porsche Cars North America
AGENCY
Fallon McElligott/Minneapolis

**139**
ART DIRECTOR
Mark Johnson
WRITER
John Stingley
PHOTOGRAPHER
Jeff Zwart
CLIENT
Porsche Cars North America
AGENCY
Fallon McElligott/Minneapolis

**140**
ART DIRECTOR
Mark Johnson
WRITER
John Stingley
PHOTOGRAPHER
Jeff Zwart
CLIENT
Porsche Cars North America
AGENCY
Fallon McElligott/Minneapolis

**141**
ART DIRECTOR
Bob Barrie
WRITER
Jamie Barrett
PHOTOGRAPHER
Rick Dublin
CLIENT
Continental Bank
AGENCY
Fallon McElligott/Minneapolis

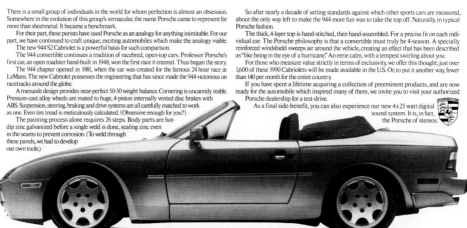

There is a small group of individuals in the world for whom perfection is almost an obsession. Somewhere in the evolution of this group's vernacular, the name Porsche came to represent far more than sheetmetal. It became a benchmark.

For their part, these purists have used Porsche as an analogy for anything inimitable. For our part, we have continued to craft unique, exciting automobiles which make the analogy viable. The new 944 S2 Cabriolet is a powerful basis for such comparison.

The 944 convertible continues a tradition of racebred, open-top cars. Professor Porsche's first car, an open roadster hand-built in 1948, won the first race it entered. Thus began the story.

The 944 chapter opened in 1981, when the car was created for the famous 24 hour race at LeMans. The new Cabriolet possesses the engineering that has since made the 944 victorious on racetracks around the globe.

A transaxle design provides near-perfect 50-50 weight balance. Cornering is uncannily stable. Pressure-cast alloy wheels are mated to huge, 4-piston internally vented disc brakes with ABS. Suspension, steering, braking and drive systems are all carefully matched to work as one. Even tire tread is meticulously calculated. (Obsessive enough for you?)

The painting process alone requires 26 steps. Body parts are hot-dip zinc galvanized before a single weld is done, sealing zinc even in the seams to prevent corrosion. (To weld through these panels, we had to develop our own tools.)

So after nearly a decade of setting standards against which other sports cars are measured, about the only way left to make the 944 more fun was to take the top off. Naturally, in typical Porsche fashion.

The thick, 4-layer top is hand-stitched, then hand-assembled. For a precise fit on each individual car. The Porsche philosophy is that a convertible must truly be 4-season. A specially reinforced windshield sweeps air around the vehicle, creating an effect that has been described as "like being in the eye of a hurricane." An eerie calm, with a tempest swirling about you.

For those who measure value strictly in terms of exclusivity, we offer this thought: just over 1,600 of these 1990 Cabriolets will be made available in the U.S. Or, to put it another way, fewer than 140 per month for the entire country.

If you have spent a lifetime acquiring a collection of preeminent products, and are now ready for the automobile which inspired many of them, we invite you to visit your authorized Porsche dealership for a test-drive.

As a final side-benefit, you can also experience our new 4 x 25 watt digital sound system. It is, in fact, the Porsche of stereos.

*Introducing the Porsche 944 S2 Cabriolet.*

# After years of buying everything from the "Porsche of toasters" to the "Porsche of stereos," perhaps you're ready for the Porsche of cars.

135

It's been over 100 years since the first noisy, bone-jarring "horseless carriages" rolled out of sheds onto dusty streets and lanes.

Through the ensuing decades, the basic principle has changed little. Now and then, however, a car has emerged so inspired in its concept, its design, its handling and use of power, that it has been labeled a milestone. A landmark point, or milestone. Worthy of preservation. Collectable. Especially when produced in limited numbers.

Today, in an era that has become sadly synonymous with homogeneity and derivative products, the Porsche 911 Carrera 4 is just such a refreshing, visionary achievement.

The world's first production sports car with electronic all-wheel drive, the Carrera 4 once again expands the boundaries of what is possible.

The all-wheel drive is an adaptive, intelligent system. Using computer-controlled sensors, it continuously monitors traction at all 4 wheels. Upon sensing wheel spin, within 25 thousandths of a second it directs power to the wheels having more traction, correcting slip usually before the driver can even sense it.

In other words, you're not really aware of the system working. Only of an incredible level of control.

This, after all, is

*The 1990 Porsche 911 Carrera 4 Coupe.*

what a landmark automobile does. Redefines the potential of the category. The Carrera 4 takes traditional sports car notions and, without changing them, elevates them. Not just power but, through adhesion, more useable power. Not just handling, but new thresholds of agility and performance on any surface.

The car is laden with other refinements and innovations as well. Like a new, self-correcting rear axle. And an integrated spoiler which rises at 50 mph and retracts again at 6 mph. Of course, there are the other collectable traits associated with Porsche for so long. The timeless 911 silhouette.

And Porsche's legendary handcrafted construction. Over 4 working days are spent for welding alone. The painting process is 26 steps. Engines are bench-built by hand.

Considering its complexity and the love and precision with which each 911 Carrera 4 is assembled, we will make relatively small numbers of these available.

For those who find that even more of an enticement, we suggest you try and find one to test-drive at your authorized Porsche dealer soon. Unless you opt to take your chances on the age-old Porsche fantasy of discovering one squirreled away in a barn somewhere. In about, let's say, the year 2017.

# Classic car collectors can now take comfort knowing there will still, in coming years, be something to collect.

136

142
**ART DIRECTOR**
Bob Barrie
**WRITER**
Jamie Barrett
**CLIENT**
Continental Bank
**AGENCY**
Fallon McElligott/Minneapolis

143
**ART DIRECTORS**
Albert Poon, Donald Ee
**WRITER**
Cozette Hendricks
**CLIENT**
IKEA Singapore
**AGENCY**
HDM/Singapore

144
**ART DIRECTOR**
Dick Pantano
**WRITER**
James Overall
**PHOTOGRAPHER**
Ronald Modra
**CLIENT**
Reebok
**AGENCY**
Hill Holliday Connors
Cosmopulos/Boston

145
**ART DIRECTOR**
Jeff Jahn
**WRITER**
Glen Wachowiak
**PHOTOGRAPHER**
Lars Hansen
**CLIENT**
Waldoch Vans
**AGENCY**
Kauffman Stewart/Minneapolis

146
**ART DIRECTOR**
Steve Beaumont
**WRITERS**
Brent Bouchez, Travis Ashby
**ILLUSTRATOR**
David Kimble
**CLIENT**
American Honda Motor
Company
**AGENCY**
Ketchum/Los Angeles

147
**ART DIRECTOR**
Neil Leinwohl
**WRITER**
Adam Goldstein
**PHOTOGRAPHERS**
Stock, Bettman Archives
**CLIENT**
Hebrew Immigrant Aid Society
**AGENCY**
Korey Kay & Partners/New York

## In the foreign exchange business, as in life, it helps to look at the bigger picture.

Foreign exchange traders put an incredible premium on speed.

Zoom! The order comes up. Wham! It's processed. Zip! On to the next one.

It's as if the entire industry had decided to binge on espresso.

At Continental Bank, we recognize the importance of expediting your trade. But we also believe in stepping back, if only for a moment, and evaluating its overall appropriateness.

Oh sure, we could be missing out on an extra transaction or two. But revolutionary as it may sound, we contend that a foreign exchange expert should function as more than a glorified order-taker.

When we examine a specific trade, for example, we always approach it from the larger perspective. Does it make good strategic sense?

Is it in synch with your long-term objectives? Does it coincide with economic and political trends?

They're basic questions, we admit. But at most banks, strange as it may seem, they're basically overlooked.

It comes down to this: at Continental, we always look after our clients' interests first. And for very selfish reasons. After all, the more we can keep you from making the wrong trades today, the more you'll be asking us to make the right ones tomorrow.

If you'd like to learn more about Continental Bank, our hedge and arbitrage functions, and our round-the-clock trading capabilities, call us at (312) 828-5753. And do it as soon as humanly possible.

Especially, we might add, if you're reading this in a canoe. **Continental Bank**
A new approach to business.

142

143

# THIS YEAR, NO ONE HIT THE WALL.

Yesterday, 26,000 people went out for a Sunday run. They ran, for the first time, from West to East in the Berlin Marathon. For 26.2 miles, they exercised perhaps the simplest of human rights: To run. To play. A small thing? Maybe. Unless it's been over half a century since you played, truly played, with a free heart and a free spirit.

**Reebok** 🇬🇧
It's time to play.™

REEBOK.® THE OFFICIAL FOOTWEAR AND APPAREL SPONSOR OF THE BERLIN MARATHON. AND MAKERS OF PERFORMANCE RUNNING SHOES SINCE 1895.

144

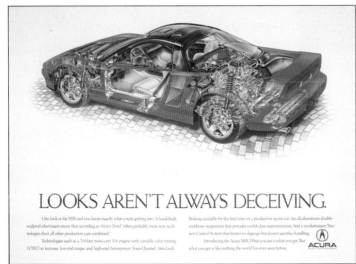

## LOOKS AREN'T ALWAYS DECEIVING.

One look at the NSX and you know exactly what you're getting into: A hand-built, sculpted-aluminum exotic that according to *Motor Trend* "offers probably more new technologies than all other production cars combined."

Technologies such as a 3.0-liter, twin-cam V-6 engine with variable valve timing (VTEC) to increase low-end torque and high-end horsepower. Four-Channel Anti-Lock

Braking available for the first time on a production sports car. An all-aluminum double-wishbone suspension that provides world-class responsiveness. And a revolutionary Traction Control System that limits tire slippage but doesn't sacrifice handling.

Introducing the Acura NSX. What you see is what you get. But what you get is like nothing the world has ever seen before.

**ACURA**

146

---

# IT HOLDS EVERYTHING. INCLUDING ITS VALUE.

One excitable Yellow Lab and kennel. | Space for anything your green thumb desires. | An evening at the Ordway.

Treasure hunting at an estate sale. | One scout troop and leader. | Remove the seats and it's a moving van.

How to handle a hungry family. | The Saturday morning golf excursion. | How to get the family bikes to new trails.

Enough room for any do-it-yourself project. | The official softball team van. | Holds yards of equipment.

A Waldoch conversion van is loads and loads of fun.

It comes with Flexsteel® seats, luxurious carpeting, oak and walnut trim, and adjustable tables—just to name a few. You can even install a TV with a video cassette player and Nintendo.

All of which makes it the perfect people mover. Excellent for traveling with family, friends, or a scout troop.

But as you can see, it's also durable enough for people who need space to carry things like bicycles, sofas, suitcases and lawnmowers. Just take out the easily removable seats and it's a moving van.

Waldochs also come in a variety of styles, competitively priced with station wagons and other sport utility vehicles. And Waldochs hold more of their resale value than any other conversion van you'll find on the market today.

So before you load up anything else, call Curt or Tom at 1-800-878-8635 for more information. Or better yet, stop by our plant and service center southwest of Forest Lake and see for yourself what goes into our vans.

We'd like nothing better than to send you packing in a Waldoch.

**WALDOCH**

145

---

# WE WERE THE ONLY TRAVEL AGENTS THEY COULD AFFORD.

They could be your grandparents. Fleeing their homes with nothing more than the clothes they wore. The things they could carry. And our help.

We're HIAS—the Hebrew Immigrant Aid Society. For 110 years we've been helping Jews around the world escape persecution.

Sadly, our mission didn't end with your grandparents. It has continued unabated, right up to the modern Exodus from Russia.

This year alone, some 200,000 Jews will emigrate to Israel. And

another 40,000 will come to the U.S. for family reunification.

We educate them about their options. We get information into the Soviet Union, where it's needed. We match immigrant families with communities here. And we navigate the vast sea of paperwork.

To accomplish these tasks, we rely on the support of our members. So please, join HIAS.

After all, if we hadn't helped your grandparents escape persecution years ago, we might be helping you do it today.

☐ Yes, I want to help HIAS serve another century of immigrants by becoming a member. Please enroll me as an individual member in the following category: ☐ $50 ☐ $100

Name_____
Address_____
City_____
State_____Zip_____

Please make checks payable to HIAS and send to: HIAS, 200 Park Ave. South N.Y., N.Y. 10003-1572. All donations to HIAS are tax-deductible within IRS rules and regulations.

## HIAS
We replanted your family tree.

147

# Most car companies have a simple view of what it takes to make a convertible.

In our opinion, taking a car, almost any car, removing the top, and calling it a convertible doesn't make it a convertible.

Any more than painting a number on the door would make it a Formula One racer.

A true convertible is designed to be a convertible from the ground up.

Not just from the top down.

The Alfa Romeo Spider has always been, and will always be, a convertible in the purest form.

It's not an idea that came from somewhere in Marketing, to capitalize on a trend.

It came from Grugliasco, Italy. Where cars still come equipped with things like history, heritage, the romance of the open roadster, love of the open road.

Very un-trendy things.

Since 1923, Alfa Romeo has captured more racing victories than any other European car company.

Which means, long before Alfa was messing up people's hair with ocean breezes, they were messing it up with finish line champagne.

If you're one of those purists who believe a true sports-car has two seats, an engine you can feel and a body that won't quit, we hope you'll see the Alfa Romeo Spider at Cornes Motors. We're at 9010 Miramar Road, or you can call us at 578-8600.

Once you test drive the Alfa, you'll understand how those other convertibles are different from the Spider.

It's not just the top, they're missing.

**CORNES MOTORS**

*Alfa Romeo    Ferrari    Bentley    Rolls-Royce*

148

**IT'S HEADED FOR BOSTON.**

And it touches down June 1."Soviet Space," an incredible array of Soviet spacecraft on display for the first time ever in the United States. Satellites, lunar rovers, space stations, and much, much more. This exhibit is Red hot. **SOVIET★SPACE** At The Museum Of Science

149

If money's the root of all evil, welcome to hell.
If there's one thing practically everyone wants more of, it's money. The only trouble is, where the devil do you find it?
The answer, of course, is your nearest branch of Nationwide. There you can now open our new CashBuilder account, a savings account which pays you quite incredible rates of interest.
In fact, for as little as £1 you'll currently earn 9.00% net pa. If, however, you have even more money to salt away, we will gladly pay you 9.50% net pa for £2,000. 9.75% net pa for £5,000. 10.25% net pa for £10,000 and a very handsome 10.75% net pa for £25,000 or more.
Naturally, all of these rates apply to your entire balance and not just to the amount that exceeds each interest tier.
To make sure you can get at your money anytime, anyplace, anywhere we also give you a cash card allowing you 24 hour access to it through most of Britain's 4,500 LINK machines.
Alternatively, if you don't want the constant temptation to spend, you can have the choice of a passbook instead.
So why not open a new CashBuilder account at Nationwide? After all, you'll have a hell of a job finding another account that can offer you all this.
Nationwide
The Nation's Building Society.

150

You can go 4 days without water. 50 days without food. Can you survive 90 days without money?
None of us wants to be starved of money.
Which is why, being the astute person you undoubtably are, you may decide to put some of yours in a high interest account at a building society.
After all, these accounts will give you an excellent return on your investment. And although you're usually required to give 90 days' notice before you can withdraw your money, this is no bad thing, since it removes that constant temptation to spend.
Trouble is, if the rainy day you've been saving for suddenly comes, most building societies are far from sympathetic.
In fact, whatever the circumstances, they'll still require you to give them 90 days' notice if you want your interest in full.
This wouldn't make your life quite so difficult if only everybody else was prepared to wait as long for their money.
But, try asking a plumber, a garage or even a dentist if they can possibly hang on 90 days before getting paid.
Not surprisingly, they'll tell you where to go in no uncertain terms.
Of course, if they had any sense, they'd tell you to go to Nationwide Anglia.
Our high interest account, CapitalBonus, not only pays you top rates of interest, it lets you take out some of your money immediately.
Once a calendar year, at a time of your choice, not ours, you can withdraw any amount up to £3,000, without having to give us any notice and without losing a penny of interest.
Unfortunately, the only way you'll get your money out of most other high interest accounts this quickly is to forego 90 days' worth of interest. Enough to leave you crying all the way to your building society.
However, if you keep a minimum of £10,000 in CapitalBonus, once it's been opened for 90 days, you can then draw on your savings as often as you wish.
Access isn't all CapitalBonus has to recommend it. It also offers you 4 rates of interest, up to 11.75% net pa for £25,000.
If patience is one of your virtues, it's possible to earn even more than this, thanks to the introduction of CapitalBonus 180. In return for giving us 180 days' notice, we'll pay you a top rate of 12% net pa.
And to make sure you are never left up stream without a paddle, so to speak, CapitalBonus 180, exactly like the 90 day option, allows you to take out up to £3,000 once a year, leaving all your hard earned interest intact.
Whilst if you keep a minimum of £25,000 in the account, as long as it's been opened 180 days, you can again have your money whenever you want.
On the other hand, for those of you who are more cautious and can afford to salt large sums away and don't need immediate access to it there's our PlatinumBond Plus.
This one year bond, currently pays you up to a very handsome 12.50% net pa. And whatever happens to the economy during the year it will always pay you at least 4.50% above our variable share account rate.
By now, you'll hopefully have realised that whichever of our accounts you decide to open, we'll make it easier for you to survive.
Because while you can go without water for 4 days and without food for 50 days, chances are you won't last long without money.
For more information or advice about which of these accounts is right for you, visit us. Or simply write today to, Claire Adams, at Nationwide Anglia Building Society, Chesterfield House, Bloomsbury Way, London WC1V 6PW.
Nationwide Anglia Building Society
CapitalBonus. Helping you make the most of your money.

151

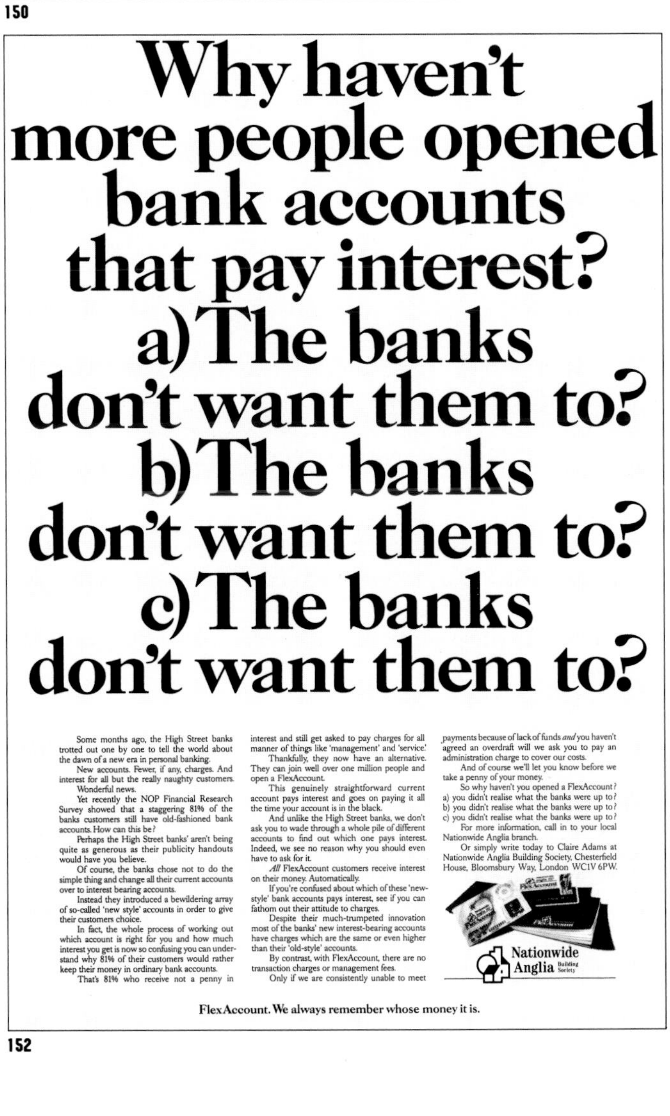
Why haven't more people opened bank accounts that pay interest?
a) The banks don't want them to?
b) The banks don't want them to?
c) The banks don't want them to?
Some months ago, the High Street banks trotted out one by one to tell the world about the dawn of a new era in personal banking.
New accounts. Fewer, if any, charges. And interest for all but the really naughty customers.
Wonderful news.
Yet recently the NOP Financial Research Survey showed that a staggering 81% of the banks customers still have old-fashioned bank accounts. How can this be?
Perhaps the High Street banks' aren't being quite as generous as their publicity handouts would have you believe.
Of course, the banks chose not to do the simple thing and change all their current accounts over to interest bearing accounts.
Instead they introduced a bewildering array of so-called 'new style' accounts in order to give their customers choice.
In fact, the whole process of working out which account is right for you and how much interest you get is now so confusing you can understand why 81% of their customers would rather keep their money in ordinary bank accounts.
That's 81% who receive not a penny in interest and still get asked to pay charges for all manner of things like 'management' and 'service.'
Thankfully, they now have an alternative. They can join well over one million people and open a FlexAccount.
This genuinely straightforward current account pays interest and goes on paying it all the time your account is in the black.
And unlike the High Street banks, we don't ask you to wade through a whole pile of different accounts to find out which one pays interest. Indeed, we see no reason why you should even have to ask for it.
*All* FlexAccount customers receive interest on their money. Automatically.
If you're confused about which of these 'new-style' bank accounts pays interest, see if you can fathom out their attitude to charges.
Despite their much-trumpeted innovation most of the banks' new interest-bearing accounts have charges which are the same or even higher than their 'old-style' accounts.
By contrast, with FlexAccount, there are no transaction charges or management fees.
Only if we are consistently unable to meet payments because of lack of funds *and* you haven't agreed an overdraft will we ask you to pay an administration charge to cover our costs.
And of course we'll let you know before we take a penny of your money.
So why haven't you opened a FlexAccount?
a) you didn't realise what the banks were up to?
b) you didn't realise what the banks were up to?
c) you didn't realise what the banks were up to?
For more information, call in to your local Nationwide Anglia branch.
Or simply write today to Claire Adams at Nationwide Anglia Building Society, Chesterfield House, Bloomsbury Way, London WC1V 6PW.
Nationwide Anglia Building Society
FlexAccount. We always remember whose money it is.

152

THE PENTAGON. AMERICA'S LAST DEFENCE AGAINST COMMUNISM, TYRANNY AND BUNIONS.
Left, right. Left, right. Left, right.
Multiply this simple leg exercise a few thousand times and you can begin to imagine what square-bashing in a new pair of US army boots does to a young man's feet.
Or can you?
Contrary to the myth, the army boot is not an instrument of torture used to initiate raw recruits.
In fact, such is the concern for the feet of men under their command that the US military issues standards for their standard issue boots.
Very high standards they are too.
The boots have to be tough and durable, naturally. They also have to be waterproof and the leather has to be flexible. In other words, the US army boot has to be an efficient part of the soldier's equipment.
Out in civvy street, few boot makers even try to match the exacting standards laid down by the Pentagon.
Up in the small town of Hampton, New Hampshire, however, there's a company that believes their boots are every bit as good as the army's.
And what's more they'll fight any man who says different.
The company is called Timberland.
To make their point, all leathers destined to become Timberland boots are subjected to a machine known as a MaserFlex.
It's designed to test just how long leathers remain waterproof in extreme circumstances.
Only if hides can withstand a minimum of 15,000 flexes can they be passed as equal to the highest standards demanded (and we mean demanded), by the US military.
Naturally, all our boots pass muster.
Only by testing the leathers in this way can we be sure that your feet won't suffer ailments caused by less well made boots.
(No less an authority than Blake's Medical Dictionary blames bunions on ill-fitting footwear in general and short or cramped boots in particular. We couldn't agree more.)
Of course, our concern for the well-being of your feet isn't left solely in the hands of a machine.
Even though we might not have quite the same budget as the Pentagon (theirs was two hundred and sixty nine thousand, nine hundred and eighty one million dollars in the fiscal year October 1989 to October 1990) we probably spend more on our hides than they do on theirs.
How come?
Remember, army boots are free. Whereas we expect our customers to invest a small fortune for a pair of Timberlands.
So we're just plain picky on their behalf.
We trek all round the country in search of tanneries that can meet our ridiculously high standards.
When we find one, we simply pay what it takes to bring every hide in the place back to Hampton.
(When the comfort of your feet is at stake, we never argue over nickels and dimes.)
We insist on premium, full grain leathers and nothing less. A rare oxhide leather called Norwegian Krymp is a particular favourite.
Back in the workshops, we dye the leathers right through. This ensures that the colour will not scuff off or crack up even under the strain of the longest march.
We could paint the colour on like other manufacturers do but pretty soon it would get a bit flaky, not unlike the manufacturers themselves.
It's at this stage of the process that we soak the leathers in silicone oil.
Impregnating them in this way keeps them supple. It also ensures that water can't seep through and give your feet a real soaking.
Rest assured, the only way you are going to get soaked with our boots is when you fork out the money for a pair.
Now you may be asking yourself if the Army can afford to give their boots away free, why on earth are ours so darned expensive?
Blame the gnarled hands and nimble fingers of the old boys who put our uppers together.
The kind of craftsmanship that can mould one piece of leather on a special geometric last doesn't come cheap.
And we'd always contend that fingers that can sew better than a machine are certainly worth shelling out a little extra for.
Mind you, while your wallet may be taking a pounding, you can take some comfort from the fact that, unlike the army, we have a policy of pampering your feet.
To make absolutely sure snow and rain can't get in, the midsoles are injection moulded to the base, creating a waterproof seal with the rubber lug sole.
A cushioned inner sole is then inserted to keep your feet snug and warm.
This is made from soft glove leather or high performance Cambrelle. Likewise those collars you get on most of our boots.
Aside from providing extra comfort, these padded collars follow the form of your ankle to help to stop the elements sneaking in.
Meanwhile, inside the boot we usually insulate the tongue, shaft and quarter with Thinsulate and the toe with Ensolite.
And we invariably add a Gore-Tex lining for good measure.
This remarkable man-made fabric has 9 billion pores per square inch, each one 20,000 times smaller than a raindrop but 700 times larger than a molecule of perspiration. As a result, your feet can actually breathe.
But just in case your feet get too cosy in there, most of our boots are fitted with a special removable polypropylene insole to absorb any excess perspiration.
What of the good old army boot? Haven't there been any concessions to the warmth and comfort to be found in a pair of Timberlands?
No sir. None at all, sir.
The US military may have finally defeated the bunion but a soldier's foot still has to live in pretty spartan surroundings.
And that, soldier, is an order.
THE REGULATION US ARMY BOOT
THE TAN BUCK BOOT
Timberland

153

**154**
ART DIRECTOR
Steve Dunn
WRITER
Tim Delaney
PHOTOGRAPHER
John Claridge
CLIENT
Timberland
AGENCY
Leagas Delaney/London

**155**
ART DIRECTOR
Steve Dunn
WRITER
Mike Lescarbeau
PHOTOGRAPHER
John Claridge
CLIENT
Timberland
AGENCY
Leagas Delaney/London

**156**
ART DIRECTOR
Steve Dunn
WRITER
Tim Delaney
CLIENT
Courtauld Institute
AGENCY
Leagas Delaney/London

**157**
ART DIRECTOR
Steve Dunn
WRITER
Tim Delaney
CLIENT
Courtauld Institute
AGENCY
Leagas Delaney/London

**158**
ART DIRECTOR
Ding Yew Moong
WRITER
Jamie Pfaff
CLIENT
Chase Manhattan Bank
AGENCY
Leo Burnett/Singapore

**159**
ART DIRECTOR
Kevin Donovan
WRITER
Amy Borkowsky
DESIGNER
Jim Gulsen
PHOTOGRAPHER
Corinne Colen
CLIENT
Bausch & Lomb/Ray-Ban
AGENCY
Levine Huntley Vick &
Beaver/New York

---

# THE ALL-AMERICAN SHOE MADE IN AMERICA VERSUS THE ALL-AMERICAN SHOE MADE IN CYPRUS.

Isn't it strange how many things which are considered typically American don't seem to be made in America anymore?

Denim jeans are more often made in Hong Kong, Italy or France.

Flat bed trucks, convertibles, motorbikes, why, you'd think the Japanese had invented them.

Even an American icon like the T-shirt is no longer able to claim sole US citizenship.

There are, of course, exceptions.

There's one small shoe company holed up in the north eastern corner of the United States that still believes in the good old American way. It's called Timberland.

Yet even as you read this, shoe companies in places that are better known for growing fruit are busily trying to fool the public into thinking that their all-American shoes are as authentic as the ones we make in the small town of Hampton, New Hampshire.

Timberland's classic hand sewn, for instance, must be about the most imitated shoe in the whole world.

That's if you discount our famous Tan Buck boot. And equally renowned boat shoe.

But like a lot of people who borrow ideas, the manufacturers of these 'knock-offs' take short cuts.

While we search the length and breadth of the country for tanneries who know how to turn out tough yet supple leathers, they simply search the length and breadth of their local wholesaler and buy what's in stock.

Naturally, they pay less for hides than we do. But we reckon that if you buy cheap, your customers feet end up paying the price.

Our imitators engage in other decidedly un-American activities.

Like painting the colour on their shoes. This pretty well ensures that after a little wear the colour will scuff or flake off.

At Timberland, we don't brush colours on, we dye them right through. But only after we've impregnated the leathers with silicone to make them completely water repellent.

As you'd expect, when the manufacturers that copy our shoes begin the labour-intensive business of constructing the upper, they begin by saving on labour. The opposite is true at Timberland.

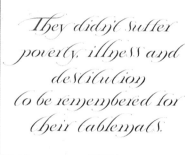

The old boys in our workshops may not be as fast as machines, or as cheap. But we believe that if you're paying top dollar for a hand-sewn, some hands should be involved in making it. Preferably experienced ones.

So each leather we use is moulded by hand on a special geometric last.

Then, a set of gnarled but nimble fingers goes to work making the uppers along the lines of the moccasin.

In all our years of turning out shoes, we haven't been able to improve on the original Red Indian design. A quick study of our two pictures and you'll see why.

That one-piece upper is a good example of their ingenuity and our workmanship. It's smooth, tidily finished off, with no unnecessary seams. You can make your own judgement about the copy.

Of course, the real test of a hand-sewn is how long the upper stays joined to the sole. Other manufacturers glue them together, sew them, then cross their fingers. Not us.

We created a permanent bonding process that's unique to us. With a patent to prove it.

What's more, each shoe is sewn with high strength nylon yarn using a double knot, pearl stitch. Then all the seams are sealed with not one but two coats of latex.

It may seem a little obsessive, but we've got a reputation to protect. Which is more than can be said of the people who copy us.

If they had any pride they'd use the same solid brass eyelets and self-oiling rawhide laces we do.

When they 'knocked-off' our Tan Buck boots, they'd put Thinsulate in the tongue, the shaft and the quarter just like us.

And if they were really worried about your feet being warm, they'd use the Gore-Tex linings we insist on in Hampton.

Truth is, the people who copy Timberland boots and shoes don't do any of these things.

Which, when you consider how little they charge for their handiwork, is hardly surprising.

And we figure it this way.

It costs a lot of money to make an item that lasts.

It isn't cheap to check out those new materials, like the Vibram EVA we now use on our new Ultra Light shoe range.

And it's pretty darned expensive to make a collection of bags and accessories to the same standard as our boots and shoes.

Thankfully, we have loyal customers who understand that you get what you pay for.

And what could be more all-American than that?

Timberland Shoes (UK) Limited, Unit Five, St. Anthony's Way, Feltham, Middlesex. TW14 0NH. Or, for any telephone enquiries, you can call us anytime on 081-890 6116.

**Timberland** ®

154

---

# TIMBERLAND GIVES YOU BACK THE COAT FOUR MILLION YEARS OF EVOLUTION TOOK AWAY.

There was a time when Man could venture into the wilderness clad in nothing but the coat God gave him.

But that was quite a while ago.

Sometime during the Lower Paleolithic Era, Homo Erectus became a creature of the great indoors. The thick hair that once covered his entire body was gone, and in its place came a man-made imitation.

Hampered by a brain the size of a walnut, man's earliest attempts at outdoor clothing were, needless to say, somewhat primitive.

Fortunately, however, our species has continued to evolve, and today can produce coats that protect us when the need for food, recreation and a disposable income forces us outside our central heated caves.

At a company called Timberland, in Hampton, New Hampshire, we design outerwear whose natural practicality rivals the coats our animal relatives were born with. Coats that provide shelter from howling wind, pelting rain and mornings as cold as an ice age.

Witness our Timberland leather coats.

They're made from the best hides we can find, and believe us, we spend a lot of time looking.

We insist upon cowhides from the open range, to avoid ugly nicks from barbed wire fences. Which means we often have to travel as far as other continents in order to find a supply that meets our standards.

We use two styles of leather on our outerwear at Timberland, Split Suede, and in the coat you see here, Weatherguard Newbuck.

Each is given a thorough dunking in waterproofing agents before getting a special finish to protect its suppleness and colour.

But we make more than leather coats that will help to keep you dry in the rain.

In other Timberland outerwear, we use a material that keeps you free of perspiration.

To let these coats 'breathe' (just like the ones Mother Nature used to make) we include a layer of Gore-Tex. This man-made fabric, with over nine billion pores per square inch, allows moisture to escape from your body, but remains waterproof.

Of course, we wouldn't take all this trouble finding perfect materials only to turn around and make a coat that doesn't last.

To make doubly certain a Timberland Trenchcoat holds together, we double stitch the seams that will be exposed to the heaviest wear, a practice that's all but extinct today.

On other Timberland coats, we overstitch many seams to prevent wind and rain from penetrating the tiny holes left behind by our sewing needles.

The result is outerwear that leaves Man as well adapted to the outdoors as he's been in millions of years.

Our sturdy coats are just one example of the Timberland Clothing range, albeit a good one, since everything we

wear, is built to last you for aeons.

Using workhorses like canvas, cotton, wool and denim, Timberland puts together sweaters, shirts and trousers, even the duffle bags to carry them in. And since practical clothing doesn't ever seem to go out of fashion, you'll be able to wear them season after season.

Naturally, if you own a pair of Timberland boots or shoes, you're already familiar with the way we do things.

You may know, for example, that we impregnate the leather of all Timberland footwear with silicone to give it a longer life and to keep your feet dry no matter what.

That we pre-stretch our leathers on a special geometric last to keep them from cracking with time.

And that seams on many Timberland boots are sealed twice with latex, because that's the only method sure to keep the water out.

The truth is, here at Timberland, we wouldn't really know how to go about things any other way.

We've even gone as far as to find a machine that can test our waterproof leathers better than we ever could by hand. It's called a Maser Flex, and it helps us make sure that our leathers will withstand 15,000 flexes. Which, by the way, is equal to the highest standard demanded by the U.S. Military.

But while we admit that our practices may seem a little obsessive, there is method to our madness.

We use solid brass eyelets in our boots, not because they look better, but because they don't rust when they get wet.

We use self oiling raw-hide laces for the simple reason that they don't get soaked with water and rot.

And we certainly don't construct our footwear using double knot pearl stitching because we think it's fun. (Even in Hampton, New Hampshire, there are more entertaining things to do.)

We do it so that the seams won't unravel, even if they're accidentally cut open on the sharp rocks and thick brush that Timberland wearers often find themselves in.

As you might suspect, all of these time consuming steps in constructing them don't serve to make Timberland boots or clothing any cheaper.

Which even someone with a shelf-like forehead and one continuous eyebrow can tell you is a very good thing.

In fact, even mankind's most distant ancestors would certainly have preferred a Timberland coat to their own hairy variety.

Ours, after all, have pockets.

Timberland (UK) Limited, Unit Four, St. Anthony's Way, Feltham, Middlesex. TW14 0NH. Telephone enquiries, please ring 081 890 6116.

**Timberland** ®

155

---

*They didn't suffer poverty, illness and destitution to be remembered for their tablemats.*

Oh, the gay romantic lives of the great artists.

Poverty drove Claude Monet to attempt suicide. And an equally impoverished Renoir to deliver him scraps of his left over food.

Van Gogh had hallucinations which terminated him throughout his life and resulted in him succeeding where Monet failed. He died of a self-inflicted gun shot wound in 1890.

Gauguin nearly starved to death in the Paris winter of 1886. He recovered long enough to allow him to visit Panama, where a fever nearly killed him.

Toulouse-Lautrec who was disfigured and stunted during his childhood died of, amongst other things, alcoholism and syphilis.

And yet these poor wretches, often scorned by both society and the artistic community are today household names.

Indeed, many are household items. Tablemats, chocolate boxes, greeting cards. Works by the great masters adorn them all.

In fact, for many people it is the only place they have ever seen some of the world's great masterpieces.

But is a tablemat really the best place to view Van Gogh's wonderfully exaggerated use of colour?

Is it possible to appreciate the tones and colours of Monet's landscapes on a greetings card measuring five inches by four?

Should Renoir's other, more delicate paintings simply be the means by which the lid of a chocolate box is made 'pretty'?

Of course not.

Now, mercifully, a new gallery has opened in London which offers everyone the chance to see many of the truest famous paintings of the Impressionist period as they were meant to be seen.

The Courtauld Collection has recently moved from Woburn Square to the North Block of Somerset House in the Strand, London.

One of England's finest monuments to neoclassical architecture, it is a fitting home for what is undoubtedly one of the most remarkable collections of paintings in the world.

Degas. Cezanne. Renoir. Gauguin. Seurat. Pissarro. Manet. Monet. Works that would have Japanese tycoons reaching for their cheque books before you could say 'Jacques Robinson' as liberally

sprinkled throughout a collection which has never been seen in its entirety before.

And who exactly bought with such taste and vision? Whose eagle-eye spotted these renowned canvases when all others were spurning them?

The man who appropriately gave his name to the collection: Samuel Courtauld.

As heir to the Courtauld textile fortune, he certainly had the wherewithal to become a collector.

But no one meeting this rather quiet, non-intellectual businessman could ever have guessed that he possessed such unerring and courageous artistic judgement.

For, as these sorry tales indicate only too clearly, the Impressionists were not always as sought after as they are today.

But this lack of endorsement by the artistic establishment did not deter Samuel Courtauld.

In the years between 1922 and 1932, he indulged in a spending spree which included the acquisition of works by practically all the major Impressionists, including the purchase of no fewer than twelve Cezannes and twelve Seurats.

He also swooped to buy recognised masterpieces from under the noses of better-known and wealthier collectors.

Renoir's 'La Loge', for instance, which was shown at the very first Impressionists Exhibition in 1874. And Manet's last great masterpiece 'A Bar at the Folies-Bergère'.

No doubt you will recognise many of these paintings when you see them hanging unceasingly on the walls of their new home.

And understand, perhaps for the first time, that for tablemats they make possible works of art.

The nearest Tube Stations to Somerset House are Temple, Holborn and Aldwych (during the rush hours). Waterloo and Charing Cross British Rail Stations are within walking distance.

Admission is £2.50. Concessions, £1.00. Open 10am to 6pm Monday to Saturday, 2pm to 6pm Sunday. Late opening Tuesdays, 6pm to 8pm. July to September by courtesy of Mobil.

Finally, the Courtauld Institute Galleries would not have been possible without the following generous sponsors: Pearson, Arthur Andersen, Courtaulds, Citibank, IBM and Toray Industries.

Courtauld Institute Galleries

156

CONSUMER NEWSPAPER
OVER 600 LINES: SINGLE

160
**ART DIRECTOR**
David Ayriss
**WRITERS**
Jim Copacino, Rick Rosenberg
**PHOTOGRAPHER**
Jonathan/Craig
**CLIENT**
Alaska Airlines
**AGENCY**
Livingston & Company/Seattle

161
**ART DIRECTOR**
Gordon Smith
**WRITER**
Laura Thomasson
**PHOTOGRAPHER**
Jon Silla
**CLIENT**
McLeod Regional
Medical Center
**AGENCY**
Loeffler Ketchum
Mountjoy/Charlotte

162
**ART DIRECTOR**
Charles Inge
**WRITER**
Jane Garland
**CLIENT**
Vauxhall
**AGENCY**
Lowe Howard-Spink/London

163
**ART DIRECTOR**
Mark Fuller
**WRITER**
Steve Bassett
**PHOTOGRAPHER**
Cathy Groth/Dean Hawthorne
Photography
**CLIENT**
Blue Cross/Blue Shield of Virginia
**AGENCY**
The Martin Agency/Richmond

164
**ART DIRECTOR**
Amy Watt
**WRITER**
Edward Boches
**ILLUSTRATOR**
Amy Watt
**PHOTOGRAPHERS**
John Huet, Cheryl Clegg
**CLIENT**
Smartfoods
**AGENCY**
Mullen/Wenham

165
**ART DIRECTOR**
Amy Watt
**WRITER**
Edward Boches
**ILLUSTRATOR**
Amy Watt
**PHOTOGRAPHERS**
Cheryl Clegg, Stock
**CLIENT**
Smartfoods
**AGENCY**
Mullen/Wenham

# A SPECIAL OFFER FOR THOSE WHO DON'T FLY ALASKA AIRLINES.

For relief of minor discomfort due to bad food, cramped seating, and the aggravation often associated with late flights, use this coupon. Or take a flight on Alaska Airlines. You'll be treated to a fresh delicious entree, roomy seating, superb on-time performance, and our award-winning service all along the way. So, if you're going to fly on another airline, take this coupon to your nearest retailer. Or, call your travel agent or Alaska Airlines at 1-800-426-0333. And take the one that's proven most effective against travel irritation.

*Alaska Airlines*

160

# Imagine For A Minute That This Is Your Spine.

Imagine that your bones are as fragile as fine china.
Imagine that every move you make could result in a debilitating bone fracture. A fracture that, if you're over 70, could lead to death from complications within a year.
And, finally, imagine that your vertebrae begin gradually collapsing until you can no longer straighten your spine.
This is what it's like to have osteoporosis. A bone disorder so widespread that by the time you're 45 you may have a 50% chance of being affected.
Unless, of course, you start doing something about it now. To find out how to prevent osteoporosis, give McLeod a call at 667-2888.
And stand up to osteoporosis. Before it brings you down.

**McLeod**
REGIONAL MEDICAL CENTER
The Choice For Medical Excellence.

161

# HEARD ABOUT THE WOMAN DRIVER IN A VAUXHALL?

She put her foot down.

She skidded on a corner.

She flew off the road.

She slithered down a hillside.

She tore through a forest.

She went through a lake.

She went through 100s of tyres.

She walked off with the 1990
FIA World Rally
Championship Ladies Cup.

Her name is Louise Aitken-Walker.

Her car is the Astra GTE 16v.

**VAUXHALL**
Once driven, forever smitten.

162

## "My grandma can beat your grandma."

Blue Cross and Blue Shield of Virginia. For ten years,
a proud sponsor of the Virginia Golden Olympics.

163

YOU CAN'T GET IT OFF YOUR MIND
Totally natural SMARTFOOD®. Air-popped popcorn smothered in white cheddar cheese.

164

YOU CAN'T GET IT OFF YOUR MIND
Totally natural SMARTFOOD®. Air-popped popcorn smothered in white cheddar cheese.

165

166

167

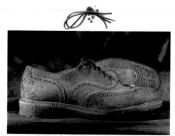

# SEE WHAT IT WAS LIKE TO BE TREATED LIKE ROYALTY 200 YEARS AGO.

## THE FRENCH REVOLUTION TONIGHT AT 9:00

It was a class struggle that turned into one of the most documented reigns
of terror in history. Watch the epic recreation of The French Revolution.
Starring Klaus Maria Brandauer, Jane Seymour and Peter Ustinov.

**172**

# We Can Tell You If You're Paying Too Much For Travel.

# You're Paying Too Much For Travel.

That is, unless you're already one of our corporate clients.
If you're not, you can be sure the above statement applies to your company.
How are we able to make such a claim? When we combined the forces of some of the largest and most prominent travel management companies in the Pacific Northwest, we not only became bigger, we gained substantial leverage and buying power with our suppliers.

The power to guarantee the lowest airfares available through any travel agency in this part of the country.
The power to negotiate significant discounts on lodging and ground transportation.
And the power of a 64-office network and more than 600 employees who promise the highest level of customer service.
All of which we suspect will capture the attention of any travel manager charged with containing corporate travel costs.

So, if the notion of reducing your travel expenditures sounds like the way to go, contact Wayne McCaulley at (206) 224-7800.
At the risk of repeating himself, the first thing he's likely to say is that you're paying too much for travel.

**US Travel Systems.
Way To Go.**

**173**

# Perhaps The First Time In History That Trading A $72,000 Car For A $35,000 Car Could Be Considered Trading Up.

In their December 1989 issue, *Popular Science* proclaimed the new $35,000 Lexus LS 400 clearly superior to its European competitors, including the $72,000 Mercedes 560 SEL.

Of course, numerical rankings alone can't tell the whole story. So here are a few astute verbal observations from the experts at *Popular Science*:

"The Lexus quickly distinguished itself as the comfort king. It glides over ragged pavement with a ride so sweet the shock absorbers seem to be filled with honey."

"Our editors practically drooled over the car's perfor-

mance, styling, ride and comfort. The Lexus radiates the rich warmth of a private sitting room."

"The Lexus has one more endearing feature—the most technically advanced and best-equipped interior of the group."

The writers also took careful note of the Lexus' 0.29 coefficient of drag, which not only gives it a sleekly contoured silhouette, but also makes it the most aerodynamic luxury sedan sold in America.

*Popular Science* summed up by declaring the Lexus

"the most nearly perfect sport sedan to date." What's more, acknowledging its M.S.R.P. of $35,000, they proclaimed it "the deal of the decade." Of course, actual retail price is established by the dealer and may vary.

So if you're a European luxury car owner who'd like to move up in the world, visit your Lexus dealer.

*Your Lexus Dealer. Pursuing Perfection.*

# Whoever Said Money Can't Buy Happiness Isn't Spending It Right.

Think of all the things you could do with $38,000.* You could dabble in the stock market. Maybe invest in some fine art.

Or, you could purchase the exhilarating feeling that can only be attained by driving a Lexus LS 400.

In just its first year, the LS 400 has redefined the term luxury car, achieving the highest "value," "workmanship," and

"overall satisfaction" ratings *Car and Driver* has ever seen.

If you think this kind of response has us smiling, you should see our customers.

*Your Lexus Dealer. Pursuing Perfection.*

176
ART DIRECTOR
John Gorse
WRITER
Nick Worthington
PHOTOGRAPHER
George Logan
CLIENT
Girobank
AGENCY
Bartle Bogle Hegarty/London

177
ART DIRECTOR
Hugh Mosley
WRITER
Simon Brooks
ILLUSTRATOR
Plum Studio
CLIENT
Thames TV
AGENCY
Butterfield Day DeVito
Hockney/London

## You're witnessing a robbery.
### (The victim's the one on the left.)

Incidents like this happen up and down the country every day.

A businessman walks into a bank armed with his day's takings, hands them to the cashier, then leaves.

Innocent enough.

What he may not realize is that often when he puts money in, the bank effectively takes money out.

Exactly how much each transaction costs him he may never know. (Banks rarely itemize all their charges.)

From the banks' point of view, this is perfectly reasonable. After all, why should they want his money? They've got vaults full of the stuff. And checking cash, credit card receipts and cheques takes time.

At Girobank, you'll find it's a slightly different story.

Our links with the Post Office mean we're always hungry for your cash.

As you may imagine, the Post Office's network of 20,000 branches needs vast amounts of cash to pay out in pensions and benefits.

Which, in turn, means we're able to offer our customers extremely competitive business rates.

But there's more to Girobank's service than competitive rates alone.

Using the Post Office also provides us with more branches than all the other clearing banks put together.

We're open until 5.30 at night and on Saturday mornings. (We don't know of many businesses that shut at 3.30pm.)

And there are no hidden charges. Our charges are agreed in advance and our statements are fully itemized.

All in all, it's a service which is now attracting over £100m a day from businesses across the country.

Clearly, when it comes to your day's takings, it would be a crime to bank anywhere else.

If you suspect you could improve your business banking, simply return the coupon or, better still, call free on **0800 444 241**, anytime.

To: Girobank plc, FREEPOST CV 1037, Stratford-upon-Avon, Warwickshire CV37 0BR.
Name _____
Title _____
Company Name _____
Address _____
_____ Postcode _____
Telephone _____
Turnover: £0 – £250,000 ☐ £250,000 – £500,000 ☐ £500,000 + ☐

 Girobank
BUSINESS BANKING

GIROBANK PLC REGISTERED IN ENGLAND NO 1950008 REGISTERED OFFICE, 10 MILK STREET, LONDON EC2V 8JH.

---

## Are people who bank with Girobank a few pence short of a shilling?

### (Hardly. We pay 9% interest on our Keyway current account.)

Shrewd is probably not the first word you'd use to describe someone who banks with Girobank. Unless, of course, you're familiar with the facts.

Girobank's new current account, Keyway, pays 9% interest.

That's 2.75% more than the Abbey National's Current Account.

3% more than NatWest's Current Plus.

2% more than the highest interest rate on Lloyds' Classic account. And, unlike some of our rivals, we pay our highest interest rate on every pound in your current account.

But, of course, there's more to banking than interest rates alone.

Our Keyway account also offers you a £100 cheque guarantee card.

A guaranteed overdraft of up to 50% of your salary.*

A cash card that gives you access to £250 a day and over 4,000 Link cash machines across the country.

A Visa card for which there is no fee. And there are no charges, even if you slip into the red by up to £20.

So where's your nearest branch?

There isn't one.

You deal with us on the telephone. You can check your account, set up an overdraft, or even discuss a mortgage, over the phone.

Anything that needs to be signed, we'll send directly to you and any cheques you need to pay in, you send to us. (We even supply you with prepaid envelopes.)

It is, we admit, a far cry from the traditional method of banking.

There are no queues. No wasted lunch hours. And we're open until 8.00 at night and midday on Saturdays.

So bear our Keyway account in mind next time you're asked to pay a whole month's charges for slipping £10 into the red. Or are refused an overdraft. Or find your bank closed. Or work out the interest you might have earned.

When you do open a Keyway account, you don't have to close your existing bank account straight away, just judge us against it.

We think you might find that people who bank with Girobank are a good deal shrewder than you thought.

For an information pack, simply return the coupon. Or, better still, pick up the phone and call us free on **0800 262 614**.

To: Keyway Information Centre, PO Box 46, Stratford-upon-Avon, Warwickshire CV37 0TU. I am over 18. I am/am not a Girobank Current Account Customer.

Mr/Mrs/Miss/Ms/Title _____ Initials _____
Surname _____
Address _____
Postcode _____ Phone/STD _____

Girobank
**You'll have the last laugh.**

*IF MONTHLY INCOME IS CREDITED TO YOUR KEYWAY ACCOUNT. £400 MINIMUM TO BE PAID IN MONTHLY. ALL INTEREST RATES QUOTED ARE ANNUAL AND NET OF LIABILITY TO BASIC RATE TAX. RATES CORRECT AT TIME OF GOING TO PRESS. APPLICANTS MUST BE AGED 18 OR OVER. YOUR HOME IS AT RISK IF YOU DO NOT KEEP UP REPAYMENTS ON A MORTGAGE OR OTHER LOAN SECURED ON IT. GIROBANK PLC, 10 MILK STREET, LONDON EC2V 8JH. REG. NO. 1950008.

---

## If they're looking after your money, why are they taking it to a bank?

The idea of employing a security carrier so you don't lose your day's takings makes a lot of sense.

But there is a flaw.

Few people realize that when your money's actually paid into the bank, the bank itself effectively takes money out.

Exactly how much you'll probably never know. (Banks rarely itemize all their charges.)

From the bank's point of view, of course, this is perfectly reasonable. After all, why should they want your money? They've got vaults full of the stuff. And checking cash, credit card receipts and cheques takes time.

At Girobank, it's a slightly different story.

Our bank's unique links with the Post Office mean we're always hungry for cash.

As you can imagine, the Post Office's network of 20,000 branches needs vast amounts of cash to pay out in pensions and benefits.

Which, in turn, means we're able to offer extremely competitive business rates.

But there's more to Girobank's service than competitive rates alone.

Using the Post Office also provides us with more branches than all the other clearing banks put together. So there's usually one close to hand.

We're open until 5.30 at night and on Saturday mornings. (We don't know of many businesses that shut at 3.30pm.)

And there are no hidden charges. Our charges are agreed in advance and our statements are fully itemized.

All in all, it's a service which is now attracting over £100m a day from businesses across the country.

Every penny of which is present and accounted for.

If you want to be sure you're not being taken for a ride, simply return the coupon or, better still, call free on **0800 444 241**, anytime.

To: Girobank plc, FREEPOST CV 1037, Stratford-upon-Avon, Warwickshire CV37 0BR.
Name _____
Title _____
Company Name _____
Address _____
Postcode _____ Tel: _____
Turnover: £0 – £250,000 ☐ £250,000 – £500,000 ☐ £500,000 + ☐

 Girobank
BUSINESS BANKING

GIROBANK PLC REGISTERED IN ENGLAND NO 1950008. REGISTERED OFFICE, 10 MILK STREET, LONDON EC2V 8JH.

**178**
**ART DIRECTOR**
Sally Bond Ours
**WRITER**
Paul Spencer
**CLIENT**
Barking Spider Tavern
**AGENCY**
Big Bob's Ad Ranch/New York

**179**
**ART DIRECTOR**
Cabell Harris
**WRITER**
Jamie Barrett
**CLIENT**
New York Life
**AGENCY**
Chiat/Day/Mojo, New York

Hell, this place is just an excuse
to get some friends together to hang out
and drink.

I'm sure if I weren't on this side
of the bar I'd be over there on
the other side.


Dave,
bartender Monday nights, sometimes
Tuesdays.

Stop by the Spider for music (live and juke box),
poetry, and sometimes even stand up comedy
(usually Tom).

The Barking Spider Tavern. 11310 Juniper. Cleveland.

---

First time a friend brought me to
the Spider I walked over to that box
and I just screamed.

"Crosstown Traffic", "Bell Bottom
Blues", "Crying", "Take Five."
F---ing Dave Brubeck on a jukebox.

Man, you just don't find that kind
of music anywhere outside your
living room.


Paul,
regular.

If you feel like it come by the Spider and hang out
with Martin, Tom, Suzanne, and Dave (and sometimes
Arthur).

The Barking Spider Tavern. 11310 Juniper. Cleveland

---

They built this hotel a couple doors
down. Kind of a pricey bed and breakfast
deal.

So every now and then some folks from
there will stumble in here and say
like "Whoa, what is this place?

And those who dig it really dig it.
I mean they hang out and make a point
of coming back whenever they're back
in town.

Those who don't dig it...well, one look
and they're out of here.


Martin,
owner, and bartender most nights.

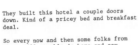

Come in and visit Martin, Tom, Suzanne, and Dave
at the Spider. You'll probably like it.

The Barking Spider Tavern. 11310 Juniper. Cleveland.

# 1 out of 315 disability cases involves someone falling off a ladder. 1 out of 5 involves someone climbing up.

We don't want to cause you any undue stress, but there are a few things you should know about disability insurance.

For one thing, it's not just about industrial accidents anymore. In fact, according to New York Life statistics, 20% of all disability cases involve mental/nervous disorders.*

To the point where they have now become the leading cause of disability—ahead of back pain, heart disease, high blood pressure and, needless to say, falling off a ladder.

At New York Life, we anticipated this trend. We recognized that there are any number of ways a person can become disabled.

So we designed our products to protect you—whether your disability is due to pressure in your lower back, or simply the pressures of everyday life.

For example, if you work full-time, but have an income loss of 20% or more due to your disability, you can still receive benefits. If you're unfortunate enough to lose 80% of your income or more, we still pay you in full.

And if you're receiving total disability benefits, and are confined to a nursing facility, there are certain New York Life policies under which your benefit payments can actually be increased by 50%.

Let's face it. We live in an all too stressful world. And no one, not even you, is immune to the pressures that are often brought to bear.

So if you'd like to remove one of your worries, contact New York Life at 1-800-331-7622.

We can tell you everything you need to know. Like the difference between long-term disability and the short-term coverage you may be receiving at work. Or how we can design a policy that meets your specific needs.

Once that's taken care of, you can concentrate on reaching the next few rungs.

**NEW YORK LIFE**
The Company You Keep.®

---

# Get well cards aren't the only things disabled people receive in the mail.

If you become disabled, and lose your source of income, how long would your money last?

Two years? One year? Six months? Six weeks? How long, for example, would it take to deplete your savings account? At what point would you have to sell your car? Or worse still, your home?

Many Americans are just a few paychecks away from financial disaster. And yet the majority of us continue to live on the edge, failing to consider the consequences of losing our income through disability.

At New York Life, we're getting more of our customers to think seriously about long-term disability insurance. And notice, by the way, that we said "long-term."

You see, although many of you may receive disability insurance through work, chances are you're covered for just three to six months.

Long-term disability, on the other hand, can cover you for as long as you're unable to work. And rather than duplicate an existing policy, it can pick up wherever your short-term coverage leaves off—which means you won't have to pay any premiums twice.

And what are the chances you'll ever be disabled long-term? Far greater, in fact, than you might suspect.

According to recent statistics, one out of seven people is disabled for more than a year by the time they're 65.[1] And surprising as it may seem, less than 20% of employees have long-term disability coverage.[2]

If you're among the uninsured 80%, and you're starting to feel a bit uneasy about it, it's time we talked. Simply call New York Life, toll-free, at 1-800-331-7622.

We can help you feel a lot more secure about what the future—or your mailman—may bring.

**NEW YORK LIFE**
The Company You Keep.®

INSUFFICIENT FUNDS

---

# At one time or another everything in your office has broken down. Why should you be any exception?

"It'll never happen to me."
"I don't know anyone who's ever needed it."
"I think I'm covered at work."

It's easy to come up with reasons why you shouldn't have long-term disability insurance. It's even easier to come up with reasons why you should.

After all, disability insurance is not just for people who have lost a limb. The fact is, most cases involve people who suffer from problems far less tangible. Like back pain. High blood pressure. Or heart disease.

And yes, it really could happen to you. If you're not convinced, just sample some of these recent disability statistics.

One out of seven people will be disabled for more than a year by the time they're 65.[1]

One out of five New York Life disability claims involves mental/nervous disorders, which are the leading cause of disability.[2]

And to top it all off, less than 20% of employees have group long-term disability coverage.[3]

Of course, we could go on at length about the importance of disability coverage. And we could point out the various financial consequences of having no source of income for what could be an indefinite period of time.

But these kinds of issues, given the fact that they concern your own personal situation, are probably best left to a discussion between you and a New York Life agent.

If you'd like to set up an appointment, simply call us toll-free at 1-800-331-7622. We may not be able to help you when your copier breaks down, but if anything should ever happen to you, we'll be there.

**NEW YORK LIFE**
The Company You Keep.®

## TOADY WILLIAMS
### OUT AND ABOUT WITH TOADY

Brat packer **Blink Cheddar** is terribly despondent over his ruptured romance with *Oh that Girl from Norway* co-star **Midge Kerchief**. Didn't I tell you this would happen? (I did, I did.) In fact, say my sources, the beleaguered teen idol turned up on Kerchief's lawn twice last week wearing nothing but combat boots and diapers, and waving his you know what around. Ah well, one more career down the dumper.

Downtown gallery owner and restaurateur **Leash Pedagod** appeared to have it all. A gorgeous wife, two beautiful children, and the respect and admiration of his community. Until, that is, he threw it all away in a sordid, vile, base, low-lying, despicable, hideous, depraved, unimaginably sick, impossibly disgusting... despite the unabated rumors, **Diane Pedagod** says she will continue to stand by her husband.

People are talking about the oh-so-chummy relations between the oh-so-married staple tycoon **Cranberry Papadapolis** and the oh-so-voluptuous daughter of village idiot Stephan Stephan, **Isabella Stephan**. The two were recently spotted at the Chow Chow Chow room, bathing each other like cats and whistling a medley of Madison Avenue favorites. Stephan, who bears a striking resemblance to Oh There... met with a terse "no comment."

Society grand dame **Buffy Muffyton** and prosthetic left chin device manufacturer **Skip Skipperson** are embroiled in a preposterously bitter and protracted custody battle-royale over their snotty little offspring, Skipper. Give him an inch and he'll take a mile.

Perennial rock-and-roll bad boy **Stink Jones** strolled up to the mike at Fong's during a charity benefit for people with abnormally high voices. Those in the know claim Jones, who was stinking like a cesspool... the sheep is recovering nicely.

**Baron Heimleich Maneuver**'s kid. Solipsistic and her pal pal **Mushy Lee** were caught bobbing for live salmon... refused to post bail. Kisses and hugs.

*Toady* xx

# The Bissell Power Steamer gets all the dirt.

And, for that matter, all the grease and all the chocolate and all the strained beets. And on and on. Because The Power Steamer packs a fiendishly aggressive little motor. Which helps it effortlessly flush away deep-down dirt vacuums can't reach. With fewer passes on the carpet. And, for that matter, the floor, the sofa, and the stairs. And on and on.

**BISSELL**

---

## *Environmental Scientists Search For Simple, Effective, Cleanup Solutions.*

### by Davis McShane

Special to The Times

Aspen: In this town of designer skiwear and designer causes, concern for the environment is often expressed over a cup of "fabulous" cappuccino.

So few locals were surprised when the international scientific community selected Aspen as the site of a week-long conference dealing with the increasingly "cause celebre" issue of global pollution.

Researchers began arriving as early as last Tuesday, from such unlikely places as Botswana and Newark. Virtually all of them expressed guarded optimism when asked what they could reasonably hope to accomplish.

Leading the American delegation is Tobias Riis, of The Berkeley Institute of Metaphysics. Like his colleagues from abroad, he has come to Colorado with some definite notions about cleaning up the planet. "Basically," Riis told reporters, "we advocate combining a number of disparate disciplines. Right now we're trying nuclear physics and acupuncture. The stumbling block has been finding financial backing for the construction of a forty-story steel needle which we could insert into the ground near various environmental hot spots."

Members of the Dutch team; from left, Harris, Fong, Langdon and Platt.

When reminded that his keynote speech had been met with blank stares and nervous laughter in The Whitney Milne Conference Hall, Riis snickered derisively. "I mock them," he said, between long draws on his trademark unfiltered Turkish cigarettes, adding that his critics suffered from "typical Western provincialism."

One of the conference's biggest surprises came with the arrival of Drs. Smith and Casey, the pair of embattled scientists who stunned the world two years ago with their controversial discovery of Freezing Point Fission. "Did we say Freezing Point Fission? What we meant to say was that it was kind of a Lukewarm Fission. Sorry."

# The Bissell Power Steamer is a breeze to use.

Because it effortlessly flushes away deep-down dirt imbedded in the nucleus of the carpet shaft. Dirt vacuums simply can't get to. And its array of handy attachments lets it work similar magic on sofas, chairs, stairs and couches. Best of all, owning a Bissell Power Steamer means never again having to deal with the hassle and expense of renting. So if you've been looking for the easiest way to deep clean carpets and upholstery, look no further.

**BISSELL**

---

# The Bissell Power Steamer is loaded with features.

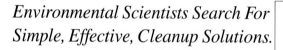

Two-speed motor gives you extra power for really tough jobs.

3½-gallon capacity tank lets you clean whole room without stopping.

Upholstery attachment deep cleans sofas and chairs as well as stairs and other hard to reach places.

Built-in brush scrubs stubborn dirt away.

50-foot water hose provides long reach for hard to reach places.

25% more suction than the previous Bissell units means more cleaning and less drying time.

Built-in caddy allows easy wand storage while wrap system neatly packs away all hoses and cords.

Flush away deep-down dirt from carpets, sofas, chairs and stairs.

**BISSELL**

*(continued from page 31)*

Spiegelman stirred. He worked his eyes open, first one, then the other. Where was he? Certainly not in his office.

He looked around. A gecko clung to the white-washed ceiling.

To his right stood a thin, angular man. Spiegelman recognized him at once. It was former game show host turned international terrorist Wink Ché.

Behind Ché sat a sturdily built thug, nursing a semi-automatic. He regarded Spiegelman with a disinterested stare.

"I had very much hoped to settle this matter quietly," said Ché nodding in the goon's direction. "To avoid calling in bothersome outside professionals. But you left me with little choice."

With that, the bruiser began shuffling forward. Despite his size, he was surprisingly nimble, one of those big men who moves across any surface easily.

"Now, Mr. Spiegelman," said Ché, "this can be extremely easy or this can be difficult. It's entirely up to you. One way or another, I assure you, our rather imposing friend here gets all the dirt."

The gorilla raised the semi-automatic, perching the bore of the barrel precariously on the bridge of Spiegelman's nose.

"You're just one man, Spiegelman," said Ché disdainfully. "A sad and misguided man. Did you actually think you could singlehandedly bring down my operation? That you could do it yourself?"

Spiegelman smiled through clenched teeth. "You may stop me, you loathsome toad, but know this: The forces of good will never rest until every last ounce of filth is flushed out of this town. And on that, I give you my full, two-year guarantee."

Ché pulled a handkerchief from his pocket and mopped his brow, slowly, deliberately. He smiled wanly.

"Such insolence. I'm afraid you've just signed your death warrant."

Spiegelman grew still. He could see the goon's massive knuckles begin to whiten on the weapon's built-in handle.

He knew from reading enough dime store novels that this was about the time fate, fortuitous or not, would play her hand. Sure enough, she was right on time. Like an overly-ripe cantaloupe in the hands of

*(continued on page 36)*

180

## With haircuts like these, it's no wonder we offer 26 different styles of hats.

Some of the worst atrocities of the war weren't committed on the battlefield. They were committed in the barbershop.

Naturally, this left a few good men looking for a few good hats. And the military was happy to oblige. In fact, over the past 40 years, the armed forces have issued over 40 different hat styles. Many of which can still be found resting comfortably atop the shelves of Bunker Hill surplus. Walk down any aisle and you're likely to spot a classic.

"Boonie" hats. Jungle hats. Drill Instructor hats. Pith helmets. Arctic hoods. Class A dress caps. Even our camouflage baseball caps. In short, we've got enough hats to cover up a whole regiment of Army-issue haircuts.

And once you select a cap, you'll also find a great selection of boots, military jackets, and gear.

So next time you're in the neighborhood, stop by Bunker Hill and pick up a new hat. After all, remember those military barbers we were talking about? Well, most of them are civilian barbers now. Scary thought, huh?

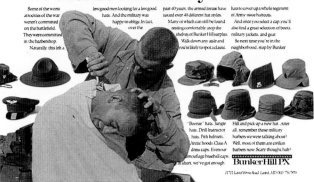

**Bunker Hill PX**

11711 Laird Berre Road, Laird, MD 000-776-7876


## We may be the only clothing store whose suits clash with everything.

At Bunker Hill PX, our clothes don't make statements. They make threats.

In fact, over the past fifty years, these uniforms have managed to clash with the Germans, the Japanese, the North Koreans, and the Viet Cong. And, barring a few nicks and scrapes, they've survived it all.

Today you'll find them, resting peacefully at Bunker Hill. These are not fashions created by sissy designers, mind you. These are clothes built by real men. Men with guns. And tattoos. Rugged 100% cotton pants. Authentic fatigue shirts. Field jackets. Parkas.

the latest accessories to complement your new outfit. Jungle "Boonie" hats. Combat boots. Utility belts. Mess kits. Canteens. Helmets.

Camouflage. All you'd need is an M-16 and a few grenades, and you've got one fashion statement that no one better ignore.

So the next time you're in the neighborhood, stop by Bunker Hill surplus and pick up some of our authentic tangues. Pick up a few accessories, too. But remember, no matter how carefully you put your outfit together, one thing is certain. It's going to clash.

**Bunker Hill PX**

11711 Laird Berre Road, Laird, MD 000-776-7876


## They say an army travels on its stomach. No wonder our boots are in such good shape.

Traditionally, the average American foot soldier spends more time on his face than he does on his feet. (This can usually be attributed to bullets, mortar shells, and other low-flying chunks of metal.)

We're not complaining, mind you. This unusual method of traveling has helped the military preserve thousands of lives.

Not to mention, thousands of boots. Many of which can be found right here at Bunker Hill Surplus.

We proudly offer a truly impressive collection of rugged military footwear. Some vintage. Some new. But all in prime fighting condition.

You'll find hundreds of black leather combat boots. Lightweight camouflage jungle boots. Hiking boots. All those great military styles that have been kicking butt for the past 40 years.

And that's not all. We also carry field jackets. Fatigues. Unit patches. Canteens. Mess kits. Camouflage caps. Jungle "Boonie" hats. Thermal underwear. Parkas. Ponchos. And much, much more.

So if you're in the market for some really tough boots, or some really tough clothes, stop by Bunker Hill today.

After all, with all the action this stuff has seen, anything you throw at them will seem like a walk in the park.

**Bunker Hill PX**

11711 Laird Berre Road, Laird, MD 000-776-7876

**182**
**ART DIRECTOR**
Bill Schwab
**WRITER**
Dean Buckhorn
**PHOTOGRAPHERS**
Michael Pohuski, National
Archives, Merril Dello Iacono
**CLIENT**
Bunker Hill PX
**AGENCY**
Earle Palmer Brown/Bethesda

**183**
**ART DIRECTOR**
Carolyn Tye McGeorge
**WRITER**
Kerry Feuerman
**ILLUSTRATOR**
Lu Matthews
**CLIENT**
Kentlands
**AGENCY**
Earle Palmer Brown/Richmond

## To prove she was innocent of witchcraft, Grace Sherwood had to do only one thing: Die.

It was called "trial by ducking." Bound hand and foot, a woman accused of witchcraft was rowed into a deep body of water and promptly pushed overboard.

And without the need of judge or jury her guilt or innocence was immediately determined. Unfortunately, she died either way.

Such was the predicament in which Grace Sherwood of Princess Anne County, Virginia found herself.

The year was 1706.

In theory, trial by ducking worked something like this:

Water, being pure, would reject the impure. And so a true witch would float. If innocent, however, the accused would sink, thus mixing her purity with that of the water, and drowning in the process. A fate only slightly preferred to being burned at the stake.

Grace Sherwood had the dubious distinction of being the first woman in the colony of Virginia tried for witchcraft. Her troubles began several years earlier.

According to county records, Mrs. Sherwood was first branded a witch by neighbor Richard Capps in 1698. Grace and her husband sued for slander and Mr. Capps reluctantly settled the matter out of court. He had, however, started a scandalous ball rolling.

Soon neighbors accused Grace of performing a wide variety of witchy activities, including sailing to England and back in one night in an eggshell, wearing men's clothing, making cows give bad milk, and exiting a room through the keyhole of a door "like a black cat."

Grace was brought to trial in 1701. But finding a jury of twelve women brave enough to sit against her proved to be all but impossible. After more than five years of confinement, and for some unknown reason, she agreed to undergo trial by ducking.

It's safe to say that things were now looking rather gloomy for this mother of three. On the day of her ducking a huge storm blew up soaking all on-lookers and postponing the event. Grace, of course, was accused of causing it.

Her destiny was determined one week later from the bow of a small rowboat bobbing gently in the Lynnhaven River. With spectators gathered on a protrusion of land still known to this day as Witch Duck Point, Grace Sherwood was thrown overboard . . . and floated. Gasps and nervous murmurs were heard from shore.

Perhaps fearful of being in contact with a witch, boatmen tried to influence the verdict by tying a heavy Bible around Grace's neck in hopes that she would sink.

No such luck.

In fact, Grace actually managed to untie the waterlogged Bible and floated around the cove on her back singing a song.

The conclusion of this bizarre episode in Virginia history is unexplained in court records. Grace was not burned at the stake. Nor hanged. She was, instead, confined to jail for nine years and then released.

34 years later, at the ripe old age of 80, Grace Sherwood died a natural (or was it supernatural?) death.

In the collections of the Virginia Historical Society, Grace Sherwood's story is preserved along with over six million other rare manuscripts relating to this state's long and colorful past.

Hanging on the walls is the largest collection of portrait paintings in the South. One of only three known life masks of Robert E. Lee stares ominously through the glass of a lighted display case. George Washington's spectacles, Patrick Henry's cane, and gold buttons from Pocahontas' dress are just a fraction of what's here.

To house these treasures, a new wing is being added to the Society's Richmond building. A campaign called the Fifth Century Fund has been started to help pay for the cost of expansion. For information on how you can help or to become a member of the Society call us in Richmond at (804) 358-4901.

**Virginia Historical Society**
*The Center for Virginia History*

## Dr. James Ambler saved 13 men from freezing to death. Unfortunately, he wasn't one of them.

While awaiting reassignment at Portsmouth, Virginia Naval Hospital, Dr. James Ambler, USN, received a telegram that would change his life. In fact, it would end it.

Lieutenant Commander George W. DeLong, USN, was assembling a crew of 33 brave and talented men for the most ambitious arctic exploration ever attempted. Destination: North Pole.

On July 8, 1879, their ship, the *Jeannette*, set sail from San Francisco Bay.

The *Jeannette* lumbered slowly northward. Too slowly. Forced to stop in Alaska to pick up dog sleds, dog teams and Indian drivers, the *Jeannette* didn't reach the Arctic Ocean until early September. Too late.

She was greeted by ice packs.

Surrounded and unable to escape, the expedition had come to a sudden, frozen halt. It was going to be a long winter.

Fortunately, James Ambler was one of the first doctors to understand the importance of preventive medicine. Lime juice was now ordered for each crew member.

(There would be no scurvy on his ship.) He made sure the drinking water was pure. Ambler himself led a daily exercise classes on the ice. He also organized games and competitions.

And when Lieutenant John Danenhower, USN, developed snow blindness, Dr. Ambler performed eye surgery by lantern light.

With the arrival of summer the men still had their health and their sanity. But not their freedom. The towering ice floes that gripped the *Jeannette* had refused to melt.

Time passed.

Anything was welcomed to break the monotony. Except what happened on June 10, 1881.

Just before midnight shockwaves ripped through the ship. All hands on deck! All hands on deck! The *Jeannette* was being crushed.

The order to abandon ship came at night the following evening. Each man performed magnificently. Supplies, dogs, sleds and three small boats were all calmly transported to the ice.

In the eerie light of an arctic summer night the *Jeannette* listed slowly to starboard, took on one gallon too many, and sank.

The following day, Dr. Ambler started an "ice diary."

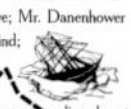

He first noted the condition of the men: Mr. Chipp could not move; Mr. Danenhower was almost blind; Captain DeLong's head was wrapped in bandages from an earlier, almost fatal accident; several of the sailors were now suffering from lead poisoning.

In the hands of a lesser physician they most certainly would have died. Yet Ambler nursed them all to health and for the first time in almost two years to move. Progress was painfully slow. Roads had to be cut through the jagged ice. Bridges were built by hand using tons of snow. When the dogs exhausted themselves pulling the heavy sleds, men took their place in the harnesses.

Throughout it all only one of the officers volunteered for manual labor: James Ambler. Ice diary: "I worked hard all day yesterday with a pick . . . then sleeping in wet clothes in a wet bag on wet ice makes every bone and separate muscle ache in the morning. Today I have not been able to draw a breath without pain."

A month later they reached open water and launched the three small boats. Siberia lay to the southwest.

A heavy gale blew for days. But the boat carrying Ambler and DeLong finally managed to ground itself in shallow water and they waded the last chilling mile to shore.

The others were nowhere in sight.

By this time frostbite had taken its toll on seaman Hans Ericksen. Flesh stripped from his feet until muscle and tendons were exposed to the frigid arctic air. Still Ambler refused to leave the crippled man behind.

With only four days' rations left, seamen William Niedemann and Louis Noros were sent to find help. Ambler, DeLong and nine others waited as long as they could. Then they died.

As it turned out, one of the other boats also made it to shore. Natives came across the half-starved men and brought them to safety in the Siberian village of Buhn.

Later that spring, Dr. Ambler's body was found with the others beneath a foot of snow. In his hand was the captain's pistol. In his pockets were the ice diary and a letter to his brother back home in Virginia.

A single line in it tells all. "I am resigned to bow my head in submission to the divine will."

In 1883, a naval board of inquiry determined that those men who had survived owed their lives in great part to Dr. James Markham Marshall Ambler, USN.

In the vast collections of the Virginia Historical Society, Dr. Ambler's ice diary is sitting on display along with thousands of other precious artifacts relating to this state's long and extremely colorful past.

To house these treasures a new wing is being added to the Society's Richmond building.

**Virginia Historical Society**
*The Center for Virginia History*

A campaign called The Fifth Century Fund has been started to pay for the expansion. For information on how you can help or to become a Society member call us in Richmond at (804) 358-4901.

## 75,000 Germans shooting at him and he's worried about finding his suicide pill.

The Messerschmitts roared in with their machine guns blazing. But if the pilots had known who they were shooting at, they would have held their fire. Two of the scrambling figures on the beach were far more valuable captured than killed.

Colonel David Bruce of Charlotte County, Virginia, had not expected to be at Normandy. As chief of OSS in Europe, his talents lay in the field of espionage. Spying, code breaking, cloak and dagger stuff. Yet here he was, part of the largest amphibious invasion in history, Operation Overlord.

Bruce was there on orders from the man bleeding next to him on the beach, General William "Wild Bill" Donovan. Ironically, the General was not there on orders. In fact, Allied high command had given specific instructions forbidding General Donovan from stepping foot anywhere near the beaches of Normandy. He was, after all, head of the entire OSS organization and privy to some of the most sensitive secrets of the war.

As the General's nickname would imply, however, Wild Bill Donovan was something of an adventurer. So twenty-four hours earlier he put on his Medal of Honor, collected Colonel Bruce and proceeded to talk his way onto the USS *Tuscaloosa*.

If Ike found out, there would be hell to pay.

Meanwhile, Field-Marshal Erwin Rommel intended to make their arrival as unpleasant as possible. Over six million mines were laid along the coastline from Holland to France. Huge concrete bunkers faced the sea with heavy guns that could sink a ship fifteen miles away. Anti-tank obstacles littered every possible landing beach. Stationed in the immediate vicinity were Cherbourg and Le Havre were eight infantry divisions. And three Panzer divisions, including the 12th *"Hitlerjugend"* S.S. Panzer Division with dreaded Tiger tanks, could roll in at the first sign of an invasion.

It was appropriately called the Atlantic Wall.

The Allies controlled the skies. But the Messerschmitts slipped through just in time to welcome Bruce and Donovan coming ashore.

Donovan leaped for cover behind their landing craft. Bruce did the same, landing bravely on the General and gashing Donovan's chin with his steel helmet. With blood running down his neck, General Donovan turned to Bruce and happily exclaimed, "Now it will be like this all the time."

They made a run for it.

Shortly after passing through Allied lines the two officers practically ran into a hail of enemy machine gun fire. Ack ack ack. Ack ack ack. Between bursts the General reminded Bruce that neither of them could be taken alive, "We know too much." Bruce nodded. The General continued, "Have you your pills with you?" Bruce thought: pills? . . . pills? Then it dawned on him. OSS officers had been issued suicide pills for just such an occasion.

Not expecting to be in the field, Bruce realized that, indeed, he did not have his pills. Embarrassed, he apologized to the General. Donovan forgave him at once and told the Colonel that he would give him one of his own suicide pills. (Whether or not Bruce thanked the General is unknown.)

As it turned out, Donovan searched his pockets and also came up empty-handed. With alarm, the General realized he left his pills in a hotel room in London. When . . . if they got back to the ship, Bruce was to radio Claridge's and have the General's "medical supplies" gathered up and safely deposited with the hall porter.

They began their retreat.

The next time that David Bruce met  the Germans things would be considerably different. Instead of Colonel Bruce, he would be called Ambassador Bruce.

In the collections of the Virginia Historical Society, David Bruce became ambassador to both Great Britain and France. He was senior U.S. representative to the People's Republic of China. During the Vietnam War, he was America's representative at the Paris peace talks. And in 1976, he ended his remarkable career as Ambassador to NATO.

David K. E. Bruce was one of the most distinguished diplomats in modern American history. But history might have been different had it been for a single bullet. Or a single pill.

In the collections of the Virginia Historical Society, Ambassador Bruce's Presidential Medal of Freedom is standing on display. Many of his official papers and personal diaries are waiting to be read.

The Virginia Historical Society is literally overflowing with history. Virginia's Liberty Bell, Stonewall Jackson's bookcase, rare paintings and maps are just a fraction of what's here.

**Virginia Historical Society**
*The Center for Virginia History*

To house these treasures a new wing is being added to the Society's Richmond building. A campaign called the Fifth Century Fund has been started to pay for the expansion. For information on how you can help or to become a Society member please call us in Richmond at (804) 358-4901.

Not long ago, a soon-to-retire Porsche engineer reflected dreamily over dinner with a friend. "You know," he said with a grin, "I never worked a day in my life."

If one thing separates a Porsche from any other car on the road, it is this. A Porsche is created not out of need, but out of love. By a handful of gifted individualists who are almost like children at play. Very intense play. Enjoying a rare opportunity few get: To not only dream of, but actually be asked to seek perfection; to freely explore new principles; to frolic among the laws of physics, challenging their limitations. The creation of the new 944 S2 Cabriolet was just such an experience.

Our newest convertible, it places you exhilaratingly in touch with the open air. At the same time, the unique 944 S2 design places you sensitively in touch with the road. As only a Porsche can.

A transaxle layout provides near-perfect 50-50 weight balance front to rear, for virtually unrivaled handling and razor-sharp control. Huge, 4-piston disc brakes with ABS haul you from 60 mph to a standstill in a paltry 120 feet. (Porsche engineers say the perfect brakes should provide such control, it feels almost as if you are touching the brake discs with your fingertips.)

Suspension, steering, braking and drive systems are all carefully matched to work as one. Even tire tread is meticulously calculated.

Precision pervades the cosmetics and finishing as well. The painting process alone requires 26 steps. Body panels are hot-dip zinc galvanized before a single weld is performed to prevent corrosion. The 4-layer cabriolet top is hand-stitched, then hand-assembled, for an exacting fit on each individual car.

And, since the Porsche philosophy toward performance requires that nothing distract the driver, attention to detail here is so extreme that side mirrors and windshield washer nozzles have heaters to prevent icing.

The most incredible thing is, all of this is done, and tested, and perfected in the name of fun.

It is often said by Porsche engineers that if you have any desire to work somewhere else in your life, you should do that first. Because once you experience Porsche, everything else seems commonplace and uninspiring.

One test-drive in the new 944 S2 Cabriolet at your authorized Porsche dealer, and you'll see very clearly what they mean. However, if you work in any type of a serious atmosphere, we suggest you come in early on a weekend. It may take a couple of days to wipe the grin off your face.

*Introducing the Porsche 944 S2 Cabriolet.*

# We don't introduce a new Porsche until we hear some of the most sophisticated engineers in Germany giggling like children.

---

A true sports car has always been, in a sense, modern society's version of a broadsword in the hands of a paladin. Still, at Porsche we have always felt that to co-exist in a civilized world, power alone is not enough. In this belief, we have spent over 2 generations in search of the perfect synergy between performance and refinement.

The new-generation 911 Carrera 2 may, in fact, have achieved just such perfect harmony.

In terms of pure potency, the fabled rear-engine now produces more breathtaking capacity than ever. A new, sophisticated engine management system and twin spark plugs combine with other refinements to realize 247 horsepower.

It is in an attempt to make this raw potential more useable, however, that we have achieved new levels of handling, manners and sophistication that allow the car to mingle in even the most polite circles. The suspension is totally redesigned to further enhance balance and control.

A new rear axle self-corrects in hard cornering. To avoid any possible distraction, a goal we take seriously, outside mirrors and windshield washer nozzles are actually heated to prevent icing.

Our revolutionary Carrera 2 with Tiptronic dual-function transmission lets the driver choose either full automatic or clutchless manual shifting. The Tiptronic in manual mode shifts faster than 95% of drivers are capable of with a clutch.

Focus on cosmetics is equally copious. Over 26 steps are dedicated to the painting process alone. Convertible tops are hand-stitched, then hand-assembled.

The list could continue on at length. But the simplest way to gain an understanding of what we have achieved is with a 911 Carrera 2 test-drive at your authorized Porsche dealership. Prepare yourself to feel the power of a legendary conqueror. But one who, now, would always say "pardon me" while laying foes to waste.

*Introducing the Porsche 911 Carrera 2 Cabriolet.*

# To understand the difference in our new 911, imagine Genghis Khan after having read "Miss Manners."

---

Incomprehensible as it may seem, in any given month, we rarely build two Porsche cars that are identical.

The simple fact is, it was never Professor Porsche's intention to build a lot of cars. Just a limited number of very special sports cars, for perfectionists like himself who could appreciate them.

It is this fierce individuality and self-expression which has always made a Porsche a Porsche. First, we do things our own way technologically. Seeking the most perfect solution. Then, we virtually sculpt each vehicle into a distinctive statement for the individual who will occupy it.

The new generation 911 Carrera 2 Cabriolet is the latest evolution in this rather unconventional philosophy.

Simply by virtue of its Porsche heritage and construction, it stands uniquely apart. Welding alone takes over 4 working days for each body. The painting process requires 26 steps. Engines are bench-built by hand. Convertible tops are individually hand-stitched, then hand-assembled.

With its legendary rear-engine now boasting 247 hp, a redesigned suspension and new self-correcting rear axle, performance and handling take yet another leap forward.

It is after all this, however, that each Porsche truly becomes singular. With every car, we seek a distinctive identity and purpose, employing myriad combinations of features and materials.

This type of exclusive, handcrafting also allows for individualization almost unheard of in this day and age. We offer over 350 different seat variations. Our current exterior color palette numbers 13, but we have available over 200 selections, including every production color we have ever used. You could even have the same silver Professor Porsche used on his first roadster in 1947.

Or, send us a sample to match. One gentleman provided us with his girlfriend's lipstick. A woman sent a swatch of her favorite dress. An eastern sheik went so far as to order a solid gold stick shift.

After a tour, one customer wrote, "In many ways, your plant has more in common with an artist's workshop than with a 'normal' automobile factory."

Of course, all this takes time. Which is why we can only promise 1,235 Carrera 2 Cabriolets to the U.S. this year. Ample reason to make time soon for a test-drive at your authorized Porsche dealership.

But be forewarned: If you acquire one, and can't wait to exchange a knowing wave with someone on the road in a car just like yours, don't hold your breath. You may never see one.

*The new Porsche 911 Carrera 2 Cabriolet.*

# Maybe we'll build another like it next month. Maybe not.

Germany is a land of fables and legends. Many passed down for generations. But for pure magic and mystique, perhaps none equals the legendary independence surrounding Porsche cars.

In the warm spring sun of 1948, Professor F. Porsche rolled out an automobile which, simply put, ignored virtually every convention of the day. The engine was just ahead of the rear axle. The body lightweight. The hood sloped steeply for optimal road vision. Everything was designed to duplicate the feel of road-contact achieved in an open-wheeled race car.

For over 40 years, Professor Porsche and his followers have been refining this concept. Retaining what is sacred. Improving what can be. Never feeling limited by the typically accepted solutions.

For 1990, Porsche introduces a new showcase for this philosophy. A new-generation 911; the Carrera 2. With 85% new components, it is designed to once again set standards for what a car can, and should, be.

Outside, the now classic 911 silhouette lives on. Yet, subtle aerodynamic improvements reduce drag. New integrated bumpers soften the lines, harkening back to Professor Porsche's first car. And, since stylists felt that the

*The new Porsche 911 Carrera 2 Coupe.*

aesthetic ideal would be to have a spoiler only when needed, a typically Porsche solution was found: An automatic spoiler which rises at 50 mph, but retracts again at 6 mph.

The rear engine remains, but now with twin spark plugs and a sophisticated new engine management system, resulting in 0 to 60 times a full half-second faster than its predecessor. Inspired by Porsche's remarkable Weissach axle created for the 928, a new live rear axle self-corrects for toe-in under hard acceleration and cornering.

But perhaps most remarkable is the 911 Carrera 2 with Tiptronic dual-function transmission. This model boasts Porsche's breakthrough gearbox which lets the driver choose either full automatic, or clutchless manual shifting. Based on the electronic shifter in Porsche's legendary 962 racing car, the Tiptronic shifts faster than 95% of drivers are capable of with a clutch. With no let-up in power.

Experience this latest package of non-conformity at your authorized Porsche dealership. We do not, however, recommend that during your test-drive you break any rules yourself.

# Legend has it that whenever a new Porsche is being created, you can hear the sound of rules breaking.

For over a quarter century, the Porsche 911 has been a hallmark of power and performance. A rear-engine, race-inspired car which has often been said to be almost alive. And which would allow gifted drivers to coax from it an experience nothing else on the road could offer.

For anyone who took part, the rewards were nearly spiritual. For others, it remained an enticing enigma: desirable, yet with all that power hooked to a 5-speed stick, not quite right for their daily lives and commutes.

It is for both groups that we now introduce our new-generation 911 Carrera 2 with Tiptronic dual-function transmission. The breakthrough Tiptronic lets you choose either full automatic, or clutchless manual shifting. Making this Carrera 2 truly a car for any time, any place and any driver.

A two-channel shifter puts a traditional automatic channel on the left. Just put it in drive and go. (For you, simple. What it actually does is highly complex. We'll get back to that.)

For manual shifting, slip the shifter to the right, into a channel marked "+" for upshifts, and "–" for downshifts. Then simply "tip" the shifter up or back. Based on the electronic gearbox in our legendary 962 race car, the Tiptronic allows instantaneous, clutchless manual shifts with no let-up in power. In actual track testing with our seasoned Porsche test-drivers, 8 of 10 had faster lap times with the Tiptronic in manual mode than they had with a straight stick.

Meanwhile, back to the automatic. A sophisticated match of computer and sensors, it is what we call a "thinking" or "adaptive" transmission. Unlike simple automatics that might let you select normal, sport or economy driving with a lever or switch, the Tiptronic every 30 to 100 milliseconds measures vehicle speed, engine speed, throttle action and both forward and lateral acceleration.

Then, the computer automatically selects from five different shifting programs or maps, continuously adapting its shift patterns to the speed and style with which you are driving.

We could tell you more, but this is one of those things where you really have to be there. The only way to fully appreciate the revolutionary performance of the Tiptronic is to feel it, with a test-drive at your authorized Porsche dealership.

We promise you'll find it a stimulating experience. Except, perhaps, for your left leg.

*Porsche's revolutionary Tiptronic clutchless transmission.*

# Now you can drive it with one leg tied behind your back.

It's been over 100 years since the first noisy, bone-jarring "horseless carriages" rolled out of sheds onto dusty streets and lanes.

Through the ensuing decades, the basic principle has changed little. Now and then, however, a car has emerged so inspired in its concept, its design, its handling and use of power, that it has been labeled a turning point, or milestone. Worthy of preservation. Collectable. Especially when produced in limited numbers.

Today, in an era that has become sadly synonymous with homogeneity and derivative products, the Porsche 911 Carrera 4 is just such a refreshing, visionary achievement.

The world's first production sports car with electronic all-wheel drive, the Carrera 4 once again expands the boundaries of what is possible.

The all-wheel drive is an adaptive, intelligent system. Using computer-controlled sensors, it continuously monitors traction at all 4 wheels. Upon sensing wheel spin, within 25 thousandths of a second it directs power to the wheels having more traction, correcting slip usually before the driver can even sense it.

In other words, you're not really aware of the system working. Only of an incredible level of control.

This, after all, is

*The 1990 Porsche 911 Carrera 4 Coupe.*

what a landmark automobile does. Redefines the potential of the category. The Carrera 4 takes traditional sports car notions and, without changing them, elevates them. Not just power but, through adhesion, more useable power. Not just handling, but new thresholds of agility and performance on any surface.

The car is laden with other refinements and innovations as well. Like a new, self-correcting rear axle. And an integrated spoiler which rises at 50 mph and retracts again at 6 mph. Of course, there are the other collectable traits associated with Porsche for so long. The timeless 911 silhouette. And Porsche's legendary handcrafted construction. Over 4 working days are spent for welding alone. The painting process is 26 steps. Engines are bench-built by hand.

Considering its complexity and the love and precision with which each 911 Carrera 4 is assembled, we will make relatively small numbers of these available.

For those who find that even more of an enticement, we suggest you try and find one to test-drive at your authorized Porsche dealer soon. Unless you opt to take your chances on the age-old Porsche fantasy of discovering one squirreled away in a barn somewhere. In about, let's say, the year 2017.

# Classic car collectors can now take comfort knowing there will still, in coming years, be something to collect.

CONSUMER NEWSPAPER
OVER 600 LINES: CAMPAIGN

188
ART DIRECTOR
Tom Lichtenheld
WRITER
John Stingley
PHOTOGRAPHERS
Stock, Tom Connors
CLIENT
World Monitor
AGENCY
Fallon McElligott/Minneapolis

189
ART DIRECTOR
Steve Dunn
WRITER
Tim Delaney
CLIENT
Courtauld Institute
AGENCY
Leagas Delaney/London

# One of our writers on China knows so much, we can't begin to tell you about him.

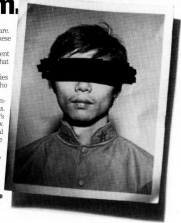

In June 1989, he was a student protesting in Tiananmen Square. He avoided the tanks. He avoided arrest. Now, incredibly, he's a Chinese ministry official, pushing democracy from the inside.

When we wanted an article on China one year after the student uprising, he was perfect to write it. Who is he? We can't tell you. That was part of the deal.

At World Monitor magazine, we believe highly involved stories call for highly involved writers. Experts who have been there. Who possess unique knowledge, and understand its significance.

We go wherever we have to in the world to find them. From Communist officials, to American schoolteachers, to former presidents. Then, we let them explain things in their own words. For an insider's perspective no journalist could uncover in a traditional interview.

It's the kind of insight needed to understand complex global issues. That's why the people you find reading World Monitor, like the people who write for it, are leaders. Individuals looking for informed assessments and speculation on what may come next, so they can prosper in the global village we all now share.

World Monitor. Conceived, created and followed by those who understand that in today's world there is, more than ever, no substitute for experience.

**WORLD MONITOR** THE CHRISTIAN SCIENCE MONITOR, MONTHLY **Where the people in the news report the news.**

# "I'm sorry this article is late. I've had a little trouble writing."

As eastern European dictatorships fell, Romania remained one of the last to repress its people.

Just before Ceausescu was toppled, we at World Monitor magazine sought to shed some light on totalitarianism, focusing on this isolated country. We searched, and found a writer who's spent a lot of time in tyrannical regimes. And a lot of time under arrest. She was jailed repeatedly while working on this article. And provided a first-hand account of the paranoia which ultimately brings such governments down. (In Romania, she discovered that a sample from every single typewriter in the country was kept on file by the secret police.)

At World Monitor, we believe it's this inside perspective that's needed to comprehend complex global issues. Because only through such personal experience can there be true understanding.

We find experts who have been a part of the story. Then we have them tell it in their own words. Be it a Communist official, a former president or an American schoolteacher. All three of whom have written for us. Sharing valuable insights.

That's why those who read World Monitor, like those who write for it, are leaders. People who want the most accurate international assessments, as well as speculation on what to expect next. So they can survive and thrive as the world becomes smaller for all of us.

World Monitor. For those who know that power comes from knowledge. And that the most powerful knowledge comes, unquestionably, from experience.

**WORLD MONITOR** THE CHRISTIAN SCIENCE MONITOR, MONTHLY **Where the people in the news report the news.**

# Frequently, our writers are people who lost their previous job.

On the eve of the 1988 presidential election two former presidents, Carter and Ford, penned letters of advice and counsel to be delivered to the winner.

But they didn't mail them. They gave them to us.

That's because they wrote the letters in response to a request from World Monitor magazine. A request to share their vision of what the new leader could expect. A vision that could come only from having held the job.

At World Monitor, we believe that to truly understand today's complex global issues, you go to the people who have been involved behind closed doors. And let them explain things in their own words.

That's why whatever the story, we search for an expert to write it. From an insider's perspective. And go wherever in the world we have to in order to find them. Be it a Chinese government official, a former KGB officer or an American schoolteacher.

It's a search for insights no journalist could ever uncover in a newsroom.

For instance, Gerald Ford foresaw that the Berlin Wall could come down in the upcoming presidency. (Remember, this was in October of 1988, even before the election.)

And that's why the people you find reading World Monitor, like the people who write for it, are leaders. Individuals trying to grasp all the dynamics at play; to survive and prosper in the global village we now share.

World Monitor. Where those who have been there, and those on their way, come together. To write. To read. And to think. Bound by the notion that there is still no substitute for experience.

**WORLD MONITOR** THE CHRISTIAN SCIENCE MONITOR, MONTHLY **Where the people in the news report the news.**

# They didn't suffer poverty, illness and destitution to be remembered for their tablemats.

Oh, the gay romantic lives of the great artists.

Poverty drove Claude Monet to attempt suicide. And an equally impoverished Renoir to deliver him scraps of his left over food.

Van Gogh had hallucinations which terrorised him throughout his life and resulted in him succeeding where Monet failed. He died of a self-inflicted gun shot wound in 1890.

Gauguin nearly starved to death in the Paris winter of 1886. He recovered long enough to allow him to visit Panama, where a fever nearly killed him.

Toulouse-Lautrec who was disfigured and stunted during his childhood died of, amongst other things, alcoholism and syphilis.

And yet these poor wretches, often scorned by both society and the artistic community are today household names.

Indeed, many are household items.

Tablemats, chocolate boxes, greeting cards. Works by the great masters adorn them all.

In fact, for many people it is the only place they have ever seen some of the world's great masterpieces.

But is a tablemat really the best place to view Van Gogh's wonderfully exaggerated use of colour?

Is it possible to appreciate the tones and colours of Monet's landscapes on a greetings card measuring five inches by four?

Should Renoir's softer, more delicate paintings simply be the means by which the lid of a chocolate box is made 'pretty'?

Of course not.

Now, mercifully, a new gallery has opened in London which offers everyone the chance to see many of the most famous paintings of the Impressionist period as they were meant to be seen.

The Courtauld Collection has recently moved from Woburn Square to the North Block of Somerset House in the Strand, London.

One of England's finest monuments to neo-classical architecture, it is a fitting home for what is undoubtedly one of the most remarkable collections of paintings in the world.

Degas. Cézanne. Renoir. Gauguin. Seurat. Pissarro. Manet. Monet. Works that would have Japanese tycoons reaching for their cheque books before you could say 'Jacques Robinson' are liberally sprinkled throughout a collection which has never been seen in its entirety before.

And who exactly bought with such taste and vision? Whose eagle-eye spotted these renowned canvasses when all others were spurning them?

The man who appropriately gave his name to the collection: Samuel Courtauld.

As heir to the Courtauld textile fortune, he certainly had the wherewithal to become a collector.

But no one meeting this rather quiet, non-intellectual businessman could ever have guessed that he possessed such unerring and courageous artistic judgement.

For, as their sorry tales indicate only too clearly, the Impressionists were not always as sought after as they are today.

But this lack of endorsement by the artistic establishment did not deter Samuel Courtauld.

In the years between 1922 and 1932, he indulged in a spending spree which included the acquisition of works by practically all the major Impressionists, including the purchase of no fewer than twelve Cézannes and twelve Seurats.

He also swooped to buy recognised masterpieces from under the noses of better-known and wealthier collectors.

Renoir's 'La Loge', for instance, which was shown at the very first Impressionists Exhibition in 1874. And Manet's last great masterpiece 'A Bar at the Folies-Bergère'.

No doubt you will recognise many of these paintings when you see them hanging unassumingly on the walls of their new home.

And understand, perhaps for the first time, that for tablemats they make possible works of art.

The nearest Tube Stations to Somerset House are Temple, Holborn and Aldwych (during the rush hours). Waterloo and Charing Cross British Rail Stations are within walking distance.

Admission is £2.50. Concessions, £1.00. Open 10am to 6pm Monday to Saturday, 2pm to 6pm Sunday. Late opening Tuesdays, 6pm to 8pm, July to September by courtesy of Mobil.

Finally, the Courtauld Institute Galleries would not have been possible without the following generous sponsors: Pearson, Arthur Andersen, Courtaulds, Citibank, IBM and Toray Industries.

**Courtauld Institute Galleries**

---

# Like a lot of millionaires, Samuel Courtauld surrounded himself with beautiful women.

Samuel Courtauld had a somewhat puritanical upbringing.

As heir to the Courtauld textile business, he was neither short of money nor pressures to conform.

Thus, the early years of his life followed a traditional path.

Public school, then travel to broaden the mind. Exactly how broad a mind it was did not come fully to light until he started collecting paintings.

In the ten years between 1922 and 1932, this non-intellectual, rather self-effacing industrialist purchased one of the most remarkable collections of paintings in the world.

Degas. Cézanne. Monet. Gauguin. Seurat. Pissarro. Toulouse-Lautrec. Renoir. Works by all the masters of Impressionism were snapped up, either for his own collection or by the Tate Gallery using a donation he made in 1923.

He bought with conviction and vision.

Late 19th century French paintings, many of which are beyond even Japanese tycoons' pockets today, were deemed brave and innovative purchases in the 1920's.

Which is probably why during his spending spree, he was able to acquire no fewer than twelve Cézannes and twelve Seurats, including Seurat's outstanding 'Une Baignade, Asnières'.

He was also prepared to buy recognised masterpieces.

Renoir's 'La Loge' for which the artist's brother posed with a Montmartre model, was originally sold by Renoir for a mere 425 francs, money he desperately needed to pay the rent.

It cost considerably more than that when it joined the Courtauld Collection in 1925 but somewhat less than the tens of millions of dollars it would fetch at auction in New York today.

And when Manet's last great masterpiece 'A Bar at the Folies-Bergère' became available in 1926 it was Samuel Courtauld who bought it, not the Louvre.

This splendid picture, full of deliberate spatial and iconic ambiguities, is perhaps the greatest work in a unique collection which also includes such masterpieces as 'Nevermore' by Gauguin, 'Portrait of the Artist with Bandaged Ear' Vincent van Gogh's famous self-portrait, along with works by Modigliani, Gainsborough, Daumier, Tiepolo

Monet and many other great painters.

Until recently, a great number of these important pictures were not on permanent display. But fortunately that has changed.

Now, after years of restricted access, the entire Courtauld Collection is moving to a magnificent new home and going on public view.

Appropriately, its new setting is itself a work of rare importance which has been saved for the nation by generous benefactions.

The North Block of Somerset House in the Strand, London, is one of the great monuments of neo-classical architecture in England.

After an Appeal was launched in 1984, this previously empty and neglected building has been restored to its former glory.

It is now a fitting place to house both the Courtauld Institute Galleries and the Institute itself with its 250 students, extensive photographic archives, the Witt and Book Libraries and conservation research laboratories.

A university institute and a gallery, both of international standing, will be combined for the first time under one roof.

Fortunately, the example set by Samuel Courtauld has meant that many other collections given by benefactors will also be shown at the new Gallery.

So whether you are a scholar wishing to be further educated and enlightened, or someone who gains intellectual and aesthetic pleasure from works of art, or simply someone who admires beautiful paintings, there is now a new place in the centre of London for you to pursue your particular pleasure.

The nearest Tube Stations to Somerset House are Temple, Holborn and Aldwych (during the rush hours). British Rail Stations are within walking distance.

Admission is £2.50. Concessions, £1.00. Open 10am to 6pm Monday to Saturday, 2pm to 6pm Sunday. Late opening Tuesdays, 6pm to 8pm, July to September by courtesy of Mobil.

Finally, the Courtauld Institute Galleries would not have been possible without the following generous sponsors: Pearson, Arthur Andersen, Courtaulds, Citibank, IBM and Toray Industries.

**Courtauld Institute Galleries**

---

# Christ has risen again. This time from a basement in Woburn Square.

It happened one June day this year in one of the quieter corners of Central London.

Only a handful of people knew about it. Even fewer witnessed it.

The fact that it occurred at all was undoubtedly a miracle.

A priceless collection of paintings, drawings and prints, including some of the most important masterpieces of religious art, were taken out of storage, painstakingly wrapped, crated and transported two miles across town to the Strand.

That they arrived safely was not the point. That their new home was ready to accept them certainly was.

For the destination of the world-famous Courtauld Collection was the North Block of Somerset House.

Despite its significance as one of the country's finest monuments to neo-classical architecture, the building had been empty and neglected for years.

Built in 1780, its magnificent rooms had been the original home of the Royal Academy.

What better place than for a collection that had its inception in Woburn Square gallery than many of the works owned by the Courtauld were rarely, if ever, seen by the public. So, as in the custom nowadays, an Appeal was launched.

Save the North Block. And provide a fitting home for the renowned Courtauld Institutes' Collection in the process.

Six years and many millions of pounds of benefactors' money later, a series of meticulously renovated galleries now house one of the most remarkable collections of art in the world.

Walking around, it is as though every universally-known painting is on view.

Manet's last great work 'A Bar at the Folies-Bergère', van Gogh's faintly macabre 'Portrait of the Artist with bandaged ear'. Gauguin's 'Nevermore'. Cézanne's 'The Card Players'. Seurat's 'The Bridge at Courbevoie'. Renoir's 'La Loge'. Degas' 'Two Dancers on the Stage'.

Room after room. Masterpiece after masterpiece. From Bernardo Daddi's richly coloured 'Polyptych: S. Giorgio a Ruballa', which has not been on view for over a decade, to John Hoyland's 'Downland' painted in 1978.

From the religious art of Albertinelli, Rubens and Van Dyck to the Impressionists Manet and Toulouse-Lautrec; to works by Nicholson and Sutherland.

And who do we have to thank for the privilege of surveying so many wonderful works of art?

The man who rightly gave his name to the Institute: Samuel Courtauld.

The head of the famous textile firm, he patiently used the same shrewd commercial sense to acquire paintings as he did to run his company.

In the years between 1922 and 1932, he purchased works by all the major Impressionists despite the fact that they were by no means as popular then as they are now.

In a particularly far-sighted splurge, he bought no fewer than twelve Cézannes and twelve Seurats, including the famous 'Une Baignade, Asnières', which now hangs in the National Gallery.

But Courtauld was not only a perceptive and enthusiastic collector, he also acted as a catalyst for other benefactors.

Viscount Lee of Fareham, bequeathed many important paintings including Bellini's 'Assassination of St Peter Martyr'.

Count Antoine Seilern's bequest, comprised oils by Rubens, Pissaro and Tiepolo.

Roger Fry, Lillian Browse and Thomas Gambier Parry also donated rare collections.

The results of their generosity, and that of many others, can now be seen hanging on the walls of Somerset House. A visit is definitely recommended.

Who knows, when you see Rubens' 'The Entombment of Christ' you may have a deeply profound religious experience.

And then, like the subject, you'll come back one day.

The nearest Tube Stations to Somerset House are Temple, Holborn and Aldwych (during the rush hours). Waterloo and Charing Cross British Rail Stations are within walking distance.

Admission is £2.50. Concessions, £1.00. Open 10am to 6pm Monday to Saturday, 2pm to 6pm Sunday. Late opening Tuesdays, 6pm to 8pm, July to September by courtesy of Mobil.

Finally, the Courtauld Institute Galleries would not have been possible without the following generous sponsors: Pearson, Arthur Andersen, Courtaulds, Citibank, IBM and Toray Industries.

**Courtauld Institute Galleries**

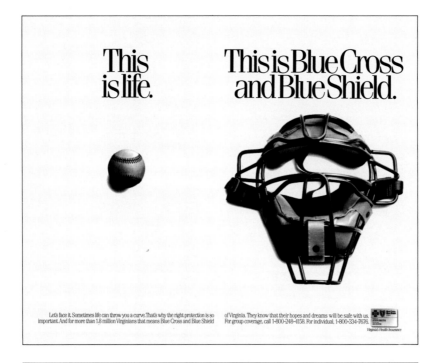

# A good leather coat should have two arms and fifty feet.

In this world, there are many things that can be mass-produced.

But not a coat like this.

Not a coat that requires over fifty feet of the finest calfskin available anywhere on earth. Calfskin so perfect it can be tanned as is with vegetable oils. Never painted or color corrected.

Not a coat whose every square inch has undergone the most expensive, most effective waterproofing known to man. A process in which we flood the leather with a special waterproof compound while it is being tanned in the drum, not afterwards.

This is the only technique that insures total penetration of the waterproofing agent. The only technique good enough for a garment that bears our name.

Not a coat whose comfort seems to increase the more you put it under the stress of active use. Because of the extra feet of calfskin, the extra hours of tailoring we spend opening up the back and shoulder dimensions. Adding features such as two-piece underarm gussets to maximize your freedom of movement.

And certainly not a coat whose detailing is so meticulous that every zipper is milled and tumbled smooth so as to not injure the leather, every button is genuine horn or brass, and every buttonhole is both calfskin bound and clean-finished with stitching inside and out.

In leather coats that lack this latter feature, shreds of lining will begin to emerge in a matter of months. But Timberland designers do not think in terms of months. They take a longer view of product longevity. Setting their sights on a decade or two. Or more.

There is a method to our madness, and it is perfectly clear. We will do anything for the extra comfort and confidence of our customers.

Confidence, for example, that getting caught in a sudden downpour won't spoil your day or your valuable calfskin investment. Confidence that on the night your buddy spills a beer on your sleeve, you'll need to do nothing more than find a little water and a sponge.

The way we see it, consumer confidence is as hard to come by, in this age of shoddy products, as the world's highest quality calfskin.

Like our leather coats and jackets, it can't be mass-produced.

**Boots, shoes, clothing, wind, water, earth and sky.**

---

# The Marines say Parris Island is the world's toughest boot camp. We beg to differ.

Everyone knows it takes weeks of hell to turn out a few good Leathernecks.

But how many people know what it takes to turn out a few good leather boots? Boots as waterproof as canteens, yet as comfortable as slippers.

You can find out fast at the world's toughest boot camp. A place called Timberland.

There we have devised tests that make the Chinese water torture seem like a walk in the park.

In one particularly grueling ordeal, we put a mass of water behind pieces of boot leather.

We then flex the leather again and again, simulating the movements the human foot might make were it slogging through a similar mass of water deep in no man's land.

After flexing each piece sixteen thousand times, we accept only one result. No leakage whatsoever. A single drop and the leather is rejected. No appeals, no second chances.

The truth is, rejections don't happen very often. Our method of waterproofing leather has been perfected over a period of twenty years, and it's the most expensive process known to man.

First, we cherrypick the world's leather supply, selecting only the cream of the crop. Then we flood every fiber of the leather, inside and out, with a special silicone waterproofing agent. We do this during the actual tanning so as not to miss a single space big enough for a water molecule to sneak in.

(We could practice shortcuts, such as brushing the surface of the leather with silicone. But then we'd be like any other boot company.)

Another torture test involves our so-called "boot within a boot," your ultimate insurance of dry, comfortable feet under the worst, wettest, coldest conditions.

The boot within a boot is actually a sock constructed of waterproof Gore-Tex, Thinsulate® insulation and smooth Cambrelle.

We take this innocent-looking sock and give it the infamous bubble test. We fill it with air, submerge it in a glass water tank, and we watch. One air bubble and the sock is sacked. Period.

Besides these and a multitude of other trials and tests, we construct our boots by impermeably bonding the upper to the midsole, creating a water-tight cradle around your foot. We keep seams to a minimum, and sew each stress point with no fewer than four rows of waterproof nylon lock stitching.

So, when a size 12 guide boot says Timberland on it, you know you can put it through anything.

Because it's already been there.

**Boots, shoes, clothing, wind, water, earth and sky.**

---

# This shoe has 342 holes. How do you make it waterproof?

Wherever you look in our footwear line, you find holes.

You find wingtips with scores of stylishly arranged perforations.

You find handsewns with scores of needle holes. Moccasins. Canoe moccasins. Boat shoes. Ultralights for easy walking. Lightweight comfort casuals for weightless walking.

Built by a lesser waterproofer, each of these styles has enough openings to admit a deluge.

But we're the Timberland company, and you have to understand where we got our start. Over twenty years ago, we were exclusively a boot manufacturer, and we were the first people to successfully produce fine leather sporting boots that were totally waterproof.

The lessons we learned then are why we're able, today, to build wingtips and handsewns you could go wading in.

Lesson one. Select only the cream of the world's leather crop, then spend the money to impregnate every pore with silicone at the same time the leather is being tanned in the drum. (We leave the shortcuts to our competitors, the ones who merely brush the surface with silicone after the leather is tanned. And the consequences, unfortunately, we leave to their customers.)

Lesson two. Be inventive. It takes more than one technology to stop water.

For example, to build a waterproof wingtip, we take a page right out of the old Timberland bootmaker's manual. We bond the upper directly to the midsole, creating an impermeable seal around your foot.

Then we build a special umbrella under those stylish wing perforations. It's actually a "shoe within a shoe."

A bootie lining of our softest saddle glove leather, fully waterproofed with silicone. Guaranteed to stop a monsoon.

Handsewns require a different solution, but one that also harks back to our boot days, when we became an early collaborator of the W.L. Gore Company, creators of waterproof, breathable Gore-Tex™ fabric.

To waterproof the needle holes of a handsewn moc, we use an exclusive technique in which Timberland saddle glove leather is laminated to a Gore-Tex bootie. Once we place this inside the moc, you have a shoe that's an open and shut success. Open to air and shut tight to water. Climate-controlled, in other words, both inside and out.

So even if it never leaves the canyons of Wall Street, every Timberland waterproof shoe owes its character to a world that will never see a sidewalk. The canyons, tundras and marshlands where our boots were born.

Which makes Timberland shoes more than waterproof.

They're water proven.

**Boots, shoes, clothing, wind, water, earth and sky.**

191

CONSUMER NEWSPAPER
OVER 600 LINES: CAMPAIGN

192
**ART DIRECTOR**
John Schmidt
**WRITER**
Jim Doherty
**PHOTOGRAPHER**
Stock
**CLIENT**
Heartlink
**AGENCY**
Zwiren Collins Karo Trusk &
Ayer/Chicago

CONSUMER NEWSPAPER
600 LINES OR LESS: SINGLE

193
**ART DIRECTOR**
Michael J. Campbell
**WRITER**
Mark S. Burk
**CLIENT**
Atlanta Pawn Center
**AGENCY**
Adguys/New York

194
**ART DIRECTOR**
Paul Norwood
**WRITER**
Court Crandall
**ILLUSTRATOR**
Paul Norwood
**CLIENT**
Atlantic Exterminators
**AGENCY**
Admen Against Big Logos/
El Segundo

195
**ART DIRECTOR**
Barton Landsman
**WRITER**
Amy Krouse Rosenthal
**CLIENT**
Riverside Chocolate Factory
**AGENCY**
Boy & Girl Advertising/Chicago

196
**ART DIRECTOR**
Barton Landsman
**WRITER**
Amy Krouse Rosenthal
**CLIENT**
Riverside Chocolate Factory
**AGENCY**
Boy & Girl Advertising/Chicago

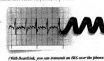

192

# Are pawn shops reputable?

## Let's just say we're no Savings & Loan.

If you've ever wondered whether pawn shops were
reputable places to borrow money, think about this.
Last year American banks made billions of dollars in bad loans.
We haven't made a bad one yet. Because when we loan you money
it's in exchange for something that's already yours.
And we'll hold it for you until you pay us back.
In fact, 90% of people who bring in items for loans do exactly that.
So, if you need money, come visit us for a loan. And if you're
still hung up about pawn shops, just think of us as a bank that says yes.

## ATLANTA PAWN CENTER

Main Location
2581 Piedmont Road
Lindbergh Plaza
266-2300

4960 Buford Highway
458-5777

3328 Buford Highway
633-0020

193

# It wouldn't be the first time you used the newspaper to kill bugs.

$10.00              $10.00

## $10.00 Off

Why take things into your own hands, when you
can call Atlantic Exterminating at 985-7716 instead?
We'll save you a few bucks and a lot of hassle.

**Atlantic EXTERMINATING** COMPANY INC

$10.00

194

---

No one ever went
to their death bed saying,
"You know, I wish
I'd eaten more rice cakes."

Riverside Chocolate Factory
An old-fashioned candy shop at 2234 N. Clark. Open 7 days 10-7.

195

---

Not until you've
tried one of our homemade
ice cream bars will you
fully understand the purpose
of having a mouth.

Riverside Chocolate Factory
An old-fashioned candy shop at 2234 N. Clark. Open 7 days 10-7.

196

# Most vacations are designed to leave your troubles behind.
# Ours will help you deal with them when you get back.

You can't run away from your problems, because sooner or later they'll find you. So stop running and deal with them before they deal with you.

The Canadian Outward Bound Wilderness School provides you with a vacation alternative that can help you cope with anything life throws you.

We combine outdoor challenges, skills training and adventure to enhance your self-reliance, confidence and compassion.

The courses take place on Black Sturgeon Lake, 160 km northeast of Thunder Bay. Far from traffic, pollution and the rat race they create. You'll undertake a voyage of self-discovery in the middle of unspoiled nature.

In the winter, the lakes and forests of Northern Ontario take on a seldom seen beauty and present a slew of special challenges. They include cross country skiing, snow shoeing, dog sledding, building snow shelters, learning first aid, orienteering and spending up to 24 hours alone reflecting.

We provide all special winter gear and course fees are tax deductible. For more information on the Canadian Outward Bound Wilderness School call toll free 1-800-268-7329 (in Toronto call 787-1721). This course isn't easy, but then again neither is life.

## The Outward Bound Winter Experience.

197

# Most of you will have cold feet before you finish this ad.

The temperature on an Outward Bound Winter Experience ranges from 0 to minus 30 degrees celsius. The snow accumulates to approximately 336 centimeters. Activities on the trail include cross country skiing, snowshoeing, dogsledding, building snow shelters, learning first aid, orienteering and spending up to 24 hours alone reflecting.

So why would you spend your winter vacation on frigid Black Sturgeon Lake, 160 km northeast of Thunder Bay when you could be lying on a beach in Florida?

Because the only thing you'll have to bring back from your week stay in the sunshine state is a bag of oranges and the sand you'll never quite get out of your shoes.

With Outward Bound the souvenirs you take home will last a lifetime. You'll learn more about yourself than how good you look with a tan. You'll learn how to lead and how to follow, how to succeed in a team and as an individual.

You might also be asking yourself, who will teach all of this? Well, the wilderness is our classroom. Rocks, forests, rivers and lakes are our teaching tools. It is through this environ-ment and Outward Bound activities we strive to develop an understanding and appreciation of ourselves, others and our fragile planet. In other words, with a little help from us you'll discover most of it on your own.

This course isn't something you do on a whim, it's physical, challenging and demands commitment. But then again, you only get out of life what you put in. If you still have cold feet

after reading this ad, don't worry, we'll provide the mukluks and parkas. Course fees are tax deductible. So, for more information on the Canadian Outward Bound Wilderness School call toll free 1-800-268-7329 (in Toronto call 787-1721).

## The Outward Bound Winter Experience.

198

Melt Hearts, Not Walls.
Lavoris
Helps remove plaque. Absolutely obliterates bad breath.

199

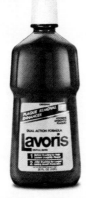

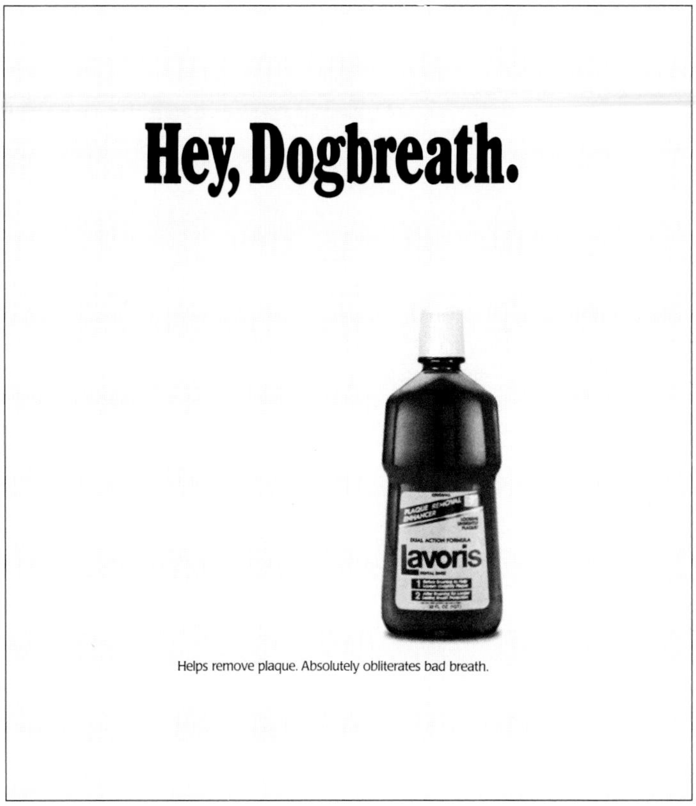

Hey, Dogbreath.
Lavoris
Helps remove plaque. Absolutely obliterates bad breath.

200

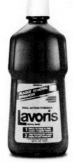

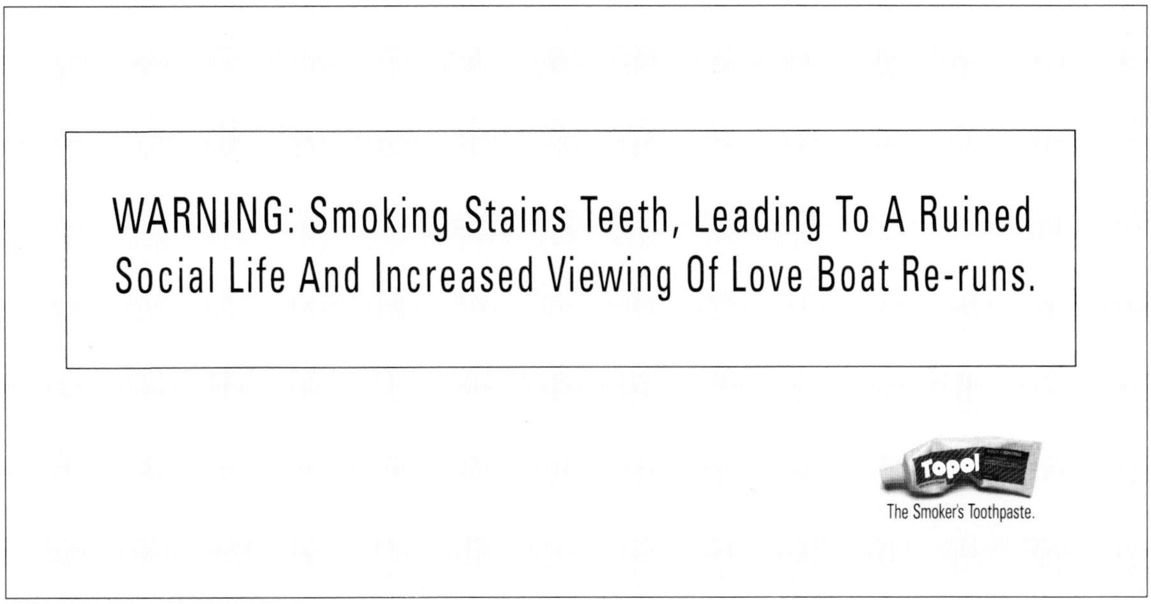

WARNING: Smoking Stains Teeth, Leading To A Ruined Social Life And Increased Viewing Of Love Boat Re-runs.
Topol
The Smoker's Toothpaste.

201

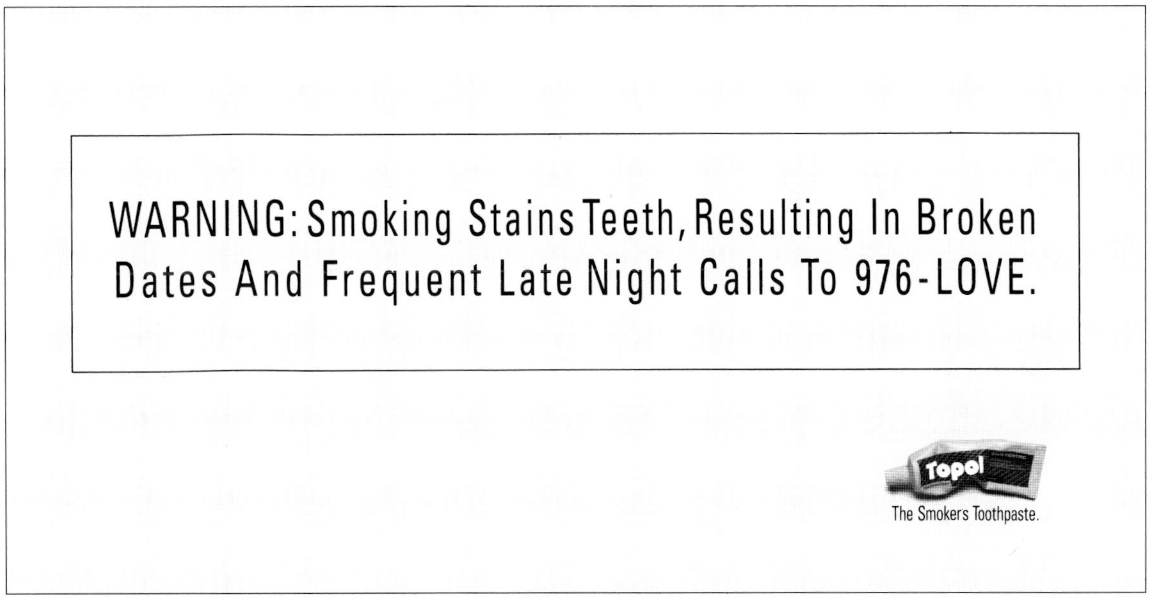

WARNING: Smoking Stains Teeth, Resulting In Broken Dates And Frequent Late Night Calls To 976-LOVE.
Topol
The Smokers Toothpaste.

202

# I DON'T DO FLOORS.
# I DON'T DO TOILETS.
# I DON'T DO DUSTING.
# I DON'T DO TUBS.
# I DON'T DO LAUNDRY.
# I DON'T DO WOODWORK.
# I DON'T DO VACUUMING.
# I DON'T DO BRASS.
# I DON'T DO DRAPES.
# I DON'T DO SILVER.
# I DON'T DO CARPETS.
# I DON'T DO OVENS.
# I DON'T DO SWEEPING.
# I DON'T DO DISHES.
# I DON'T DO TILE.
# I DON'T DO WAXING.
# I DON'T DO GROUT.
# I DON'T DO CHROME.
# I DON'T DO IRONING.
# I DON'T DO LUNCH.

**WINDOW CLEANERS**
Call 353-4087 anytime.
Ask for Dave.

203

## Can you guess the weight of this ten-ton elephant?

Correct answers and near misses
are entitiled to $1 bar drinks and $.50 tap beers any
Monday through Friday between 4 and 6.

### Meister's
SCANDIA
Where smart people go to get stupid.

204

**CONSUMER NEWSPAPER**
**600 LINES OR LESS: SINGLE**

**209**
**ART DIRECTOR**
Bob Brihn
**WRITER**
Bruce Bildsten
**PHOTOGRAPHER**
Rick Dublin
**CLIENT**
Porsche Cars North America
**AGENCY**
Fallon McElligott/Minneapolis

**210**
**ART DIRECTOR**
Kim Cable
**WRITER**
Guy Lowe
**PHOTOGRAPHER**
Bryan Moreheade
**CLIENT**
Opti-World
**AGENCY**
Fitzgerald & Company/Atlanta

**211**
**ART DIRECTOR**
Don Miller
**WRITER**
Gary Cohen
**PHOTOGRAPHER**
Carl Furuta
**CLIENT**
Range Rover of North America
**AGENCY**
Grace & Rothschild/New York

**212**
**ART DIRECTOR**
Steve Sweitzer
**WRITER**
Todd Tilford
**PHOTOGRAPHER**
Dennis Fagan
**CLIENT**
Tabu Lingerie
**AGENCY**
GSD&M/Austin

**213**
**ART DIRECTOR**
Bob Barrie
**WRITERS**
Luke Sullivan, Pete Smith
**PHOTOGRAPHER**
Richard Boyd
**CLIENT**
Texas Tavern
**AGENCY**
Jack Smith Agency/Roanoke

**214**
**ART DIRECTOR**
Chris Poulin
**WRITER**
Jim Garaventi
**PHOTOGRAPHERS**
John Huet, Roger Birn
**CLIENT**
Anderson Little
**AGENCY**
Leonard Monahan Lubars & Kelly/Providence

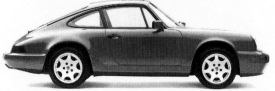

On January 1, the government is going to throw you a curve.
(Nobody handles curves better than Porsche.)
Avoid being put in a corner with a new luxury tax. Buy a Porsche before January 1 and you'll be able to handle that corner just fine.
PORSCHE®
PORSCHE ®

209

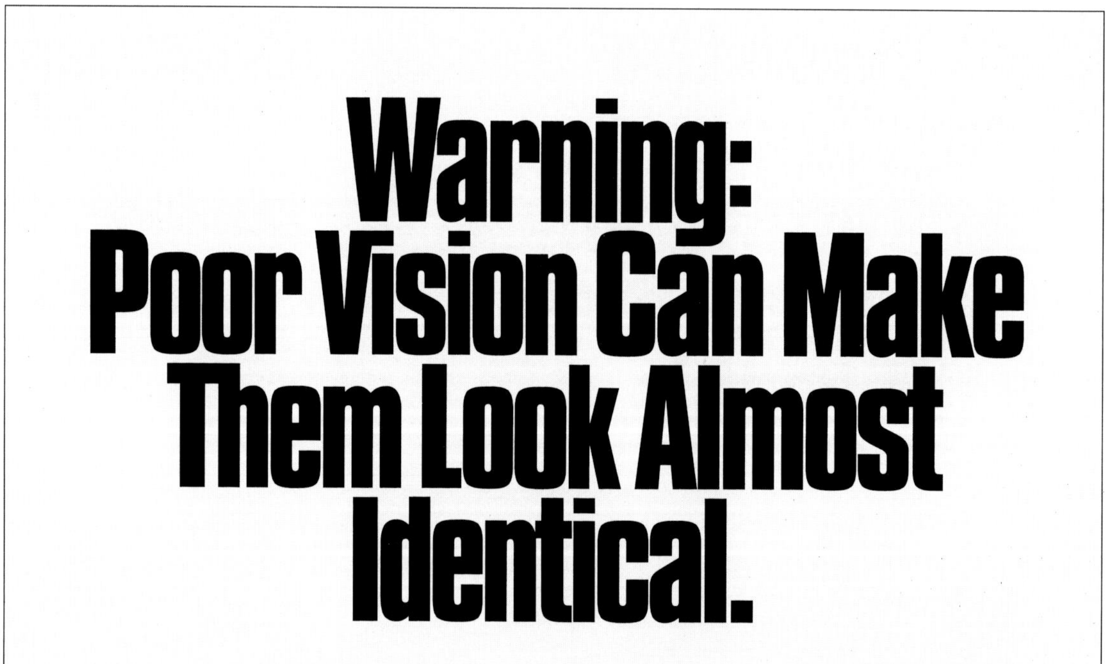

Warning: Poor Vision Can Make Them Look Almost Identical.
REGULAR-STRENGTH
Aim
GEL
PROVEN CAVITY PROTECTION
PREPARATION H
HEMORRHOIDAL OINTMENT
Pensacola • Tradewinds Shopping Center • 477-4500
OPTI-WORLD

210

Aim® is the registered trademark of Chesebrough-Pond's, Inc. PREPARATION H® is the registered trademark of WHITE HALL LABORATORIES, INC.

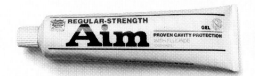

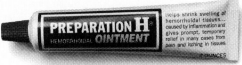

# The British have always driven on the wrong side of the road.

It's not that we can't get it right. We simply have our own way of doing things.

While other automobiles are either unusually rugged, or extravagantly civilized, we've made the one luxury car that isn't dependent on the luxury of a road.

Short of going across endangered terrain, there are very few places you won't see it.

Why not come in and test drive a Range Rover?

While it's hardly inexpensive, it's an investment you'll feel perfectly comfortable with. Whichever side of the road you're on.

TREAD LIGHTLY—DRIVE RESPONSIBLY OFF-ROAD.    PLEASE BUCKLE UP FOR SECURITY. © 1990 RANGE ROVER OF NORTH AMERICA, INC.

**RANGE ROVER**

**MONDAY NIGHT FOOTBALL HAS MET ITS MATCH.**

*Crossroads Center, 183 & Burnet, Mon.-Sat. 10-8, Sun. 12-6, 452-TABU*

**TABU**
*Lingerie*

# OUR CHILI RECIPE IS SO SECRET, EVEN WE DON'T KNOW WHAT'S IN IT.

**Texas Tavern**

*Serving the same old thing since 1930.*

Texas Tavern, 114 Church Avenue, Roanoke, VA 24011. Phone 342-4825. ©1990.

# SAVE 5% ON SWEATERS. OH HECK, IT'S CHRISTMAS— MAKE IT 50%.

While we're in this warm holiday spirit, we want everyone else to feel warm

**50% off sweaters now through Sunday.**

all over too. So between now and Sunday, we're taking 50% off our entire stock of $35 and $40 men's and women's sweaters. Whether you're giving or receiving, you'll find a wide selection of beautiful cardigans and pullovers to

keep everyone on your list warm. For women, there's ramie and cotton blends, lambswool and angora, hand-embroidered styles, and more. For men, there's handsome jacquard styles, vibrant patterns and colorful solids in cotton, cotton blends, wool and acrylic/wool blends. So what are you waiting for, Christmas?

**ANDERSON LITTLE**

*We're the perfect fit.*

# Why Should The Rich Get All The Brakes?

How much money you have in your bank account shouldn't determine how safe you feel on the road.

And if you purchase the new 1990 Subaru® Legacy,™ it won't.

The Subaru Legacy is one of the few affordable cars in the world with anti-lock brakes (ABS). A feature that pumps your brakes for maximum maneuverability under heavy braking.

It's a safety feature so valuable, some insurance companies will give you a refund on your premium if you buy a car with the ABS system.

Even without anti-lock brakes, the Subaru Legacy offers you one of the most advanced systems for controlling your car on the road today. With full time four wheel drive — a more civilized form of four wheel drive that gives you better handling and traction on four lane highways as well as one lane dirt roads. Power-assisted front and rear disc brakes. And four wheel independent suspension.

Of course, to many drivers, how fast they go is just as important as how fast they stop. So every Subaru Legacy is powered by a horizontally-opposed (for reduced vibration), aluminum (for more even heat distribution), single overhead camshaft, multi-point electronic fuel injected, 16 valve engine.

*Mercedes 190E with ABS Brakes, $31,600‡*

*Jaguar XJ6 with ABS Brakes, $39,700‡*

*BMW 535i with ABS Brakes, $42,310‡*

The Subaru Legacy was also designed to stand up to the very same conditions that have driven many cars into the ground.

In fact, 93% of all Subaru cars registered in America since 1979 are still on the road.* And a new Subaru may last even longer. A Subaru Legacy has broken the FIA world speed/endurance record by running 19 days at an average speed of 138.8 mph for more than 60,000 miles.**

Since the Subaru Legacy was designed to last a long time, it's available with a lot of things to make that time pass pleasantly. Including power sunroof, power windows and locks, lumbar support seats and an 80 watt AM/FM stereo radio.

And you get all of this for thousands of dollars less than the cost of many European luxury cars.

But the way we figure, along with the anti-lock brakes, you deserve a few other breaks as well.

*R.L. Polk & Co. Statistics, July 1, 1988. **Validated by the Federation Internationale De L'Automobile. ‡Suggested retail price. Does not include dealer preparation, inland transportation, taxes, license and state or title fees. Dealer's actual price may vary. †Based on manufacturer's suggested retail price.

## Subaru Legacy™
*We Built Our Reputation By Building A Better Car.*

*1990 Subaru Legacy with Full Time Four-Wheel Drive and ABS Brakes, from $18,914.†*

215

# MOST BALLPLAYERS NOLAN RYAN'S AGE ARE PITCHING HORSESHOES.

 TWINS VS. NOLAN RYAN & THE RANGERS. WED, 7:35 PM.

A FAMILY • TRADITION

216

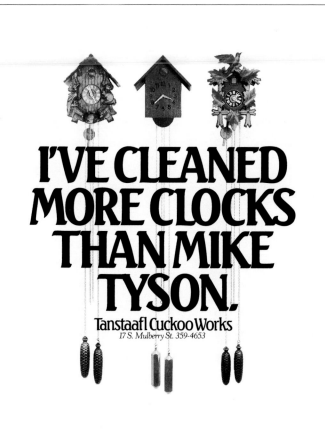

# I'VE CLEANED MORE CLOCKS THAN MIKE TYSON.

**Tanstaafl Cuckoo Works**
*17 S. Mulberry St. 359-4653*

217

---

# If You Think Your Office Furniture Is Such A Good Investment, Try Selling It.

The moment new furniture is driven off the showroom floor and parked in your office, serious depreciation sets in. That's why it rarely makes sense for a business to buy.

At more than 80 coast-to-coast showrooms, we'll show you how a modest monthly lease rate provides the same brand-name furniture with no large cash outlay, solid tax breaks, and a guarantee of satisfaction.

So call Cort today. It's one of the smartest investments you'll ever make.

**CORT. Furniture Rental**
*You handle the business. We'll handle the furniture.*

218

---

# A FEW YEARS AGO, WE LET THE BOYS STOP WEARING TIES. NEXT YEAR, WE'RE ALLOWING DRESSES.

This fall, Providence Country Day School is ready to enroll girls in grades 9–12, as well as boys in grades 5-12. If you're a student who would be interested in attending a school which has a friendly, caring environment, small classes, and outstanding teachers, we urge you to call our Director of Admissions Jack Kurty for additional information, at 401-438-5170. And no matter what clothes you wear on the outside, we think you'll find this is one school that will genuinely appreciate you for what you have on the inside.

**PROVIDENCE COUNTRY DAY SCHOOL IS NOW ENROLLING WOMEN.**

219

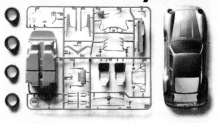

# I've had articles about awnings in *Fabrics* magazine. It's possible you missed them.

Thinking of awnings? Consult a published awning scholar.
I just happen to have the number of one right here. 841-0507.

## SOMMER AWNING COMPANY

---

**Some people inherit athletic ability.
Some people inherit musical talent.
Some people inherit mechanical skill.**

## I got awnings.

I'm a 4th generation awning man. You should see
what I learned growing up in their shadow. Call 841-0507.

### SOMMER AWNING COMPANY

---

**I know so much about awnings, you better hope you don't get stuck talking to me at a party.**

I've traveled the world learning my craft. Ask me anything.
If you have a few minutes. 841-0507.

### SOMMER AWNING COMPANY

**CONSUMER NEWSPAPER**
**600 LINES OR LESS: CAMPAIGN**

**225**
**ART DIRECTOR**
Paul Norwood
**WRITER**
Court Crandall
**ILLUSTRATOR**
Paul Norwood
**CLIENT**
Atlantic Exterminators
**AGENCY**
Admen Against Big Logos/
El Segundo

**226**
**ART DIRECTOR**
Barton Landsman
**WRITER**
Amy Krouse Rosenthal
**CLIENT**
Riverside Chocolate Factory
**AGENCY**
Boy & Girl Advertising/Chicago

# It wouldn't be the first time you used the newspaper to kill bugs.

$10.00      $10.00

## $10.00 Off

Why take things into your own hands, when you
can call Atlantic Exterminating at 985-7716 instead?
We'll save you a few bucks and a lot of hassle.

**Atlantic EXTERMINATING** COMPANY INC.

$10.00

# If this is your problem.

If you're looking for a way to solve your cockroach problem,
just call Atlantic Exterminating at 985-7716. We'll turn things around.

# This is our solution.

# A restaurant is often judged by who eats there.

Before a few bad customers ruin your restaurant's reputation,
call us at 985-7716. We'll make sure their next meal is their last.

**Atlantic EXTERMINATING** COMPANY INC.

# No one ever went to their death bed saying, "You know, I wish I'd eaten more rice cakes."

Riverside Chocolate Factory
An old-fashioned candy shop at 2234 N. Clark. Open 7 days 10-7.

---

# Not until you've tried one of our homemade ice cream bars will you fully understand the purpose of having a mouth.

Riverside Chocolate Factory
An old-fashioned candy shop at 2234 N. Clark. Open 7 days 10-7.

---

# Remember, aside from Shirley MacLaine, we only live once.

Riverside Chocolate Factory
An old-fashioned candy shop at 2234 N. Clark. Open 7 days 10-7.

CONSUMER NEWSPAPER
600 LINES OR LESS: CAMPAIGN

227
ART DIRECTORS
Steve St. Clair, Karen Prince
WRITERS
Jeff Odiorne, Jr., Isidoro Debellis
PHOTOGRAPHER
Supplied by Outward Bound
CLIENT
Outward Bound
AGENCY
Chiat/Day/Mojo, Toronto

228
ART DIRECTOR
Arty Tan
WRITER
Mike Gibbs
PHOTOGRAPHER
Jim Arndt
CLIENT
Icebox
AGENCY
Fallon McElligott/Minneapolis

# Most of you will have cold feet before you finish this ad.

The temperature on an Outward Bound Winter' Experience ranges from 0 to minus 30 degrees celsius. The snow accumulates to approximately 336 centimeters. Activities on the trail include cross country skiing, snowshoeing, dogsledding, building snow shelters, learning first aid, orienteering and spending up to 24 hours alone reflecting.

So why would you spend your winter vacation on frigid Black Sturgeon Lake, 160 km northeast of Thunder Bay when you could be lying on a beach in Florida?

Because the only thing you'll have to bring back from your week stay in the sunshine state is a bag of oranges and the sand you'll never quite get out of your shoes.

With Outward Bound the souvenirs you take home will last a lifetime. You'll learn more about yourself than how good you look with a tan. You'll learn how to lead and how to follow, how to succeed in a team and as an individual.

You might also be asking yourself, who will teach all of this? Well, the wilderness is our classroom. Rocks, forests, rivers and lakes are our teaching tools. It is through this environ-

ment and Outward Bound activities we strive to develop an understanding and appreciation of ourselves, others and our fragile planet. In other words, with a little help from us you'll discover most of it on your own.

This course isn't something you do on a whim, it's physical, challenging and demands commitment. But then again, you only get out of life what you put in. If you still have cold feet

after reading this ad, don't worry, we'll provide the mukluks and parkas. Course fees are tax deductible. So, for more information on the Canadian Outward Bound Wilderness School call toll free 1-800-268-7329 (in Toronto call 787-1721).

## The Outward Bound Winter Experience.

---

# Hell, frozen over.

Welcome to Dante's world. Otherwise known as Black Sturgeon Lake. 160 km northeast of Thunder Bay. Home to the Outward Bound Winter Experience. Where

you leave the comforts and securities of family and friends behind as you voyage into a world of adventure and self-discovery.

You'll travel through profound silence and remark at the chilling beauty that surrounds you. All the while, taking advantage of opportunities (some would call them that, anyway) that can only be found in the unspoiled wilderness of this distant land in the great white north.

Just you, nine other brave souls and two instructors. Outfitted with food, parkas, mukluks, overnights, cross country skis, snowshoes, sleeping bags, and back packs we provide. The courage, drive and stamina, you'll have to bring yourself.

As you journey through the land of fire and ice, you'll learn cross country skiing, snowshoeing, building snow shelters, and safety/ first aid procedures necessary to endure (and maybe even enjoy) this winter wilderness experience.

There are also two special experiences you may never get to do again in your life. One is the opportunity to work with our specially trained Huskies. You'll learn to mush, feed, and care for them while out on the trail. The other is to do a solo (up to 24 hrs.) where you go off alone to reflect. You're on your own on this one.

All course fees are tax deductible and you may even qualify for tuition assistance. Our number is 1-800-268-7329 (in Toronto 787-1721). So give us a shout. It's not like you have to sell your soul or anything.

## The Outward Bound Winter Experience.

---

# The alternative to Outward Bound is to head south for a tan.
## But a tan only lasts two weeks.

There are any number of ways to spend your precious holiday, so think carefully. After all, you only get a couple of weeks a year.

You could pack up and take a vacation somewhere warm. Or you could sign up for the Outward Bound Winter Experience and feel warm all over. Not just on the outside. It's a holiday where the temperatures will dip well below zero but your insides will glow with a burning desire to get to know other people

in a completely new way.

Just you, nine others, and two instructors. Facing the challenges and opportunities that can only be found on Black Sturgeon Lake (160 km northeast of Thunder Bay) in the winter. On the trail, you'll learn winter first aid, cross country skiing, snowshoeing, and the thrill of mushing a team of Huskies through

the profound silence of Canada's great white north. Ending in a solo (up to 24 hrs.) where you'll meet someone new. Yourself.

We provide all special winter gear and course fees are tax deductible. So, call 1-800-268-7329 (in Toronto 787-1721) for more information.

After all, which would you rather come back with? Some bad seashell souvenirs and a change of color on the outside. Or a complete change of you on the inside.

## The Outward Bound Winter Experience.

ICEBOX Custom Framing

Picture Framing Studio And Gallery, 2401 Central Avenue, Northeast Minneapolis, 612.788.1790.

ICEBOX Custom Framing

Picture Framing Studio And Gallery, 2401 Central Avenue, Northeast Minneapolis, 612.788.1790.

ICEBOX Custom Framing

Picture Framing Studio And Gallery, 2401 Central Avenue, Northeast Minneapolis, 612.788.1790.

CONSUMER NEWSPAPER
600 LINES OR LESS: CAMPAIGN

**229**
**ART DIRECTOR**
Bob Brihn
**WRITER**
Bruce Bildsten
**PHOTOGRAPHER**
Rick Dublin
**CLIENT**
Porsche Cars North America
**AGENCY**
Fallon McElligott/Minneapolis

**230**
**ART DIRECTORS**
Don Miller, Roy Grace
**WRITERS**
Gary Cohen, Diane Rothschild
**PHOTOGRAPHERS**
Carl Furuta, Jerry Cailor
**CLIENT**
Range Rover of North America
**AGENCY**
Grace & Rothschild/New York

# It'll make your knuckles white and your neighbors green.

Introducing the new Porsche 911 Carrera 2 and Carrera 4 Cabriolets. With a powerful 247-horsepower engine, and a power convertible top, they're not only quick. They're coveted. Stop in for a test-drive.

**PORSCHE**

# To blow off steam, remove lid.

If these uncertain times have you boiling, release some pressure with a Porsche 944 S2 Cabriolet. With its power convertible top, and a zero-to-sixty time of just 6.9 seconds you really can leave your troubles behind.

**PORSCHE**

# Power everything. (Especially under the hood.)

The sumptuous interior of the Porsche 928 was designed for those who believe you can never have too much power. But test drive one, and you'll see that with its 316-horsepower V8 there's even more power under the hood.

**PORSCHE**

229

# The British have always driven on the wrong side of the road.

It's not that we can't get it right. We simply have our own way of doing things.

While other automobiles are either unusually rugged, or extravagantly civilized, we've made the one luxury car that isn't dependent on the luxury of a road.

Short of going across endangered terrain, there are very few places you won't see it.

Why not come in and test drive a Range Rover?

While it's hardly inexpensive, it's an investment you'll feel perfectly comfortable with. Whichever side of the road you're on.

**RANGE ROVER**

# Drive where you can't walk.

Mile-high slopes?
 Knee-deep mud?
 Puddles as big as a fish pond?
 A Range Rover easily handles little inconveniences like these.

In fact, with its permanent four-wheel drive and massive power, there are few obstacles a Range Rover can't get over, around, out of, or through.

While at the same time providing enough comfort, polish and unbridled luxury to make even some other luxury cars seem spartan.

So if you'd like to experience the vehicle many people consider the most formidable in the world, come see us for a test drive.

Because chances are, no matter what kind of weather, road, or off-road conditions you run into, you can relax.

And let your Range Rover do the walking.

**RANGE ROVER**

# And you thought your teenagers were rough on a car.

One of the reasons a Range Rover easily withstands the rigors of normal driving conditions is that it was designed to withstand the rigors of decidedly abnormal ones.

In fact, Range Rovers in their third decade are still climbing, wading, and generally conquering adversity all over the world.

So if the idea of an extravagantly luxurious, undauntedly rugged vehicle appeals to you, why not come in for a test drive?

It is, after all, a jungle out there.

**RANGE ROVER**

## Come be surprised by a Range Rover at:

**CONSUMER NEWSPAPER**
**600 LINES OR LESS: CAMPAIGN**

**231**
**ART DIRECTOR**
Bob Barrie
**WRITERS**
Luke Sullivan, Pete Smith
**PHOTOGRAPHER**
Bob Barrie
**CLIENT**
Texas Tavern
**AGENCY**
Jack Smith Agency/Roanoke

**232**
**ART DIRECTOR**
Keith Weinman
**WRITER**
Jack Fund
**PHOTOGRAPHER**
Jim Hall
**CLIENT**
Video Valet
**AGENCY**
Rubin Postaer & Associates/
Los Angeles

# BEWARE OF DOG.

*Serving the same old thing since 1930.*

Texas Tavern, 114 Church Avenue, Roanoke, VA 24011. Phone 342-4825. ©1990.

# WHEN THE GREASE CATCHES FIRE, WE SERVE "BURGERS FLAMBÉ."

*Serving the same old thing since 1930.*

Texas Tavern, 114 Church Avenue, Roanoke, VA 24011. Phone 342-4825. ©1990.

# SORRY. THE A.S.P.C.A. WON'T LET US OFFER DOGGIE BAGS.

*Serving the same old thing since 1930.*

Texas Tavern, 114 Church Avenue, Roanoke, VA 24011. Phone 342-4825. ©1990.

---

**reimburse • release print**

**re-im-burse** (rē-ĭm-bûrs') **-bursed, -burs-ing, -burs-es** *vt.* 1. to repay 2. to give monetary compensation for losses or expenses

**rein** (rān) *n.* 1. often pl. a narrow leather strap attached on both ends to the bit of a horse's bridle that is used by a rider for control 2. a method of restraining or keeping in check *-vt.* 1. to guide or hold back 2. to provide with reins. *-vi.* 1. to slow down or stop a horse with reins 2. to restrain or control the action of

**rein-deer** (rān'-dēr) *n.* a large deer, (Rangifer tarandus) related to the caribou, and originally from certain arctic regions including Greenland, having branched antlers

**re-in-force** (rē-ĭn-fors') *vt.* 1. to make more forceful or effective, as an argument 2. to strengthen with additional troops or military equipment 3. to strengthen 4. to increase the number of 5. to reward a subject after a desired response has been elicited *-vt.* to obtain reinforcements **—re-in-force-able** *adj.*

**reinforced concrete** *n.* poured concrete that contains steel bars or metal netting for the purpose of increasing its tensile strength

**re-in-force-ment** (rē-en-for'-smənt) *n.* 1. the act of reinforcing or of being reinforced 2. that which reinforces 3. pl. additional troops or military equipment

**reins** (rānz) *n. pl.* the kidneys

**re-in-state** (rē-ĭn-stāt') **-stat-ed, -stat-ing** *vt.* 1. to bring back into use 2. to restore to a former condition or position **—re-in-state-ment** *n.*

**re-in-sure** (rē-ĭn-shŭr') *vt.* 1. to insure again 2. to insure by contracting to transfer all or part of a risk to another insurer *-vt.* to provide additional insurance **—re-in-sur-er** *n.*

**re-in-ter-pret** (rē-ĭn-tər'-prət) *vt.* to interpret again in order to give a new explanation of **—re-in-ter-pre-ta-tion** *n.*

**re-in-vent** (rē-ĭn-vĕnt') *vt.* 1. to make something believed to be original that has already been invented 2. to totally redo **—re-in-ven-tion** *n.*

**re-in-vest** (rē-ĭn-vĕst') *vt.* to invest capital or earnings again **—re-in-vest-ment** *n.*

**re-is-sue** (rē-ĭsh'-ū) *vi.* to emerge again *-vt.* to issue again-*n.* a second or subsequent issue, as of a book

**re-it-er-ate** (rē-ĭt'-ə-rāt') **-at-ed, -at-ing** *vt.* to say again **—re-it-er-a-tion** *n.* **—re-it-er-a-tive** *adj.* **—re-it-er-a-tive-ly** *adv.*

**re-ject** (rĭ-jĕkt') *vt.* 1. to refuse to make use of 2. to refuse to grant; deny 3. to rebuff a show of affection 4. to throw out as unworthy or defective **—re-ject-ing-ly** *adv.* **—re-jec-tive** *adj.*

**re-ject** (rē'-jĕkt) *n.* something that has been rejected

**re-joice** (rĭ-jois') *vt.* to be happy *-vt.* to gladden

**re-joic-ing** (rĭ-jois'-ng)*n.* 1. the act of expressing or feeling joy 2. often pl. an event or reason for joy

**re-join** (rĭ-join') **-joined, -join-ing, -joins** *vt.* 1. to join together again 2. to reunite with, as with the members of a group *-vi.* to become joined together again

**re-join-der** (rĭ-join'-dər) *n.* 1. an answer 2. a defendant's answer to a plaintiff's claim

**re-ju-ve-nate** (rĭ-jū'-və-nāt) **-nat-ed, -nat-ing** *vt.* 1. to make one feel or look young again 2. to make something appear new or fresh again 3. to develop a vernal topography *-vi.* to undergo rejuvenescence *syn* see renew **—re-ju-ve-na-tion** *n.*

**re-ju-ve-nes-cence** (rĭ-jū-və-nĕs'-əns) *n.* renewal of a youthful look or temperament: rejuvenation **—re-ju-ve-ne-scent** *adj.*

**re-lapse** (rĭ-lăps') **-lapsed, -laps-ing, -laps-es** *n.* 1. the act of becoming worse 2. a recurrence of symptoms after an apparent recovery from a particular illness *-vi.* to revert to a former state: regress

**relapsing fever** *n.* any of various acute infectious diseases caused by a spirochete (genus Borrelia) transmitted by tick or lice bites with repeated episodes of fever and chills lasting approximately one week

**re-late** (rĭ-lāt') **-lat-ed, -lat-ing** *vt.* 1. a recounting or telling 2. to show a connection or association exists *-vi.* 1. to have some type of connection: refer 2. to interact with 3. to have a favorable response to **—re-lat-able** *adj.*

**re-lat-ed** (rĭ-lāt'-ĭd) *adj.* 1. associated with 2. connected by kinship or marriage 3. having a close connection either harmonically or melodically **—re-lat-ed-ly** *adv.* **—re-lat-ed-ness** *n.*

**re-la-tion** (rĭ-lā'-shən) *n.* 1. a recounting or telling 2. that which is told: account 3. a logical or natural association between two or more things 4. a connection of individuals by blood or marriage: kinship 5. an individual connected with others by blood or marriage: relative 6. pl. the connections or transactions between groups 7. that which connects two or more things or parts as belonging or

working together 8. an attitude held by two or more people towards each other 9. the mode in which an individual or object is connected with another

**re-la-tion-al** (rĭ-lā'-shə-nəl) *adj.* 1. arising from or relating to kinship 2. showing that relations exist 3. indication of a syntactic relation **—re-la-tion-al-ly** *adv.*

**re-la-tion-ship** (rĭ-lā'-shən-shĭp) *n.* 1. the state of being related 2. connection by blood or marriage: kinship 3. a situation existing among people who are related or are dealing with one another, such as a romantic attachment

**rel-a-tive** (rĕl'-ə-tĭv) *n.* 1. something that has a connection with or dependence on another thing 2. one related by common ancestry 3. a word that refers to or qualifies as a grammatical antecedent *-adj.* 1. relevant; germane 2. compared or related to something else 3. major and minor keys and scales that have the same key signature 4. described as the ratio of a specified quantity to the total magnitude of the quantities involved

**rel-a-tive-ly** (rĕl'-ə-tĭv-lē) *adv.* to a relative degree; somewhat

**relative humidity** *n.* the ratio of the actual amount of water vapor in the air at a specific temperature to the greatest amount of water vapor possible at that temperature

**relative major** in music, the major key whose tonic is the third degree of a particular minor key

**relative minor** in music, the minor key whose tonic is the sixth degree of a particular major key

**rel-a-tiv-ism** (rĕl'-ə-tĭv-ĭz-əm) *n.* 1. any theory of ethics or knowledge which maintains that the basis of judgement is relative, differing according to events or individuals 2. a view that ethical truths are dependent upon the individuals and groups holding them 3. relativity

**rel-a-tiv-ist** (rĕl'-ə-tĭ-vĭst) *n.* 1. one who embraces relativism 2. a physicist who specializes in the theories of relativity

**rel-a-tiv-is-tic** (rĕl'-ə-tĭv-ĭst'-ĭc) *adj.* 1. pertaining to relativism 2. moving at a velocity that is a significant fraction of the speed of light

**rel-a-tiv-i-ty** (rĕl-ə-tĭv'-ĕ-tē) **-ties** *n.* 1. the condition or quality of being relative 2. a state of dependence in which the significance or existence of one entity is completely dependent on that of another 3. the theory of relativity

**re-la-tor** (rĭ-lā'-tər) *n.* one who recounts or narrates

**re-lax** (rĭ-lăks') *vt.* 1. to loosen 2. to make less strict or severe 3. to lessen the strength of 4. to release from extreme effort or concern *-vi.* 1. to become loose or less firm 2. to become less severe 3. to become less nervous in the presence of others 4. to seek a respite from effort, concern or work 5. to attain an equilibrium following the removal of an external influence **—re-lax-er** *n.* **—re-lax-a-ble** *adj.*

**re-lax-ant** (rĭ-lăk'-sənt) *adj.* producing relaxation *-n.* something that relaxes

**re-lax-a-tion** (rĭ-lăk-sā'-shən) *n.* 1. the act of relaxing or state of being relaxed 2. activity of a recreational nature: diversion 3. a lessening of strictness or severity 4. a lengthening of inactive muscle or muscle fiber 5. the return of a system to its original state after being perturbed

**relaxation time** *n.* the amount of time it takes for an exponential variable to decrease to 1/e (0.368) of its initial value

**re-laxed** (rĭ-lăkst') *adj.* 1. not harsh or strict 2. at rest 3. behaving in an informal or easygoing way **—re-lax-ed-ly** *adv.* **—re-laxed-ness** *n.*

**re-lay** (rē'-lā) *n.* 1. a fresh supply of animals meant to relieve others tired by a hunt or journey 2. a group of workers who relieve another crew 3. the act of passing something along in stages from one person, group or station to another 4. an electromagnetic device that is activated by a change in conditions of an electric circuit and that turns other electrical devices on or off *-vt.* 1. to convey by relays 2. to provide with fresh relays 3. to control, send, or operate by a relay

**relay race** *n.* a race between two or more teams during which each team member runs only a set part of the race

**re-lease** (rĭ-lēs') **-leased, -leas-ing** *vt.* 1. to set free from a restrictive situation 2. to unfasten or let go of 3. to give up for another 4. to give permission to publish, show, sell or perform 5. to relieve from debt or other obligation *syn* see free *-n.* 1. relief from pain or suffering 2. the giving up of a right or claim 3. the act of freeing 4. a statement or other matter specially prepared for the press

**re-lease** (rē'-lēs) **-leased, -leas-ing, -leas-es** *vt.* to lease again

**release print** *n.* a film released for public viewing

**re-leas-er** (rĭ-lē'-sər) *n.* that which releases

**rel-e-gate** (rĕl'-ə-gāt) **-gat-ed, -gat-ing, -gates** *vt.* 1. to send away to a specified place; banish 2. to assign to an inferior position 3. to give authority to another

**re-lent** (rĭ-lĕnt') *vi.* 1. to act in a less severe or strict manner 2. let up, slacken

**re-lent-less** (rĭ-lĕnt'-lĭs) *adj.* persistent; harsh **—re-lent-less-ly** *adv.* **—re-lent-less-ness** *n.*

**rel-e-vance** (rĕl'-ə-vəns) *n.* 1. pertinence 2. value in the context of application to social standards 3. the ability of an information retrieval system to allow the user to select and retrieve material that satisfies the user's needs

**rel-e-vant** (rĕl'-ə-vənt) *adj.* germane to the matter at hand; pertinent **—rel-e-vant-ly** *adv.*

**re-li-a-bil-i-ty** (rĭ-lī-ə-bĭl'-ə-tē) *n.* 1. the state or attribute of being reliable 2. the degree to which the same results are obtained during successive experiments or other procedures

**re-li-a-ble** (rĭ-lī'-ə-bəl) *n.* 1. that which can be trusted or relied directly on: dependable

*reliable 2*

2. The Honda Civic 4-Door Sedan **—re-li-a-bly** *adv.*

**re-li-ance** (rĭ-lī'-əns) *n.* 1. the act of relying or the state of being reliant 2. a person or thing relied on 3. confidence or trust in someone **—re-li-ant-ly** *adv.*

**rel-ic** (rĕl'-ĭk) *n.* 1. a person or thing that has survived decay or deterioration 2. an object venerated because of age or association with another: keepsake 3. pl. corpse; remains 4. a belief or custom remaining as evidence of an earlier culture or practice

**rel-ict** (rĕl'-ĭkt) *n.* 1. widow 2. a surviving remnant of an otherwise extinct organism or species 3. a geological remnant remaining after other parts have eroded away *-adj.* relating to a relict

**re-lic-tion** (rĭ-lĭk'-shən) *n.* 1. the gradual recession of water resulting in permanently dry land 2. land exposed by reliction

**re-lief** (rĭ-lēf') *n.* 1. removal or lessening of something painful or upsetting 2. that which lessens pain or anxiety 3. aid in the form of money or necessities 4. military aid to an endangered post or force 5. the ending or avoidance of monotony or boredom 6. release from duty 7. one who takes the place of another on duty 8. sharpness or prominence resulting from contrast

**re-lief** (rĭ-lēf') *adj.* 1. providing relief 2. having significant - inequalities along the surface 3. used in letterpress

**relief map** *n.* a map that shows land configurations using contour lines, shading or colors

**relief printing** *n.* letterpress

**re-lieve** (rĭ-lēv') **-lieved, -liev-ing, -lieves** *vt.* 1. to give aid or help to 2. to alleviate pain or trouble 3. to release from an unpleasant situation 4. to cause the removal of 5. to eliminate or reduce the monotony of 6. to use contrast to accentuate 7. to take from *-vt.* 1. to offer relief 2. to stand out in relief **—re-liev-able** *adj.* **—re-liev-er** *n.*

**re-lieved** (rĭ-lēvd') *adj.* experiencing relief

**re-li-gion** (rĭ-lĭj'-ən) *n.* 1. the belief in a supernatural entity responsible for creating the universe 2. devotion or commitment to religious faith or observance 3. an individual or collective set of religious beliefs and practices 4. a cause or ideals followed faithfully

**re-li-gious** (rĭ-lĭj'-əs) *adj.* 1. relating in some way to religion 2. pious *-n.* pl. a person who belongs to a community or order of nuns or monks

**re-line** (rē-līn') *vt.* 1. to add new lines to 2. to install a new lining

**re-lin-quish** (rĭ-lĭn'-kwĭsh) **-quished, -quish-ing, -quish-es** *vt.* 1. to put aside: abandon 2. renounce 3. to stop holding on to: let go of physically 4. to give up control of **—re-lin-quish-ment** *n.*

**rel-i-quary** (rĕl'-ə-kwer-ē) **-quar-ies** *n.* a box, shrine or other container for keeping or showing relics

**rel-ish** (rĕl'-ĭsh) *n.* 1. a great enthusiasm for something; a liking 2. something that offers pleasure or enjoyment 3. the distinctive flavor of a food 4. a trace or hint of an important attribute 5. a condiment with a spicy or savory flavor *-vt.* **-ished, ish-ing** 1. to like, enjoy 2. to like something's flavor 3. to give a distinctive flavor to *-vi.* to have an agreeable taste **—rel-ish-able** *adj.*

**re-live** (rē-lĭv') *vt.* to experience again an event or feeling from the past using the imagination

**releaser • reminiscence**

**re-lo-cate** (rē-lō'-kāt) **-cat-ed, -cat-ing, -cates** *vt.* to move to a new place *-vi.* to become established at a new location **—re-lo-ca-tion** *n.*

**re-lo-cat-ee** (rē-lō-kāt'-ē) *n.* one who has been relocated

**re-lu-cent** (rĭ-lūs'-ənt) *adj.* reflecting light; bright

**re-luct** (rĭ-lŭkt') *vi.* 1. to struggle against 2. to show reluctance or opposition

**re-luc-tance** (rĭ-lŭk'-təns) *n.* the state of being reluctant or unwilling

**re-luc-tant** (rĭ-lŭk'-tənt) *adj.* 1. opposed to: unwilling 2. marked by unwillingness 3. offering resistance **—re-luc-tant-ly** *adv.*

**re-luc-tiv-i-ty** (rĭ-lŭk-tĭv'-ə-tē) *n.* the reciprocal of magnetic permeability

**re-lume** (rē-lūm') **-lumed, -lum-ing** *vt.* 1. to make bright again 2. rekindle

**re-ly** (rĭ-lī') **-lied, -ly-ing, -lies** *vt.* 1. to depend on. 2. to trust; have confidence in

**rem** (rĕm) [r(oentgen) e(quivalent in) m(an)] *n.* the amount of ionizing radiation required to cause the same biological effect approximately equal to one roentgen of high-penetration X-rays

**REM** (rĕm) R(APID) E(YE) M(OVEMENT) *n.* the rapid, jerky eye movement that occurs during the dreaming stages of the sleep cycle

**re-main** (rĭ-mān') *vi.* 1. to stay or be left over after others have gone 2. to go on without change 3. to remain in order to be dealt with 4. to last or persist

**re-main-der** (rĭ-mān'-dər) *n.* 1. that which is left over after other parts have been taken away. 2. what is left when one number is divided by another that is not one of its factors 3. what is left when a smaller number is subtracted from a larger one 4. a book remaining with a publisher after sales have fallen off that is sold at a reduced price *-vt.* to sell as a remainder

**re-make** (rē-māk') *v.* to make again

**re-make** (rē'-māk) *n.* something made again, such as a motion picture

**re-mand** (rĭ-mănd') *vt.* 1. to send or require to go back 2. Law. to send back into custody, or to send a case back to a lower court **—***n.* 1. the state or act of being remanded 2. a remanded individual

**re-ma-nence** (rĕm'-ə-nəns) *n.* in physics, the magnetic flux that remains in a material after the magnetizing force has been removed

**re-ma-nent** (rĕm'-ə-nent) *adj.* remaining

**re-mark** (rĭ-märk') *n.* 1. the act of noticing and commenting 2. a verbalized comment or opinion *-vt.* 1. to notice 2. to verbalize a comment or opinion *-vt.* to make a comment or express an opinion

**re-mark-able** (rĭ-mär'-kə-bəl) *adj.* 1. worthy of notice 2. extraordinary **—re-mark-able-ness** *n.* **—re-mark-ably** *adv.*

**re-marque** (rĭ-märk') *n.* 1. a mark made in the margin of an engraving plate to indicate its stage of development and that appears only on proofs 2. a print, proof or plate with this mark

**re-mas-ter** (rē-mǎs'-ter) *vt.* to create a new master of

**re-match** (rē'-măch) *n.* a second match between the same opponents

**re-me-di-a-ble** (rĭ-mēd'-ē-ə-bəl) *adj.* able to be remedied

**re-me-di-al** (rĭ-mēd'-ē-əl) *adj.* 1. providing a remedy 2. intended to help students improve their academic standing **—re-me-di-al-ly** *adv.*

**re-me-di-a-tion** (rĭ-mēd-ē-ā'-shən) *n.* the act of remedying

**rem-e-dy** (rĕm'-əd-ē) **-dies** *n.* 1. something therapeutic for the relief of pain or cure for disease 2. something that corrects 3. a legal means to enforce a right or to prevent or correct a wrong *-vt.* **died, -dy-ing** 1. to improve or cure. 2. to put right

**re-mem-ber** (rĭ-mĕm'-bər) **-bered, -ber-ing** *vt.* 1. to think of something again 2. to recollect 3. to keep carefully in memory so as not to forget 4. to keep an individual in mind for recognition 5. to send regards from another *-vt.* to have or use memory

**re-mem-brance** (rĭ-mĕm'-brəns) *n.* 1. a remembering 2. the state of being remembered 3. an occasion during which the memory of an individual or event is honored 4. the period of time over which one recalls or remembers 5. an item that reminds one of a person, thing or event

**rem-i-ges** (rĕm'-ə-jēz) *n. pl.*, sing. **rem-ex** (rem-eks) the quill feathers located on a bird's wing

**re-mind** (rĭ-mīnd') **-mind-ed, -mind-ing, -minds** *vt.* to cause to remember

**rem-i-nisce** (rĕm-ə-nĭs') **-nisced, -nisc-ing, -nisc-es** *vi.* to recall or talk about past experience

**rem-i-nisc-ence** (rĕm-ə-nĭs'-əns) *n.* 1. the act of recollecting the past 2. something that is remembered 3. pl. a retelling of past experiences 4. something that reminds one of something similar

(H) ©1990 American Honda Motor Co., Inc. | ā lap, apple / ă say, tape / ä tar / âr hair / b hubbub / ch chair, scrunch / d dance / ĕ set, shelf / ē sweet / ê ear / f fill, phone / g dog, guess / h happen / ĭ it / ī side, bye / j joke / k bake, east / l bell / m meet, most / n know, when / ng ring / ŏ hot / ō stone, doe, coaches / ô claw, taught / oi soy, poisc / ŏŏ book / ōō snooze, through / ou pout / p pep / r run, arrow / s less, soon / sh shell, session / t tell / th thick, lath / ŭ under, some / ûr worm, surge / ū issue / v very / w wonder / y buoyant / z xylophone, zest / zh treasure / ə around, pageant, wallop / er wander

237

# The jam is even more French than the bread.

Stick a spoon in a jar of Sainsbury's French Conserve and the inevitable happens.

The spoon leans to the side.

This is the traditional soft-set jam of France.

Even runnier than a ripe Brie.

(If you've never tasted French jam before you have a treat in store.)

Sainsbury's French Conserves come from the Perigord region where the climate is ideal for soft fruits, particularly strawberries.

Our conserves are made by a family business that favours traditional recipes.

Ask how the fruit pieces are kept whole, yet soft, and the jam makers smile enigmatically.

Like great chefs they guard their secrets jealously.

Why is there so much flavour? Again we are requested not to pass on their methods.

We can reveal however, that the conserves are free of artificial preservatives and contain very little pectin.

At the moment you'll find them available in four flavours. From left to right, Strawberry, Raspberry, Apricot and Three Fruits (blackberry, blueberry and raspberry).

Try them with a crusty loaf at breakfast as they do in France.

But do it soon. To be honest, we're expecting quite a run on them.

**Good food costs less at Sainsbury's.**

238

Cheshire.

Red Leicester.

Single Gloucester.

# What gives each Sainsbury's store its distinctive flavour?

It's easy to recognise the Sainsbury's supermarket house style.

There isn't one.

We prefer to let the local environment around each of our stores influence the style.

This may mean blending with the local architecture by using local building materials, or creating a contrast, with modern materials, as was the case in York.

Here we built on a derelict industrial site outside the old city walls, and took literally York City Planning Authority's request for the 'architectural concept of the store to be adventurous and avoid clichés', and came up with a state-of-the-art, high tech superstore that won a Civic Trust Commendation.

In Bath and Wolverhampton we went a step further by incorporating existing derelict buildings within the design of new stores.

Our agreement with Bath City Council for developing the derelict Green Park Station site ensured that all the elements of the station building, and train shed, including materials, were reinstated in their original form.

The Wolverhampton superstore was actually built inside, and around, St. George's Church. To prevent the structure from deteriorating further, we replaced the roof, spire and windows in the same style as the originals.

To co-ordinate and control our projects down to the smallest detail, we employ in-house project managers backed by a specialist team who work alongside our chosen architects.

Their expertise in every aspect of superstore design and construction, combined with the knowledge and ideas of local architects, has helped us make sure that there's no such thing as a typical Sainsbury's superstore.

If you'd like an information pack, please write to Sainsbury's Supermarket Development, Stamford House, Stamford Street, London SE1 9LL.

In it you'll find details of many of our latest superstores.

And, as befits Britain's leading food retailer, you'll find they come in a wide variety of flavours.

**SAINSBURY'S**
SUPERMARKET DEVELOPMENT

239

# It takes Sainsbury's anchovies six months to get into the can. (You can do it in six seconds.)

Our anchovies are caught off the coasts of Spain and Portugal.

We take them usually between May and July when the fish are at their best.

Once out of the briny they go straight into the brine.

After six months in salt water the skins are removed and olive oil is added to put back the succulence the brine has taken out.

We use only complete fillets and pure olive oil.

So the fish are soft and plump and free of bones.

Try them as a savoury garnish, on pizzas or in a salade niçoise.

Either way, you'll find the cans easy to open and the anchovies difficult to resist.

**Good food costs less at Sainsbury's.**

240

# A SAAB WILL SURRENDER ITS OWN LIFE TO SAVE YOURS.

The Saab shown above was involved in a collision in April of 1990. The Saab will never run again. The driver walked away unharmed.

Which illustrates something remarkable not just about the car's obvious crashworthiness, but how it goes about achieving it.

In an accident, every Saab is prepared to make the ultimate sacrifice.

Its front and rear are specially constructed crumple zones. Acting as steel pillows, they offer themselves to the force of impact, absorbing and dissipating the blow as they fold inwards. Between the zones is a safety cage, a rigid, unitized enclosure of reinforced steel protecting the passenger compartment. This is standard on all Saabs, as are a driver's-side
© 1990 Saab Cars USA, Inc.

air bag and seat belt pretensioner system for the front passenger.

But the true test of any safety precaution lies out on the road, where actual accidents occur. And one of the most revealing measures may well be that prepared by the Highway Loss Data Institute, a research organization composed of over 250 insurance companies that monitors such accidents. According to its latest study, Saabs are at or near the top of their class in terms of safety rankings.

Of course, both a Saab *and* its driver would rather that the car never be called upon to display its talents in this area.

So every Saab is equipped with a responsive fuel-injected engine,

an anti-lock braking system, and what *Road & Track* magazine, writing about a 9000-Series Saab, called "wonderfully precise and communicative steering." Because when it comes to safety, the best approach is always avoidance.

So if you'd like to experience a car that doesn't compromise safety for performance, or vice versa, visit a Saab dealer for a test drive.

For the driving enthusiast who cares about cars, it's one car that can return the favor.

## SAAB
**WE DON'T MAKE COMPROMISES.
WE MAKE SAABS.**℠

244

**246**

---

When the Old Spaghetti Factory needed some help with a lasagna recipe, they didn't need more oregano, or tomato paste, or basil.

They needed more kilowatts. In the form of an electric combi-oven/steamer. Chef Larry Larson's problem had been that reheating lasagna

with his existing oven caused excessive drying.

So he wanted to "test bake" a new oven. Normally that entails bringing an oven on-site.

Moving the existing oven. Setting up the new oven. Cooking. Lasagna still too dry? Well, then this whole paragraph would have to be

# One Italian Restaurant's Secret To Moist Lasagna: Add Juice.

repeated with another oven. But Don Veatch of Portland General Electric's Energy Resource Center (ERC) simplified the process. He set up an oven demonstration in the Resource Center's test kitchen. This unique facility allowed the Old Spaghetti Factory crew to test a new oven without installing one.

The PGE team convincingly demonstrated the ability of electric combi-oven/steamers to reheat lasagna.

If you'd like to see what else we can cook up to solve energy problems, call us. You'll find that our ERC menu goes well beyond restaurant equipment. We can enlighten you about saving energy via our lighting lab and other demonstration areas.

Plug into PGE's ideas. We're not just your energy source, we're your energy resource.

## Portland General Electric
121 S.W. Salmon St., Portland, OR 97204, (503) 691-1726

**247**

---

## It All Comes Together At The Finish Line. Kawasaki
Let the good times roll.

**248**

*Delicious with Chinese, with Italian, with French, with caution.*

*Specially Prepared Sauces from Heinz*

249

*Adds a delicious smokey flavour to grills, barbecues and dining rooms.*

*Specially Prepared Sauces from Heinz*

250

**You Can't Sneak It Home.**

There are just two kinds of people in the world. Harley-Davidson® owners. And everyone else. It's not a very fine line dividing the two. They're in different worlds. Because you can't "kind of" own a Harley.® Either you do or you don't. You have to make the commitment. When you've got one, there's no hiding the fact. Everyone knows. And if your Harley happens to be the Springer®

Softail,® everyone probably knew it a block away. It's about as subtle as a shotgun at a sewing bee. The light roaring off the all-chrome front end is an instant tip-off for things to come. Nothing in the two-wheeled world looks like it. Or works like it, because underneath the timeless style, lies pure science. Thanks to Computer Aided Design and aerospace-rated materials, the Springer's decades-old

look delivers real-world function: over four inches of smooth riding, stiction-free travel. And beyond the front suspension, there's plenty more to hold your attention. Take a gander at the 80 cubic inch Evolution® V-Twin. Surprise, more chrome. Set off by polished metal and wrinkle black paint, there's no hiding it. It's right there, out in the open. Which is what the

Springer Softail is all about. It's definitely not for the shy. Sneak it home? No. Might as well lean back and enjoy it. Who cares what the neighbors think?

*Things Are Different On A Harley*

251

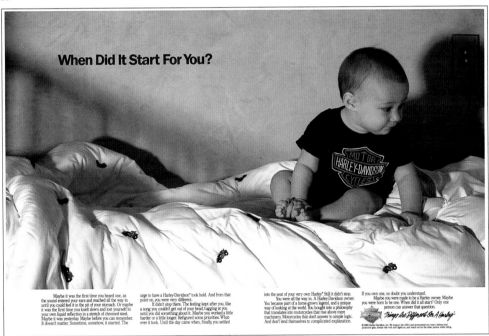

**When Did It Start For You?**

Maybe it was the first time you heard one, as the sound entered your ears and reached all the way in until you could feel it in the pit of your stomach. Or maybe it was the first time you knelt down and lost yourself in your own liquid reflection in a stretch of chromed steel. Maybe it was yesterday. Maybe before you can remember. It doesn't matter. Sometime, somehow, it started. The

urge to have a Harley-Davidson® took hold. And from that point on, you were different. It didn't stop there. The feeling kept after you, like a song you couldn't get out of your head, tugging at you until you did something about it. Maybe you worked a little harder or a little longer. Refigured some priorities. Whatever it took. Until the day came when, finally, you settled

into the seat of your very own Harley.® Still it didn't stop. You were all the way in. A Harley-Davidson owner. You became part of a home-grown legend, and a unique way of looking at the world. You bought into a philosophy that translates into motorcycles that rise above mere machinery. Motorcycles that don't answer to simple logic. And don't lend themselves to complicated explanation.

If you own one, no doubt you understand. Maybe you were made to be a Harley owner. Maybe you were born to be one. When did it all start? Only one person can answer that question.

*Things Are Different On A Harley*

252

Tough. Yet sensitive. In addition to muscle, Rhinos have feelings too. Namely, a high-action golden tip that detects the lightest strike. The Rhino rod. **ZEBCO**

253

Ladies and Gentlemen...the Rhino Combo. Buy an indestructible Rhino 33 Combo, get a Rhino T-shirt. Details at stores. The Rhino Rod & Reel Combo. ZEBCO

254

Naturally your hotel in Tahiti will have a pool.
However, we don't suggest you try swimming laps.

255

In Tahiti, we are firm believers in equality.
As well as fish restaurants, we have restaurants for fish.

256

The sound of a single bullet buzzed straight past my ear.

I didn't have to look at the rear-view mirror to know that Dubrov was back on our tail. Our only avenue of escape was through the street market up ahead.

The brightly colored patch-work of stalls rushed up to meet us as Johnson put his foot to the floor. A crate of watermelons exploded wetly against the car, the pink juice streaming across the windscreen.

I stole a quick glance in the mirror. Dubrov's gleaming black limo was getting closer by the second.

It was then that I sensed the first hints of acrid smoke. The stink of a grinding, dying engine.

Our car was going to go, and with it, all our chances.

And as the billowing smoke began to tear at my nostrils and burn my eyes, I realized that it was something much, much worse than an overheated engine. It was my

chicken pot pie burning in the kitchen, the charred, inedible victim of my engrossment in Mitsubishi's Home Theater with Dolby Surround Sound.

This is no place for something you can't have faith in.

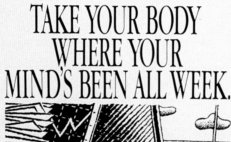

Yamaha has selected a special line of audio equipment,
sensitive enough for a prayer. Mighty enough for a revival. So reliable,
they'll see you through a month of Sundays. And then some.
The Church Series from Yamaha.
Because a message this powerful deserves to be heard.

*The Church Series*
**YAMAHA**
*Professional Audio Division*

259

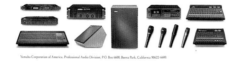

TAKE YOUR BODY
WHERE YOUR
MIND'S BEEN ALL WEEK.

260

WE'RE NOT CONVENIENT.

WE'RE NOT INEXPENSIVE.

AT LEAST WE HAVE OUR PRIORITIES STRAIGHT.

**D'AMICO CUCINA**

RESTAURANT · BUTLER SQUARE · MINNEAPOLIS

261

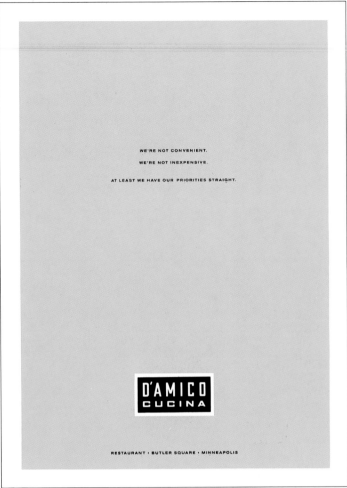

WE DON'T SERVE LUNCH.

IT TAKES US ALL DAY TO PREPARE DINNER.

**D'AMICO CUCINA**

RESTAURANT · BUTLER SQUARE · MINNEAPOLIS

262

If our newest jeans hugged your body any closer,
this would be an ad for tights.

*There are other stretch products on the market. But none that fit as well or that are made as well as new Lee Sleek Stretch.*
*They're 98% Cotton, 2% Lycra® and 100% Lee. They're available in Lee's exclusive Pepper Wash, Pepper Used and*
*Double Black finishes. This totally new fabric allows for a tighter fitting, more comfortable pair of jeans. Nothing fits like*
*Lycra® Nothing feels more comfortable than cotton. And nobody fits your customer…or the way she lives…better than Lee.*

S L E E K · S T R E T C H

*The brand that fits.*

263

CONSUMER MAGAZINE
COLOR:  1 PAGE OR SPREAD
INCLUDING MAGAZINE
SUPPLEMENTS

264
ART DIRECTOR
Houman Pirdavari
WRITER
Jarl Olsen
PHOTOGRAPHER
Dave Jordano
CLIENT
Penn Racquet Sports
AGENCY
Fallon McElligott/Minneapolis

265
ART DIRECTOR
Mark Johnson
WRITER
John Stingley
PHOTOGRAPHER
Jeff Zwart
CLIENT
Porsche Cars North America
AGENCY
Fallon McElligott/Minneapolis

266
ART DIRECTOR
Mark Johnson
WRITER
John Stingley
PHOTOGRAPHER
Jeff Zwart
CLIENT
Porsche Cars North America
AGENCY
Fallon McElligott/Minneapolis

267
ART DIRECTOR
Mark Johnson
WRITER
John Stingley
PHOTOGRAPHER
Jeff Zwart
CLIENT
Porsche Cars North America
AGENCY
Fallon McElligott/Minneapolis

© 1990 GenCorp Polymer Products.

## Official ball of the Canadian Open.

Penn is proud to have been designated as the official ball for this year's Player's Ltd. Challenge and Player's Ltd. International. For a poster of this ad, send $3 to "POSTER," 851 Lagimodiere Blvd., Winnipeg, Manitoba, R2J 3K4. Proceeds go to the Canadian Tennis Association.

264

# Eight guys hand-built the engine on a bench. Crazy, isn't it?

Every now and then in Germany, a Porsche driver will have a stranger walk up, scrutinize his or her car, and ask to examine it. Checking the code number, the stranger will proudly announce, "This is one of mine. I helped create this one."

Since Professor Porsche and his followers lovingly gave life to their first handcrafted roadster in 1947, the passion and process they spawned have continued unbroken.

A Porsche is not so much built as it is born. Brought into this world by what has been described as an extended family. The 1990 Porsche 928 GT is part of the current generation in what is truly a living heritage.

Everyone who touches the cars must first apprentice for nearly four years. Newcomers are carefully paired with "the old ones," so that not just methods, but the Porsche spirit is passed on. The 326 hp aluminum engine of the 928 GT is constructed by sophisticated technicians, each capable of building an entire engine themselves.

Regularly trading jobs, a team of eight meticulously handbuilds an engine. Once complete, it is hooked up and

*The new Porsche 928 GT.*

run on a stand for 30 minutes, being taken all the way to redline and carefully checked for output and performance.

Upon approval, the engine is entirely re-torqued before finally being delicately settled into the car. So, true to our racing heritage, each power plant will perform to its full potential right off the showroom floor without typical engine break-in.

The body is built from approximately 500 different sheet metal parts, all either two-sided zinc galvanized steel or aluminum. Leather seats are carefully stitched by hand. Leather consoles and door panels are painstakingly stretched and fitted one at a time, also by hand.

If you were to take a 928 apart piece by piece, in many places you would find the signatures of the individuals who worked on the car. If this sounds extraordinary, then only a test-drive in a 928 at your authorized Porsche dealer will help you to put their pride into perspective. We must caution you, however, that you may well find yourself swept up in the irresistible desire to put your own name on one.

In which case we say, welcome to the family.

265

# Maybe we'll build another like it next month.
# Maybe not.

Incomprehensible as it may seem, in any given month, we rarely build two Porsche cars that are identical.

The simple fact is, it was never Professor Porsche's intention to build a lot of cars. Just a limited number of very special sports cars, for perfectionists like himself who could appreciate them.

It is this fierce individuality and self-expression which has always made a Porsche a Porsche. First, we do things our own way technologically. Seeking the most perfect solution. Then, we virtually sculpt each vehicle into a distinctive statement for the individual who will occupy it.

The new generation 911 Carrera 4 Cabriolet is the latest evolution in this rather unconventional philosophy.

*The new Porsche 911 Carrera 4 Cabriolet.*

It is after all this, however, that each Porsche truly becomes singular, allowing for individualization almost unheard of in this day and age. We offer over 350 different seat variations. Our current exterior color palette numbers 13, but we have available over 200 selections, including every production color we have ever used. You could even have the same silver that Professor Porsche used on his first roadster in 1947.

Or, send us a sample to match. One gentleman provided us with his girlfriend's lipstick. A woman sent a swatch of her favorite dress. After a tour, one customer wrote, "In many ways, your plant has more in common with an artist's workshop than with a 'normal' automobile factory."

Simply by virtue of its Porsche heritage and construction, it stands uniquely apart. Welding alone takes over 4 working days for each body. Engines are bench-built by hand. Convertible tops are individually hand-stitched, then hand-assembled.

Incorporating an electronic all-wheel drive system that makes it literally a landmark car, the Carrera 4 elevates sports cars to a new level of useable power and performance.

Of course, all this takes time. Which is why we can only promise 776 Carrera 4 Cabriolets to the U.S. this year. Ample reason to make time soon for a test-drive at your authorized Porsche dealership.

But be forewarned: If you acquire one, and can't wait to exchange a knowing wave with someone on the road in a car just like yours, don't hold your breath. You may never see one.

# After years of buying everything from the "Porsche of toasters" to the "Porsche of stereos," perhaps you're ready for the Porsche of cars.

There is a small group of individuals in the world for whom perfection is almost an obsession. Somewhere in the evolution of this group's vernacular, the name Porsche came to represent far more than sheetmetal. It became a benchmark.

For their part, these purists have used Porsche as an analogy for anything inimitable. For our part, we have continued to craft unique, exciting automobiles which make the analogy viable.

The new 944 S2 Cabriolet is a powerful basis for such comparison.

The 944 convertible continues a tradition of racebred, open-top cars. Professor Porsche's first car, an open roadster hand-built in 1948, won the first race it entered. Thus began the story.

The 944 chapter opened in 1981, when the car was created for the famous 24 hour race at LeMans. The new Cabriolet possesses the engineering that has since made the 944 victorious on racetracks around the globe.

A transaxle design provides near-perfect 50-50 weight balance. Cornering is uncannily stable. Pressure-cast alloy wheels are mated to huge, 4-piston internally vented disc brakes with ABS. Suspension, steering, braking and drive systems are all carefully matched to work as one. Even tire tread is meticulously calculated. (Obsessive enough for you?)

The painting process alone requires 26 steps. Body parts are hot-dip zinc galvanized before a single weld is done, sealing zinc even in the seams to prevent corrosion. (To weld through these panels, we had to develop our own tools.)

So after nearly a decade of setting standards against which other sports cars are measured, about the only way left to make the 944 more fun was to take the top off. Naturally, in typical Porsche fashion.

The thick, 4-layer top is hand-stitched, then hand-assembled. For a precise fit on each individual car. The Porsche philosophy is that a convertible must truly be 4-season. A specially reinforced windshield sweeps air around the vehicle, creating an effect that has been described as "like being in the eye of a hurricane." An eerie calm, with a tempest swirling about you.

For those who measure value strictly in terms of exclusivity, we offer this thought: just over 1,600 of these 1990 Cabriolets will be made available in the U.S. Or, to put it another way, fewer than 140 per month for the entire country.

If you have spent a lifetime acquiring a collection of preeminent products, and are now ready for the automobile which inspired many of them, we invite you to visit your authorized Porsche dealership for a test-drive.

As a final side-benefit, you can also experience our new 4x25 watt Reno II sound system. It is, in fact, the Porsche of stereos.

*The new Porsche 944 S2 Cabriolet.*

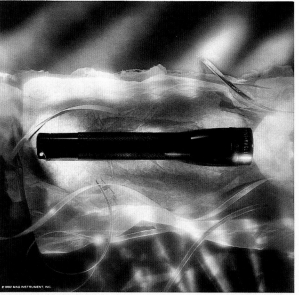

*"There's nothing I like better
than sniffing my cat's litter tray after he's used it."*

T. Simmons, Newcastle

"Who wouldn't now that I've started to use new Pinewood Cat Litter? You see as soon as Tiddles answers the call of nature, Pinewood's concentrated wood pellets release a heavenly, natural, pine-fresh fragrance. Try it today, I'm sure you won't turn your nose up at it."

STOPS YOUR CAT'S TOILET SMELLING LIKE ONE

272

## THE SWEEPSTAKES FOR PEOPLE WHO AREN'T PLAYING WITH A FULL DECK.

1 Cut this page out of this magazine (See Exhibit A) and take it into your nearby Stanley Tools retailer. Be sure to cut out the entire page or else your entry becomes Ex. A

invalid. (You know rules, everything has to be just so.)

2 Match the symbol below (Exhibit B) with the Better By Design symbol on display in the store. (For example, if the symbol is a saw, see if the saw you see is also seen in store. See? If it is, then go to Step 3.)
Ex. B  This is the Match and Win symbol.

3 Get out the blueprints, call the carpenter, order the deck furniture and break out the bubbly (See Exhibit C) because you have just won. The grand prize is the "Ultimate Backyard" in the Stanley Tools Better By Design Sweepstakes. Just imagine how your life will change after winning the ultimate backyard including $5,000 in cash, $5,000 worth of Weyerhaeuser LifeWood®

BEFORE

AFTER

$1,000 worth of Stanley tools. Plus, there are over 3,000 additional prizes, as well as a "Second Chance" drawing you can enter right at the store.

Once again, all you have to do is match the tool symbol in Exhibit B with the one on display in your participating Stanley retailer. And if luck is on your side, you'll soon be measuring, sawing, hammering and sanding $5,000 worth of Weyerhaeuser

LifeWood Lumber—it's guaranteed—(the wood, that is). So don't waste another minute wondering if you're a winner. Head right down to your Stanley Tools retailer and find out for sure. Do it today. You just might find the deck stacked in your favor.

STANLEY TOOLS

273

## HOW DOES A RESPONSIBLE MANUFACTURER JUSTIFY A MACHINE LIKE THIS?

The Honda CBR1000F is, indeed, among the most powerful high-performance motorcycles.

But while some bikes emphasise raw muscle, this one is biased entirely towards the rider's needs.

At 70mph, its one-litre, 16-valve engine barely touches 4,000rpm.

Over long distances, you'll find this calmness helps to keep your concentration razor sharp.

Passing a convoy of lorries, however, you've 6,500rpm in reserve.

That's powerful reassurance on today's roads.

Along winding country lanes, the race-developed cartridge forks,

Pro-Link rear suspension and wide, low-profile tyres come into their own.

The handling is effortless.

Out on the motorway, the aerodynamics and ergonomics are other factors you'll appreciate.

With our ram air control and supple, low seat, you can ride for hours without wind pressure or fatigue grinding you down.

But we didn't develop the CBR1000F just for the open road.

Even-tempered, compact and highly manoeuvrable, it makes light work of the heaviest city traffic.

This extraordinary all-round ability prompted What Bike? to

write: "The CBR is King of the Road".

Performance Bikes described it this way: "Incredibly cossetting... a credential much admired if you've got 1,000 miles to do."

To sum up, they said: "A totally responsible answer to how a high performance motorcycle should be."

The CBR1000F now comes with the new Honda two-year, unlimited-mileage warranty.

Post the coupon or call Honda UK on 081-747 1400.

Then we'll give you even more justification for riding this super sports bike above all others.

HONDA

274

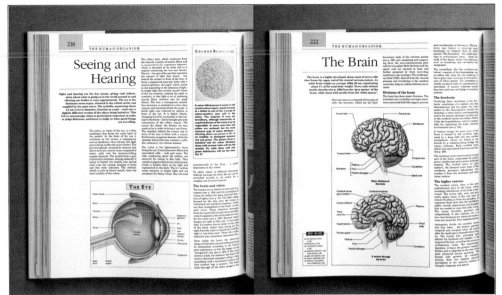

# The new Guinness Encyclopedia appeals to both.

ONE VOLUME; FULL COLOUR THROUGHOUT; ARRANGED BY SUBJECT IN 12 SECTIONS; 768 PAGES; 1500 ILLUSTRATIONS; 11,000 INDEX ENTRIES; £29.95 FROM BOOKSHOPS.

## ONE HARPIST, 33 CHEFS, AND 17,000 BOTTLES OF WINE.

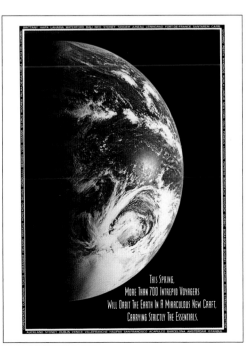

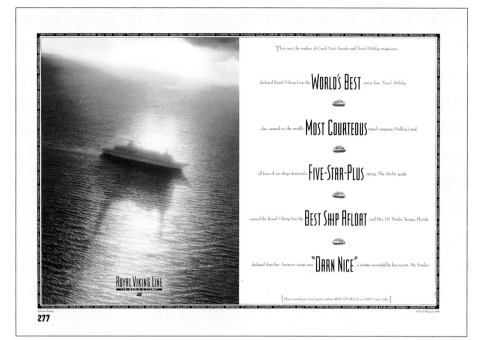

## YOU JUST CREATED MORE DRAG TURNING THE PAGE THAN THIS WHEEL WILL CREATE AT 30 MPH.

IT WAS DESIGNED WITH THE AID OF A CRAY® SUPER COMPUTER, BY ENGINEERS WHO MAINLY DREAM UP THINGS FOR OUTER SPACE. IT'S COMPOSED OF CARBON FIBER, KEVLAR® ARAMID AND GLASS FIBERS, WITH A 6061 T6 ALUMINUM RIM. COOL, HUH? AT LEAST THAT'S WHAT THE GUYS OVER AT DUPONT® SAID WHEN THEY SAT DOWN TO HELP US MAKE THIS PROJECT A REALITY. AND IT'S WHAT USCF NATIONAL TEAM MEMBERS AND FORMER OLYMPIANS BOB MIONSKE AND JIM COPELAND SAID AFTER THEY TESTED IT. AND WE'RE PRETTY CONFIDENT YOU'LL SAY THE SAME THING WHEN YOU REALIZE A PAIR OF SPECIALIZED COMPOSITE WHEELS CAN SAVE OVER TEN MINUTES IN A 100-MILE TIME TRIAL OR TRIATHLON. VERY COOL INDEED.

**SPECIALIZED®**

280

### And you thought your teenagers were rough on a car.

One of the reasons a Range Rover withstands the rigors of normal driving conditions so stupendously is that it was designed to withstand the rigors of decidedly abnormal ones.

The sands of the Sahara. The snows of Kilimanjaro. Jungles. Craters. Mud-covered savannahs.

With a unique 14 gauge steel chassis, Range Rovers not only get through mile

after mile of arduous terrain, they get through year after year of it.

In fact, Range Rovers in their third decade are still climbing, wading and

generally conquering adversity all over the world.

So if the idea of an extravagantly luxurious, undauntably rugged vehicle appeals to you, call 1-800 FINE 4WD for the name of a dealer near you.

It's not surprising that even at roughly $38,000 many people consider a Range Rover well worth the price.

It is, after all, a jungle out there.

281

### ISN'T IT NICE TO LIVE IN A TIME WHEN WOMEN AREN'T BEING PUSHED AROUND SO MUCH ANYMORE?

Women have spent the last ten centuries conforming to their lingerie. Fortunately, lingerie has finally gotten around to conforming to women.

**MAIDENFORM®**

282

Last year, the U.S. Department of Transportation reported more traffic fatalities on normal weather days than on rainy and snowy days combined. Unfortunately, the sun's glare and haze can create a blind spot right where a driver needs visibility most: the front windshield. Ordi-

## 78° And Not A Cloud In The Sky. What A Hazardous Day For A Drive.

nary sunglasses give drivers only partial protection from the sun's distractions. After all, they were designed more for viewing the curves on the beach than the ones on the road. That's exactly why we've developed Ray-Ban Sunglasses for Driving, sunglasses created specifically to help you keep your eyes on the road. With brown B-15 Top Gradient Mirror lenses and 100% UV protection, they're highly effective at screening out blue light. Which simply means they clear up road haze and sharpen detail without any color distortion. What's more, the top portion of the lens is mirrored to help reduce overhead glare, while the uncoated lower lens still gives you a crisp and clear view of the instrument panel. And unlike photochromic lenses that require ultra-violet sunlight to darken fully, Ray-Ban B-15 lenses always stay dark enough to reduce dangerous glare.

All of which help make Ray-Ban Sunglasses for Driving the safest thing you could wear in your car next to a seat belt. Of course it doesn't hurt if the car you're driving is also designed for safety—like the Volvo 740, the Grand Prize in our Test-Drive Sweepstakes. To enter, just pick up an official entry form at your Ray-Ban dealer. And while you're there, test-wear a pair of Ray-Ban Sunglasses for Driving. They can turn 78° and sunny back into what it was always meant to be: a beautiful day for a drive.

*Ray-Ban*
**Sunglasses For Driving.**

283

| MANUFACTURER COUPON | EXPIRES 02-28-91 |
|---|---|

PROTECTIVE COATING ACTION
ORIGINAL FORMULA
Pepto-Bismol
Soothing relief for:
• Indigestion • Upset Stomach
• Heartburn • Diarrhea • Nausea
12 FL. OZ.

# 30¢ OFF
one any size

CONSUMERS: Redeem ONLY by purchasing the brand size(s) indicated. May not be reproduced. Void if transferred to any person, firm or group prior to store redemption. You pay any sales tax. Any other use constitutes fraud. LIMIT ONE COUPON PER PURCHASE. DEALER: Sending coupons to Procter & Gamble, 2150 Sunnybrook Drive, Cincinnati, Ohio 45237 signifies compliance with "Requirements for Proper Coupon Redemption." Copy available by writing to the above address. Cash Value 1/100 of 1 cent. 9011

90704

PROCTER & GAMBLE

5 00149 66130 3

# A SPECIAL OFFER FOR THOSE WHO DON'T FLY ALASKA AIRLINES.

For relief of minor discomfort due to bad food, cramped seating, and the aggravation often associated with late flights, use this coupon.

Or take a flight on Alaska Airlines. You'll be treated to a fresh delicious entree, roomy seating, superb on-time performance, and our award-winning service all along the way.

So, if you're going to fly on another airline, take this coupon to your nearest retailer. Or, call your travel agent or Alaska Airlines at 1-800-426-0333. And take the one that's proven most effective against travel irritation.

284

# £167,000 for a can of soup?

# Heaven only knows what a can of Stella would fetch.

'The main body and substance of the work stems mainly, one would suspect, from the so called "Barley School" of France, Belgium and Germany.' Marina Vaizey, Sunday Times

'The work appears to have matured dramatically over the past eight weeks, leaving its contemporaries floundering.' Bruce Bernard

'The Czechoslovakian influence is very much in evidence. One can detect the use of "Saaz" in the artist's approach to his work.' Sue Davies, Photographers Gallery

'Hop Art?' Brian Sewell, Evening Standard

'Gee.' Andy Warhol

'Such is the overwhelming interest in this particular work, one would not expect the bidding to stop until at least 11pm.' Jocelyn Stevens, Royal College of Art

'I'm sure it's not my round.' Hunter Davies

**Stella Artois. Reassuringly expensive.**

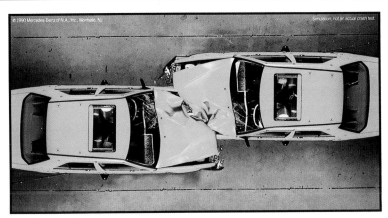

© 1990 Mercedes-Benz of N.A., Inc., Montvale, NJ.  Simulation, not an actual crash test.

# The perfect accident?

The front left corner of the eastbound car has abruptly met the front left corner of the westbound car in an offset frontal impact.

If two cars had to meet this way, how fortunate that they were both Mercedes. Because every new Mercedes-Benz has been designed from the drawing board up with this specific type of crash in mind.

Mercedes-Benz studies show that serious accidents far more often involve offset than direct head-on impacts. So the forward chassis and body structure of a Mercedes-Benz is ingeniously configured to absorb, channel and distribute impact forces in *both* offset and head-on collisions. Aiming to blunt the thrust of kinetic energy before it reaches the passenger area.

ENGINEERED LIKE NO OTHER
CAR IN THE WORLD

Aiming to reduce the occupants' risk of serious injury.

Even with this defense against offset impacts, the absolutely no-risk, no-damage, no-injury accident is and probably always will be unattainable.

But that has never discouraged the engineers of Mercedes-Benz from trying. And never will.

For further information on Mercedes-Benz safety, call 1-800-243-9292 anytime.

289

290        291

292

293

DON'T ROUGH IT.          LIVE LIFE IN COMFORT.

**294**

DON'T ROUGH IT.          LIVE LIFE IN COMFORT.

**295**

**296**

## OF COURSE, YOU COULD GO TO A MORE FAMOUS ISLAND THAN LANA'I. MILLIONS OF OTHERS DO.

Imagine spending the day on a golden beach where your footprints are the only ones left in the sand.

imagination you say. Hardly.

All it really takes is a trip to Lana'i. Hawaii's Private Island.

late 1990), a grand beachfront resort. Both are quite exclusive, offering exceptional accommodations, exquisite dining, and championship golf.

The island itself is all yours to explore. There are reef-protected coves, perfect for snorkeling. Ancient petroglyphs to discover and ponder. And a 3,370-foot summit where you can gaze

Imagine exploring misty forests of Norfolk pines and stark red moonscapes all in one afternoon.

Imagine picking ripe mangoes for lunch, then enjoying an elegant dinner that evening.

It takes a rather vivid

On this 140-square-mile playground, getting away from it all is anything but a worn cliché.

In fact, there are but two luxurious retreats on the entire island. The Lodge at Koele, an elegant country estate, and the Manele Bay Hotel (opening

down upon the islands of Oahu, Maui, Molokai, Hawaii and Kahoolawe.

The truth is, Lana'i has something for everyone.

Only everyone won't be there.

For an invitation to Rockresorts on Lana'i, call us: 1-800-54-LANAI.

HAWAII'S PRIVATE ISLAND

**297**

## ON LANA'I, TWO'S COMPANY, THREE'S A CROWD, AND FOUR IS PRACTICALLY UNHEARD OF.

Imagine having 140 square miles of paradise practically to yourself.

Welcome to Lana'i, Hawaii's Private Island. There are just two

need to hurry up and enjoy Hawaii.

No hurry at all.

Travel by horseback to the ancient ruins of Kaunolu Village, once the per-

championship golf courses with views so spectacular, keeping your eye on the ball is next to impossible. A marine preserve where you can snorkel face to fin with Hawaii's state fish, the humuhumunukumukuapua'a. And secluded beaches where you'll be interrupted only by the presence of your own shadow.

luxurious resorts here. The Lodge at Koele, a grand country estate. And an elegant beachfront villa known as the Manele Bay Hotel (opening late 1990). Each of these resorts hosts a limited number of guests. So there is never any pressure to beat the crowds, no

sonal playground of King Kamehameha the Great. His warriors proved their bravery by leaping from the cliffs into the water 60 feet below.

Please don't attempt this yourself.

Instead, enjoy the many amenities this island affords. We have

Is this the Hawaii you long to experience?

Don't ponder the question too long. Others have already made up their minds.

For an invitation to Rockresorts on Lana'i, call us: 1-800-54-LANAI.

### LANA'I
HAWAII'S PRIVATE ISLAND.

**298**

GREAT·BRITAIN

## In Britain, you can stay at an 18th-century inn. Or you can stay at a really old one.

Step over the threshold of a British inn, and you'll step back hundreds of years. Back to the times of the Tudors and the Stuarts, of saints, of smugglers and of highwaymen.

Only in Britain can you stay in a grand Georgian house one night and a rose-smothered country cottage the next. You can wake up in a seaside Bed and Breakfast to tea, toast and honey.

You can take the old adage "a man's home is his castle" literally and hang your hat in one of Britain's majestic castles-turned-hotels. Or wander off the beaten track for a fireside chat and a pint in a cozy family-run farmhouse.

OVER 200 INNS AND HOTELS ON BRITISH AIRWAYS HOLIDAYS

Whether you prefer staying in centuries-old inns or modern hotels, the British Airways Holidays "London Plus ..." brochure offers you a multitude of options. For example, "Britain Auto-Hotel Holiday" gives you a rental car with unlimited mileage for five days and accommodations with private bath at your choice of more than 200 inns and hotels in England, Scotland and Wales. All from just $323 to $464 per person, double occupancy.

Prices include your room for five nights, delicious full English breakfasts, hotel service charges and taxes. Extra-night rates are also available.

For a great way to get to know

the British as well as Britain, there's the "Bed and Breakfast Fly/Drive Holiday." This unique program combines an unlimited-mileage rental car with a choice of hundreds of Bed and Breakfast locations, from farmhouses and country cottages to small private homes in sub-

urban settings. The cost is just $41 to $69 per person per night, double occupancy, lodging taxes included.

For vacations that take you off the beaten path to some of the most distinguished inns and hotels in Britain, look into the British Airways Holidays "Preferred Vacations" brochure. For example, "Fine Country House Hotels of Britain" offers a select collection of outstanding country house hotels, providing comfortable, often luxurious accommodations, excellent service and fine food in a peaceful country setting. All of these exclusive arrangements are

more affordable than you'd imagine. The cost is merely $80 to $183 per person per night, double occupancy, and includes a room with private bath, a full English breakfast, service charges, taxes and special amenities. Or for a unique adventure in nice, clean country air, consider "English Walking Tours" in the Cotswolds, Cornwall or Derbyshire. These five-day walks include six nights' accommodations, full breakfast, lunch and dinner daily for $1005 per person. Prices shown do not include airfare.

To take advantage of any of these British Airways Holidays vacation arrangements, you must fly one of British Airways transatlantic services and book before you leave. So call 1-800-628-8997 or send the coupon today. Then see your travel agent.

Britain
We speak your language. Everywhere you go in the lands of Britain you will meet interesting and friendly people.

**BRITISH AIRWAYS**
The world's favourite airline®

**299**

## "I'D BE AN expert ON THIS BY NOW if I didn't have to take SO MANY naps."

SARAH BAGWELL, AGE 4
*Cardome Center, Georgetown, Kentucky*

NO, SARAH'S NOT MASTERING a new video game. It's a computer.

What's a four year old doing in the same room as a computer, you ask? "Why not? It's long overdue," replies Bill McKinney, director of the Georgetown community center that houses a new early childhood development program. "At first glance, we look like your everyday day care center. But what our kids do here between naps is quite remarkable."

Pre-schoolers here are taught a second language: Spanish. And when they're not playing in

the sandbox (still the most popular activity) they can be found in the computer room.

"By the time these children go to school they will be well prepared and ready to learn.

They'll know their colors, numbers and the alphabet. It gives them a tremendous advantage," says Bill.

Giving every youngster a

running start in life is the dream of Bill McKinney and his dedicated staff of 25.

And although it's still in its infancy, the program is already regarded by experts as a model for the nation.

Toyota is proud to have donated the $1.3 million

Georgetown needed to start this important community and childcare center.

Naturally, we're happy that the children of so many of our employees are benefitting from this superb day care.

But we are even more excited by the long-term value of Bill's vision to the country as a whole.

How great will the impact of this project be? We're not sure.

Although we hope that some day Sarah and her trusty computer will be able to give us the answer.

**TOYOTA**
INVESTING IN THE INDIVIDUAL

---

THERE'S BEEN A LOT OF TALK about the environment lately. But out on Chesapeake Bay, sailing around on a vintage skipjack, a group of school kids are learning that when it comes to the environment, actions speak louder than words.

Myrtha Allen, Environmental Sciences teacher at P.S. 405, Baltimore, explains, "Most of my kids are city born and bred. They live in apartments, they get their milk in cartons, their eggs in those styrofoam containers. They were about as interested in the environment as they are in

## "IT WAS THE FIRST FISH Jawan had seen that WASN'T SURROUNDED by french fries."

MYRTHA ALLEN, Teacher

homework." She smiles at a nearby eight-year-old. "And who can blame them? Some of them, like Jawan here, had never even seen a live fish before."

That's where the Chesapeake Bay Foundation stepped in. Since 1966, when it started in Annapolis, Maryland, with a rented fishing trawler and little else, the Foundation has taken more than 300,000 students out into the Bay to experience the environment first hand. And at the same time making them aware of how important their contribution is to the future of the planet.

Myrtha puts it simply. "To get these kids wanting to clean up the world, we've got to get their hands dirty."

And they do. They get very dirty.

"Oh yeah," chuckles Myrtha, "we do it all. Once we threw a net in just to see what we'd get. When we pulled it up, sure enough there were the milk cartons, the soda cans, the egg containers. And flapping around in the middle of it all was this big, cranky striped bass. You should've seen their faces.

"We took 20 little consumers out on a boat that day. We came back with 20 budding environmentalists."

At Toyota, we're proud that through the

support we give to the Foundation more kids like Jawan will be able to experience our fragile environment first hand. And hopefully start playing an active part in preserving it.

Is the program working? "These kids are organizing neighborhood recycling drives,

they're writing letters to Senators. Take a look at these posters some of my students have been doing."

The classroom walls are alive with crayon and pencil. Bright orange crabs. Smiling oysters. Families of ducks.

And one poster that stops everyone. It's of a smiling little boy holding hands with a big striped bass. And boldly scrawled above both their heads is one word: "Brothers".

And it's signed by Jawan. Age eight.

**TOYOTA**
INVESTING IN THE INDIVIDUAL

In a sport where you spend
so much time looking at your feet,
you should like what you see.

302

303

304

Pella® windows are one of the great

classified secrets of all times.

Mention in the

## PELLA SELLS WINDOWS. APPARENTLY, WE SELL HOUSES, TOO.

classifieds that a house has Pella windows, and it somehow seems to sell better.

It's amazing.

Then again, maybe not so amazing. Because Pella windows speak volumes about any house they're in. They tell people that a house is top of the line. That whoever built it probably didn't cut corners.

**BUILT TO IMPOSSIBLY HIGH STANDARDS. OUR OWN.**™

That in addition to being a comfortable place to live, it's probably a good long-term investment.

So if you're building or renovating a house, be sure to choose Pella windows.

Because a Pella window is the handiest tool of all. A selling tool.

For a free copy of our Window-scaping® Idea Book, and the location of The Pella Window Store® nearest you, please call 1-800-524-3700.

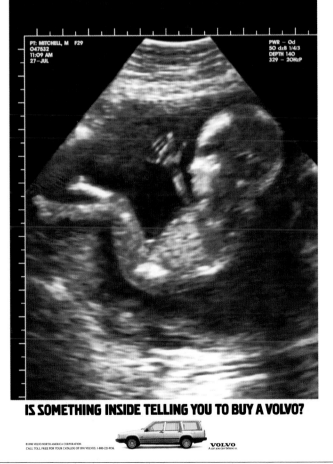

# How to keep a dog looking for birds instead of the pick-up truck.

Any reasonable hunter would admit that, out here, your dog is the one doing most of the work.

A good pointer can run 20 miles for every 5 his owner walks.

It's no jog in the park, either. In and out of brambles, over and under logs, trailing scent through enough bogs, barbed-wire fences and sharp-cut silage to make a triathlon look like a cakewalk.

But if he hasn't stoked up on the extra nutrition a working dog needs, your dog can flat run out of gas before you run out of birds.

When it comes to nutrition for hunting dogs, no dog food, no matter where it's bought, brings more to the table than Purina' Puppy Chow, Dog Chow, and HiPro dog foods.

Extra nutrition should start extra young with hunting dogs. Because the last thing you want is to shortchange developing bones, muscles, and nosepower you'll be relying on years later.

Puppy Chow provides all the extra protein, calcium and iron needed to help a pup reach its potential his papers promise.

It also supplies those extra calories he'll burn. Especially if his first year's training calls for a lot more than playing catch with a rubber ball.

Once a hunting dog is grown, he needs a dog food that's not only 100% nutritionally complete and balanced, but highly digestible.

So more nutrition ends up in the dog than on your lawn.

Purina Dog Chow leads the pack with a full 1650 digestible calories to the pound.

Its balanced formula contains 43 essential nutrients. Including a healthy 21% protein to help keep a dog's muscles, bones and foot pads tougher than the terrain.

For the hunter who likes to get the most out of a box of shells, and expects as many rounds out of his gun dog, Purina developed an even higher octane dog food.

Purina' HiPro Dog Meal. With 29% more protein than the average dog food, HiPro helps build muscles and the red blood cells needed to fuel those muscles.

It also delivers all 43 essential vitamins, minerals and nutrients, and packs more energy per pound than the bulk of dog foods on the shelf. 1750 digestible calories.

There are only three kinds of hunting dogs. Growing. Full-grown. And full-bore.

By now, you no doubt have an idea which of these brands from Purina is right for your kind of dog and your style of hunting.

Combine it with good training and the right conditioning, and you're bound to have less trouble keeping that gun dog pointed safely in the right direction.

Away from the truck.

Field tested, time proven.

308

---

YOUR ONLY COMPLAINT IS YOU CAN'T DO IT AGAIN TOMORROW.

Seventeen degrees and icing. Only one hunter you know is crazy enough to be out here. But you brought along a few dozen decoys for company, and your feathered friends ought to be dropping in any time now. Soon you'll be warm and they'll be frozen.

AMMUNITION THAT WORKS AS HARD AS YOU DO

309

---

"Every driver has his own dream of luxury, and most don't dare dream this high. 'World's finest' is an elusive crown to capture, but the Lexus LS 400 is definitely in the running."
*Car and Driver, September 1989*

"Our auto editors practically drooled over the car's performance, styling, ride, and comfort."
*Popular Science, December 1989*

"Lexus offers a concert hall, seven-speaker Nakamichi stereo option that's just devastating."
*Automotive Industries, August 1989*

"Breathtaking."
*Motor Trend, August 1989*

"Imagine a high-speed cloud with a leather interior."
*Car and Driver, September 1989*

"Manufacturers usually require years to refine their cars to Lexus' level of competence, and almost none ever gets this far."
*U.S. News & World Report, January 8, 1990*

"You might not be able to hear a mighty V-8 roar, but this 4.0-liter, 32-valve DOHC powerplant puts out 250 horsepower that you can feel from the bottom to the top of the rev range."
*Automobile Magazine, January 1990*

"These guys have thought of everything."
*Road & Track, September 1989*

"The engine is as tempting as sin. It'll push you through the wind with an ease normally reserved for things with wings."
*Car and Driver, September 1989*

"The 1990 Lexus LS 400 is our choice for the best car of 1989."
*Popular Science, December 1989*

# Who Needs An Advertising Agency?

"Our panel was almost unanimous in its admiration for the new Lexus LS 400."
*Playboy, March 1990*

"A driving experience that can only be called marvelous."
*Car and Driver, January 1990*

"Accelerates like a train (on very smooth rails) all the way to its top speed."
*Road & Track, September 1989*

"The LS 400 is a pioneering vehicle."
*Automobile Magazine, January 1989*

"There are countless details in a luxury sedan. Lexus, particularly, seems to have lavished attention on every one of them."
*Car and Driver, December 1989*

"The Lexus LS 400 quickly distinguished itself as the comfort king."
*Popular Science, December 1989*

"There's a new player on the field, and a very good one."
*Road & Track, September 1989*

"At full power, as it rushes toward its redline, its spirit cannot be fully suppressed and there issues forth a most exquisite sound—an ethereal texture on the ears, a tear of silk. Seldom does luxury have such an audible dimension."
*Car and Driver, January 1990*

"Another masterstroke from the land of the perfect machine."
*Automobile Magazine, January 1990*

"A very thoughtful, beautifully crafted luxury sedan."
*Automobile Magazine, January 1989*

"One word I bring away from my four-day experience with the Lexus LS 400: 'Harmony.'"
*Asia Week, June 26, 1989*

"Lexus transports you literally and figuratively into another dimension. The car's smoothness and air of total integration is both a wonder and a delight."
*Car and Driver, January 1990*

"You can bet there are some nervous folks over on the Continent right about now."
*Motor Trend, August 1989*

"The Lexus LS 400 may be the first perfect car."
*Playboy, March 1990*

"The only way Toyota can improve its new Lexus LS 400 is by figuring out how the car can make wake-up calls and brew fresh coffee."
*"M" Magazine, February 1990*

"A remarkable engineering achievement."
*Road & Track, September 1989*

"This is a car that knows its business, whether the mission is a leisurely cruise or a flat-out charge up a mountain."
*Popular Science, December 1989*

"Toyota, in its first time at bat in the major leagues, slams one out of the park. The Lexus LS 400 is a formidable stroke."
*Car and Driver, December 1989*

"The LS 400 is about to kick some serious tail in the luxury-car market."
*Automobile Magazine, January 1990*

"This is quite possibly the smoothest, most refined driveline that isn't on the drawing board."
*Motor Trend, August 1989*

"The Lexus LS 400 is an exquisite automobile."
*U.S. News & World Report, January 8, 1990*

"This car applies high technology in a most endearing manner: to create the most nearly perfect sport sedan to date."
*Popular Science, December 1989*

"Nothing close to the Lexus flagship—in price, size and class—will be unaffected by the new standards the LS 400 has set."
*Automobile Magazine, January 1990*

The Lexus LS 400. A luxury sedan so rare and innovative that it's inspired something equally rare in the automotive industry: a public display of affection. For more information, call 800-USA-LEXUS.

LEXUS
The Relentless Pursuit Of Perfection.

310

# Sorry About Your Seats.

No matter what your Super Bowl tickets say, you could be sitting front row. That is, if you had a pair of Tasco binoculars. We have all kinds – standard binoculars, wide angles, zooms. **tasco**® We have compacts small enough to fit inside your shirt pocket. And our new In-Focus® binoculars never need focusing no matter who picks them up. Next time, bring Tasco binoculars to the game.® You'll have the best seats in the house.

TASCO –
BINOCULAR
SUPPLIER
TO THE NFL

For more information, write Tasco, P.O. Box 520080, Miami, Florida 33152 (add $3.00 for color catalog). Or call (305) 591-3670, Ext. 274.

Nike Air Trainer SC

Early morning, calling from a car phone. I know it's two thirty in the morning. And I apologize for calling so late. But I just had to call. Whataya mean who's this? Don't you know Diddley, this is Bo Jackson. Yeah, That Bo Jackson. I know I've never called you before. It's just that I'm having trouble sleeping and I was wondering if you wanted to play football. Come on, I got my new cross-training shoes on. OK, so you don't want to play football. Then how about a little kickboxing? No. How about lawn bowling? No. Pole vaulting? Contact bridge? Water ballet? A triathlon? Come on, I got my cross-training shoes on. Don't give me no jive about having to get sleep before work. I mean, how many jobs do you think I have and you don't hear me crying about it, do you? Alright then, wiffle ball? Wind sprints? Bulgarian folk dancing?

**CONSUMER MAGAZINE
COLOR: 1 PAGE OR SPREAD
INCLUDING MAGAZINE
SUPPLEMENTS**

**313**
**ART DIRECTOR**
David Jenkins
**WRITER**
Jim Riswold
**PHOTOGRAPHER**
Dan Lamb
**CLIENT**
Nike
**AGENCY**
Wieden & Kennedy/Portland

**314**
**ART DIRECTOR**
Charlotte Moore
**WRITER**
Janet Champ
**PHOTOGRAPHER**
Michael O'Brien
**CLIENT**
Nike
**AGENCY**
Wieden & Kennedy/Portland

**315**
**ART DIRECTOR**
Warren Eakins
**WRITER**
Peter Wegner
**PHOTOGRAPHER**
Pete Stone
**CLIENT**
Nike
**AGENCY**
Wieden & Kennedy/Portland

**316**
**ART DIRECTOR**
Rick McQuiston
**WRITER**
Steve Sandoz
**PHOTOGRAPHER**
Stock
**CLIENT**
Oregon Tourism
**AGENCY**
Wieden & Kennedy/Portland

313

314

# HAWAIIAN SHIRTS FOR YOUR FEET.

So, you're hanging ten in Maui or you're just stepping into your hot tub. Fine. You'll need a few things. First, you'll need a solid rubber outsole for traction. Then you'll need a spandex upper for breathability. Like gills, sort of. And you'll definitely need some wacky colors to make the fish think you're one of them. In short, you'll need NIKE Aqua Socks. Remember: when the going gets wet, the wet go Hawaiian.

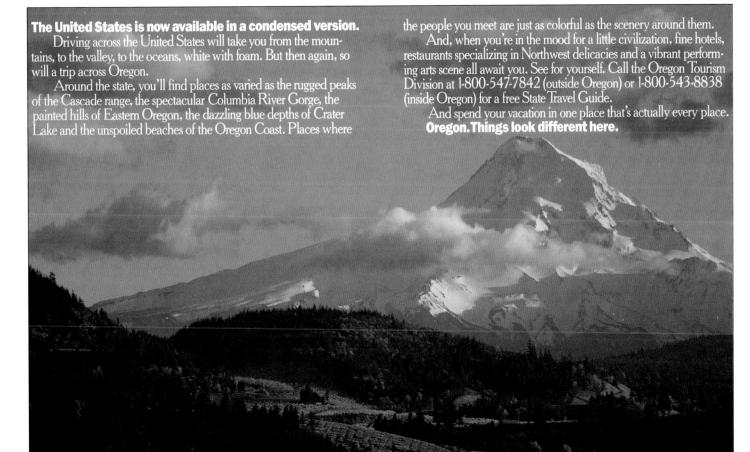

**The United States is now available in a condensed version.**

Driving across the United States will take you from the mountains, to the valley, to the oceans, white with foam. But then again, so will a trip across Oregon.

Around the state, you'll find places as varied as the rugged peaks of the Cascade range, the spectacular Columbia River Gorge, the painted hills of Eastern Oregon, the dazzling blue depths of Crater Lake and the unspoiled beaches of the Oregon Coast. Places where the people you meet are just as colorful as the scenery around them.

And, when you're in the mood for a little civilization, fine hotels, restaurants specializing in Northwest delicacies and a vibrant performing arts scene all await you. See for yourself. Call the Oregon Tourism Division at 1-800-547-7842 (outside Oregon) or 1-800-543-8838 (inside Oregon) for a free State Travel Guide.

And spend your vacation in one place that's actually every place.
**Oregon. Things look different here.**

## Global Warming. Acid Rain. Root Canal.
## Things could be worse, you could be a pension sponsor.

A world of trouble notwithstanding, pension management can be a lot to bear. Unless you're with

MassMutual. We provide quality investments, services and solutions for defined contribution and

defined benefit plans. And we do so with unwavering attention, uncompromising response. Our

financial strength is top-rated, and our expertise honed over forty years in the pension plan arena.

All told, we manage more than $13 billion in assets. We'd like to manage yours. Call Peter Vogian,

Senior Vice President, at (413) 788-8411, today. You'll find he can do you a world of good.

**MassMutual**
*Pension Management*
We help you keep your promises.℠

©1990 Massachusetts Mutual Life Insurance Co., Springfield, MA 01111.

## Our small company fund.
## Being greeted with wild enthusiasm by CFO's everywhere.

Thanks to a superior return potential at reduced risk, MassMutual's Small Company Fund

has prompted uncharacteristic zeal in certain quarters. Its diversified portfolio consists of

stocks selected on the basis of a unique product, market position or operating characteristic.

This value-oriented investment style minimizes volatility, maximizes return—the ideal way

to diversify while enhancing overall pension fund growth potential. Call Peter Vogian, Senior

Vice President, at (413) 788-8411 today. You'll barely be able to contain yourself.

**MassMutual**
*Pension Management*
We help you keep your promises.

©1990 Massachusetts Mutual Life Insurance Co., Springfield, MA 01111.

## The MassMutual 401(k). The most significant contribution
## to pension management since antacid.

A stressful world becomes all the more so in the arena of pension management. One form of relief is

MassMutual's exceptionally well administered 401(k). We deliver a variety of reports on time, accurately

and to specification. To maximize plan participation, we provide comprehensive communications

support. And we offer a range of proven investment funds including a guaranteed fund. All with the

benefit of top-rated financial strength and 40 years of retirement plan expertise. Call Peter Vogian,

Senior Vice President, (413) 788-8411, today. You'll find all he has to say easily digestible.

**MassMutual**
*Pension Management*
We help you keep your promises.℠

©1990 Massachusetts Mutual Life Insurance Co., Springfield, MA 01111.

CONSUMER MAGAZINE
B/W: CAMPAIGN
INCLUDING MAGAZINE
SUPPLEMENTS

319
ART DIRECTOR
Stuart Baker
WRITER
Tom Jenkins
PHOTOGRAPHER
Jack Bankhead
CLIENT
Majestic Wine Warehouses
AGENCY
HDM Horner Collis &
Kirvan/London

CONSUMER MAGAZINE
COLOR: CAMPAIGN
INCLUDING MAGAZINE
SUPPLEMENTS

320
ART DIRECTORS
John Horton, Ron Brown
WRITERS
Richard Foster, David Abbott
PHOTOGRAPHERS
John Brown, Tony Evans,
Christine Hanscomb
CLIENT
Sainsbury's
AGENCY
Abbott Mead Vickers.
BBDO/London

# At our prices you'll want to buy 12 bottles at a time.

## (That's just as well, because you'll have to.)

At Majestic you'll find a whole lot more to choose from, and whole lot less to pay, because we're wholesalers.

Unfortunately, this means you won't be able to buy less than 12 bottles at a time.

The good news is that you can take 12 bottles of anything. Choose a couple of mellow vintage clarets (the kind you wouldn't dream of offering guests), with half a dozen sparkling wines for that family get-together.

Add a bottle of sherry for the cleaner's birthday, a bottle of Taylor's Port for grandad, a 10 year old Macallans to help while away the autumn evenings, some Gordon's Gin (we also sell the tonic) and a bottle of VSOP Armagnac.*

That makes 13. But that's alright. After the first 12 you can buy as many as you like.

**The wine connoisseur is the one in the jeans.**

You won't find any stuffed shirts behind the counter at Majestic, just tee shirts.

But don't let that fool you. Our staff may not be wine snobs, but they're wine enthusiasts. They taste every wine that comes into their Warehouse.

They can also be very opinionated. Don't be surprised if they suggest what they consider to be a better wine at a cheaper price. They want to give their customers the best value, even if it means giving our finance director sleepless nights.

**Free wine tasting. (Now you've only got yourself to blame.)**

You'll always find at least 6 bottles of wine and one of Champagne open for tasting.

If there's anything you'd particularly like

to try, we'll be happy to open a bottle. (However, we do draw the line at vintage Krug and the Beaune '82.)

**The Ultimate Bribe - 15% off Champagne.**

We buy and sell in massive quantities, so we can afford to make extra-massive reductions in our profits on certain lines, in a ruthless and underhand gambit to get you into our Warehouses.

For the next few weeks it's 15% off a case of Champagne. And not off one you've never heard of, but off 24 you know and love.

Would you believe Bollinger RD 1979 reduced from £479.88 a case to £407.90, Louis Roederer Brut Premier (nv) from £227.88 to £193.70, Pommery (nv) from £197.88 to £168.20, Joseph Perrier (nv) from £167.88 to £142.70 etc., etc., etc. Is there no end to our generosity? (Offer ends Dec 16 1990.)

Call us on 0839 600547** for details of more reductions in our 'Weekend Specials'.

**We'll get you loaded.**

Every Majestic Wine Warehouse has free parking. And when you buy your case (or preferably, cases) our staff will be only too happy to carry it (them) to your car for you.

If you live locally, they'll even carry it home for you free, in one of our vans.

For more details about the world's most wonderful way to buy wine (and spirits) phone your local Majestic. They're open late 7 days a week. For your very own free guide to the world's most famous wine regions, see the bottom of this ad.

## Majestic Wine Warehouses

Now you can get it wholesale.

---

Life is tough for the customer at a Majestic Wine Warehouse.

We won't let you get away with simply grabbing the first bottle that happens to come to hand.

First of all you'll be faced with at least 6 open bottles of wine, and one of Champagne, which we'd dearly love you to taste.

If these wines are not to your taste, we'll open just about any bottle that takes your fancy. (Er, no... not the Beaune '82. Sorry.)

Then begins your epic journey around the Warehouse, with it's mind-boggling array of sherries, ports and spirits. And so many wines, from so many countries, all with comprehensive and critical descriptions written by our staff. (Take a course in speed reading.)

Never has so much been opened, by so few, for so many. (Opening hours are 7 days a week till late.)

**Connoisseur. Not, 'Can I con you, sir?'**

The way some wine salespeople go on, you'd think they were being paid a very tasty commission for pushing certain lines. Our sales staff will never sell you that old line.

They're wine enthusiasts who taste all the wines as they come into their Warehouse. Quiz them on any of our vintages, or even non-vintages.

We're a wholesaler, which means you have to buy at least 12 bottles at a time. (A mixed case of wines and spirits* will do). When you buy in these quantities,

we like to be sure you've made the right choices.

Our staff won't always try to sell you the most expensive wine, and if it's only good enough for the punch, they'll tell you.

Some of our much respected competitors think this disarming honesty is bad for business. That's their business.

**The Ultimate Bribe -15% off Champagne.**

We buy and sell in massive quantities, so we can afford to make extra-massive reductions in our profits on certain lines, in a ruthless and underhand gambit to get you into our Warehouses.

For the next few weeks it's 15% off a case of Champagne. And not off one you've never heard of, but off 24 you know and

love. Would you believe Bollinger RD 1979 from £479.88 a case to £407.90, Louis Roederer Brut Premier (nv) from £227.88 to £193.70, Pommery (nv) from £197.88 to £168.20, Joseph Perrier (nv) from £167.88 to £142.70 etc., etc., etc. Offer ends Dec 16 1990.

(Call Majestic now on 0839 600547** and find out about even more reductions on even more wines in our 'Weekend Specials'.)

**Off the back of a lorry.**

If you live in the area, Majestic will deliver your wine free. If you just can't wait to

get your booty home, you can pop it straight into the boot of your car, which you'll have parked free of charge at one of our 33 Warehouses' 33 car parks. Come round now. We're probably open.

erm... no! not bad. maybe? I'll take it.

## Majestic Wine Warehouses

Now you can get it wholesale.

---

# Three new concepts in wine salesmanship.

### The truth.

### The whole truth.

### And nothing but the truth.

So honest! Are we crazy? Not really.

You see, Majestic Wine Warehouses are wholesalers to the general public. This means you can buy wine at low, wholesale prices from a huge, wholesale selection.

It also means you'll have to buy 12 bottles at a time. (A mixed case of wines and spirits* will do.) And when you're buying in these quantities we feel we can't afford to let you make a mistake.

**An awful lot of nonsense is talked about wine. Just talk to our staff.**

Wine snobs have a language all of their own. Fortunately, it's not a language we speak at Majestic.

Our sales staff are wine enthusiasts, not wine snobs. They taste all the wines that come into their Warehouse, and they're used to talking about them in layman's language.

If your boss is coming to dinner and you're looking for a nice Premier Cru, just say, 'My boss is coming to dinner and I'm looking for a nice Premier Cru'.

If your son's home from university and is having some friends round, say, 'My son's home from university and is having some friends round. Anything over £1.60 a bottle would be wasted on them'. We understand.

**Ample Free Samples.**

Free samples at a wine store may seem as unlikely as a sale at the bank. But Majestic is unlike any other wine store.

There are always at least 6 wines open for tasting, as well as one Champagne. If there's a particular wine you'd like to try, our sales staff will open it for you, though we have to draw the line at

the more expensive vintages. After all, business is business, even at Majestic.

**Special Reductions on Quality Wines. Unfair competition? Yes.**

Of all the sneaky, underhand...

We've bought massive quantities (even more massive than our usual massive quantities) of some very special wines. This means we can sell them to our customers at very special low prices. Our customers are overjoyed. Our competitors are undercut. Happiness.

The wines include Bourgogne Hautes Cotes de Nuits 1988 (Domaine Gonet) reduced from £4.99 a bottle to £3.99, Beaujolais Villages 1989 (Domaine des Esseries) from £4.69 to £3.49, Chateau Richotey 1986 (AC Fronsac) from £4.29 to £2.99 and Vouvray Tete de Cuvee (Methode Champenoise) from £6.49 to £5.25. Offer ends November 25, 1990.

(Call Majestic on 0839 600547** and they'll tell you about even more reductions on our 'Weekend Specials'. Now that's really below the belt.)

**Cashchequecreditcard n'Carry.**

We don't mind how you pay, as long as you pay. And once our staff have got your cashchequecreditcard, they'll be only too happy to deliver your wine free if you live locally. If you've parked free of charge at one of our 33 Warehouses' 33 car parks, they'll carry it to the car for you.

If you'd like to look us up, look down at the bottom of this page for the phone number of your local Majestic. We're open late, 7 days a week.

## Majestic Wine Warehouses

Now you can get it wholesale.

# Sainsbury's present 100 year-old bacon.

What you see in the picture was a common sight in the Sainsbury's of yesteryear.

But while counter service is now a fond memory, the flavour of good old-fashioned bacon lingers on.

Sainsbury's Traditional Bacon is made the way bacon used to be made 100 years ago.

Slowly.

The entire curing process takes nearly a month. The joints are rubbed with salt, immersed in brine, drained and matured for 3 weeks.

As you can imagine, Sainsbury's Traditional Bacon has a meatier texture and flavour than standard bacon.

You can buy middle and streaky unsmoked, and back unsmoked or smoked.

The smoking process, like the cure, is done in the time-honoured way–in kilns over oak chips.

If you hanker for the flavour of a bygone age, take a trip to your local Sainsbury's.

You'll find us in Memory Lane.

**Good food costs less at Sainsbury's.**

---

George Eliot.

Bombay Duck.

German Shepherd.

Sparkling Riesling.

# A name can often create the wrong impression. (Even at Sainsbury's.)

A sparkling Riesling sounds as though it ought to be sweet and fruity.

In actual fact, this one is crisp, dry and elegant.

Made only from Riesling grapes it has a faint flavour of lemons and a pleasing richness.

It also has a history.

The wine makers of Schloss Wachenheim can be traced back to the Romans and they are sticklers for tradition.

Their Riesling gets its sparkle from a second fermentation in the bottle.

(The time-honoured secret of all great sparkling wines.)

In cool cellars under the centre of Wachenheim thousands of bottles are tended by hand as the wine rests and matures.

The finished wine is perfect served chilled as an aperitif or at celebrations.

And thanks to Sainsbury's you don't need to wait for one to try it.

At just £4.65 it has the style of wines costing three times as much.

One wrong impression we're sure you can live with.

**Good wine costs less at Sainsbury's.**

---

# Sainsbury's new boy and girl nappies. For people who don't want to spend all their disposable income on disposables.

If your baby gets through five nappies a day that's over 1,800 a year. (A lot of money to throw away.)

Which is why Sainsbury's have designed the best possible nappies at the lowest possible prices.

Our new range features all the latest developments in nappy technology.

We've improved the absorbency; with superabsorber granules placed where they're needed most – in the front for boys, lower for girls.

We've fitted new tapes that reseal every time, so it's always easy to check that your baby is feeling comfortable.

Our elasticated waistband fits more snugly.

We've introduced a Teddy Bear wetness indicator and we've even managed to pack the nappies more neatly, so they take up less room.

Best of all, our nappies cost much less than the major brands.

And isn't that a nice bottom line to end with? **SAINSBURY'S.**

CONSUMER MAGAZINE
COLOR: CAMPAIGN
INCLUDING MAGAZINE
SUPPLEMENTS

321
**ART DIRECTOR**
David White
**WRITER**
Daniel Searle
**PHOTOGRAPHER**
Stuart Crossett
**TYPOGRAPHER**
Peter White
**CLIENT**
Stuart Alexander
**AGENCY**
The Ball Partnership/
North Sydney

322
**ART DIRECTOR**
Kathy Delaney
**WRITER**
Greg DiNoto
**PHOTOGRAPHERS**
Duane Michals, Ken Shung
**CLIENT**
Mass Mutual Life Insurance
**AGENCY**
Bozell/New York

A promise to let you color a red rose green.

A promise that a secret whispered is as good as kept.

A promise you can always rely on me.

Nothing binds us one to the other like a promise kept. Nothing divides us like a promise broken. At MassMutual we believe in keeping our promises. That way all the families and businesses that rely on us can keep theirs.

**MassMutual**®
We help you keep your promises.℠

A promise not to tell who really picked out the prom corsage.

A promise to keep the dreaded Aunt Edna from checking in when I'm away on business.

A promise to make things easier for you than they were for me.

Nothing binds us one to the other like a promise kept. Nothing divides us like a promise broken. At MassMutual we believe in keeping our promises. That way all the families and businesses that rely on us can keep theirs.

**MassMutual**®
We help you keep your promises.℠

A promise two wheels will replace three, once your feet can reach the pedals.

A promise that you won't be the only one wearing galoshes in the rain.

A promise you'll feel as safe tomorrow as you do today.

Nothing binds us one to the other like a promise kept. Nothing divides us like a promise broken. At MassMutual we believe in keeping our promises. That way all the families and businesses that rely on us can keep theirs.

**MassMutual**®
We help you keep your promises.℠

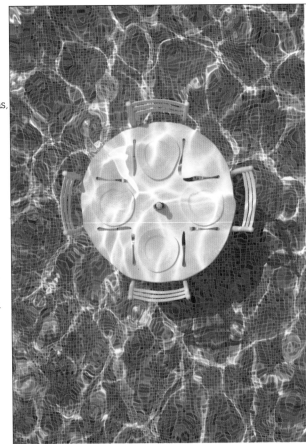

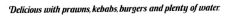

*Delicious with prawns, kebabs, burgers and plenty of water.*

*Specially Prepared Sauces from Heinz.*

*Delicious with Chinese, with Italian, with French, with caution.*

*Specially Prepared Sauces from Heinz.*

*Delicious on steak, on chicken, on fish, on your own.*

*Specially Prepared Sauces from Heinz.*

## Smoking or non-smoking?

Never before has freedom of choice been more joyfully apparent than in the two Volkswagen Golfs before you.

On your left is the Golf GTi 16V. If you've ever wondered where the expression, "smokin' down the highway" originated, you'll have your answer after one test-drive. This GTi 16V is gutsy.

It boasts a 2 litre, 16-valve, 134 hp engine and comes with BBS alloy wheels and a calibrated sports suspension.

If, however, speed is not of the essence, there is our popular Golf, on your right. A sporty, fun-to-drive car, just slightly less powerful. Being Golfs, they are versatile and roomy.

Being Volkswagens, they display the sure, responsive road handling typical of German engineering. So why endow one model with different driving personalities?

Because Volkswagen engineers have long observed that no two people are alike in their driving personalities.

So offering options within the Golf model range is simply par for the course.

**Golf**

## After 40 years on the road we still haven't worked out all the bugs.

You'd think they'd be long gone by now.

But no. Venture out onto any highway and chances are you'll still spot a Beetle scooting merrily down the road.

Not bad for a car that made its debut in the early 1950's.

You can thank our German engineers for its staying power. They've always been obsessed with building durable, reliable cars. Just look at the current Volkswagen line-up displayed here.

Each one has been inspected by hand, eye and computer. They've even been x-rayed. (Obsession knows no bounds.)

The Passat's valves are self-adjusting to keep its power up and fuel consumption down.

The Jetta's dash can survive temperatures from −41°C to 54°C. no sweat.

Every Volkswagen is the product of hours of gruelling, torturous tests even Hercules couldn't survive.

All because our engineers believe a car isn't worth its salt unless you can depend on it not only day after day, but year after year.

Just ask any Beetle owner.

## Mighty oaks from little acorns grow.

Who would have dreamed that from that cute, little acorn of a Beetle way back in the 50's would evolve an entire line of sophisticated automobiles typified by the new Passat you see before you.

Yet here the Passat stands. With enough space to accommodate 51 university students (compared to the Beetle's 23). Or 5 sane adults, whichever comes first.

Here is an automobile that rivals in comfort and handling, the legendary road sedans of Germany (without, of course, rivalling their staggering price tags).

Although the Passat is one of the more expensive Volkswagens we've ever built, its litany of features more than compensates for its starting price of under twenty-thousand dollars.*

There is, by way of example, air conditioning, a tilt steering wheel, power heatable mirrors and a sophisticated track-correcting rear suspension system that must be experienced to be appreciated. Plus interior space so vast the rear seats actually recline.

But enough. Suffice it to say, this mighty oak stands proudly in your Volkswagen dealer's showroom.

**Passat**

*Based on our new Passat GL which has a manufacturer's suggested retail price of $22,710.00. Options, destination charge and dealer preparation extra. Dealer may sell for less.

CONSUMER MAGAZINE
COLOR: CAMPAIGN
INCLUDING MAGAZINE
SUPPLEMENTS

325
ART DIRECTOR
Beth Kosuk
WRITER
Robin Raj
CLIENT
WQXR 96.3 FM
AGENCY
Carroll Raj Stagliano/
New York

326
ART DIRECTOR
Angela Dunkle
WRITER
Dion Hughes
PHOTOGRAPHERS
Bo Hylen, Steven Raber
CLIENT
Mitsubishi
AGENCY
Chiat/Day/Mojo, Venice

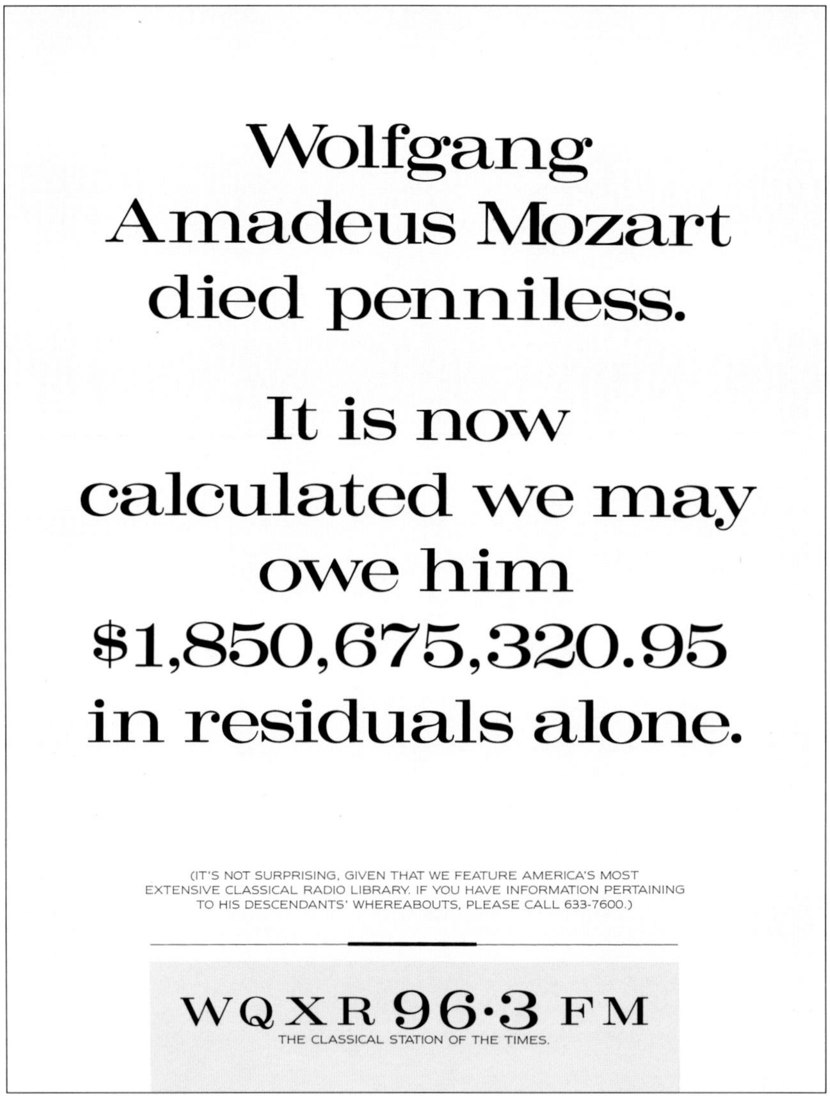

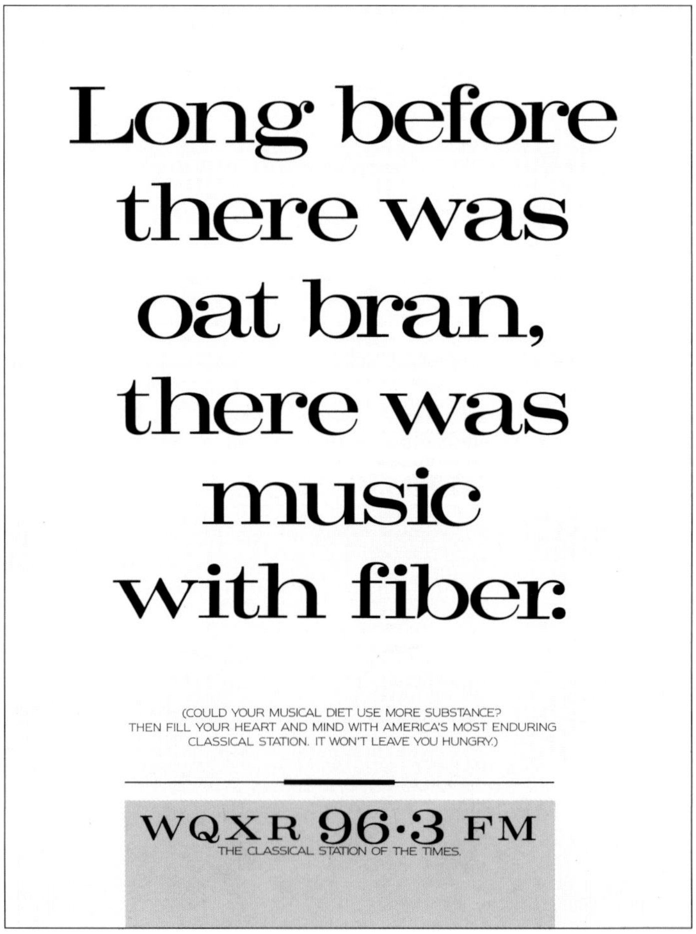

Wolfgang
Amadeus Mozart
died penniless.

It is now
calculated we may
owe him
$1,850,675,320.95
in residuals alone.

(IT'S NOT SURPRISING, GIVEN THAT WE FEATURE AMERICA'S MOST
EXTENSIVE CLASSICAL RADIO LIBRARY. IF YOU HAVE INFORMATION PERTAINING
TO HIS DESCENDANTS' WHEREABOUTS, PLEASE CALL 633-7600.)

WQXR 96·3 FM
THE CLASSICAL STATION OF THE TIMES.

We can't
comment on
whether Elvis
is alive.
But we can
confirm that
Beethoven's
doing quite well.

(WE HEAR FROM HIM SEVERAL TIMES A DAY.
AND HE'S NOT JUST GETTING OLDER. HE'S GETTING BETTER. LISTEN FOR
YOURSELF ON "AMERICA'S CLASSICAL STATION OF THE YEAR.")

WQXR 96·3 FM
THE CLASSICAL STATION OF THE TIMES.

Long before
there was
oat bran,
there was
music
with fiber.

(COULD YOUR MUSICAL DIET USE MORE SUBSTANCE?
THEN FILL YOUR HEART AND MIND WITH AMERICA'S MOST ENDURING
CLASSICAL STATION. IT WON'T LEAVE YOU HUNGRY.)

WQXR 96·3 FM
THE CLASSICAL STATION OF THE TIMES.

325

The sound of a single bullet buzzed straight past my ear.

I didn't have to look at the rear-view mirror to know that Dubrov was back on our tail. Our only avenue of escape was through the street market up ahead.

The brightly colored patchwork of stalls rushed up to meet us as Johnson put his foot to the floor. A crate of watermelons exploded wetly against the car, the pink juice streaming across the windscreen.

I stole a quick glance in the mirror. Dubrov's gleaming black limo was getting closer by the second.

It was then that I sensed the first hints of acrid smoke. The stink of a grinding, dying engine.

Our car was going to go, and with it, all our chances.

And as the billowing smoke began to tear at my nostrils and burn my eyes, I realized that it was something much, much worse than an overheated engine. It was my chicken pot pie burning in the kitchen, the charred, inedible victim of my engrossment in Mitsubishi's Home Theater with Dolby Surround Sound.

The insane laughter faded away behind me. To one side of the clearing sat a deserted house, as decomposed and forgotten as the people who'd once lived there.

The door opened, and I was in the front room, a room so dark I felt I could reach out and run my fingers through its inky stillness.

From outside the window came the sounds of the night. Owls. Crickets. And from across the room…drip, drip, drip.

My eyes, adjusting to the light, made out what appeared to be a coat hanging from a hat rack, but as the haze dissolved from my sight I saw that from the neck of the coat stared the lifeless face of Kuperman, his eyes frozen in horror. A shrieking laugh, as inescapable as a nightmare, rang out around me.

My heart, already shaking at the cage of my chest, exploded as a hand fell upon my shoulder.

"So how do you like the Mitsubishi Home Theater's surround sound?" asked the sales guy.

"Uhhh, great" I said, as I stumbled to the door of the showroom for a breath of fresh air.

Swimming at night had never bothered me before. But as I watched the sun retreat behind the horizon, an overwhelming sense of loneliness swept over me.

I peered into the heavy black water and knew that this was now an alien world, no longer a turquoise playground, but something dark, mysterious, uncaring.

The peaceful murmur of waves and seagulls, sounds I usually found so comforting, had taken on a sinister and mocking air.

Suddenly, there was a splash somewhere off to my right. I turned, but could see nothing. My breath quickened as I heard another ripple, this time behind me.

I was fighting to keep the rush of adrenaline from pushing me into a blind panic when, my God! I felt something brush against the soles of my feet.

As my terror found voice in a bellowing scream I realized it was only my cat Columbus, and that watching a movie such as this on a Mitsubishi Home Theater with Dolby Surround Sound was not, repeat not, good for my nerves.

CONSUMER MAGAZINE
COLOR: CAMPAIGN
INCLUDING MAGAZINE
SUPPLEMENTS

327
ART DIRECTOR
Dennis Stevens
WRITER
Johanna Quinn Templeton
ILLUSTRATOR
Michael Schwab
PHOTOGRAPHER
Bermuda Government
Information Services
CLIENT
Bermuda Department of
Tourism
AGENCY
DDB Needham Worldwide/
New York

328
ART DIRECTOR
Houman Pirdavari
WRITER
Bruce Bildsten
PHOTOGRAPHER
Hiro
CLIENT
Timex Corporation
AGENCY
Fallon McElligott/Minneapolis

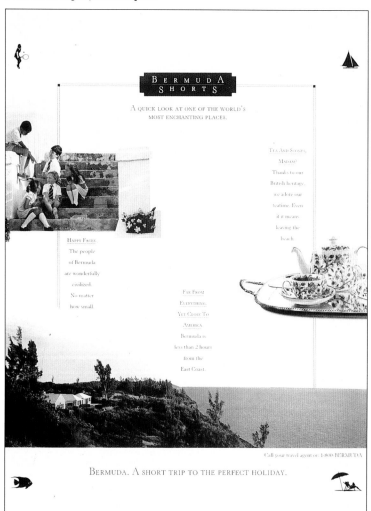

Lynn Hill, the world's top female rock climber, fell 85 feet and landed on her tailbone after she failed to secure the knot in her safety harness. A twenty-foot fall can be fatal. Her worst injuries were a dislocated elbow and a "sore butt." Lynn is wearing a dress watch from the Timex women's fashion collection. It has a very secure buckle. It costs about $45.

**TIMEX**

Edwin Robinson became blind and deaf after a truck accident. Nine years later he was struck by lightning and within hours his vision and hearing were restored. Edwin is wearing a dress watch from the Timex men's fashion collection. Water-resistant, it stands up to all kinds of weather. It costs about $45.

**TIMEX**

Raul Garcia has dived off the famous La Quebrada cliff in Acapulco, Mexico 37,348 times. The cliff is 87 feet high. The water below is 12 feet deep. The watch that Raul is wearing is water-resistant to 82 feet. It's from the Timex men's fashion collection. It costs about $40.

**TIMEX**

CONSUMER MAGAZINE
COLOR: CAMPAIGN
INCLUDING MAGAZINE
SUPPLEMENTS

329
ART DIRECTOR
Michael Fazende
WRITER
Bill Miller
PHOTOGRAPHER
Michael Johnson
CLIENT
The Lee Company
AGENCY
Fallon McElligott/Minneapolis

330
ART DIRECTOR
Bob Brihn
WRITER
Bruce Bildsten
PHOTOGRAPHER
Jim Arndt
CLIENT
Continental Granite
AGENCY
Fallon McElligott/Minneapolis

We think jeans should fit your waist, hips and thighs.
But most importantly, your head.

*Wearing Lee Relaxed Rider™ jeans is a nice thing to do for your body. But it's an even nicer thing to do for your head. They're made well. They fit right. They don't cost a bundle. And they won't try to make you into something you're not. Nobody fits your body...or the way you live...better than Lee.*
R E L A X E D · R I D E R S

Our new stretch jeans solve two major problems.
Inhaling and exhaling.

*Lee Pepper Stretch jeans are cut to fit your body, not to cut off your circulation. With a comfortable, relaxed fit, they move when you move. And they look exactly like regular denim jeans. The only person who will know you're wearing stretch jeans is you. Promise. Nobody fits your body...or the way you live...better than Lee.*
P E P P E R · S T R E T C H

Save yourself the trip.
Our newest jeans have already been through hell.

*You don't have to wait until the fourth or fifth time through the washer and dryer before you can wear these jeans in public. Lee's new Pepper Used jeans look and feel like your favorite pair of jeans the first time you try them on. Just the way you like them. Nobody fits your body...or the way you live...better than Lee.*
P E P P E R · U S E D

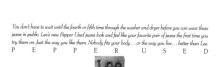

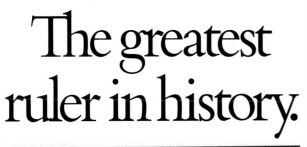

# The sound was jazz, the atmosphere was smoky, and the mood was martinis.

On the South Side of Chicago it was Lincoln Gardens, up in Harlem it was the Cotton Club. But it could have been just about anywhere there was a bar, a dance floor, and jazz.

We're not talking about jazz piano suites or orchestrated jazz stylings that passed for jazz in the mainstream. We're talking about real ear-piercing, heart-pounding New Orleans jazz, born from the souls of penniless musicians who traveled from club to club in rattletrap cars, luggage tied to the roof, and a makeshift bed in the back seat.

Young black artists like Johnny Dodds and Papa Joe Oliver were among the first of the new jazz stars. Night after night, they played to packed, smoke-filled houses, bringing with them this new form of music they invented.

Jazz was so new, the people went mad for it. "Night Clubbers," as they were called, poured into the hot spots to hear the new sounds from the South, to dance, and to drink. And the drink of choice was the martini.

However, the martini was more than the king of cocktails, it was a symbol for the thinking that was sweeping the nation after World War I. People were after things that were fun, new and exciting. And that's just what they got. Black met white, jazz bands played where orchestras once reigned, and cocktails were mixed in spite of prohibition.

Today the martini is back. And though you can't return to the Cotton Club or hear live jazz from the horn of Papa Joe Oliver, you *can* taste a martini just the way it was back then.

Gilbey's. Taste what it was all about.

### Gilbey's. The Authentic Gin.

# The dress was chiffon, the stockings were silk, and a martini was the height of fashion.

There's never been a time when fashion was invisible. Yet never a time was it so obvious as the 1920's. In fact, to the elegant Parisian or New Yorker fashion was considered vital.

These were the early days of great designers who still influence the fashion industry today. Their bold interpretations of the art deco style set the world on fire. New color, new material all brought out new looks. Looks that changed as quickly as the weather.

Perhaps it was a reaction to the drab gray of war. To the sacrifice. The sorrow. Whatever the reason, it seemed everyone was intent on outshining their friends and acquaintances.

But whether or not a dress was a designer original was just part of the story. Everything that was "in fashion" became part of one's own personal style. Viewing the latest portrait from Tamara de Lempicka, driving your Bugatti out on Long Island or listening to jazz on a gramophone were all fashion statements unto themselves.

Even ordering the right cocktail was part of fashion. And in the 1920's nothing was more fashionable than the martini. Today fashion is just as obvious. And though the times may call for a Patrick Kelly instead of a Paul Poiret, the martini is still made the same way.

Gilbey's. Good taste never goes out of style.

### Gilbey's. The Authentic Gin.

# The lighter was Sandoz, the jewelry Cartier, and a martini was the perfect accessory.

It was a game really. From her handbag the woman would reveal her silver Chaumet cigarette case. Slowly she'd roll a cigarette through her fingers giving her escort just enough time to reach inside his breast pocket for his gold Sandoz lighter. Then, just as the tip of the cigarette would part her lips, he'd strike the lighter illuminating her face for the entire room to see.

This game was played out in restaurants, ballrooms and clubs every night. And all the players were carefully selected long before the evening began. What cigarette case would suit the mood? What lighter would spark the flame? What necklace or ring would catch just a glint of the fire and send it racing back across the room?

The right accessory could say everything about you. No disposable items here. Make-up cases, pens, watches, everything that could help describe a person were beautifully finished down to the last detail. This attitude even spilled over into the drink one held. Most likely a martini.

But not just any martini. "A martini very dry with a dash of bitters," "A martini sweet, no olive," "A dry Gibson, stirred."

Today, personal accessories are making a comeback. Fountain pens cling to lapel pockets, timeless watches tick from wrists and elegant jewelry once again adorns necklines.

Even the martini is back. And the gin that made them then still makes them now. Gilbey's. A very tasteful accessory.

### Gilbey's. The Authentic Gin.

## The British have always driven on the wrong side of the road.

It's not that we can't get it right. We simply have our own way of doing things.

While other automobiles are either unusually rugged, or extravagantly civilized, we've made the one luxury car that isn't dependent on the luxury of a road.

Short of going across endangered terrain, there are very few places you won't see it.

With its massive chassis, and permanent 4-wheel drive, a Range Rover can go through anything from a desert to a snowstorm. In fact, it can even go through time, gracefully.

Range Rovers in their third decade are still performing automotive impossibilities from the Serengeti to the Himalayas.

**RANGE ROVER**

Lest we remain complacent, though, we always manage to make improvements that improve even a Range Rover.

The 1991, for example, has a quieter ride, along with a larger fuel tank for increased touring range.

Why not call 1-800-FINE 4WD for a dealer near you? Obviously, at around $42,400, a Range Rover isn't inexpensive.

But it's an investment you'll feel quite comfortable with.

Whichever side of the road you're on.

## No other luxury car makes as favorable an impression.

Granted, there are other luxury cars that boast an impressive array of amenities including leather seats, a multi-speaker sound system and burl walnut trim. Just like a Range Rover.

And, yes, there are other luxury cars that are capable of comfortably cruising at over 100 mph on the test track. Just like a Range Rover.

But no other luxury car can carve its way through blankets of road-closing snow. Take on puddles that could sink a canoe. Or conquer boot-swallowing mud. Just like a Range Rover.

Because no other luxury car is built like a Range Rover.

With its tenacious permanent 4-wheel drive and stump-pulling V-8 engine, a Range Rover can help you see your way through virtually anything. Even when there's no road in sight.

So why not call 1-800-FINE 4WD for the name of a Range Rover dealer near you?

At around $42,400, a Range Rover isn't something you'd buy every day.

It is, however, something you can drive every day.

**RANGE ROVER**

## And you thought your teenagers were rough on a car.

One of the reasons a Range Rover withstands the rigors of normal driving conditions so stupendously is that it was designed to withstand the rigors of decidedly abnormal ones.

The sands of the Sahara. The snows of Kilimanjaro. Jungles. Craters. Mud-covered savannahs.

With a unique 14 gauge steel chassis, Range Rovers not only get through mile after mile of arduous terrain, they get through year after year of it.

In fact, Range Rovers in their third decade are still climbing, wading and generally conquering adversity all over the world.

So if the idea of an extravagantly luxurious, undauntedly rugged vehicle appeals to you, call 1-800-FINE 4WD for the name of a dealer near you.

It's not surprising that even at roughly $38,000 many people consider a Range Rover well worth the price.

It is, after all, a jungle out there.

**RANGE ROVER**

CONSUMER MAGAZINE
COLOR: CAMPAIGN
INCLUDING MAGAZINE
SUPPLEMENTS

335
ART DIRECTOR
Jud Smith
WRITER
Kerry Casey
PHOTOGRAPHER
Rod Pierce
CLIENT
Federal Cartridge
AGENCY
Carmichael Lynch/
Minneapolis

336
ART DIRECTOR
Cathi Mooney
WRITER
Ken Mandelbaum
ILLUSTRATOR
Greg Winters
PHOTOGRAPHERS
Jill Sabella, Robert Ammirati
CLIENT
Dakin
AGENCY
Mandelbaum Mooney Ashley/
San Francisco

# The Leaves Turn, The Hunters Gather And The Bull Begins To Fly.

# Is It A Bigger Target You Need? Or Better Ammunition?

# Are You Killing The Sport Of Hunting?

**CONSUMER MAGAZINE COLOR: CAMPAIGN INCLUDING MAGAZINE SUPPLEMENTS**

**337**
**ART DIRECTOR**
Brian Fandetti
**WRITER**
Paul Silverman
**PHOTOGRAPHER**
George Petrakes
**CLIENT**
The Timberland Company
**AGENCY**
Mullen/Wenham

**338**
**ART DIRECTOR**
Woody Kay
**WRITER**
Steve Bautista
**PHOTOGRAPHER**
Aaron Jones
**CLIENT**
Dexter Shoe
**AGENCY**
Pagano Schenck &
Kay/Providence

## A good leather coat should have two arms and fifty feet.

In this world, there are many things that can be mass-produced.

But not a coat like this.

Not a coat that requires over fifty feet of the finest calfskin available anywhere on earth. Calfskin so perfect it can be tanned as is with vegetable oils.

Never painted or color corrected.

Not a coat whose every square inch has undergone the most expensive, most effective waterproofing known to man. A process in which we flood the leather with a special waterproof compound while it is being tanned in the drum, not afterwards.

This is the only technique that insures total penetration of the waterproofing agent. The only technique good enough for a garment that bears our name.

Not a coat whose comfort seems to increase the more you put it under the stress of active use. Because of the extra feet of calfskin, the extra hours of tailoring we spend opening up the back and shoulder dimensions. Adding features such as two-piece underarm gussets to maximize your freedom of movement.

And certainly not a coat whose detailing is so meticulous that every zipper is milled and tumbled smooth so as to not injure the leather, every button is genuine horn or brass, and every buttonhole is both calfskin bound and clean-finished with stitching inside and out.

In leather coats that lack this latter feature, shreds of lining will begin to emerge in a matter of months. But Timberland designers do not think in terms of months. They take a longer view of product longevity. Setting their sights on

a decade or two. Or more.

There is a method to our madness, and it is perfectly clear. We will do anything for the extra comfort and confidence of our customers.

Confidence, for example, that getting caught in a sudden downpour won't spoil your day or your valuable calfskin investment. Confidence that on the night your buddy spills a beer on your sleeve, you'll need to do nothing more than find a little water and a sponge.

The way we see it, consumer confidence is as hard to come by, in this age of shoddy products, as the world's highest quality calfskin.

Like our leather coats and jackets, it can't be mass-produced.

**Timberland**

Boots, shoes, clothing, wind, water, earth and sky.

---

## The Marines say Parris Island is the world's toughest boot camp. We beg to differ.

Everyone knows it takes weeks of hell to turn out a few good Leathernecks.

But how many people know what it takes to turn out a few good leather boots? Boots as waterproof as canteens, yet as comfortable as slippers.

You can find out fast at the world's toughest boot camp. A place called Timberland.

There we have devised tests that make the Chinese water torture seem like a walk in the park.

In one particularly grueling ordeal, we put a mass of water behind pieces of boot leather.

We then flex the leather again and again, simulating the movements the human foot might make were it slogging through a similar mass of water deep in no man's land.

After flexing each piece sixteen thousand times, we accept only one result. No leakage whatsoever. A single drop and the leather is rejected. No appeals, no second chances.

The truth is, rejections don't happen very often. Our method of waterproofing leather has been perfected over a period of twenty years, and it's the most expensive process known to man.

First, we cherrypick the world's leather supply, selecting only the cream of the crop. Then we flood every fiber of the leather, inside and out, with a special silicone waterproofing agent. We do this during the actual tanning so as not to miss a single space big enough for a water molecule to sneak in.

(We could practice shortcuts, such as brushing the surface of the leather with silicone. But then we'd be like any other boot company.)

Another torture test involves our so-called "boot within a boot," your ultimate insurance of dry, comfortable feet under the worst, wettest, coldest conditions.

The boot within a boot is actually a sock constructed of waterproof Gore-Tex, Thinsulate® insulation and smooth Cambrelle.

We take this innocent-looking sock and give it the infamous bubble test. We fill it with air, submerge it in a glass water tank, and we watch. One air bubble and the sock is sacked. Period.

Besides these and a multitude of other trials and tests, we construct our boots by impermeably bonding the upper to the midsole, creating a water-tight cradle around your foot. We keep seams to a minimum, and sew each stress point with no fewer than four rows of waterproof nylon lock stitching.

So, when a size 12 guide boot says Timberland on it, you know you can put it through anything.

Because it's already been there.

**Timberland**

Boots, shoes, clothing, wind, water, earth and sky.

---

## This shoe has 342 holes. How do you make it waterproof?

Wherever you look in our footwear line, you find holes.

You find wingtips with scores of stylishly arranged perforations.

You find handsewns with scores of needle holes. Moccasins. Canoe moccasins. Boat shoes. Ultralights for easy walking. Lightweight comfort casuals for weightless walking.

Built by a lesser waterproofer, each of these styles has enough openings to admit a deluge.

But we're the Timberland company, and you have to understand where we got our start. Over twenty years ago, we were exclusively a boot manufacturer, and we were the first people to successfully produce fine leather sporting boots that were totally waterproof.

The lessons we learned then are why we're able, today, to build wingtips and handsewns you could go wading in.

Lesson one. Select only the cream of the world's leather crop, then spend the money to impregnate every pore with silicone at the same time the leather is being tanned in the drum. (We leave the shortcuts to our competitors, the ones who merely brush the surface with silicone after the leather is tanned. And the consequences, unfortunately, we leave to their customers.)

Lesson two. Be inventive. It takes more than one technology to stop water.

For example, to build a waterproof wingtip, we take a page right out of the old Timberland bootmaker's manual. We bond the upper directly to the midsole, creating an impermeable seal around your foot.

Then we build a special umbrella under those stylish wing perforations. It's actually a "shoe within a shoe."

A bootie lining of our softest saddle glove leather, fully waterproofed with silicone. Guaranteed to stop a monsoon.

Handsewns require a different solution, but one that also harks back to our boot days, when we became an early collaborator of the W.L. Gore Company, creators of waterproof, breathable Gore-Tex™ fabric.

To waterproof the needle holes of a handsewn moc, we use an exclusive technique in which Timberland saddle glove leather is laminated to a Gore-Tex bootie. Once we place this inside the moc, you have a shoe that's an open and shut success. Open to air and shut tight to water. Climate-controlled, in other words, both inside and out.

So even if it never leaves the canyons of Wall Street, every Timberland waterproof shoe owes its character to a world that will never see a sidewalk. The canyons, tundras and marshlands where our boots were born.

Which makes Timberland shoes more than waterproof.

They're water proven.

**Timberland**

Boots, shoes, clothing, wind, water, earth and sky.

# The exclusive waterproof

*In creating these waterproof shoes, we've given them two features steeped in Scottish tradition.*

# fabric is Scottish.

*One is a unique and beautiful material, used for the last 100 years, that's amazingly effective at repelling water.*

# So is the price.

*The world's finest waxed cotton fabric. While the other is something the Scots have respected for centuries. A fair price.*

*The Argyle, with Highland Green waterproof waxed fabric and Thinsulate® thermal insulation, at $85 a pair.*

---

# After buying some dress

*If you're paying so much to dress up below the ankles that it affects what you can wear above them,*

# shoes, can you still afford

*then we have several solutions. They're called Dexter dress shoes. Footwear that provides what you want in a shoe—*

# to get dressed?

*the finest materials and workmanship—without tacking on precisely what you don't want. A premium at the cash register.*

*The Royale and the Ritz, part of the Dexter Contemporary Dress Collection, priced about $70 a pair.*

---

# One shoe maker says it's

*They make a handsome and rugged casual tie shoe. We make a handsome and rugged casual tie shoe.*

# made of wind, water, earth and sky.

*They feature the finest oiled and waxy leathers. We feature the finest oiled and waxy leathers.*

# At $125 a pair

*Underneath, they put a long-wearing, lightweight sole. That's where we put our long-wearing, lightweight sole.*

# they should throw in the moon.

*They have a price tag of $125 or more. We don't.*

*The Spenser, from the Dexter New American Brogues Collection, is available in a variety of oiled leathers and priced about $75 a pair.*

CONSUMER MAGAZINE
COLOR: CAMPAIGN
INCLUDING MAGAZINE
SUPPLEMENTS

339
ART DIRECTORS
Mark Decena, Ron Walter
WRITERS
David Munroe, Tom Molitor
ILLUSTRATOR
Lawrence Duke
PHOTOGRAPHER
Michelle Clement,
Kevin Sanchez
CLIENT
Kikkoman International
AGENCY
Saatchi & Saatchi DFS/Pacific,
San Francisco

340
ART DIRECTOR
Rick McQuiston
WRITER
Steve Sandoz
PHOTOGRAPHERS
Gary Braasch, Stock
CLIENT
Oregon Tourism
AGENCY
Wieden & Kennedy/Portland

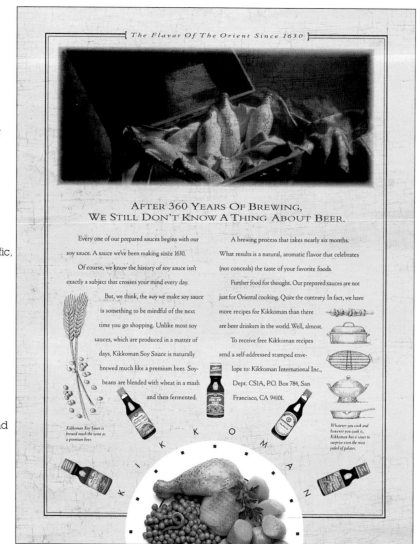

*The Flavor Of The Orient Since 1630*

### AFTER 360 YEARS OF BREWING, WE STILL DON'T KNOW A THING ABOUT BEER.

Every one of our prepared sauces begins with our soy sauce. A sauce we've been making since 1630.

Of course, we know the history of soy sauce isn't exactly a subject that crosses your mind every day.

But, we think, the *way* we make soy sauce is something to be mindful of the next time you go shopping. Unlike most soy sauces, which are produced in a matter of days, Kikkoman Soy Sauce is naturally brewed much like a premium beer. Soybeans are blended with wheat in a mash and then fermented.

A brewing process that takes nearly six months. What results is a natural, aromatic flavor that celebrates (not conceals) the taste of your favorite foods.

Further food for thought. Our prepared sauces are not just for Oriental cooking. Quite the contrary. In fact, we have more recipes for Kikkoman than there are beer drinkers in the world. Well, almost.

To receive free Kikkoman recipes send a self-addressed stamped envelope to: Kikkoman International Inc., Dept. CS1A, P.O. Box 784, San Francisco, CA 94101.

*Kikkoman Soy Sauce is brewed much the same as a premium beer.*

*Whatever you cook and however you cook it, Kikkoman has a sauce to surprise even the most jaded of palates.*

*The Flavor Of The Orient Since 1630*

### THANKS TO VEGETARIANS, MEAT HAS NEVER TASTED BETTER.

Teriyaki all began with soy sauce. The very seasoning Buddhist monks brought to Japan from China in the 6th century A.D.

Although soy sauce was originally served to enliven an all-vegetable diet, the rice-weary monks couldn't resist a brush with the occasional fish. Enter a wondrous marinade.

Teriyaki (translated means "glaze broil") became a delicious partnership of soy sauce and sweet Japanese cooking wine. Centuries later, Japanese farmers landed on the shores of Hawaii. There they found ginger, brown sugar and green onions to be just the right complement to their homeland blend. Years later, in quest of the perfect teriyaki, Kikkoman married the Hawaiian and Japanese versions by blending a clever palette of herbs, spices, sugar and wine.

If, perchance, you meet a Buddhist monk, thank him on behalf of barbecue history. You might find that a chicken breast brushed with Kikkoman Teriyaki is a religious experience in itself.

To receive free Kikkoman recipes send a self-addressed stamped envelope to: Kikkoman International Inc., Dept. CS4A, P.O. Box 784, San Francisco, CA 94101.

*Naturally brewed soy sauce, the key ingredient in our Teriyaki, begins with Buddhism.*

*Teriyaki Marinade & Sauce penetrates meats for an island flavor. For thick and tasty teriyaki flavor, brush on Teriyaki Baste & Glaze.*

*The Flavor Of The Orient Since 1630*

### SALT WAS THE FIRST CONDIMENT KNOWN TO MAN. DO YOU KNOW THE SECOND?

The earliest ancestor of present day soy sauce was documented in classics centuries ago. Making soy sauce perhaps the second condiment ever to attend a meal.

Of course, we know the history of soy sauce isn't a subject that crosses your mind every day.

But, we think, the *way* we make soy sauce is a story to be mindful of the next time you go shopping. Unlike most soy sauces, which are produced in a matter of days, Kikkoman Soy Sauce is naturally brewed for nearly six months. Soybeans are blended with wheat in a mash and then fermented.

What results is a natural, aromatic flavor that celebrates (not conceals) the taste of your favorite foods. For those of you watching your sodium intake, we offer Kikkoman Lite. The same naturally brewed flavor, but with forty percent less salt.

Further food for thought. Kikkoman Soy Sauce isn't only for Oriental cooking. Quite the contrary.

How many ways can one use Kikkoman? Have fun answering that one. To receive free Kikkoman recipes send a self-addressed stamped envelope to: Kikkoman International Inc., Dept. CS2A, P.O. Box 784, San Francisco, CA 94101.

*Once stored in cedar barrels, Kikkoman Soy Sauce is among the oldest living brands in history.*

*Whatever you cook and however you cook it, Kikkoman Soy Sauce elevates the essence of meats to a glorious level.*

**Don't let your child grow up thinking the natural habitat for an animal is the zoo.**

These days many zoos are recreating natural habitats for their animals. In Oregon, we never got rid of ours.

Across the state you'll find over 1,250,000 acres of land set aside for the many creatures who call Oregon home. Which is why you can spot residents like bighorn sheep, deer, elk and eagles all year long. Sometimes just a few feet from a paved road.

Along the coast, you'll thrill to the sight of killer and gray whales spouting their way north or south. And in the spring and fall, the skies above Southern Oregon's Klamath wildlife areas are literally filled with immense clouds of Canadian geese, whistling swans and other birds who stop to rest here during their migration.

If those are the kind of crowds you'd like to see for a change, call the Oregon Tourism Division at 1-800-547-7842 (outside Oregon) or 1-800-543-8838 (inside Oregon) for a free state travel guide. And get back to nature in a place that never left it.

**Oregon. Things look different here.**

**The United States is now available in a condensed version.**

Driving across the United States will take you from the mountains, to the valley, to the oceans, white with foam. But then again, so will a trip across Oregon.

Around the state, you'll find places as varied as the rugged peaks of the Cascade range, the spectacular Columbia River Gorge, the painted hills of Eastern Oregon, the dazzling blue depths of Crater Lake and the unspoiled beaches of the Oregon Coast. Places where the people you meet are just as colorful as the scenery around them.

And, when you're in the mood for a little civilization, fine hotels, restaurants specializing in Northwest delicacies and a vibrant performing arts scene all await you. See for yourself. Call the Oregon Tourism Division at 1-800-547-7842 (outside Oregon) or 1-800-543-8838 (inside Oregon) for a free State Travel Guide.

And spend your vacation in one place that's actually every place.

**Oregon. Things look different here.**

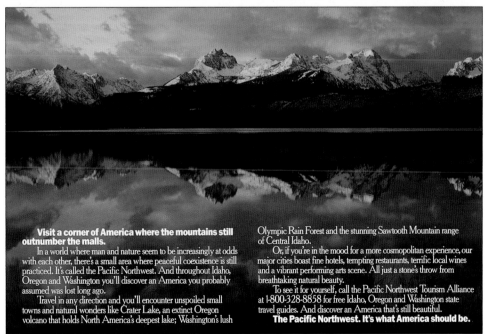

**Visit a corner of America where the mountains still outnumber the malls.**

In a world where man and nature seem to be increasingly at odds with each other, there's a small area where peaceful coexistence is still practiced. It's called the Pacific Northwest. And throughout Idaho, Oregon and Washington you'll discover an America you probably assumed was lost long ago.

Travel in any direction and you'll encounter unspoiled small towns and natural wonders like Crater Lake, an extinct Oregon volcano that holds North America's deepest lake; Washington's lush Olympic Rain Forest and the stunning Sawtooth Mountain range of Central Idaho.

Or, if you're in the mood for a more cosmopolitan experience, our major cities boast fine hotels, tempting restaurants, terrific local wines and a vibrant performing arts scene. All just a stone's throw from breathtaking natural beauty.

To see it for yourself, call the Pacific Northwest Tourism Alliance at 1-800-328-8858 for free Idaho, Oregon and Washington state travel guides. And discover an America that's still beautiful.

**The Pacific Northwest. It's what America should be.**

340

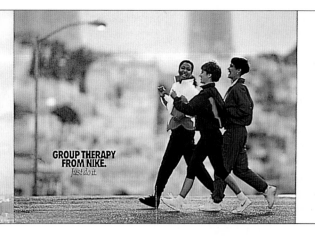

FEAR OF FAILURE
FEAR OF SUCCESS
FEAR OF LOSING
YOUR HEALTH
FEAR OF LOSING
YOUR MIND
FEAR OF BEING TAKEN
TOO SERIOUSLY
FEAR OF NOT BEING TAKEN
SERIOUSLY ENOUGH
FEAR THAT YOU
WORRY TOO MUCH
FEAR THAT YOU DON'T
WORRY ENOUGH
YOUR MOTHER'S FEAR
YOU'LL NEVER MARRY
YOUR FATHER'S FEAR
THAT YOU WILL.

GROUP THERAPY
FROM NIKE.
*Just do it.*

YOUR PADDED BRA
YOUR PUSH-UP BRA
YOUR 48-HOUR BRA
YOUR CONTROL TOP
PANTYHOSE
YOUR SUPPORT PANTYHOSE
YOUR CONTROL TOP
SUPPORT PANTYHOSE
YOUR BAGGY PANTS
YOUR BAGGY SHIRTS
YOUR SHIRT WITH THE
VERTICAL STRIPES
YOUR SWEATER WITH THE
VERTICAL STRIPES
YOUR DRESS WITH THE
VERTICAL STRIPES
YOUR BLACK ANYTHING

SELF-SUPPORT
FROM NIKE.
*Just do it.*

THE NEW YEAR'S
RESOLUTION DIET
THE FIRST-REAL-DATE-
IN-TWO-YEARS DIET
THE WEDDING DAY DIET
THE HONEYMOON DIET
THE IT-CAN'T-BE-SUMMER-
I-HAVEN'T-LOST-
ANY-WEIGHT-YET DIET
THE BEFORE-THE-BABY DIET
THE AFTER-THE-BABY DIET
THE I-CAN'T-CUT-OFF-
MY-THIGHS-BUT-I-CAN-
STOP-EATING DIET
THE 10-YEAR REUNION DIET
THE I-WISH-I-WAS-HER DIET
THE LAST-DITCH DIET

FOOD FOR THOUGHT
FROM NIKE.
*Just do it.*

341

342

"So Boo Boo's big brown eyes are staring at me through a face full of vanilla frosting."

"My little cousins, Melissa and Matthew, were playing soccer with the Chicken Kiev."

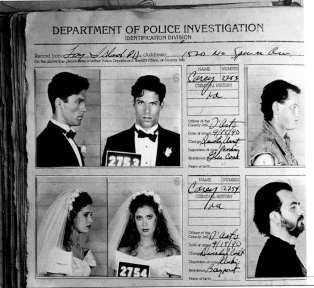

"I didn't exactly remember the Long Island Police Department being on the guest list."

343

# There are 800 reasons for sending flowers. Guilt is 700 of them.

Call 1·800·FLOWERS today for birthdays and anniversaries, Mother's Day, holidays, anyday. Including the day you had a fight, the night you got home at 11:00, the promotion you forgot to acknowledge. Call today, forgiveness tomorrow, guaranteed.

## CALL 1·800·FLOWERS©
### (1-800-356-9377)
### YOUR 24 HOUR WORLDWIDE FLORIST

# Introduce your husband to a younger woman.

It's a scientific fact that poor moisture retention makes skin look dry, lined, and aged. That's why many dermatologists recommend Formula 405˜ deep-action moisturizers, from Doak Pharmacal. The exclusive, European ingredient in Formula 405˜ increases moisture retention and minimizes fine lines for healthier, younger-looking skin.

Scientifically Formulated
## formula 405™

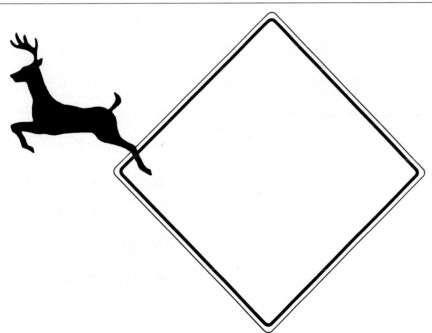

## Attract more deer.
"Dr. Juice's Deer Scent Secrets," Sept. 23 on Ch. 28 after the Dolphins/Giants game.

Another day. Another miracle.

About 400 times a year, a baby is born at the Wild Animal Park. But we never quite get used to it.

Because every time it happens, we know we're one cheetah, one okapi, one lowland gorilla closer to saving another species from extinction.

And that's why this place is here. To provide a 2,100-acre sanctuary where endangered animals can live their lives and raise their families, safe from harm.

By visiting us and supporting our efforts, you'll help more miracles happen.

So come on out—and see them with your own eyes.

Take I-15 to Escondido's Via Rancho Parkway exit and follow the signs. (619) 234-6541. Open daily at 9 a.m.

San Diego Wild Animal Park

347

# CHARIVARI

*Never coming to a mall near you.*

348

349

# HERE'S A CLIP FROM TONIGHT'S MOVIE.

See Clint Eastwood get the lead out when "Dirty Harry" returns to clean up a gang of renegade cops.

## "MAGNUM FORCE" TONIGHT AT 8.

### WJZY 46
Charlotte

---

### Next Time You're Wine Shopping, Check Out These Convenient Aisles.

Shopping for wine can be more [                    ] than just an errand. It can be an adventure. One to share with family and friends, all year around. After trying Ohio wines from your favorite store or restaurant, come sample the activities, tours, tastings, and culture Ohio's 42 wineries have to offer. Many are just a short drive away. For your free Ohio winery guide, call 1-800-BUCKEYE.

**OHIO** *the heart of it all!*®

*The Wines of Ohio*

---

## Before age five, the average child has experienced guerilla warfare, auto wrecks and homicide.

©DAKIN, Inc. Dakin stuffed animals are available at fine gift and toy shops everywhere.

At Dakin, we've always designed toys that would let your children have some other experiences.

How it feels to love something. To care. And what it's like to use their imagination.

Which may be why many books on how to raise a child have had something interesting to say about stuffed animals like the Dakin you see here:

That they can play an important role in helping your children develop into secure, well-adjusted individuals.

Now, how many toys can promise you that?

Gifts you can feel good about...™

**DAKIN**

YOU CAN'T GET IT OFF YOUR MIND

Totally natural SMARTFOOD®. Air-popped popcorn smothered in white cheddar cheese.

355

YOU CAN'T GET IT OFF YOUR MIND

Totally natural SMARTFOOD®. Air-popped popcorn smothered in white cheddar cheese.

356

YOU CAN'T GET IT OFF YOUR MIND

Totally natural SMARTFOOD®. Air-popped popcorn smothered in white cheddar cheese.

357

*Life is full of
unexpected bumps.
Ours you'll like.*

© 1990 Pepperidge Farm, Inc.

*Lumps of macadamia nuts. Chunks of milk chocolate.*

*Sausalito. Every bump even better than expected.*

PEPPERIDGE FARM ®   *PEPPERIDGE FARM REMEMBERS*

358

# I know so much about awnings, you better hope you don't get stuck talking to me at a party.

I've traveled the world learning my craft. Ask me anything.
If you have a few minutes. 841-0507.

## SOMMER AWNING COMPANY

359

IF THEY CAN FLY IN IT, YOU CAN HUNT IN IT.

A day like this will have most hunters hunting for the next bowl game on television.     Leaving the two of you with all the birds.     AMMUNITION THAT WORKS AS HARD AS YOU DO.

360

Could Johann Sebastian Bach make it to the top today without being endorsed by Coke or Pepsi?

LONG AFTER THE POP FIZZLES, TRUE ART
ALWAYS SEEMS TO ENDURE. DISCOVER WHY ON AMERICA'S
MOST ENDURING CLASSICAL RADIO STATION.

WQXR 96·3 FM
THE CLASSICAL STATION OF THE TIMES.

The Guinness Book states Julio Iglesias has sold more records than anyone else in history.

Tell Tchaikovsky the news.

(LONG AFTER THE POP FIZZLES, TRUE ART ENDURES.
HEAR IT PRESENTED DAILY BY "AMERICA'S CLASSICAL STATION OF THE YEAR.")

WQXR 96·3 FM
THE CLASSICAL STATION OF THE TIMES.

Bach, Handel, Scarlatti, Telemann & Vivaldi.

In 1701, they were the New Kids On The Block.

(LONG AFTER THE POP FIZZLES, TRUE ART ENDURES.
DISCOVER WHY ON AMERICA'S MOST ENDURING CLASSICAL STATION.
FEATURING RADIO'S MOST EXTENSIVE CLASSICAL LIBRARY.)

WQXR 96·3 FM
OR 1560 AM. THE CLASSICAL STATIONS OF THE TIMES.

361

## OUTDOOR: SINGLE

**362**
**ART DIRECTOR**
Ron Brown
**WRITER**
David Abbott
**TYPOGRAPHER**
Joe Hoza
**CLIENT**
The Economist
**AGENCY**
Abbott Mead Vickers.
BBDO/London

**363**
**ART DIRECTOR**
Ron Brown
**WRITER**
David Abbott
**TYPOGRAPHER**
Joe Hoza
**CLIENT**
The Observer
**AGENCY**
Abbott Mead Vickers.
BBDO/London

**364**
**ART DIRECTOR**
Ron Brown
**WRITER**
David Abbott
**TYPOGRAPHER**
Joe Hoza
**CLIENT**
The Observer
**AGENCY**
Abbott Mead Vickers.
BBDO/London

**365**
**ART DIRECTOR**
Ron Brown
**WRITER**
David Abbott
**TYPOGRAPHER**
Joe Hoza
**CLIENT**
The Observer
**AGENCY**
Abbott Mead Vickers.
BBDO/London

**366**
**ART DIRECTORS**
Clem McCarthy, Randy Rosand
**WRITER**
Tom Nelson
**PHOTOGRAPHER**
David Langley
**CLIENT**
United Parcel Service
**AGENCY**
Ammirati & Puris/New York

**367**
**ART DIRECTOR**
Sig Gross
**WRITER**
Bertrand Garbassi
**PHOTOGRAPHER**
Chris Collins
**CLIENT**
Austin Nichols/Wild Turkey Bourbon
**AGENCY**
Angotti Thomas Hedge/
New York

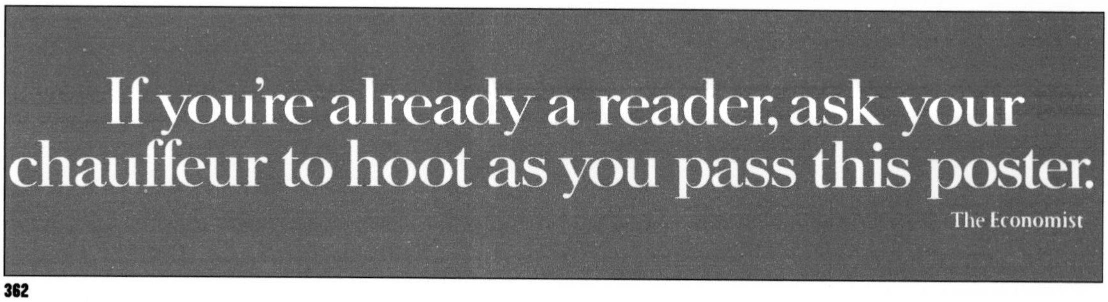
If you're already a reader, ask your
chauffeur to hoot as you pass this poster.
The Economist

362

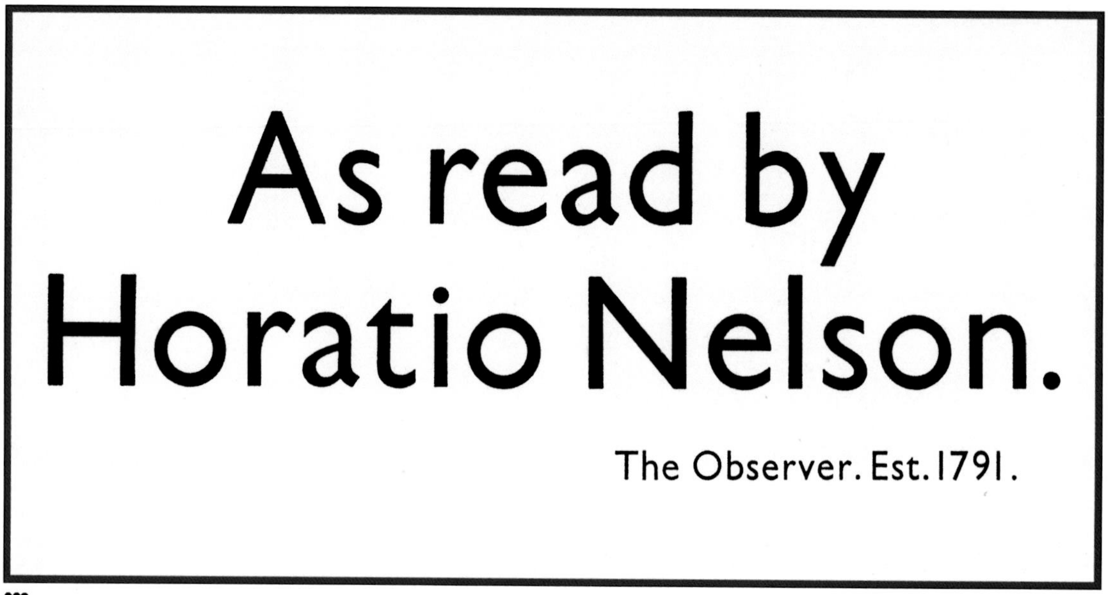
As read by
Horatio Nelson.
The Observer. Est. 1791.

363

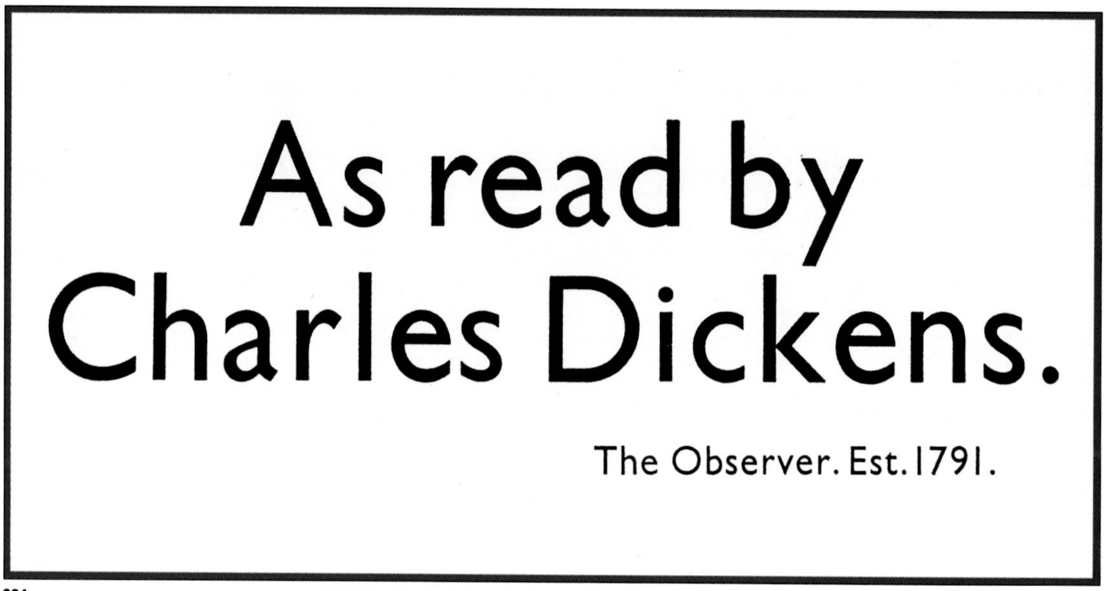
As read by
Charles Dickens.
The Observer. Est. 1791.

364

# As read by Jane Austen.

The Observer. Est. 1791.

365

# It comes when you call it.
## 1-800-PICK-UPS

UPS AIR SERVICE

© 1990 United Parcel Service of America, Inc.

United Parcel Service

UPS

310812

366

# Accept no decoys.

**WILD TURKEY**
8 years old. 101 proof. pure Kentucky.

367

## OUTDOOR: SINGLE

**368**
**ART DIRECTORS**
Bryan Buckley, Stan Poulos,
Tanya Hotton
**WRITERS**
Tom DeCerchio, Bryan Buckley
**PHOTOGRAPHER**
Steve Hellerstein
**CLIENT**
Discover Magazine
**AGENCY**
Buckley DeCerchio Cavalier/
New York

**369**
**ART DIRECTORS**
Bryan Buckley, Stan Poulos,
Tanya Hotton
**WRITERS**
Tom DeCerchio, Bryan Buckley
**PHOTOGRAPHER**
Steve Hellerstein
**CLIENT**
Discover Magazine
**AGENCY**
Buckley DeCerchio Cavalier/
New York

**370**
**ART DIRECTOR**
Jeff Terwilliger
**WRITER**
Kerry Casey
**CLIENT**
Metropolitan Transit Commission
**AGENCY**
Carmichael Lynch/Minneapolis

**371**
**ART DIRECTOR**
Warren Johnson
**WRITER**
Kay Jurkovich
**CLIENT**
Minnesota State Lottery
**AGENCY**
Carmichael Lynch/Minneapolis

**372**
**ART DIRECTORS**
Geoffrey Roche, Duncan Milner
**WRITER**
Joe Alexander
**CLIENT**
Metro Toronto Zoo
**AGENCY**
Chiat/Day/Mojo, Toronto

368

369

370

371

372

**373**
ART DIRECTORS
David Angelo, Gary Rozanski
WRITERS
David Angelo, Gary Rozanski
CLIENT
Seagram's Crown Royal
AGENCY
DDB Needham Worldwide/
New York

**374**
ART DIRECTOR
Tom Fincham
WRITER
Jeff Abbit
PHOTOGRAPHER
Redding/Cooper
CLIENT
Orange County Transit District
AGENCY
dGWB/Irvine

**375**
ART DIRECTOR
Joe Paprocki
WRITER
Patrick Hanlon
PHOTOGRAPHER
Stock
CLIENT
High Museum of Art
AGENCY
Earle Palmer Brown/Atlanta

**376**
ART DIRECTOR
Dick Brown
WRITER
Dick Brown
CLIENT
Gus Paulos Chevrolet
AGENCY
Evans/Salt Lake City

**377**
ART DIRECTOR
Tom Lichtenheld
WRITER
Luke Sullivan
CLIENT
General Mills/Bringer's
AGENCY
Fallon McElligott/Minneapolis

**378**
ART DIRECTOR
Bob Brihn
WRITER
Mike Gibbs
CLIENT
Star Tribune
AGENCY
Fallon McElligott/Minneapolis

373

374

375

# DRINK AND D~~RIV~~E.

**G** **Gus Paulos Chevrolet**
3500 South 4050 West

376

# Hungry? Tired? Divorced?
# BRINGER'S
## CALL 941-FOOD

377

# COMPLETE COLOR COVERAGE OF THE NFL.

**Star Tribune**

378

**OUTDOOR: SINGLE**

**379**
ART DIRECTOR
Michael Fazende
WRITER
Jarl Olsen
PHOTOGRAPHER
Rick Dublin
CLIENT
Jim Beam Brands
AGENCY
Fallon McElligott/Minneapolis

**380**
ART DIRECTOR
Peter Holmes
WRITER
Donna McCarthy
CLIENT
CJCL 1430 Radio
AGENCY
Franklin Dallas Kundinger/
North York, Ontario

**381**
ART DIRECTOR
Jeremy Postaer
WRITER
Rob Bagot
PHOTOGRAPHERS
Robert Mizono, Stock
CLIENT
San Francisco Examiner
AGENCY
Goodby Berlin & Silverstein/
San Francisco

**382**
ART DIRECTOR
James Jung
WRITER
Brian Harrod
PHOTOGRAPHER
Bert Bell
CLIENT
Levi Strauss
AGENCY
Harrod & Mirlin/Toronto

**383**
ART DIRECTOR
Bill Murphy
WRITER
Margaret Wilcox
CLIENT
Museum of Fine Arts
AGENCY
Hill Holliday Connors
Cosmopulos/Boston

MELLOWED SINCE 1983
(HAVEN'T WE ALL?)

7-YEAR-OLD JIM BEAM BLACK

379

ISN'T IT TIME
YOU LISTENED TO MUSIC THAT
ANNOYS THE KIDS?

Frank Sinatra, Sarah Vaughan, Nat King Cole. **CJCL 1430**

380

A Lot Can Happen Between 9 & 5.

**San Francisco Examiner** The Afternoon Paper.

381

# Ouchless.

**LEVI'S 501**

MEDIACOM

382

# Spend the day where there's nothing to do but stare at the walls.

MUSEUM·OF·FINE·ARTS/BOSTON

383

384

385

*Madonna tickets.*
*071 872 0220.*

The Courtauld Institute Galleries' priceless collections of paintings can finally be seen in their entirety at Somerset House, the Strand. 10am-6pm Monday to Saturday and 2pm-6pm Sunday. Also 6pm-8pm on Tuesdays, July to September. Admission £2.50. Concessions £1.

Courtauld Institute Galleries

# PAY HALF NOW AND NOTHING LATER.

A range of five fitted kitchens with every unit at half price.

TEXAS HOMECARE

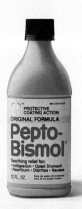

**OUTDOOR: SINGLE**

**388**
**ART DIRECTOR**
David Ayriss
**WRITER**
Jim Copacino
**PHOTOGRAPHER**
Jonathan/Craig
**CLIENT**
Alaska Airlines
**AGENCY**
Livingston & Company/Seattle

**389**
**ART DIRECTOR**
Alan Waldie
**WRITER**
Mark Wnek
**PHOTOGRAPHER**
Stock
**CLIENT**
Photographer's Gallery
**AGENCY**
Lowe Howard-Spink/London

**390**
**ART DIRECTOR**
Charles Inge
**WRITER**
Jane Garland
**ILLUSTRATOR**
David Lawrence
**CLIENT**
Henri Wintermans
**AGENCY**
Lowe Howard-Spink/London

**391**
**ART DIRECTOR**
Amy Watt
**WRITER**
Edward Boches
**ILLUSTRATOR**
Amy Watt
**PHOTOGRAPHERS**
John Huet, Cheryl Clegg
**CLIENT**
Smartfoods
**AGENCY**
Mullen/Wenham

**392**
**ART DIRECTORS**
Rob Rich, Woody Kay
**WRITER**
Wayne Winfield
**ILLUSTRATOR**
Pauly Becker
**PHOTOGRAPHER**
Ira Garber
**CLIENT**
Smithsonian Air/Space Magazine
**AGENCY**
Pagano Schenck & Kay/Providence

ORIGINAL FORMULA
Pepto-Bismol
ON YOUR AIRLINE, IS THIS AN AFTER-DINNER DRINK?
For soothing relief from the hassles of business travel, next time fly Alaska Airlines.
Alaska Airlines


**388**

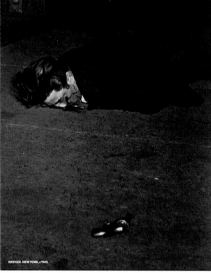

SHOT IN NEW YORK. HUNG IN SOHO.
THE PHOTOGRAPHERS' GALLERY
5 & 8 GREAT NEWPORT STREET, LONDON WC2.


**389**

Our finest hour.
Our finest seven minutes.
CAFÉ CRÈME
by HENRI WINTERMANS


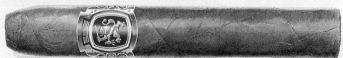

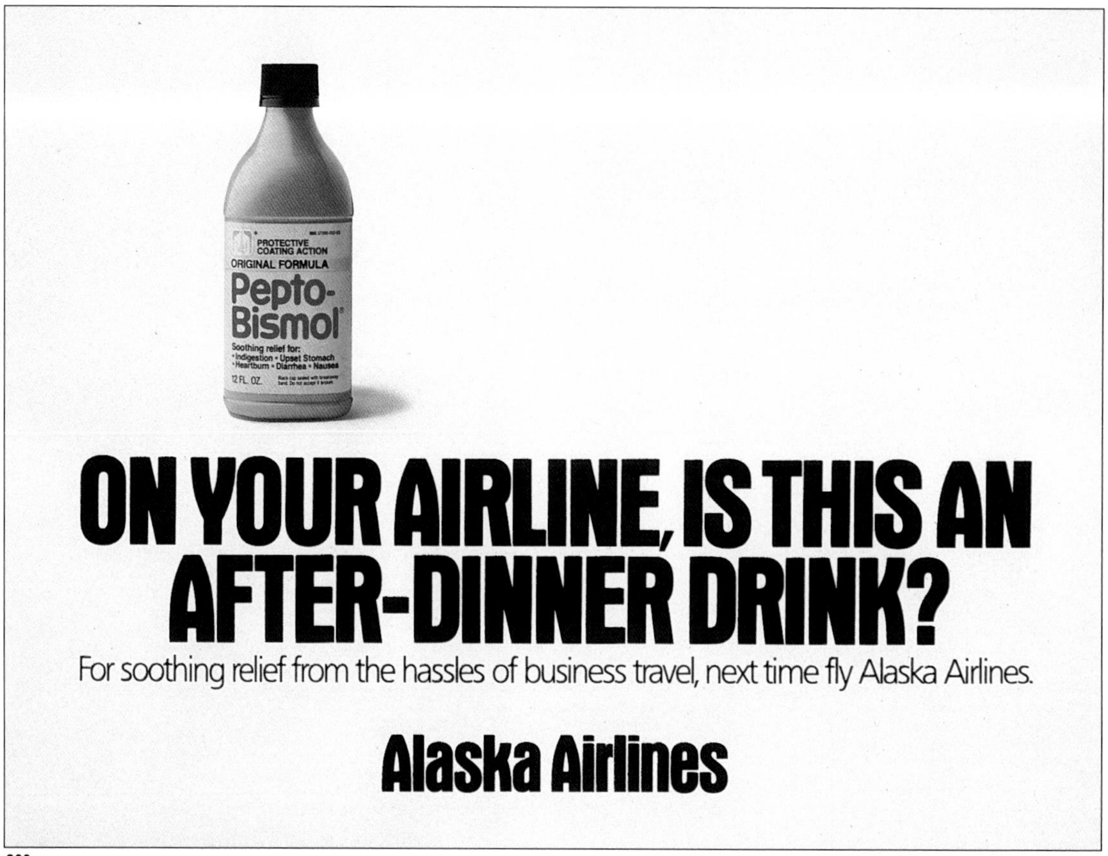

**390**

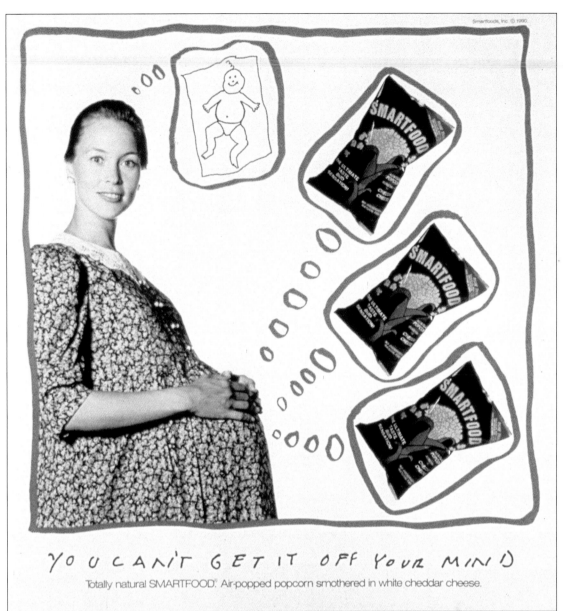

YOU CAN'T GET IT OFF YOUR MIND

Totally natural SMARTFOOD® Air-popped popcorn smothered in white cheddar cheese.

391

# For One Day In 1969, The Earth Revolved Around The Moon.

**Air & Space Smithsonian Magazine Celebrates Man's Landing On The Moon.**

392

See what the world was like when your parents were young.

Find out what things were really like in the good old days. See "Dinosaurs in the Dark of Night" at The Minneapolis Planetarium from March 31 through November 4. Sponsored by The Friends of the Minneapolis Public Library. Adults: $3. Children under 12: $1.50 and babies under 2: free. At 300 Nicollet Mall. Call 372-6644 for showtimes. And tell your parents. If they like living in the past, they'll love our new show.

Dinosaurs at The Minneapolis Planetarium

393

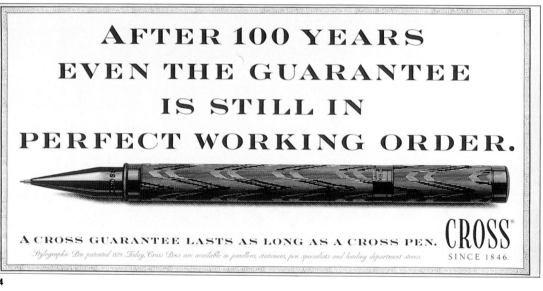

AFTER 100 YEARS
EVEN THE GUARANTEE
IS STILL IN
PERFECT WORKING ORDER.

A CROSS GUARANTEE LASTS AS LONG AS A CROSS PEN. CROSS

SINCE 1846.

Stylographic Pen patented 1879. Today, Cross Pens are available in jewellers, stationers, pen specialists and leading department stores.

394

OUTDOOR: CAMPAIGN

**397**
**ART DIRECTOR**
John Staffen
**WRITER**
Marty Cooke
**PHOTOGRAPHER**
Harry DeZitter
**CLIENT**
NYNEX Information Resources
**AGENCY**
Chiat/Day/Mojo, New York

**398**
**ART DIRECTORS**
Duncan Milner, Geoffrey Roche
**WRITER**
Joe Alexander
**CLIENT**
Metro Toronto Zoo
**AGENCY**
Chiat/Day/Mojo, Toronto

# Traffic Isn't The Only Thing That Crawls Around Here.

THE METRO TORONTO ZOO

## See The Loch Ness Monster. Honest.

PREHISTORIC SEA CREATURES.
THE METRO TORONTO ZOO

## Discover How Sheiks Got Around Before Mercedes And BMW.

CAMEL RIDES AT THE
METRO TORONTO ZOO.

398

**399**
**ART DIRECTOR**
David Meador
**WRITERS**
Bruce Davidson, Alison Grant
**CLIENT**
Burger King Corporation
**AGENCY**
D'Arcy Masius Benton &
Bowles/New York

**400**
**ART DIRECTOR**
Marcee Ruby
**WRITER**
Shelley Ambrose
**ILLUSTRATOR**
Bob Fortier
**CLIENT**
Dalin-Junior Caramels
**AGENCY**
J. Walter Thompson/Toronto

# This Is One Ad Where The Product Can't Hide Behind A Clever Headline.

RAND TYPOGRAPHY

401

There are plenty of excellent reasons for leaving the country.

Frankly, 'The chance to do better ads' isn't usually regarded as one of them.

The D&ADA jury thought this was a pretty good ad.
Unfortunately, none of them was looking for a job at the time.

402

# IS THIS THE BEST AD EVER WRITTEN?

MEN WANTED for Hazardous Journey. Small wages, bitter cold, long months of complete darkness, constant danger, safe return doubtful. Honour and recognition in case of success. — Ernest Shackleton.

When this little advertisement ran, in 1900, Ernest Shackleton was snowed under with replies.

Why? Surely, by all the accepted rules, he shouldn't have been. For a start, the 'promise' is entirely negative. And there's no picture.

So let's rewrite the ad, according to the rules.

"Men wanted for exciting journey. Good money, excellent conditions, certainty of massive royalties from publishing and movie rights. Reply now!"

Brilliant. Run it.

And if they had, you know instinctively that, even though they might have had a bagful of replies, it's very doubtful that they'd have got anywhere near the South Pole.

And certainly, no-one would have returned, to cash in on the deal.

And we wouldn't now be talking about the ad either. Would we?

Isn't the strength of that advertisement, then, in its simplicity? Isn't it sheer power in its honesty?

And is not its most brilliant quality the way it appeals precisely, and absolutely exclusively, to the very specialised section of the market it addresses?

'Wimps need not apply' would be superfluous. It's written large enough between the lines.

No doubt Shackleton wrote the ad straight off the cuff, pausing only to count the words, and the cost. It works because it has passion, and belief, and you can feel the leadership, if not fanaticism, in every phrase.

But this advertisement is written for an agency. An advertising agency. We produce ads, every day, for a living.

And frankly, rarely for as romantic a cause, or as inspiring a journey, as Ernest's.

But we do like to think that, at times, our work is as focussed, and as simple, as his: We know for certain that it can be as effective.

To help us, we've evolved systems that force us to take a fresh look at every problem; to wring the very last drop of information out of the product and the market; and to avoid at all costs, the trite, the formula-led, and especially the downright boring.

We've even produced an example, to show how, in all likelihood, our system would have led us to the same conclusion to which Shackleton's inspiration led him. (To his ad, that is. Not to the South Pole.)

If you'd be interested in finding out how we work, give us a call. We're in Hong Kong, Malaysia, Thailand, Taiwan, and Singapore.

We're The Ball Partnership.

---

403

---

# THERE IS A SPELLING MISTAKE IN THIS ADVERTISEMENT. THE FIRST PERSON TO SPOT IT WILL RECIEVE $500.

No, it's not in this line.

Or, you'll have guessed, in this line, either.

You're going to have to read this entire page, with the eyes of a school examiner, to spot it.

Which, when you think, makes it rather a good advertisement, doesn't it? Since ads, like the editorial they sidle up to, are written to be read.

How many of the other ads in this week's 'Media' are going to get this amount of attention?

One, maybe? Two?

It's more than likely that you haven't read any of them. Be honest, now.

You've given them the same treatment you give those suspiciously friendly encyclopaedia salesmen, who knock on your door and ask for five minutes of your time.

No, thank you: Slam the door. (Or in this case, turn the page.)

No sale. And we don't blame you. You saw the sell coming. Why waste your time?

The majority of ads are like that, too. Predictable, dull, and not very well presented.

They resolutely ignore the fact that the average consumer sees one thousand, six hundred advertising messages every day, and would be perfectly content not to see any at all.

You see, with the possible exception of seven year old brats with a passion for Teenage Mutant Ninja Turtles, PEOPLE DON'T LIKE ADS. There, we've said it. In a publication dedicated to the creed that advertising is a profession comparable only in its saintliness and altruism with being one of Mother Teresa's little helpers, we've spilt the beans:

We are not universally popular: If spacemen came down and took every person connected with advertising away for dissection, it would be a long time before we were missed. And even then, it would be because people discovered that their newspapers had become more interesting, and their TV programmes more enjoyable, for our absence.

(See? Heresy spoken out loud. And still we write. No thunderbolts from on high. God doesn't like ads, either.)

And yet...

And yet, in the face of reams of irrefutable evidence to the contrary, the majority of advertising agencies (and let's spread the blame a bit, their clients, too), persist in the belief that this just ain't so.

They sincerely believe that buying a space also guarantees readership of whatever they fill it with.

Sadder still, the higher the cost of the space, the more tense and creatively constipated they become, and the more safe and generic is their message: It's a new rule: the bigger the budget, the blander the ads.

Even the relatively enlightened feel that if they find, and mention, some semblance of a benefit in that space, they've really done a good job.

That by some miracle, the consumer is going to home in on their ad, shrieking "Just what I've always wanted!"

Sure. If your benefit is "Free Beer".

OK; definitely, if your benefit is "Free Beer". But if it's not, you're in big trouble.

You're going to be thrown in there with washing powders that get clothes whiter, toothpastes that taste nicer, tires that grip better ...

In other words, you're going to be ignored.

Don't misunderstand us, please. If your product has a substantial benefit over its competitors, you'd be mad not to tell everyone. The point is, it'd be mad to think that's all you had to do.

The public, as we've said, has become immune to everyday advertising.

For an ad to succeed these days, it has to work on many levels. It has to be relevant to the reader: It has to speak to him in language he can relate to: If there is a benefit to crow about, it has to be a benefit that's important to the consumer, not just to the manufacturer: To revert to the door-to-door salesman analogy, it has to look good ...the sort of person you'd invite into your home: the sort of advertisement you'd welcome into your mind...

But most of all, it has to be 'different'.

It has to jump from the page, or leap off the screen, screaming "Read me! Watch me!"

And it has to do so with a degree of seduction in its voice, rather than the foot-in-the-door brazen insistence, that leads only to the zap, the flip, and the broken toe.

Now. Doubtless there are sceptics out there who may say that this particular advertisement meets none of the criteria that it has been at such pains to expound.

That it is visually dull, dull, dull.

That it's criminally overwritten: That it's also a stupid concept, and that the one and only reason that they're reading it is to find the spelling mistake and qualify for $500 in the currency of their choice.

They may, of course, be right. (Found it yet, by the way? Keep going; concentrate.)

But at the Ball Partnership we'll do anything to get people to read ads.

Ours. Or yours.

This advertisement has cost us $22,336 to run. As you can imagine we're more than happy to give away $500 to make sure that everybody reads it. If you've found the spelling mistake (and if you haven't by now, you've missed it), call The Ball Partnership in Hong Kong, Malaysia, Singapore, Taiwan or Thailand and ask to speak to the Managing Partner. Of course, you're almost certainly too late to get the five hundred bucks, but call anyway. We like to chat about ads.

---

404

---

# TO GIVE YOU AN IDEA OF HOW SLOW IT WAS,

Solid Firestone rubber tires, a hand-operated windshield swipe, and a doorless cab made this 1924 Kenworth L-2 somewhat lacking in the comfort department. It made up for it, though, with a blazing 25 mph top speed.

"SPEED GETS 'EM"

## THE BUGS USED TO SMASH INTO THE REAR WINDOW.

We can't say this Kenworth went on to become a best-seller. But every truck we've ever designed— in its time and for its reason—was built precisely the same way: To be the World's Best.

KENWORTH
The World's Best.

Kenworth Truck Co., a division of PACCAR
For more information call 1-800-426-0694

---

405

---

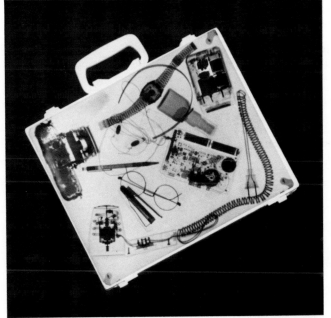

## There are fifty known terrorist groups in the world, unfortunately, this is the best picture we have of them.

If you've ever wondered how a security guard can distinguish a toiletry from a time bomb, the sad fact is sometimes he can't. But with the latest technology comes new hope.

First in the form of a luggage scanner that can determine not only what an object is, but what it is made of.

And now there is a camera that scans your face while a computer attempts to match it with one of the 500 terrorists in its memory bank.

Thus making it virtually impossible for a bomb to go undetected. And making it just as unlikely that a false alarm will cause a stranger to rummage through your undergarments. Month after month, Discover is the first to break stories like these that affect our lives.

In fact, 5.1 million readers turn to us for a clear picture of the most complicated issues of our times. Quite simply, there's no better vehicle to reach today's concerned citizens. Discover Magazine. It may be the only way to understand this world.

DISCOVER

---

406

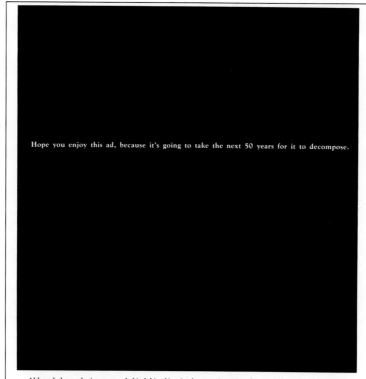

Hope you enjoy this ad, because it's going to take the next 50 years for it to decompose.

Although the marketing strategy behind this ad is a timeless creation, it's unfortunate that the ad itself will likely last into the next century.

Which causes one to wonder how long other refuse lasts in a landfill. For example, the pen that this ad was written with will indeed see the next millennium.

At Discover, we've been telling our readers for the past ten years about America's perilous landfill shortage.

However, the world's brimming garbage dumps are only one of the many pertinent stories that you'll find in the pages of Discover Magazine.

Each month, we inform our readers of pressing issues facing our world. From the environment to the latest medical breakthroughs, our staff of award-winning writers breaks stories first.

Perhaps that's why over 5.1 million people scan our magazine's pages each month. With numbers like that, there's no better vehicle in which to reach today's concerned citizens.

Discover Magazine. It may be the only way to understand this world.

**DISCOVER MAGAZINE**

407

Glasnost Hush Puppies.

In an historic gesture, Hush Puppies' Shoes was invited to be the first American company to manufacture and sell footwear in the Soviet Union. Thank you, Mr. Gorbachev.

408

## Competing with independent television is getting tough. Just ask this 25-year-old network executive.

Ms. Sarah Michaels has a tough job.

"*You* just try selling against independent television's audience share of 25%. It's awful. These guys have a full 25% sign-on-to-sign-off share of all television viewing. And you should see some of the nasty looks I get when I tell buyers my rates are way up, even though my network's audience share is dropping like a brick through the floor straight on its way to China.

They ask me, 'Well, why shouldn't I buy the indies? They got great numbers in prime time, they've got great demos. The indies are hot, babe.' And all I can say is, 'Wanna do lunch?' I'm tellin' ya, it gets old real fast."

### Independent Television

409

---

"These shows are political.

The judges are hacks.

The trophies are ugly.

The dinners are lousy.

The ads are abysmal.

What's that?

I won?

This is definitely the

best show in New York."

410

---

*MICHAEL CAN'T MAKE IT. PLAYING ON THE COAST —TED*

## COME SEE ~~MICHAEL JORDAN~~ IN PERSON.

*NBA Commissioner David Stern*

~~MICHAEL JORDAN~~ *David Stern*

**I**n his speech, he'll tell all about those exciting ~~high-flying death-defying slam dunks~~! *global markets* Listen spellbound as he fondly recalls his most exciting ~~collegiate~~ *corporate* moments. He'll tell with painstaking detail exactly what it's like to ~~win the~~ *attend a* National Championship! He'll also reveal why he never thought he'd be a professional basketball superstar! And describe the sensation of driving past the ~~likes of~~ *New York Connecticut Jersey* ~~Ewing, Laimbeer~~ and ~~Malone~~. Why are kids wild about his ~~Air Jordans~~? *wing tips* Find out...IN PERSON! This luncheon will take place on November 19th at the Chicago Hilton and Towers. Doors open promptly at 11:45 a.m. See you there.

**CAC**

Tickets are ~~$35~~ *$25* for members, ~~$45~~ *$35* for non-members. Call the Chicago Advertising Club at 312-819-2959 for reservations and information. Tickets must be purchased in advance by check, Visa/Mastercard or American Express. ~~No~~ tables of ten and ~~No~~ season discounts are available. Cancellations will ~~Not~~ be accepted. *→ through 11/13/90.*

411

---

412

413

414

**S YOUR AGENCY BETTER AT CHASING HEADLINES THAN WRITING THEM?**

*Fig 1. A bit messy.*

THE PERFECT SUICIDE should be quiet, painless and above all, neat. This rules out many time-honored methods, including guns, knives, hanging, electrocution and long falls onto unyielding surfaces. One excellent method is a strong tea made from poisonous toadstools. Another popular, but particularly gruesome method is to stay far too long in a dead end job. THE CREATIVE REGISTER. Advertising Talent Scouts. (212) 533-3676.

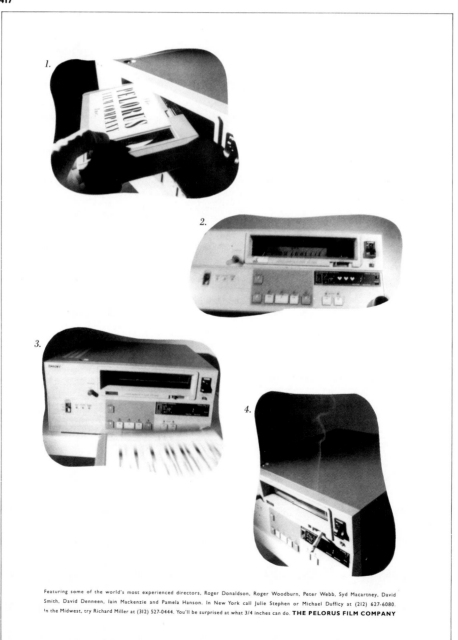

417

418

---

A column disrupts a trade show or convention in the worst ways. Columns make it hard to set up – they always seem to be right where your booth should be. They ruin sight lines and can mess up major media presentations. Not to mention the double-ugly, elevated outlets overflowing with electrical cords at perfect tripping height. We took all of this into consideration when we built the new, 500,000 sq. ft. Oregon Convention Center. To make sure that nothing gets in the way of your event's success, our exhibit floor has 150,000 column-free sq. ft. Oregon Convention Center. 503-235-7575.

422

# Can you identify these convention sites from the air?

Lots of cities can offer you more than Portland, Oregon. More traffic. More litter. More smog. Which is why Portland is indeed a breath of fresh air. Long ranked as one of America's cleanest cities by the EPA, Portland passed the nation's first anti-litter bottle bill. And all 365 days in 1989 were well below the federal standards governing ozone and particulate pollution.

One reason is Portland's light rail system. Trains silently pull up alongside the new Oregon Convention Center 164 times per day to pick up thousands of visitors. All of whom reap the benefits of our pristine river city: quiet meals in waterfront cafes, and long walks that are easy on the lungs. Some even opt to fish downtown for chinook salmon (and yes, they're safe to eat).

If you're tired of convention sites that all blend together, you really should look into Portland. And now you know you won't have to squint to see it.

**Portland, Oregon**
Things look different here

*All 500,000 sq. ft. of the Oregon Convention Center opens in September, 1990.*

423

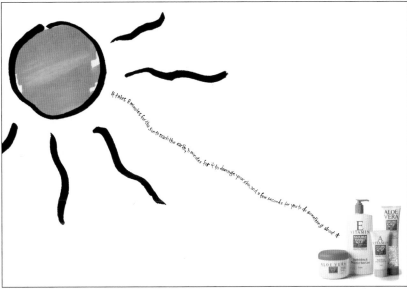

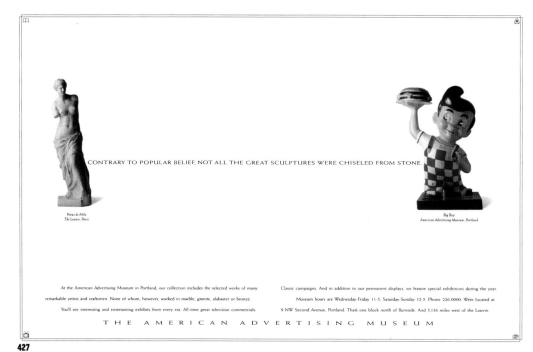

427

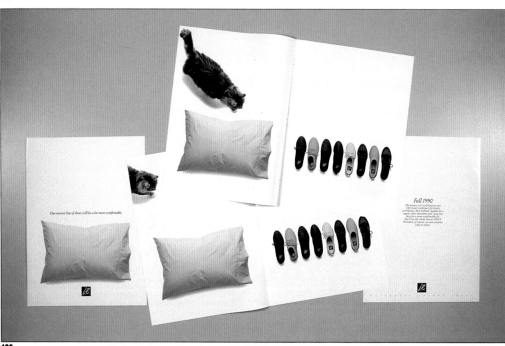

428

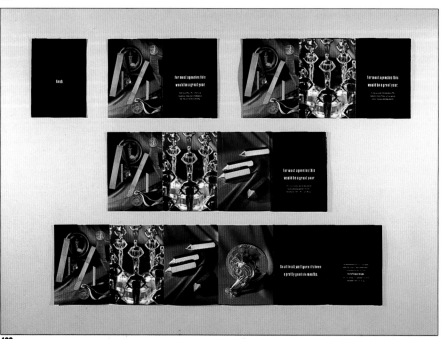

429

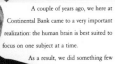

A couple of years ago, we here at Continental Bank came to a very important realization: the human brain is best suited to focus on one subject at a time.

As a result, we did something few

of which business banking legends are made. The only true measure of greatness, we believe, is how well one responds to a customer's business banking needs.

At Continental, we've committed our substantial resources to that very goal. And, perhaps sensing our uncommon singleness of purpose, some of the industry's finest business bankers have committed themselves to us.

## It's not easy for a bank to serve consumer and business customers at the same time.

banks have had the foresight to do. We relinquished our consumer banking interests and became "business only."

For us, it's meant that we no longer mess up our hair. But for you, the business banking customer, it can mean even more.

After all, while rubbing one's belly and patting one's head may be an impressive physical feat, it is not the stuff

To the point where, today, we've bolstered the bank's strengths in virtually every department: from corporate finance and financial risk management to foreign exchange and cash management.

Of course, we could go on at length about our personnel. We could extol endlessly upon their considerable and varied credentials.

And while we're at it, we could expound effusively on such matters as our high level of responsiveness, our creative use of financial instruments, and our exhaustive attention to detail.

But rather than attempt to woo you with rhetoric, we thought we'd invite you to talk to a Continental banker yourself. Simply call (312) 828-5799. We think you'll find our focused expertise can make a real difference for your company. And we're not just patting ourselves on the back. **Continental Bank**
A new approach to business.

## Continental Bank proudly reminds you that we have a really lousy passbook savings program.

As you may know, Continental has left the consumer banking and become "business only." Now, on the surface, that merely means we

offer such things as passbook savings, credit cards and long lines marked off by felt ropes.

Beyond that, however, it has meant a singleness of purpose for our entire organization.

Today, instead of greeting our customers with a team of tellers, we're greeting them

Citicorp's     Chemical's     Bank of America's     Chase Manhattan's     Ours.

with a team of experienced, sophisticated, business banking professionals.

Instead of offering our clients toasters, blenders and cuddly stuffed animals, we're offering them customized financial risk management products like swaps, caps and corridors.

And instead of trotting out some dusty old product like passbook savings, we're introducing them to our latest credit, restructuring and capitalization ideas.

Mind you, it's not that we haven't provided these kinds of services before. It's just that now, having left the daily demands of mass market banking to our competitors, we're providing them exclusively.

Has all this emphasis on business banking translated into fewer customers? Frankly, yes. About 60,000, to be precise. And with 60,000 fewer customers to worry about, you'd be amazed how much more focused a bank can be.

If it's a passbook savings account you're after, there are any number of fine financial institutions we could recommend—just a few of which are listed here. But if it's a disciplined, dynamic and responsive business bank, we suggest you call (312) 828-5799 and speak directly to us.

We may be lousy in some areas. But when it comes to business banking, we're proud to remind you that we're anything but. **Continental Bank**
A new approach to business.

# A DEMONSTRATION OF WHAT CAN HAPPEN TO ELECTRIC MOTOR PARTS IF YOU DON'T USE AMOCO RYKON PREMIUM GREASE.

(OPEN HERE)

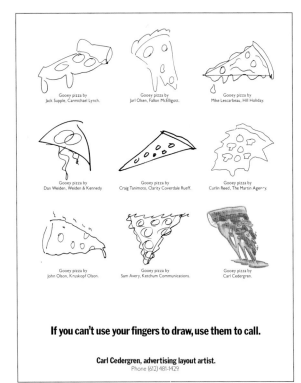

**433**

**434**

WITH THE RISING COST OF POSTAGE,
THE REASONS FOR A LIGHTWEIGHT PUBLICATION
PAPER JUST KEEP ADDING UP.

Choctaw Gloss from Weyerhaeuser. Call 1-800-447-0722 for all the numbers.

# "I'm sorry this article is late. I've had a little trouble writing."

As eastern European dictatorships fell, Romania remained one of the last to repress its people.

Just before Ceausescu was toppled, World Monitor magazine sought to shed some light on totalitarianism, focusing on this isolated country. We searched, and found a writer who's spent a lot of time in tyrannical regimes. And a lot of time under arrest.

She was jailed repeatedly while working on this article. And provided a first-hand account of the paranoia which ultimately brings such governments down. (In Romania, she found that a sample from every typewriter in the country was kept on file by the secret police.)

At World Monitor, we believe it's this inside perspective that's needed to comprehend complex global issues. Because only through personal experience can there be true understanding.

We find experts who have been a part of the story. Then we have them tell it in their own words. Be it a Communist official, a former president or an American schoolteacher. All three of whom have written for us.

That's why those who read World Monitor, like those who write for it, are leaders.

People who want the most accurate international assessments, as well as speculation on what to expect next. So they can survive and thrive as the world becomes smaller for all of us. World Monitor. For those who know that power comes from knowledge. And that the most powerful knowledge comes, without question, from experience.

**WORLD MONITOR**
THE CHRISTIAN SCIENCE MONITOR · MONTHLY
Where the people in the news report the news.

436

---

# A baby is brought into the cold world kicking and screaming. Sounds like somebody already warned it about rectal thermometers.

*The ear is recognized as the ideal site to take a temperature.*

Let's be honest. No one really likes to be on the giving—or receiving end of a rectal thermometer. They're dangerous. They're slow. And they make everyone feel uncomfortable.

So it seems logical that if it were at all possible to avoid them completely and forever, we would.

Agreed? Fine.

But what about the alternatives? The mouth relies on patient cooperation for accuracy. That leaves infants, toddlers and the elderly out of the picture. And under the arm? Well, you might be better off just guessing.

Fortunately, there is a better way. It's called the Thermoscan™ Pro-1 Instant Thermometer. It fits in the palm of your hand. No cords. No bulky box or wires. And it's easy to use. You simply position the probe tip inside the ear canal—press a

button—and you're done. It takes less than two seconds to get a precise reading.

Sound a little like something from a science-fiction movie? Not really.

We've known for years that the ear is the ideal site for obtaining an accurate reflection of the body's "core" temperature. Mainly because of the close relationship

*Introducing the Thermoscan Pro-1 Instant Thermometer. Designed to change the future of thermometry.*

of the hypothalamus and the tympanic membrane. And the ear isn't affected by things like eating, drinking, smoking or cross-contamination from contact with mucous membranes.

Combine this with infrared technology and you end up with a breakthrough. Add the fact that we own a patent that enables us to use a unique temperature sensing system, and you end up with an even

bigger breakthrough—it sells for about half the price of other infrared units.

But don't just take our word for it. Find out for yourself how great this thermometer is. The sooner you use it, the sooner you'll be convinced.

For more information, please call us at 1-800-327-7226.

**THERMOSCAN**
INSTANT THERMOMETER

437

---

## IN 1989, WE SURPASSED EVERY CRUISE LINE ON EARTH. NOT TO MENTION PARIS, ROME, LONDON AND VENICE.

Recently, the readers of *Condé Nast Traveler* were asked to rate what they thought to be the most satisfying travel experiences in all the world.

As you might guess, many of the world's greatest cities finished near the top. As you might not guess, a certain cruise line surpassed them all.

Now ask yourself, what could have possibly provoked your clients to rate Royal Viking Line, a fleet

of ships, far above the world's most fabulous cities? The answer to this question is really quite simple: we resorted to our usual tactics.

We hired chefs trained at Europe's finest culinary academies, and put them to work preparing all manner of tantalizing delicacies. We built the most spacious cruise vessels on earth and staffed them with the highest crew-to-passenger ratio of any ship, anywhere.

We stocked our wine cellars with over 17,000 bottles, and employed six sommeliers to watch over each and every one. We flew fresh Maine lobster halfway around the globe, and provided a gracious couple from Nantucket with a '58 Bordeaux in the middle of the Aegean when the time and circumstance was nothing short of perfect.

These methods not only worked on the readers of *Condé Nast Traveler* but on other unsuspecting souls as well. In 1989, we won more awards than any other cruise line on earth.

For the sixth time in seven years, *Travel-Holiday* magazine named Royal Viking the "World's Best" cruise line. *Berlitz* said our newly-christened Royal Viking Sun was the "Best Ship Afloat." The esteemed critics at *Fielding's Guide*, never to be outdone, gave all our ships the distinguished rating of five-stars-plus. And the readers of *Condé Nast Traveler* overwhelmingly voted Royal Viking Line the world's "Number One" cruise line.

This, of course, is good news for us, and for you, and for travel agents like you the world over who

diligently seek out new business and an ever-growing client base. For many of these awards reflect the findings of readers' polls.

In other words, these are your clients speaking.

So next time a pair of unfamiliar faces appear in your office, do not be afraid to mention Royal Viking Line. And do not be surprised if their reply goes something like this: "Yes, of course, Royal Viking Line. They're the 'World's Finest.' We were hoping you would suggest them."

And do not be at all astonished when this nice couple, and other nice couples just like them, come to you again, and again, and again and again—after all, more experienced travelers turn and return to us than any other cruise line on earth.

Are you ready for them? To make quite certain you are, call the good people of sales assistance at (800) 346-8000. They will provide you with all the information generally required to sell and resell Royal Viking Line to clients over and over and over again.

After that, you will without a doubt be needing this number at reservations: (800) 422-8000. In Canada, we ask you to please dial (800) 448-4785. As always, we thank you and welcome your next call.

**ROYAL VIKING LINE**

"Cruise lines were judged on seven criteria: destinations served, ship size, service, cabin quality, recreational activities, food, and value for money. Royal Viking won every category overwhelmingly."

438

# It Works Better.
# It Costs Less.
# End Of Ad.

---

# WITH SALES UP 185%, IT ALMOST BEGINS TO LOOK BEAUTIFUL.

*New Zealand kiwifruit probably aren't your idea of beauty. ~ But obviously, somebody's finding them attractive: Over the past five years they've achieved the sales growth mentioned above. ~ And unlike most other fruit, kiwifruit as a* *category have increased in both household penetration and per capita consumption. In plain English: The people who've never bought kiwifruit before are buying them now. And the people who have bought them are buying more. ~ To place an order* *please contact your New Zealand Fruit Company representative. ~ We'll be the first to admit that New Zealand kiwifruit aren't going to win any beauty contests. But they're hard to beat in a competition we think is a little more important. ~ Sales.*

 **NEW ZEALAND FRUIT COMPANY**

---

# It's no wonder the world's leading *dentists* are coming to *Singapore.*

In fact, 5,000 of them are coming for the World Dental Congress. And after they've finished speaking in our superbly-equipped, modern meeting facilities, they'll be ready to bite into Singapore's world-famous cuisine. Or open their mouths in amazement at the city's exciting melange of Chinese, Malay, Indian and European cultures. Convention City Singapore. The world's dentists are going to eat it up.

Send me the free Convention Planners' Guide to Singapore.
Name & Title
Company
Address
State _____ Zip Code _____ City _____ Tel _____
Mail to: The Singapore Convention Bureau, P.O. Box 26999, Santa Ana, CA 92799, U.S.A.
or call the Incentive Travel Manager at 1-800-688-4446.

CONVENTION CITY
# Singapore
Where the world comes together.

## The Marines say Parris Island is the world's toughest boot camp. We beg to differ.

Everyone knows it takes weeks of hell to turn out a few good Leathernecks.

But how many people know what it takes to turn out a few good leather boots? Boots as waterproof as canteens, yet as comfortable as slippers.

You can find out fast at the world's toughest boot camp. A place called Timberland.

There we have devised tests that make the Chinese water torture seem like a walk in the park.

In one particularly grueling ordeal, we put a mass of water behind pieces of boot leather.

We then flex the leather again and again, simulating the movements the human foot might make were it slogging through a similar mass of water deep in no man's land.

After flexing each piece sixteen thousand times, we accept only one result. No leakage whatsoever. A single drop and the leather is rejected. No appeals, no second chances.

The truth is, rejections don't happen very often. Our method of waterproofing leather has been perfected over a period of twenty years, and it's the most expensive process known to man.

First, we cherrypick the world's leather supply, selecting only the cream of the crop. Then we flood every fiber of the leather, inside and out, with a special silicone waterproofing agent. We do this during the actual tanning so as not to miss a single space big enough for a water molecule to sneak in.

(We could practice shortcuts, such as brushing the surface of the leather with silicone. But then we'd be like any other boot company.)

Another torture test involves our so-called "boot within a boot," your ultimate insurance of dry, comfortable feet under the worst, wettest, coldest conditions.

The boot within a boot is actually a sock constructed of waterproof Gore-Tex, Thinsulate® insulation and smooth Cambrelle.

We take this innocent-looking sock and give it the infamous bubble test. We fill it with air, submerge it in a glass water tank, and we watch. One air bubble and the sock is sacked. Period.

Besides these and a multitude of other trials and tests, we construct our boots by impermeably bonding the upper to the midsole, creating a water-tight cradle around your foot. We keep seams to a minimum, and sew each stress point with no fewer than four rows of waterproof nylon lock stitching.

So, when a size 12 guide boot says Timberland on it, you know you can put it through anything.

Because it's already been there.

Boots, shoes, clothing, wind, water, earth and sky.

**442**

---

## A good leather coat should have two arms and fifty feet.

In this world, there are many things that can be mass-produced.

But not a coat like this.

Not a coat that requires over fifty feet of the finest calfskin available anywhere on earth. Calfskin so perfect it can be tanned as is with vegetable oils. Never painted or color corrected.

Not a coat whose every square inch has undergone the most expensive, most effective waterproofing known to man. A process in which we flood the leather with a special waterproof compound while it is being tanned in the drum, not afterwards.

This is the only technique that insures total penetration of the waterproofing agent. The only technique good enough for a garment that bears our name.

Not a coat whose comfort seems to increase the more you put it under the stress of active use. Because of the extra feet of calfskin, the extra hours of tailoring we spend opening up the back and shoulder dimensions. Adding features such as two-piece underarm gussets to maximize your freedom of movement.

And certainly not a coat whose detailing is so meticulous that every zipper is milled and tumbled smooth so as to not injure the leather, every button is genuine horn or brass, and every buttonhole is both calfskin bound and cleanfinished with stitching inside and out.

In leather coats that lack this latter feature, shreds of lining will begin to emerge in a matter of months. But Timberland designers do not think in terms of months. They take a longer view of product longevity. Setting their sights on

a decade or two. Or more.

There is a method to our madness, and it is perfectly clear. We will do anything for the extra comfort and confidence of our customers.

Confidence, for example, that getting caught in a sudden downpour won't spoil your day or your valuable calfskin investment. Confidence that on the night your buddy spills a beer on your sleeve, you'll need to do nothing more than find a little water and a sponge.

The way we see it, consumer confidence is as hard to come by, in this age of shoddy products, as the world's highest quality calfskin.

Like our leather coats and jackets, it can't be mass-produced.

Boots, shoes, clothing, wind, water, earth and sky.

**443**

---

## Many boots are waterproof. Few are waterproven.

For over twenty years, our customers have put Timberland boots through the worst tests imaginable. They've worn them through 1,000-mile sled dog races. They've worn them through brackish backwaters and hellish swamps.

Tough as these tests are, they're not nearly as punishing as the ones we perform ourselves.

For starters, let us walk you through our notorious flex test.

In this ordeal, we put a mass of water behind pieces of boot leather. We then flex the leather again and again, simulating movements the human foot might make were it slogging through a similar mass of water deep in no man's land.

After flexing each piece of leather a mere sixteen thousand times, we accept only one result. No leakage whatsoever. A single microscopic drop and the leather is rejected. No appeals, no second chances.

The truth is, rejections don't happen very often. Our method of waterproofing leather has been perfected over a period of twenty years, and it's the most expensive process known to man.

First, we cherrypick the world's leather supply, selecting only the cream of the crop. Then we flood every fiber of the leather, inside and out, with a special silicone waterproofing agent. We do this during the actual tanning so as not to miss a single space big enough for a water molecule to sneak in.

(We could practice shortcuts, such as brushing the surface of the leather with silicone after tanning. But then we'd be like any other boot company.)

Another torture test involves our so-called "boot within a boot," your ultimate insurance of dry, comfortable feet under the worst, wettest, coldest conditions.

The boot within a boot begins as a sock made of waterproof, breathable Gore-Tex® fabric. To which we later add Thinsulate® insulation and a durable, smooth Cambrelle® lining. But only if the sock passes the infamous bubble test. In which we fill it with air, submerge it in a glass water tank, and watch.

One air bubble and the sock is sacked. Period.

Besides these and a multitude of other trials and tests, we construct our boots by

impermeably bonding the upper to the midsole, creating a watertight cradle around your foot. We keep seams to a minimum, and sew each stress point with no fewer than four rows of waterproof nylon lock stitching. Stitching that won't break, rot or mildew.

(Competitors please note that's nylon, not cotton. And four rows, not two.)

So, when a size 12 guide boot says Timberland on it, you know you can put it through anything. Because it's already been there.

Boots, shoes, clothing, wind, water, earth and sky.

**444**

# VISIT YOUR GREAT GRANDPARENTS IN NEW YORK.

More than 100 million Americans can trace their roots to a small wooden ramp. It leads to a 24-acre landfill in New York Harbor called Ellis Island. And between 1892 and 1924, 12 million immigrants crossed over it into the American Dream.

As chronicler of that dream, LIFE proudly documents the resurrection of Ellis Island, with unlimited access to the archives and memorabilia.

It's an exclusive opportunity to see America the way these people did, the ones who left everywhere on Earth and came to a small island off Manhattan. So we could all be here today.

Photos: The Watchorn Memorial Methodist Church courtesy MetaForm, Inc.

445

It's been a bumpy road for love these past decades.

In the 60's, you had free love. In the 70's, quick love. In the 80's, I'm-in-a-meeting-could-I-get-back-to-you love.

And now the indicators are in for the 90's. The winner? Yes, good old fashioned, committed, monogamous love.

Read it and sigh in LIFE's special Romance section. A comprehensive report on the state of the heart.

# COMMITMENT IS BACK.

446

# FORMER KING LOOKING FOR WORK. WILLING TO RELOCATE.

The thoughtful gentleman sunbathing in three-piece suit and fedora on the left may look like your average retiree. In fact, he is heir to the throne of the Ottoman Empire.

Banished to France after World War I, he's one of a number of unemployed kings and queens whose portraits LIFE's photo editor discovered in Europe. LIFE interviewed them, and now we present their intriguing story to Americans: monarchs who sit on chairs and sofas, not thrones.

447

# No matter how good you are you can always be replaced.

Even Vibram® soles, so the rumor goes, eventually wear out. However, that's certainly no reason to despair. After all, even these, the most durable of soles, can be quickly and easily replaced–with new Vibram soles.

Choose from Vibram® Evaflex® sport unit soles; Evaflex® mini-lug soles for lightweight casuals; or high abrasion soles for rugged outdoor and work footwear. Of course, there's more to Vibram® than soles.

There's also our newly expanded line of Vibram® sheets–which includes a wide variety of EVA oil-resisting sheets, women's two ply toplifting, and sheets for spikeless golf shoes. So the next time your customer brings in a pair of shoes for repair, do what so many quality shoe manufacturers did in the first place. Put on genuine Vibram soles. It's the only way to make the shoes as good as new.

© 1990 QUABAUG CORPORATION, NORTH BROOKFIELD, MASSACHUSETTS 01535. MANUFACTURERS OF VIBRAM® SOLES UNDER EXCLUSIVE LICENSE IN THE UNITED STATES.

VIBRAM® AND THE YELLOW OCTAGONAL LABEL ARE THE REGISTERED TRADEMARKS OF VIBRAM SpA OF ITALY

448

---

Hurricanes. And small boys.

It's a toss-up as to which can wreck a house faster.

*Hurricane Gilbert*

So we make sure every Pella® window is prepared for both.

For example, every week in Pella, Iowa, we arrange for several large hurricanes.

contort windows, blast windows with water, and crank windows open and closed thousands of times.

All of which, to some people, may seem like overkill.

But it's merely our way of making certain that every single Pella window

*Gilbert Miller*

## WE HAVE TESTING EQUIPMENT THAT CAN SIMULATE THE DESTRUCTIVE POWER OF BOTH GILBERTS.

In our testing laboratory, we not only reproduce hurricane force winds, but arctic cold, desert heat, tropic humidity, and salt air more corrosive than you'll find on any seacoast.

We have machines that shake windows, **BUILT TO IMPOSSIBLY HIGH STANDARDS. OUR OWN.®**

can weather a whole lifetime of use and abuse.

Which we feel is important. Even if you don't live in the path of Gilbert.

For a free copy of our Windowscaping® Idea Book, and the address of The Pella Window Store® nearest you, please call 1-800-524-3700. © 1990 Rolscreen Company

449

---

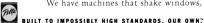

*Ordinary paint, after the equivalent of 5000 hours of 5% salt fog (AAMA 605.2)*

## AH, YES. THERE'S NOTHING LIKE THE RESTORATIVE, HEALTH-GIVING EFFECTS OF BRACING SEA AIR.

Sea air may do wonders for the human constitution. But it can absolutely destroy wood, metal and paint.

Put wood windows in a house on the seacoast, and you can count on repainting every couple years. (A swell way to spend your summer vacation, right?) Install vinyl or ordinary aluminum-clad windows, and you'll find them peeling, blistering or fading within three to five years.

*Permacoat Plus™ after the equivalent of 10,000 hours of 5% salt fog (AAMA 605.2.)*

But now, instead of choosing among the lesser of those evils, you can install something good: aluminum-clad wood windows from Pella.®

Thanks to revolutionary new coating systems **BUILT TO IMPOSSIBLY HIGH STANDARDS. OUR OWN.®**

called Permacoat™ and Permacoat Plus,™ these windows are so resistant to corrosion, we can warranty their exterior finish for twenty years.*

Not only will they not become ugly over time, these windows will be beautiful from day one. Because they're available in a stunning array of colors. You can have any shade you see here, and if you don't see what you want here, ask. We can match just about any color you send us.

So, if you're building or renovating a home on the seacoast, make sure you install Pella. The window that can weather the weather.

For a free Windowscaping® Idea Book and the location of The Pella Window Store® nearest you, call 1-800-524-3700.

*For complete terms and conditions of warranty contact your local Pella Window Store.®

450

Cover and block
scents also available.

# Oh Look, A Nice Bottle Of Forehead And Tarsal Glands.

Dr. Juice Deer Attractant™ is not a urine based sex scent. It's a forehead & tarsal gland scent that triggers curiosity and "approach behavior." So choose the science of Dr. Juice. Each bottle is loaded for deer. **Dr. Juice Deer Attractant.**

© 1990 Normark Co., 1710 East 78th St., Mpls., MN 55423

451

# Run your ads in The Oregonian instead of on TV, and eliminate the competition.

The Oregonian has some bad news to report: Studies indicate that over 50% of today's television viewers don't pay attention to commercials.

They're busy doing more interesting things. Like sprinting for the bathroom. Raiding the fridge. Exercising their thumbs on the remote control.

Problems, we'd like to remind you, you'll never encounter when running a newspaper ad. Because newspaper is the one, and probably only, medium where people actually look forward to seeing your advertising.

In study after study, consumers call the newspaper the most helpful, believable and influential source of advertising information available.

And The Oregonian delivers over 555,000 of those consumers every day—a whopping 91% of the Portland metro population after just one week.

To find out more, call Brian Bounous here at The Oregonian: 221-8279. Because not even the best TV spot can grab the consumer's mind if it's in the bathroom at the moment. **The Oregonian**

452

453

454

455

456

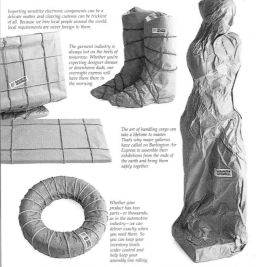   
  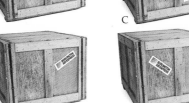    

TRADE ANY SIZE
B/W OR COLOR:
CAMPAIGN

458
ART DIRECTOR
Matt Haligman
WRITERS
Jeff Atlas, Kirk Citron
PHOTOGRAPHERS
Irving Penn, Robert Mizono
CLIENT
Allure/Conde Nast
AGENCY
Atlas Citron Haligman &
Bedecarre/San Francisco

459
ART DIRECTORS
Bryan Buckley, Stan Poulos,
Tanya Hotton
WRITERS
Tom DeCerchio,
Bryan Buckley,
Courtney Rohan
PHOTOGRAPHER
Steve Hellerstein
CLIENT
Discover Magazine
AGENCY
Buckley DeCerchio Cavalier/
New York

## 100 years ago, women would have killed for this body.

Beauty changes. Every century, every decade, every month. And Allure magazine will be there. With straight-forward reporting. And the latest news about skin care and fitness, fragrance and fashion, travel and trends. Beginning in March. For information call Diane Wichard, Advertising Director, 212-880-5554.

**allure**
The shape of things to come.

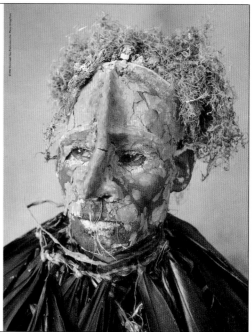

## Centuries before cosmetics, the tribesmen of New Guinea had their own idea of the mud pack.

Beauty is the most personal form of expression. What you find appealing, others may not. That's what Allure magazine explores. With news about make-up and fashion, literature and design, fragrance and fitness. Beginning in March. For information call Diane Wichard, Advertising Director, 212-880-5554.

**allure**
The new face of beauty.

## Why 6,000,000 women who used to carry a little red book now carry a little red lipstick.

Beauty makes a statement. And when nail polish becomes political, and fashion becomes philosophy, Allure magazine will be there. With reporting about fragrance and fitness, cosmetics and culture, travel and trends. Beginning in March. For information call Diane Wichard, Advertising Director, 212-880-5554.

**allure**
The revolutionary beauty.

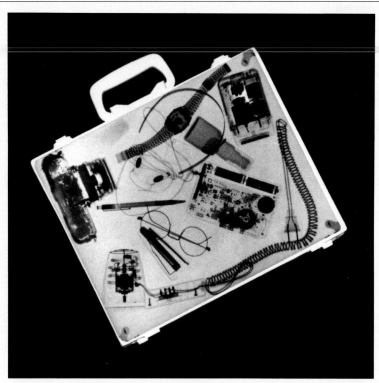

## There are fifty known terrorist groups in the world, unfortunately, this is the best picture we have of them.

If you've ever wondered how a security guard can distinguish a toiletry from a time bomb, the sad fact is sometimes he can't. But with the latest technology comes new hope.

First in the form of a luggage scanner that can determine not only what an object is, but what it is made of.

And now there is a camera that scans your face while a computer attempts to match it with one of the 500 terrorists in its memory bank.

Thus making it virtually impossible for a bomb to go undetected. And making it just as unlikely that a false alarm will cause a stranger to rummage through your undergarments. Month after month, Discover is the first to break stories like these that affect our lives.

In fact, 5.1 million readers turn to us for a clear picture of the most complicated issues of our times. Quite simply, there's no better vehicle to reach today's concerned citizens.

Discover Magazine. It may be the only way to understand this world.

*Healthy Breast*

*Total Mastectomy*

## Now there's a birth control pill without these side effects.

It is a horrifying reality shared by millions of women each year. Breast cancer is one of the leading causes of death for women in this century.

Perhaps most astounding is the fact that birth control pills have now been found to cause breast cancer in some women.

However, one of the country's top researchers recently developed a birth control pill that he believes actually prevents breast cancer.

Discover readers were the first to learn of this remarkable breakthrough and the informative and enlightening story that led to it. In each issue, Discover's top-rated writers and investigative reporters break stories that affect people's lives.

Each month, Discover gives 5.1 million readers a point of view on life that no other magazine can deliver.

Discover Magazine. It may be the only way to understand this world.

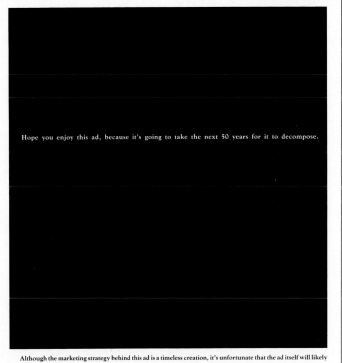

Hope you enjoy this ad, because it's going to take the next 50 years for it to decompose.

Although the marketing strategy behind this ad is a timeless creation, it's unfortunate that the ad itself will likely last into the next century.

Which causes one to wonder how long other refuse lasts in a landfill. For example, the pen that this ad was written with will indeed see the next millennium.

At Discover, we've been telling our readers for the past ten years about America's perilous landfill shortage.

However, the world's brimming garbage dumps are only one of the many pertinent stories that you'll find in the pages of Discover Magazine.

Each month, we inform our readers of pressing issues facing our world. From the environment to the latest medical breakthroughs, our staff of award-winning writers breaks stories first.

Perhaps that's why over 5.1 million people scan our magazine's pages each month. With numbers like that, there's no better vehicle in which to reach today's concerned citizens.

Discover Magazine. It may be the only way to understand this world.

459

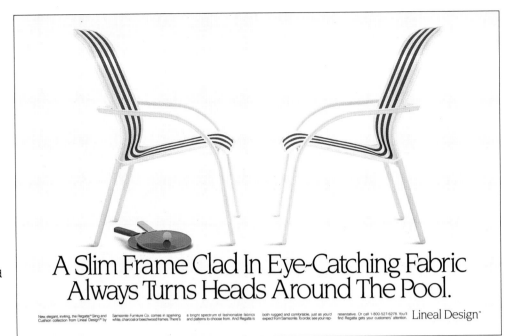

## A Slim Frame Clad In Eye-Catching Fabric Always Turns Heads Around The Pool.

New, elegant, inviting, the Regatta™ Sling and Cushion collection from Lineal Design™ by Samsonite Furniture Co. comes in sparkling white, charcoal or beechwood frames. There's a bright spectrum of fashionable fabrics and patterns to choose from. And Regatta is both rugged and comfortable, just as you'd expect from Samsonite. To order, see your representative. Or call 1-800-527-6278. You'll find Regatta gets your customers' attention.

Lineal Design™

## A Shapely Silhouette Always Draws Stares From The Poolside Crowd.

The classic Chesapeake™ Sling and Cushion collection from Lineal Design™ by Samsonite Furniture Co. has a breezy new style: frames in charcoal and beechwood as well as original white. A lively palette of the latest patterns and fabrics. Plus the comfort and durability you've come to expect from Samsonite. To order Chesapeake, or for further information, contact your representative. Or call 1-800-527-6278. You'll see we're looking better than ever.

Lineal Design™

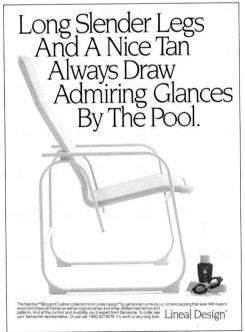

## Long Slender Legs And A Nice Tan Always Draw Admiring Glances By The Pool.

The Natchez™ Sling and Cushion collection from Lineal Design™ by Samsonite Furniture Co. is more dazzling than ever. With beechwood and charcoal frames as well as original cameo and white. Brilliant new fabrics and patterns. And all the comfort and durability you'd expect from Samsonite. To order, see your Samsonite representative. Or just call 1-800-527-6278. It's worth a very long look.

Lineal Design™

460

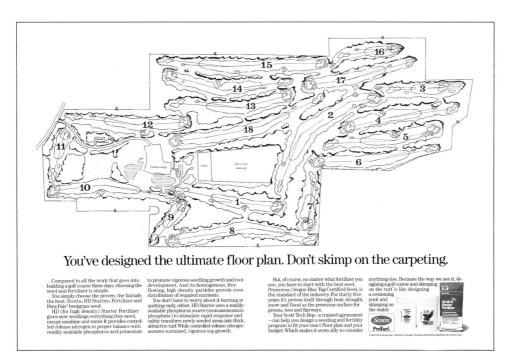

## You've designed the ultimate floor plan. Don't skimp on the carpeting.

Compared to all the work that goes into building a golf course these days, choosing the seed and fertilizer is simple.

You simply choose the proven, the failsafe, the best. Scotts® HD Starter® Fertilizer and PennPals® bentgrass seed.

HD (for high density) Starter Fertilizer gives new seedlings everything they need, except sunshine and water. It provides controlled-release nitrogen in proper balance with readily-available phosphorus and potassium to promote vigorous seedling growth and root development. And its homogenous, free flowing, high-density particles provide even distribution of required nutrients.

You don't have to worry about it burning or quitting early, either. HD Starter uses a readily-available phosphorus source (monoammonium phosphate) to stimulate rapid response and safely transform newly seeded areas into thick, attractive turf. While controlled-release nitrogen assures sustained, vigorous top growth.

But, of course, no matter what fertilizer you use, you have to start with the best seed. Penncross, Oregon Blue Tag Certified Seed, is the standard of the industry. For thirty-five years it's proven itself through heat, drought, snow and flood as the premium surface for greens, tees and fairways.

Your Scott Tech Rep—a trained agronomist—can help you design a seeding and fertility program to fit your exact floor plan and your budget. Which makes it seem silly to consider anything else. Because the way we see it, designing a golf course and skimping on the turf is like designing a swimming pool and skimping on the water.

Scotts. ProTurf.

---

## We offer more than 10 exclusive varieties of grass seed. But only one color.

At Scott we may offer a lot of exclusive seed varieties. But we have only one set of standards. The highest.

And those high standards begin with our breeding and varietal development. We not only work closely with universities and other seed developers, we have our own extensive in-house breeding program, with our own testing facilities all over the country.

The result? Seed to meet any requirement. Exclusive varieties like our Coventry, Abbey, Bristol and Victa Kentucky bluegrasses; Accolade, Caravelle, Loretta, Applause and Ovation perennial ryegrasses; Banner Chewings fescue; and Chesapeake and Aquaro tall fescues.

But seed development is only part of the story. We have the most stringent requirements and controls for clean seed in the industry. From grower selection all the way through cleaning, testing and packaging, our standards are uncompromising. In fact, we pioneered the seed business over 100 years ago.

And only our seed comes equipped with a Scott Tech Rep. They're true agronomists, who can make recommendations and develop complete seeding and fertility programs to fit your specific needs and problems.

Of course, we still aren't content. We're constantly working harder to develop even better seed varieties.

Although you can rest assured, we're going to stick with the same old color.

Scotts. ProTurf.

---

## If the dimethyl phenylene iminocarbonothlioyl thiophanate carbamate doesn't get them, the iprodione methyl ethyl dichlorophenyl carboxamide dioxo imidazolidine will.

O.K., let's rephrase that. Scotts® Fluid Fungicides stop fungus. Period. That's because each product in our Fluid Fungicide line contains not just one, but two highly effective active ingredients—active ingredients specially formulated to work together to stop diseases once and for all. And only Scotts offers them.

But not only are our unique pre-mixed formulas more effective, they're also easier to use and safer for your turf. No additives are needed. And unlike powders, there's no dust.

To further insure against resistance, we offer three different products—Fluid Fungicide, Fluid Fungicide II and Fluid Fungicide III—that work alone or in rotation. Together, they control the major disease problems you encounter: brown patch, leaf spot, dollar spot, anthracnose, rust and pythium.

But that's enough technical mumbo jumbo for now. Call your Scotts Tech Rep and he can help you design a complete disease prevention program. Scotts. The big name in fluid fungicides.

Scotts. ProTurf.

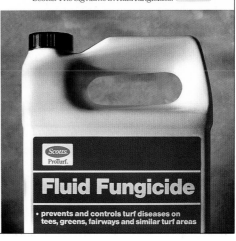

**Fluid Fungicide**

• prevents and controls turf diseases on tees, greens, fairways and similar turf areas

Lee Lites. A new line of lightweight denim.

Light, cool, comfortable jeans with a remarkably soft hand. Perfect for all seasons. Available in two different finishes: Aged Stone and Aged Blue. Call your Lee sales representative today. Because Lee Lites are just what the market ordered. And they just might take off without you.

Lee Lites. Lightweight denim.

Light, cool, comfortable jeans with a remarkably soft hand. Perfect for all seasons. Available in two different finishes: Aged Stone and Aged Blue. Call your Lee sales representative today. Because Lee Lites are just what the market ordered. And everyone will be reaching for them.

Lee Lites. Lightweight denim.

Light, cool, comfortable jeans with a remarkably soft hand. Perfect for all seasons. Available in two different finishes: Aged Stone and Aged Blue. Call your Lee sales representative today. Because Lee Lites are just what the market ordered. And they're raising eyebrows everywhere.

## Most banks don't like to be pigeon-holed. Fortunately, we do.

At Continental Bank, we're considered something of a rare bird. A reputation, we hasten to add, with which we wholeheartedly concur.

After all, we're not a renaissance bank. We're a business bank. Top to bottom, inside and out, through and through.

Now to some, that may seem like an unusual thing to crow about. But then specializing on business has never been, shall we say, a banking industry specialty.

The fact of the matter is, of the approximately 14,000 financial institutions in the United States, the overwhelming majority of them serve both the individual consumer market and business.

There is, quite clearly, a niche. So we've decided to scratch it.

We've found the exercise to be extremely liberating. No longer torn between two conflicting constituencies, we've been giving our business banking accounts the kind of round-the-clock attention they deserve.

For example, rather than use the extra time to lower our golf scores, we've been using it to lower your financial risk. Rather than pull some standard banking

solution out of the industry stockpile, we've been more than willing to tinker around and invent something new.

And rather than concentrate on the abstractions of theory alone, we've become absolute sticklers for detail. Even if it means reviewing, say, your capital structure for the umpteenth time.

Of course, you can't deliver first-rate financial service without first-rate financial people. Which is why over the last few years, we've gone on recruiting missions all over the globe—earning us not only frequent flier points, but some of the top talents in the industry.

In short, we're doing what we've always done for our business clients. Only now, we're doing it with a level of sophistication, resourcefulness and commitment that few if any banks can match. So go ahead, pigeonhole Continental Bank. Label us. Categorize us. Put us in a nice, neatly defined little banking box—we don't mind.

Just so long as you can appreciate the kind of difference that a pure, unadulterated, "business only" bank can make. And just so long as you call us at (312) 828-5799 to discuss your business banking needs.

After all, if you really want to find out how we can help your company, the best way is to hear it straight from our own beaks. **Continental Bank**
A new approach to business.

---

A couple of years ago, we here at Continental Bank came to a very important realization: the human brain is best suited to focus on one subject at a time.

As a result, we did something few

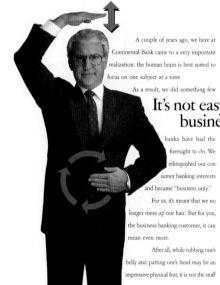

banks have had the foresight to do. We relinquished our consumer banking interests and became "business only."

For us, it's meant that we no longer mess up our hair. But for you, the business banking customer, it can mean even more.

After all, while rubbing one's belly and patting one's head may be an impressive physical feat, it is not the stuff

of which business banking legends are made. The only true measure of greatness, we believe, is how well one responds to a customer's business banking needs.

At Continental, we've committed our substantial resources to that very goal. And, perhaps sensing our uncommon singleness of purpose, some of the industry's finest business bankers have committed themselves to us.

## It's not easy for a bank to serve consumer and business customers at the same time.

To the point where, today, we've bolstered the bank's strengths in virtually every department: from corporate finance and financial risk management to foreign exchange and cash management.

Of course, we could go on at length about our personnel. We could extol endlessly upon their considerable and varied credentials.

And while we're at it, we could expound effusively on such matters as our high level of responsiveness, our creative use of financial instruments, and our exhaustive attention to detail.

But rather than attempt to woo you with rhetoric, we thought we'd invite you to talk to a Continental banker yourself. Simply call (312) 828-5799. We think you'll find our focused expertise can make a real difference for your company. And we're not just patting ourselves on the back. **Continental Bank**
A new approach to business.

---

## Continental Bank proudly reminds you that we have a really lousy passbook savings program.

As you may know, Continental has left the consumer banking industry and become "business only." Now, on the surface, that merely means we no longer offer such things as passbook savings, credit cards and long lines marked off by felt ropes.

Beyond that, however, it has meant a singleness of purpose for our entire organization.

Today, instead of greeting our customers with a team of tellers, we're greeting them

with a team of experienced, sophisticated, business banking professionals.

Instead of offering our clients toasters, blenders and cuddly stuffed animals, we're offering them customized financial risk management products like swaps, caps and corridors.

And instead of trotting out some dusty old product like passbook savings, we're introducing them to our latest credit, restructuring and capitalization ideas.

Mind you, it's not that we haven't provided these kinds of services before. It's just that now, having left the daily demands of mass market banking to our competitors, we're providing them exclusively.

Has all this emphasis on business banking translated into fewer customers? Frankly, yes. About 60,000, to be precise. And with 60,000 fewer customers to worry about, you'd be amazed how much more focused a bank can be.

If it's a passbook savings account you're after, there are any number of fine financial institutions we could recommend—just a few of which are listed here. But if it's a disciplined, dynamic and responsive business bank, we suggest you call (312) 828-5799 and speak directly to us.

We may be lousy in some areas. But when it comes to business banking, we're proud to remind you that we're anything but. **Continental Bank**
A new approach to business.

465

# Perception.

# Reality.

For a new generation of Rolling Stone readers, there's more to living in harmony with our planet than sitting still for twenty minutes. And the readers of Rolling Stone are doing their part to recycle that message. If you want to reach socially responsible, highly educated consumers, you'll like the environment in the pages of Rolling Stone.

**Rolling Stone**

---

# Perception.

# Reality.

For a new generation of Rolling Stone readers, Canada is not a place you go to avoid a draft. It gets cold up there. Besides, last year, 108,000 Rolling Stone readers were among the brave and the free who served their country proudly in an *all volunteer* armed services. If you're looking for volunteers, be all you can be in the pages of Rolling Stone.

**Rolling Stone**

---

# Perception.

# Reality.

For a new generation of Rolling Stone readers, paper products with gummed edges are used for leaving notes, not for leaving reality. These days, the readers of Rolling Stone are among those most likely to experiment with new products. From Post-It® notes to personal computers, if you've got new products to sell, we invite you to roll your own media plan in the pages of Rolling Stone.

**Rolling Stone**

TRADE ANY SIZE
B/W OR COLOR:
CAMPAIGN

468
ART DIRECTOR
Bob Barrie
WRITER
Jamie Barrett
ILLUSTRATORS
Carl Cedergren and Others
CLIENT
Carl Cedergren
AGENCY
Fallon McElligott/Minneapolis

469
ART DIRECTOR
Michael Fazende
WRITER
Bill Miller
PHOTOGRAPHERS
Mark LaFavor,
Michael Johnson
CLIENT
The Lee Company
AGENCY
Fallon McElligott/Minneapolis

Galloping horse by
George Gier, Hal Riney & Partners.

Galloping horse by
Dan Weiden, Weiden & Kennedy.

Galloping horse by
Tom McElligott, Chiat/Day/Mojo.

Galloping horse by
Greg Beaupre, BBD&O.

Galloping horse by
Joe Alexander, Clarity Coverdale Rueff.

Galloping horse by
Lyle Wedemeyer, Martin/Williams.

Galloping horse by
Rod Kilpatrick, Cole & Weber.

Galloping horse by
Jamie Barrett, Fallon McElligott.

Galloping horse by
Carl Cedergren.

**If you can't use your fingers to draw, use them to call.**

**Carl Cedergren, advertising layout artist.**
Phone (612) 481-1429.

Gooey pizza by
Jack Supple, Carmichael Lynch.

Gooey pizza by
Jarl Olsen, Fallon McElligott.

Gooey pizza by
Mike Lescarbeau, Hill Holiday.

Gooey pizza by
Dan Weiden, Weiden & Kennedy.

Gooey pizza by
Craig Tanimoto, Clarity Coverdale Rueff.

Gooey pizza by
Curlin Reed, The Martin Agency.

Gooey pizza by
John Olson, Kruskopf Olson.

Gooey pizza by
Sam Avery, Ketchum Communications.

Gooey pizza by
Carl Cedergren.

**If you can't use your fingers to draw, use them to call.**

**Carl Cedergren, advertising layout artist.**
Phone (612) 481-1429.

Frazzled housewife by
Lyle Wedemeyer, Martin/Williams.

Frazzled housewife by
Luke Sullivan, Fallon McElligott.

Frazzled housewife by
Sam Avery, Ketchum Communications.

Frazzled housewife by
Mike Lescarbeau, Hill Holiday.

Frazzled housewife by
Joe Alexander, Clarity Coverdale Rueff.

Frazzled housewife by
Bill Hillsman, Kauffman Stewart.

Frazzled housewife by
Jo Marshall, Lacey LaMaster.

Frazzled housewife by
Tom McElligott, Chiat/Day/Mojo.

Frazzled housewife by
Carl Cedergren.

**If you can't use your fingers to draw, use them to call.**

**Carl Cedergren, advertising layout artist.**
Phone (612) 481-1429.

## To sell more jeans this year, push the right buttons.

A peek at the most dramatic, new innovation in the jeans business this year.

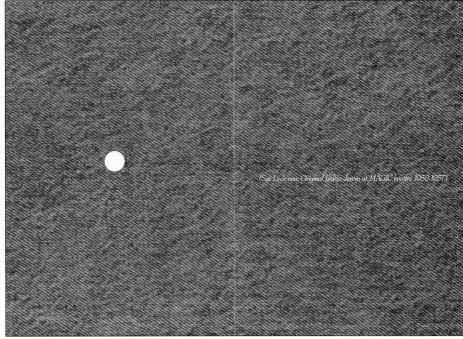

*(See Lee's new Original Indigo denim at MAGIC booths 1050-1057.)*

How to spot a real kid.

*Outfit by Lee. Spot by Heinz.*

*Outfit by Lee. Spot by Spot.*

TRADE ANY SIZE
B/W OR COLOR:
CAMPAIGN

470
ART DIRECTOR
Gary Goldsmith
WRITER
Dean Hacohen
CLIENT
Knoll
AGENCY
Goldsmith/Jeffrey, New York

471
ART DIRECTORS
Steve Matthews, Andrew Bell
WRITER
Martin Lee
PHOTOGRAPHERS
Peter Hopkins, Stock
CLIENT
Singapore Convention Bureau
AGENCY
Leo Burnett/Singapore

**Now Knoll can provide you with truly affordable office seating.** I'll believe it when I see it. **It's for everyone in the company.** I'll believe it when I see it. **From secretaries to CEOs.** I'll believe it when I see it. **It's not even named after a designer.** I'll believe it when I see it. **Bulldog. Available June 15.** I'll believe it when I see it. Maybe.

Knoll

**Now at Knoll you can choose between a wide array of systems, desks, files and chairs.** Not just between high design and higher design? **They're made to look good in executive suites as well as mailrooms.** Not just museums and design annuals? **And they're practical and affordable.** Not just expensive and more expensive? **Knoll.** Knoll?

Knoll

**Knoll introduces a new line of office chairs.** How many million do I need to buy one? **An affordable line of seating for everyone in the office.** Affordable for whom? The Princess Aga Khan? **It's affordable for companies in the Fortune 500.** I knew it wasn't cheap. **And equally affordable if you're not.** How many times are they going to repeat "affordable?" **Introducing Bulldog. Affordable.**

Knoll

# *If* you're very, *very* good at your job, this is what you *get.*

It's called Thaipusam and last year, thousands of top achievers loved the experience. They were given the ultimate incentive in Singapore, where a multi-racial, multi-cultural city provides some of the most exciting sights, sounds and scenes in the world. Incentive Isle Singapore. Anywhere else would be a real pain.

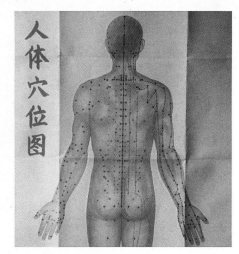

# What's the *point* of meeting in *Singapore?*

人体穴位图

From a medical point of view, it could be the knowledge that being pampered in one of our five five star hotels does wonders for the blood pressure. Or knowing that our delicious cuisine is the perfect cure for loss of appetite. Or trying to pin down the real reasons why acupuncture works. Of course, Convention City Singapore offers something rather more straight forward for medical organisers. No headaches. Whether it's a meeting for 5,000 dentists, 1,000 orthopaedic surgeons or any number of psychologists. And isn't that what healthy medical meetings are all about?

# It's no wonder the world's leading *dentists* are coming to *Singapore.*

In fact, 5,000 of them are coming for the World Dental Congress. And after they've finished speaking in our superbly-equipped, modern meeting facilities, they'll be ready to bite into Singapore's world-famous cuisine. Or open their mouths in amazement at the city's exciting melange of Chinese, Malay, Indian and European cultures. Convention City Singapore. The world's dentists are going to eat it up.

# A good leather coat should have two arms and fifty feet.

In this world, there are many things that can be mass-produced.

But not a coat like this.

Not a coat that requires over fifty feet of the finest calfskin available anywhere on earth. Calfskin so perfect it can be tanned as is with vegetable oils.

Never painted or color corrected.

Not a coat whose every square inch has undergone the most expensive, most effective waterproofing known to man. A process in which we flood the leather with a special waterproof compound while it is being tanned in the drum, not afterwards.

This is the only technique that insures total penetration of the waterproofing agent. The only technique good enough for a garment that bears our name.

Not a coat whose comfort seems to increase the more you put it under the stress of active use. Because of the extra feet of calfskin, the extra hours of tailoring we spend opening up the back and shoulder dimensions. Adding features such as two-piece underarm gussets to maximize your freedom of movement.

And certainly not a coat whose detailing is so meticulous that every zipper is milled and tumbled smooth so as to not injure the leather, every button is genuine horn or brass, and every buttonhole is both calfskin bound and cleanfinished with stitching inside and out.

In leather coats that lack this latter feature, shreds of lining will begin to emerge in a matter of months. But Timberland designers do not think in terms of months. They take a longer view of product longevity. Setting their sights on a decade or two. Or more.

There is a method to our madness, and it is perfectly clear. We will do anything for the extra comfort and confidence of our customers.

Confidence, for example, that getting caught in a sudden downpour won't spoil your day or your valuable calfskin investment. Confidence that on the night your buddy spills a beer on your sleeve, you'll need to do nothing more than find a little water and a sponge.

The way we see it, consumer confidence is as hard to come by, in this age of shoddy products, as the world's highest quality calfskin.

Like our leather coats and jackets, it can't be mass-produced.

Boots, shoes, clothing, wind, water, earth and sky.

---

# The Marines say Parris Island is the world's toughest boot camp. We beg to differ.

Everyone knows it takes weeks of hell to turn out a few good Leathernecks.

But how many people know what it takes to turn out a few good leather boots? Boots as waterproof as canteens, yet as comfortable as slippers.

You can find out fast at the world's toughest boot camp. A place called Timberland.

There we have devised tests that make the Chinese water torture seem like a walk in the park.

In one particularly grueling ordeal, we put a mass of water behind pieces of boot leather.

We then flex the leather again and again, simulating the movements the human foot might make were it slogging through a similar mass of water deep in no man's land.

After flexing each piece sixteen thousand times, we accept only one result. No leakage whatsoever. A single drop and the leather is rejected. No appeals, no second chances.

The truth is, rejections don't happen very often. Our method of waterproofing leather has been perfected over a period of twenty years, and it's the most expensive process known to man.

First, we cherrypick the world's leather supply, selecting only the cream of the crop. Then we flood every fiber of the leather, inside and out, with a special silicone waterproofing agent. We do this during the actual tanning so as not to miss a single space big enough for a water molecule to sneak in.

(We could practice shortcuts, such as brushing the surface of the leather with silicone. But then we'd be like any other boot company.)

Another torture test involves our so-called "boot within a boot," your ultimate insurance of dry, comfortable feet under the worst, wettest, coldest conditions.

The boot within a boot is actually a sock constructed of waterproof Gore-Tex, Thinsulate® insulation and smooth Cambrelle.

We take this innocent-looking sock and give it the infamous bubble test. We fill it with air, submerge it in a glass water tank, and we watch. One air bubble and the sock is sacked. Period.

Besides these and a multitude of other trials and tests, we construct our boots by impermeably bonding the upper to the midsole, creating a water-tight cradle around your foot. We keep seams to a minimum, and sew each stress point with no fewer than four rows of waterproof nylon lock stitching.

So, when a size 12 guide boot says Timberland on it, you know you can put it through anything.

Because it's already been there.

Boots, shoes, clothing, wind, water, earth and sky.

---

# This shoe has 342 holes. How do you make it waterproof?

Wherever you look in our footwear line, you find holes.

You find wingtips with scores of stylishly arranged perforations.

You find handsewns with scores of needle holes. Moccasins. Canoe moccasins. Boat shoes. Ultralights for easy walking. Lightweight comfort casuals for weightless walking.

Built by a lesser waterproofer, each of these styles has enough openings to admit a deluge.

But we're the Timberland company, and you have to understand where we got our start. Over twenty years ago, we were exclusively a boot manufacturer, and we were the first people to successfully produce fine leather sporting boots that were totally waterproof.

The lessons we learned then are why we're able, today, to build wingtips and handsewns you could go wading in.

Lesson one. Select only the cream of the world's leather crop, then spend the money to impregnate every pore with silicone at the same time the leather is being tanned in the drum. (We leave the shortcuts to our competitors, the ones who merely brush the surface with silicone after the leather is tanned. And the consequences, unfortunately, we leave to their customers.)

Lesson two. Be inventive. It takes more than one technology to stop water.

For example, to build a waterproof wingtip, we take a page right out of the old Timberland bootmaker's manual. We bond the upper directly to the midsole, creating an impermeable seal around your foot.

Then we build a special umbrella under those stylish wing perforations. It's actually a "shoe within a shoe."

A bootie lining of our softest saddle glove leather, fully waterproofed with silicone. Guaranteed to stop a monsoon.

Handsewns require a different solution, but one that also harks back to our boot days, when we became an early collaborator of the W.L. Gore Company, creators of waterproof, breathable Gore-Tex™ fabric.

To waterproof the needle holes of a handsewn moc, we use an exclusive technique in which Timberland saddle glove leather is laminated to a Gore-Tex bootie. Once we place this inside the moc, you have a shoe that's an open and shut success. Open to air and shut tight to water. Climate-controlled, in other words, both inside and out.

So even if it never leaves the canyons of Wall Street, every Timberland waterproof shoe owes its character to a world that will never see a sidewalk. The canyons, tundras and marshlands where our boots were born.

Which makes Timberland shoes more than waterproof.

They're water proven.

Boots, shoes, clothing, wind, water, earth and sky.

"Garth was a good boy. And unlike
the other kids his age, he was very sensitive.
Particularly, I thought, to the nuances
of the editorial genre and subtext.
That he's equally adept at operating the
vortran oscillator in multiple node format,
well, what more could a parent want?"

——— MRS. O'DONNELL

GARTH O'DONNELL

6344 FOUNTAIN AVENUE/HOLLYWOOD    CALIFORNIA 90028/TEL. 213·466·7063

ENCORE VIDEO

"I think Ernie's been bringing his shorts
in here for about two years, so I guess you
could say I know him where he lives.
Imagine my surprise, then, when he told me
he was mastering directly on non-linear
media, and not on the antiquated rolfman
synch dubber. It reminded me why I got
into this business in the first place."

——— MOE FEINMAN

ERNIE CAMACHO

6344 FOUNTAIN AVENUE/HOLLYWOOD    CALIFORNIA 90028/TEL. 213·466·7063

ENCORE VIDEO

"Even in high school I always knew Richard
would amount to something. Gosh, when his
fingers would fly over that Quintex x4000,
doing A-B rolls like they were straight
insert edits, well, what girl wouldn't get
goosebumps. My girlfriends were so jealous
that my guy had a mastery of cross-platform
vertical filtration and theirs didn't. I suppose
I'll never meet another editor like Ritchie.
But I'll always have my memories."

——— PATTY

RICHARD CRAWFORD

6344 FOUNTAIN AVENUE/HOLLYWOOD    CALIFORNIA 90028/TEL. 213·466·7063

ENCORE VIDEO

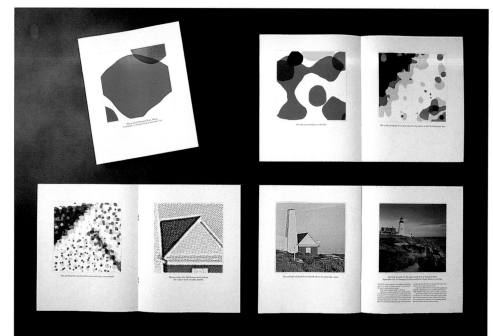

477

478

COLLATERAL BROCHURES
OTHER THAN BY MAIL

**476**
ART DIRECTOR
Steven Mitsch
WRITER
Rosalind Greene
PHOTOGRAPHER
Pamela Hanson
CLIENT
Liz Claiborne/Realities
AGENCY
Altschiller Reitzfeld/
Tracy-Locke, New York

**477**
ART DIRECTOR
Scott Zacaroli
WRITER
Clark Moss
PHOTOGRAPHER
Stock
CLIENT
Agfa Compugraphic
AGENCY
Anderson & Lembke/
New York

**478**
ART DIRECTOR
Toni Bowerman
WRITER
Lee Nash
PHOTOGRAPHERS
Deborah Turbeville,
John Holt Studios
ILLUSTRATOR
Calderwood & Preg
CLIENT
Cole-Haan
AGENCY
Cipriani Kremer
Advertising/Boston

REALITY IS THE BEST FANTASY OF ALL

Liz claiborne

REALITIES

A FRAGRANCE FROM
Liz claiborne

How to spot a real kid.

479

Outfit by Lee. Spot by Smucker's.

Outfit by Lee. Spot by Crayola.

The Power of Water

Preventing the Erosion of Assets.

480

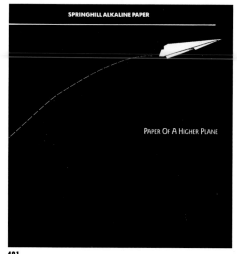

**SPRINGHILL ALKALINE PAPER**

PAPER OF A HIGHER PLANE

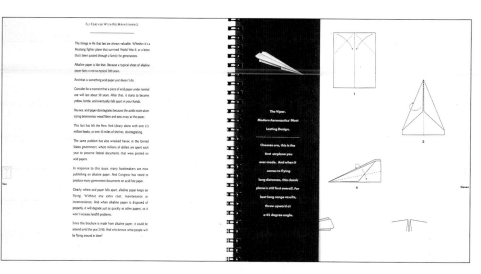

FLY FOREVER WITH NO MAINTENANCE

The things in life that last are always valuable. Whether it's a Mustang fighter plane that survived World War II, or a letter that's been passed through a family for generations.

Alkaline paper is like that. Because a typical sheet of alkaline paper lasts a not-so-typical 200 years.

And that is something acid paper just doesn't do.

Consider for a moment that a piece of acid paper under normal use will last about 50 years. After that, it starts to become yellow, brittle, and eventually falls apart in your hands.

You see, acid paper disintegrates because the acidic rosin-alum sizing deteriorates wood fibers and eats away at the paper.

This fact has left the New York Library alone with over 2.5 million books, or over 35 miles of shelves, disintegrating.

The same problem has also wreaked havoc in the United States government, where millions of dollars are spent each year to preserve federal documents that were printed on acid papers.

In response to this issue, many bookmakers are now publishing on alkaline paper. And Congress has voted to produce many government documents on acid-free paper.

Clearly, where acid paper falls apart, alkaline paper keeps on flying. Without any extra cost, maintenance or inconvenience. And when alkaline paper is disposed of properly, it will degrade just as quickly as other papers, so it won't increase landfill problems.

Since this brochure is made from alkaline paper, it could be around until the year 2190. And who knows what people will be flying around in then?

The Viper.
Modern Aeronautics' Most
Lasting Design.

Chances are, this is the first airplane you ever made. And when it comes to flying long distances, this classic plane is still first overall. For best long range results, throw upward at a 45 degree angle.

**481**

---

u n

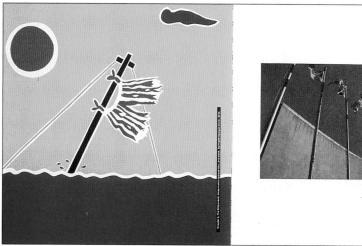

**482**

---

GARY FISHER'S PLACE IN CYCLING HISTORY IS ALREADY ASSURED.

BUT HE'S NOT TAKING ANY CHANCES.

INTRODUCING THE 1990
FISHER MOUNTAINBIKES

CR-7

PARAGON

**483**

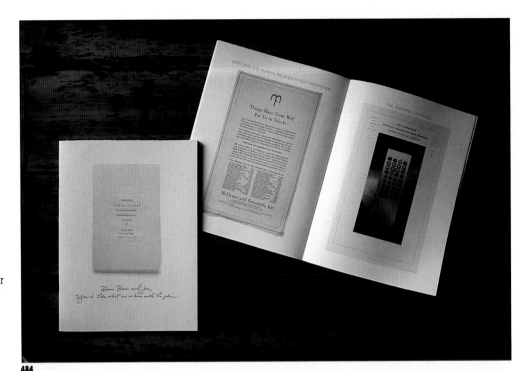

484

485

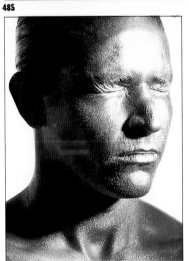

486

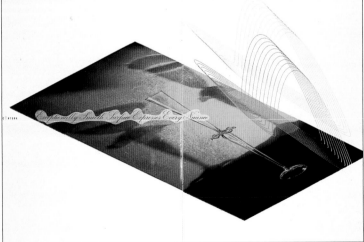

PATINA HAS THE RANGE TO HANDLE ANY CHALLENGE YOU THROW AT IT...BRIGHT OR MUTED COLORS, LIGHT OR DARK TONES, HEAVY COVERAGE OR MINUTE DETAIL.

THE CHALLENGE OF MEETING THE RANGE ON ITS OWN UNCOMPROMISING TERMS HAS PRODUCED A SPECIAL BREED OF SURVIVORS, THOSE HARDWORKING COW-HANDS WHO ALWAYS HAVE MANAGED TO THRIVE ON HARDSHIP AND ISOLATION.

**487**

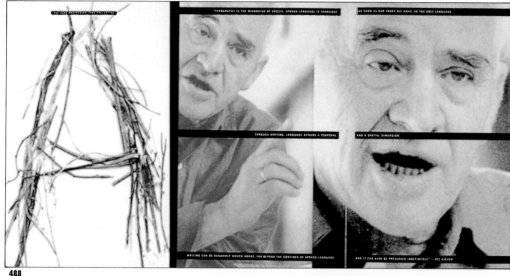

**488**

# MELVYN BRAGG CONTEMPLATES THE FUTURE OF BRITISH TELEVISION.

Will we have soaps coming out of our ears? Will we have wall to wall gameshows? Will quality programming be a thing of the past? Mr. Bragg, for one, isn't going to take it sitting down. Join him on the 25th June for a 6 o'clock start at JWT, 40 Berkeley Square. Tickets are available from your IPA rep. or on 235-7020. **The IPA Society**

**489**

490

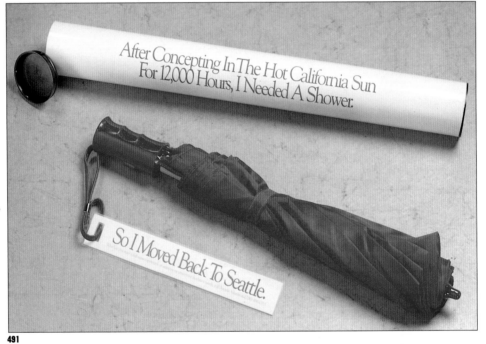

491

492

**493**

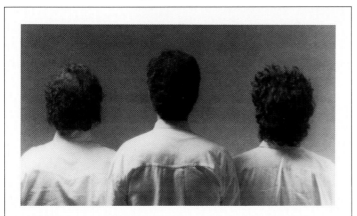

# AFTER 12 YEARS OF SHOOTING IN CHELSEA,

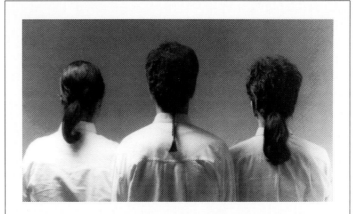

# WE'RE MOVING OUR STUDIO TO SOHO.

Steve Bronstein, Howard Berman, and Gary Hurewitz have opened a new photography studio. At 38 Greene Street. Where pubs are called "cafe's", and diners, "bistros". But while the neighborhood may take some adjusting to, their new studio won't. Because they now have more space than they ever dreamed of. If you'd like to see their new studio, or maybe just their portfolios, call 925-2999, and ask for Gary Hurewitz or Bonnie Shapiro.

**BRONSTEIN BERMAN**

**494**

**495**

COLLATERAL DIRECT MAIL:
SINGLE

**496**
**ART DIRECTOR**
Steve Fong
**WRITER**
David Shane
**CLIENT**
Bissell
**AGENCY**
Chiat/Day/Mojo, New York

**497**
**ART DIRECTOR**
Shelton Scott
**WRITER**
Mary McPhail
**CLIENT**
Carolina Acura Dealers
**AGENCY**
Crispin & Porter Advertising/
Coral Gables

**498**
**ART DIRECTOR**
Jamie Way
**WRITERS**
Jamie Way,
Caroline Srickland
**CLIENT**
Fiberglass Canada
**AGENCY**
Deacon Day Massey
Advertising/Toronto

**499**
**ART DIRECTOR**
Angela Dunkle
**WRITER**
Dion Hughes
**CLIENT**
Mitsubishi
**AGENCY**
Chiat/Day/Mojo, Venice

**500**
**ART DIRECTOR**
Alex Bogusky
**WRITER**
Chuck Porter
**CLIENT**
Personnel Pool of America
**AGENCY**
Crispin & Porter Advertising/
Coral Gables

**501**
**ART DIRECTOR**
Alex Bogusky
**WRITER**
Chuck Porter
**CLIENT**
Personnel Pool of America
**AGENCY**
Crispin & Porter Advertising/
Coral Gables

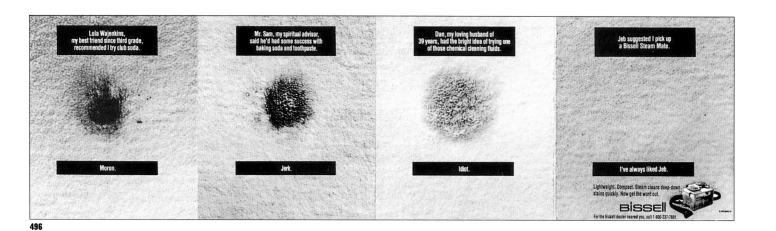

496

497

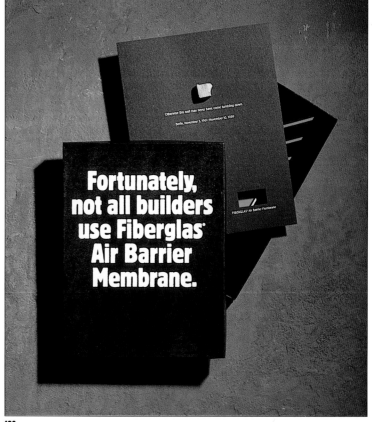

498

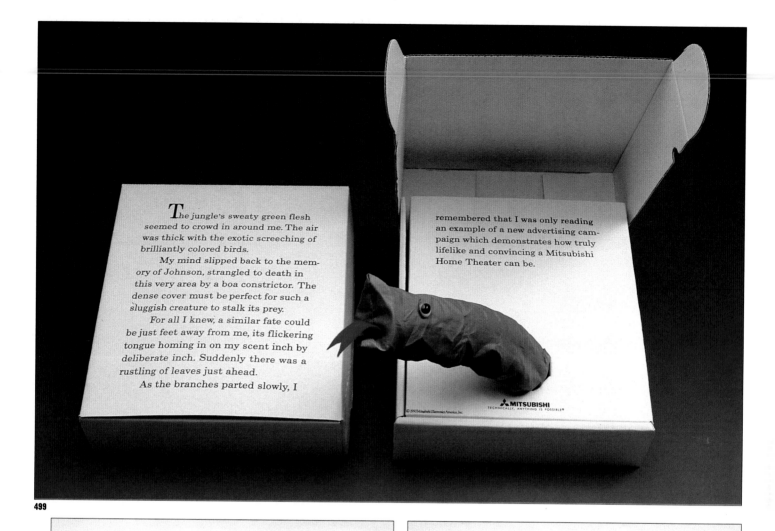

The jungle's sweaty green flesh seemed to crowd in around me. The air was thick with the exotic screeching of brilliantly colored birds.

My mind slipped back to the memory of Johnson, strangled to death in this very area by a boa constrictor. The dense cover must be perfect for such a sluggish creature to stalk its prey.

For all I knew, a similar fate could be just feet away from me, its flickering tongue homing in on my scent inch by deliberate inch. Suddenly there was a rustling of leaves just ahead.

As the branches parted slowly, I remembered that I was only reading an example of a new advertising campaign which demonstrates how truly lifelike and convincing a Mitsubishi Home Theater can be.

© 1990 Mitsubishi Electronics America, Inc.

▲ MITSUBISHI
TECHNICALLY, ANYTHING IS POSSIBLE®

499

Have you ever noticed that in the legal profession it takes a long time to attain, arrive at, achieve, come to, complete, light upon, meet, reach and get to the point?

500

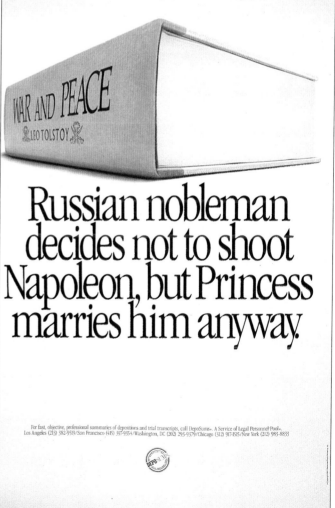

WAR AND PEACE
LEO TOLSTOY

Russian nobleman decides not to shoot Napoleon, but Princess marries him anyway.

501

**502**
ART DIRECTOR
Brian Born
WRITER
Ed Cowardin
ILLUSTRATOR
Dean Hawthorne
PHOTOGRAPHER
Dean Hawthorne
CLIENT
Virginia Historical Society
AGENCY
Earle Palmer Brown/
Richmond

**503**
ART DIRECTOR
Arty Tan
WRITER
Bruce Bildsten
CLIENT
Amoco Oil
AGENCY
Fallon McElligott/
Minneapolis

**504**
ART DIRECTOR
Bob Barrie
WRITER
Jarl Olsen
CLIENT
Fallon McElligott
AGENCY
Fallon McElligott/
Minneapolis

**505**
ART DIRECTOR
Mark Johnson
WRITER
John Stingley
CLIENT
Fallon McElligott
AGENCY
Fallon McElligott/
Minneapolis

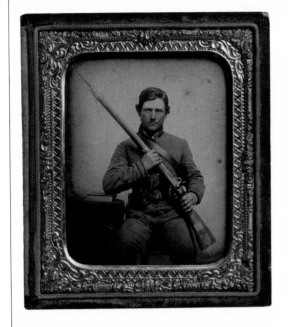

Private Anthony Barksdale survived the Civil War. But his image may become its latest casualty. As could the images of thousands of other Virginians, black and white, celebrated and obscure. ✝ With each passing year, chemicals like oxidative gases and acetic acids are becoming more and more lethal to many of the 130,000

### 129 years later, he's being exposed to chemical warfare.

historic photographs and negatives in our archives. To protect them we desperately need a modern conservation laboratory and darkroom. ✝ That way, we can properly preserve a unique archive that lets us see 150 years of Virginia history face to face.

Please, give generously. Because while old soldiers may never die, they do fade away.

**Save the photographs.**
*Virginia Historical Society, P.O. Box 7311, Richmond, Virginia 23221*

Photography: Dean Hawthorne; Typesetting, Riddick Advertising Art; Creative, EPB/Richmond.

502

A DEMONSTRATION OF WHAT CAN HAPPEN
TO ELECTRIC MOTOR PARTS IF YOU DON'T
USE AMOCO RYKON PREMIUM GREASE.

(OPEN HERE)

503

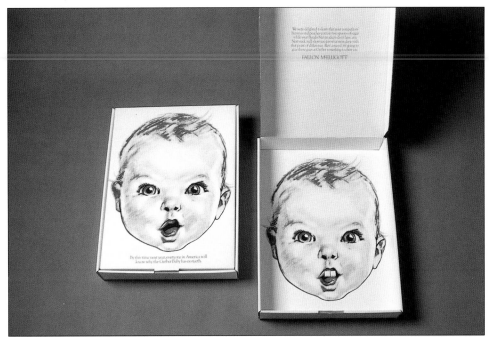

504

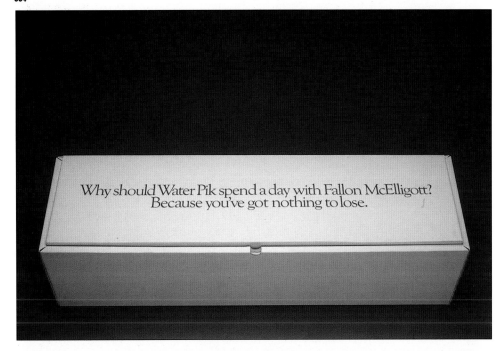

Why should Water Pik spend a day with Fallon McElligott?
Because you've got nothing to lose.

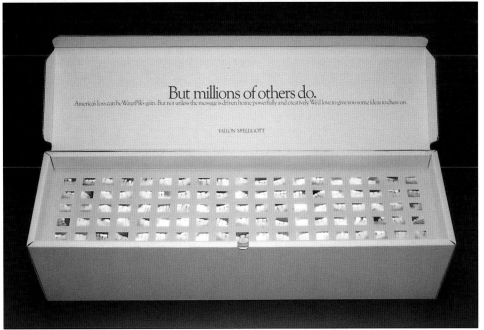

But millions of others do.

505

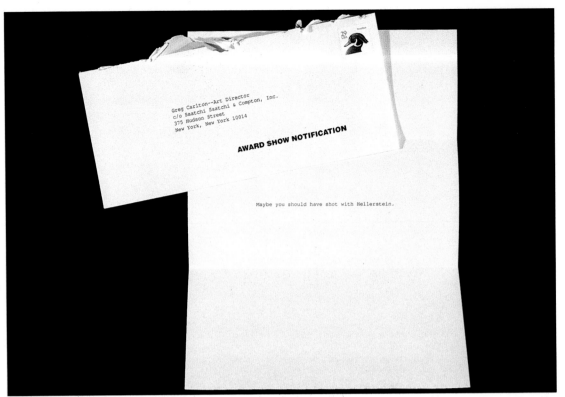

506

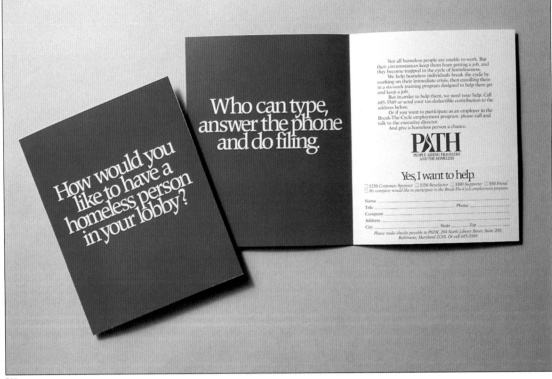

507

**509**
**ART DIRECTORS**
Michael James Wheaton,
Todd Treleven
**WRITER**
Michael James Wheaton
**ILLUSTRATOR**
For Color, Inc.
**CLIENT**
For Color, Inc.
**AGENCY**
Hoffman York & Compton/
Milwaukee

**510**
**ART DIRECTOR**
Tom Routson
**WRITER**
Tom Molitor
**PHOTOGRAPHER**
Dean Hawthorne
**CLIENT**
Richmond Ad Club
**AGENCY**
Lawler Ballard/Richmond

**511**
**ART DIRECTOR**
John Carter
**WRITER**
Kevin Endres
**PHOTOGRAPHER**
Gorden Meier
**CLIENT**
Kevin Endres
**AGENCY**
Kevin Endres Creative/
Nashville

**512**
**ART DIRECTOR**
Brett Borders
**WRITER**
Brett Borders
**CLIENT**
Brett Borders

509

510

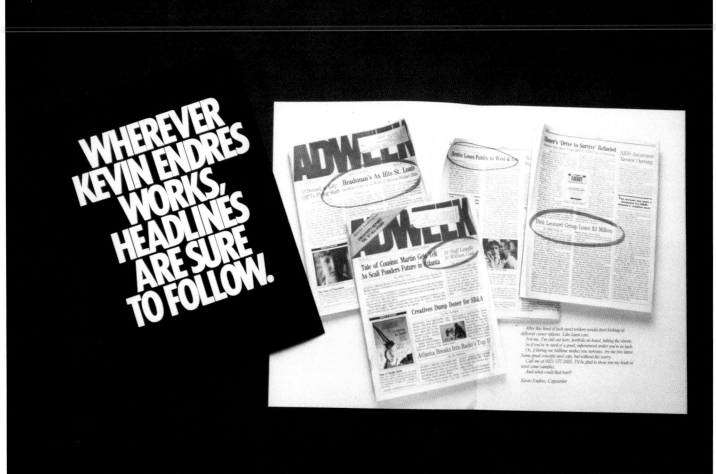

**513**
**ART DIRECTOR**
Shari Hindman
**WRITER**
Curlin Reed
**CLIENT**
The Martin Agency
**AGENCY**
The Martin Agency/
Richmond

**514**
**ART DIRECTORS**
Amy Watt, Amy Werfel
**WRITERS**
Edward Boches, Nancy
Vetstein
**PHOTOGRAPHER**
Cheryl Clegg
**CLIENT**
Smartfoods
**AGENCY**
Mullen/Wenham

**515**
**ART DIRECTOR**
Vincent Picardi
**WRITERS**
Carol Martin, Mickey Taylor
**PHOTOGRAPHER**
Stock
**CLIENT**
James Hardie Building
Products
**AGENCY**
Salvati Montgomery Sakoda/
Costa Mesa

**516**
**ART DIRECTOR**
Scott Dube
**WRITER**
Ron MacDonald
**CLIENT**
Lexus
**AGENCY**
SMW Advertising/Toronto

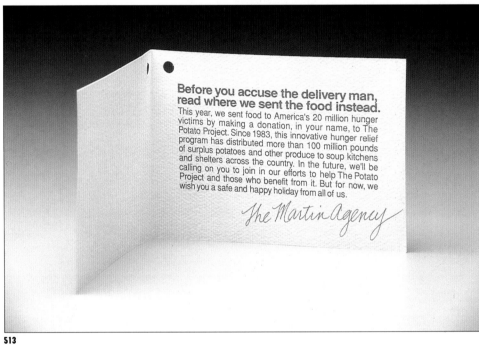

513

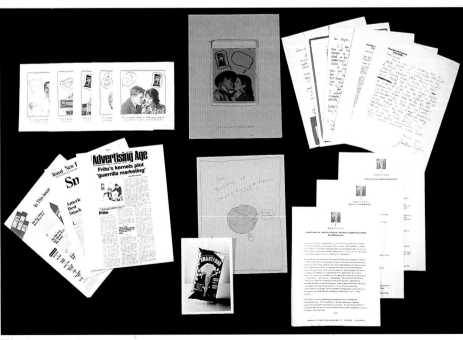

514

Last year the Martins
had a choice between installing a Hardishake roof
or putting in a swimming pool.

There are a lot of things you can do with your money
besides investing in a new roof.

Very few of which, however, are as important as a fire-
resistant Hardishake roof.

Hardishake can be installed to achieve the highest
possible fire rating. Class A. And has a transferable 50-year
limited warranty.

Which means your home stands a much better chance
of surviving a fire storm.

And, if you ask the Martins, having that peace of mind
is much better than having a swimming pool.

**◎ HARDISHAKE®**

*THE NEW YORK TIMES* **OBITUARIES**

**3,**
**ief**
**50's**

### Ex–Doyle Dane Copywriter, Tony Lamont, Dies in New Jersey

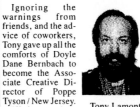

Tony Lamont

Ignoring the warnings from friends, and the advice of coworkers, Tony gave up all the comforts of Doyle Dane Bernbach to become the Associate Creative Director of Poppe Tyson / New Jersey.

His last words as he stepped onto the elevator that day were, "I'll turn that New Jersey agency into a hot creative shop or I'll die trying."

In lieu of flowers, please send job offers to: The Society for the Reincarnation of Tony Lamont, 51 Harrison Avenue, North Plainfield, NJ 07060. Or if you'd like to arrange for a private viewing call: 201-755-5780. But please hurry. We can't keep his body in the house forever.    •

1946 he taught at Cornell University Medical College.

Dr. Lewis is survived by two sons, William Hall 3d and Ogden Northrop Lewis, both of Manhattan; a sister, Helen Holley of Washington, and two grandsons.

### Ludwig von M
**Former Swiss Presi'**

BERN, Nov. 26 (AF
M'oos, a former P'
'd as Vice Pr

**Lo**
**E.**

Louis
secutive
Conn., a
Medical
years old
dent.
Mr. Cla
intestinal t
Mr. Cla
elected ma
that post un
a period of
attracted cc
of employee:
New York.
Mr. Clapes
now Pace U
1938, specia
marketing.
Stamford h
ment. Fror
member of
In 1963,
clerk and
1975, whe
incumber
After 1
the Firs'
Besid
field, C'
Christi
Ridge
two
Sta
t/

ngineer
ic works
966, died
reenwich,

a spokes-

ninistrative
s, the archi-
e had been
nen he re-
rom Mayor
was consid-
city govern-
walking a
tors, archi-
anners, bu-

s president
; Congress,
nted every
.ustry.

erve
Eggers &
d the con-
:s Canada
d Manhat-

N.Y., and
te in 1926
degree in
ned a sec-
ng from

active
' En-
m-

"You'll Never Make It To The NHL."
"You'll Never Make It To The NHL."
"You'll Never Make It To The NHL."

## It's A Good Thing Jim Kyte Had A Hearing Impairment.

Some people say that Jim Kyte is a victim of hearing impairment.

Actually, the real victims are Denis Savard, Mark Messier, or any other player who's tried to get around him for that matter.

Because sometimes a handicap is anything but. That's how Jim saw it. And that's how most of the kids who have gone through the doors of our school see it today.

We should know. We've watched it happen for four years now.

The Jim Kyte Hockey School for the Hearing Impaired is a non-profit organization where children from all across the country learn to overcome their handicap, gain confidence and have some fun at the same time. More importantly, these children are put in an environment where they can learn to rely on themselves.

That's the good news. The bad news is that it costs about $1500 to bring a child to Winnipeg, house them, feed them, provide qualified sign language interpreters, NHL instructors and an additional staff of 85 volunteers.

That's where we're hoping you (or your group) will help us out. And why we've enclosed a donation card.

It always seems that the kids that need us most are the ones that can least afford us. Simply put, we'd like your support. So that we can teach these kids that having a hearing impairment doesn't necessarily mean they're missing anything.

And who knows.

We just might turn out another Jim Kyte in the meantime.

**The Jim Kyte Hockey School For The Hearing Impaired.**
253 College St. Suite 309, Toronto Ontario, M5T 1R5

BUZZ OFF
LOT 8 FULL
PUSH SHOVE
INSUFFICIENT FUNDS
YOU'RE LATE
LET'S DO LUNCH
URGENT
WATCH IT NO ADMITTANCE
PRESSURE COOKER
GIMME A BREAK
55 M.P.H. HURRY

EXPIRED
PLEASE CALL
BOTTLENECK
MOVE IT BUDDY
RETURN TO SENDER
PAST DUE NOW RUSH
DEADLINE
OUT OF STOCK
OVERDUE
NEXT WINDOW
OUT OF ORDER

BUTTER UP REJECTED
AMOUNT DUE
OVERTIME
OFFICIAL NOTICE
BLEEP
SENDER PAY
OUT TO LUNCH
NO PARKING DRIVEWAY WRONG
NUMBER
OUT OF MY FACE

High in the Rocky Mountains, less than an hour's drive from the Salt Lake City International Airport, high-speed quads transport you well above the cares and crowds of a pressure-filled world.

Whooosh. Your skis whisper through the lightly packed snow. With each turn, stress and tension seem to float away on clouds of white crystals. Up here there's just you, clear air, frosted mountain peaks, and mile after mile of incredible snow.

Some people think Utah is America's choice to host the 1998 Winter Games because it's so quick and easy to get to. Some people think it's because Utah has so many world-class resorts. All true. In fact, our 1990-91 Utah Winter Vacation Planner can show you hundreds of other reasons why Utah was chosen. It's FREE and chock-full of pictures, places, addresses, phone numbers and rates — everything you need to know for the perfect winter vacation. But the real reason can only be found at the top of a Utah mountain. Or on your way down.

PUT YOURSELF ABOVE IT ALL.

The tension's building. I need some relief, fast. Here's what I'd like you to send me:

❑ 1990-1991 Utah Winter Vacation Planner......................Free*
❑ Gold Key Value Coupon Book.............................$20.00
❑ Ski Utah Video (VHS)......................................$14.95
❑ Overnight delivery (optional)...............................$10.00
                                                TOTAL:

Name
Address
City _____ State _____ Zip _____
❑ VISA ❑ MasterCard   Expiration Date:
Card Number: ❑❑❑❑-❑❑❑❑-❑❑❑❑-❑❑❑❑
Signature
Date

*If you're in a real rush, put this card in an envelope along with $2 and we'll send your planner by First Class Mail. Or call the Utah Travel Council at (801) 538-1030.

Utah. Let the games begin.

# Don't hang out at the gym.

We have a wide selection of sports bras and body suits.
So you can stay in shape while you're getting in shape.

**Body Language**
*In Calhoun Square.*

520

# Encourage the guys to stand at the back of the class.

In aerobics, the latest thing is the thong. And we've got it.
Wear one to class and watch all the guys stand back.

**Body Language**
*In Calhoun Square.*

521

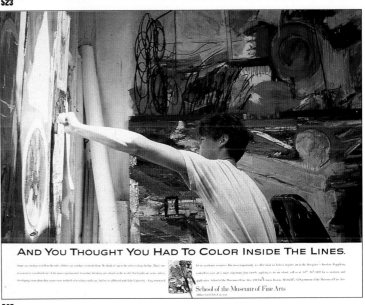

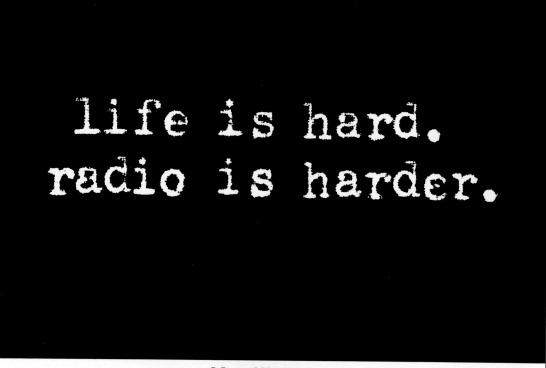

526

527

## ROAD&TRACK
### 10 BEST CARS OF '91

**Nissan Sentra XE**
Best Coupe/Sedan in its class.
**Nissan Maxima SE**
Best Coupe/Sedan in its class.
**Nissan 300 ZX**
Best Sports/GT in its class.
**Nissan 300 ZX Turbo**
Best Sports/GT in its class.
**Infiniti Q45**
Best Coupe/Sedan in its class.
**BMW M5**
Best Coupe/Sedan in its class.
**Acura NSX**
Best Sports/GT in its class.

## To put this in perspective, imagine having five children grow up to be Nobel Prize winners.

To ensure a place on this list, a car must stand for craftsmanship and reliability. But, more importantly, it should make the hair stand on the back of your neck. Which might explain why five cars from the Nissan family are represented here. After all, we've always believed a car should be much more than a form of transportation. It should be a form of pure inspiration.

## NISSAN

*Road & Track magazine, December 1990.*

**528**

## If you want clearer photos, we suggest you watch a slower racing team.

**NISSAN**
Motorsports

**529**

## Why We Have Outdoor Seating.
Pasqual's Beans Free With Any Dinner.

## WARNING: Our Pintos May Cause Rear-end Explosions.
Get Pasqual's Bean Dip To Go.

**530**

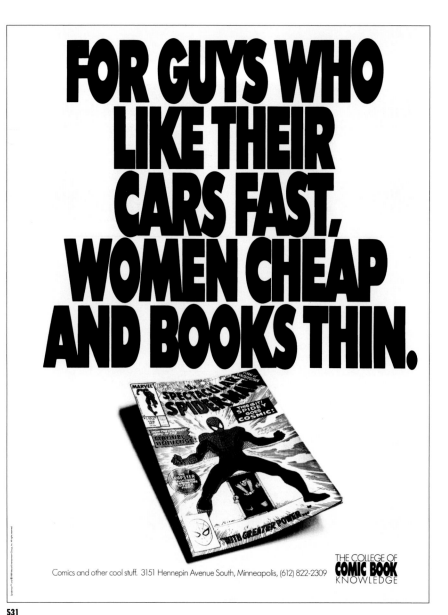

**FOR GUYS WHO LIKE THEIR CARS FAST, WOMEN CHEAP AND BOOKS THIN.**

Comics and other cool stuff. 3151 Hennepin Avenue South, Minneapolis, (612) 822-2309

THE COLLEGE OF
**COMIC BOOK**
KNOWLEDGE

531

Just what you'd expect
from a store devoted to travel:

We're moving.

Visit our new store at 444 N. Michigan (opening mid-March).
Or our other, practically new one at 150 S. Wacker.

⊕ The Rand McNally Map & Travel Store

532

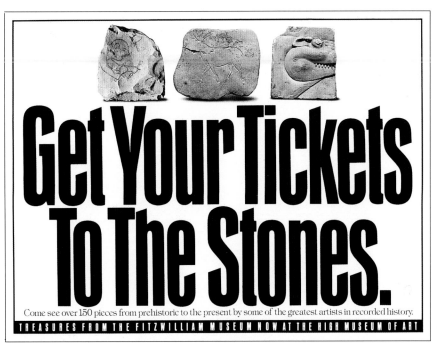

# Get Your Tickets To The Stones.

Come see over 150 pieces from prehistoric to the present by some of the greatest artists in recorded history.

**TREASURES FROM THE FITZWILLIAM MUSEUM NOW AT THE HIGH MUSEUM OF ART**

533

## How Generals cover their Privates.

We've got enough camouflage to cover you from head to toe. And everywhere in between.

**Bunker Hill PX**
War Surplus at Peacetime Prices.

534

## Whaddaya want, a medal?

We've got just the thing for that straight shooter. That real trooper. Or just your average Joe.

**Bunker Hill PX**
War Surplus at Peacetime Prices.

535

# COLLATERAL P.O.P.

**536**
**ART DIRECTOR**
Merril Dello Iacono
**WRITER**
Dean Buckhorn
**PHOTOGRAPHER**
Claude Vazquez
**CLIENT**
Hell Sauce
**AGENCY**
Earle Palmer Brown/Bethesda

**537**
**ART DIRECTOR**
Merril Dello Iacono
**WRITER**
Dean Buckhorn
**PHOTOGRAPHER**
Claude Vazquez
**CLIENT**
Hell Sauce
**AGENCY**
Earle Palmer Brown/Bethesda

**538**
**ART DIRECTOR**
Carolyn Tye McGeorge
**WRITER**
Kerry Feuerman
**CLIENT**
Earle Palmer Brown
**AGENCY**
Earle Palmer Brown/Richmond

**539**
**ART DIRECTOR**
Houman Pirdavari
**WRITER**
Jarl Olsen
**PHOTOGRAPHER**
Dave Jordano
**CLIENT**
Penn Racquet Sports
**AGENCY**
Fallon McElligott/Minneapolis

**540**
**ART DIRECTOR**
Houman Pirdavari
**WRITER**
Jarl Olsen
**PHOTOGRAPHER**
Dave Jordano
**CLIENT**
Penn Racquet Sports
**AGENCY**
Fallon McElligott/Minneapolis

**541**
**ART DIRECTOR**
Steve Sweitzer
**WRITER**
Todd Tilford
**PHOTOGRAPHER**
Dennis Fagan
**CLIENT**
Tabu Lingerie
**AGENCY**
GSD&M/Austin

536

537

British Influence on American Typography. How much leading is too much

leading? Find out at EPB's next art direction seminar, noon, August 21, 1990.

538

539

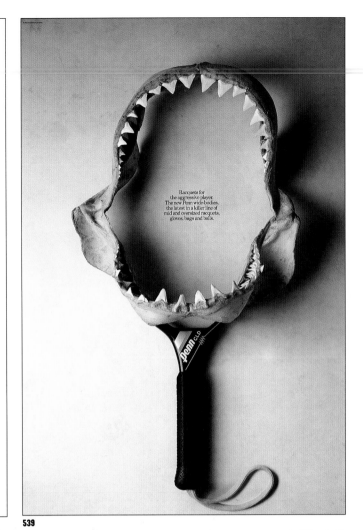

540

541

**542**
ART DIRECTOR
Steve Sweitzer
WRITER
Todd Tilford
PHOTOGRAPHER
Dennis Fagan
CLIENT
Tabu Lingerie
AGENCY
GSD&M/Austin

**543**
ART DIRECTOR
Jeff Jahn
WRITER
Glen Wachowiak
PHOTOGRAPHER
Jim Arndt
CLIENT
Arctic Cat Snowmobiles
AGENCY
Kauffman Stewart Advertising/
Minneapolis

**544**
ART DIRECTOR
Jim Mountjoy
WRITERS
Steve Skibba, Ed Jones
PHOTOGRAPHER
Steve Knight
CLIENT
Jerry's Record Mart
AGENCY
Loeffler Ketchum
Mountjoy/Charlotte

**545**
ART DIRECTOR
Hilber Nelson
WRITER
Christopher Wilson
CLIENT
Sylvio P. Lesso, D.D.S.
AGENCY
Martin/Williams, Minneapolis

**546**
ART DIRECTOR
Kevin McCarthy
ILLUSTRATOR
Dave McMacken
CLIENT
IKEA
AGENCY
Stein Robaire Helm/Los Angeles

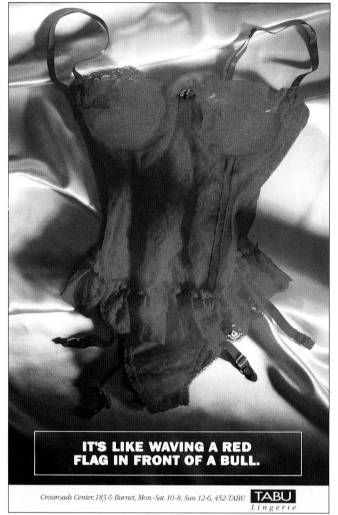

542

543

**Some Of Our Best Records Are Seriously Warped.**

It's not unusual to find some pretty strange albums at Record Mart. But then, haven't some of the best musicians always been a little off beat? 217 King Street, Alexandria, (703) 683-4583 **Jerry's Record Mart**

544

**EAT LESS SWEETS AND YOU'LL HAVE TEETH IN YOUR MOUTH, NOT IN YOUR HANDS**

SYLVIO P. LESSA, D.D.S.

545

It's a big country. Someone's got to furnish it.

546

## She's not crying because she's blind. She's crying because you're deaf.

You're looking at a picture of a very plucky little girl.

She's also a very lucky little girl.

When she was 13 months old, Michelle was found to have a tumour in her left eye.

The medical name for it is retinoblastoma and it's as nasty as it sounds.

Left alone it would almost certainly have killed Michelle, which left the doctors with no choice.

They removed her eye and replaced it with an artificial one.

Even then she wasn't out of the wood.

A tumour in one eye often leads to a tumour in the other.

For years afterwards, Michelle and her parents lived with the fear that one day her luck might run out.

Even so, it's not herself that Michelle feels sorry for.

What upsets her is that children with her condition are still being born.

That there are still over a quarter of a million people registered blind or partially sighted in this country.

And that every day another forty swell their ranks.

The cause isn't very hard to find.

Over the last twenty years, treatment to prevent or cure blindness has changed dramatically.

Curiously, the public's attitude to blindness has not.

There's a feeling that it's one of those unavoidable Acts of God, a cruel trick of fate, Kismet.

And if you're unlucky enough to go blind, then blind you stay.

Nothing could be further from the truth.

Michelle was looked after by doctors at the world famous Moorfields Eye Hospital in the City Road.

Three miles away across town in Judd Street, is the Institute of Ophthalmology, Moorfields' research arm.

And in the rarified world of ophthalmological research, it's equally famous.

The people working here have been responsible for some of the most important advances of recent years in the treatment of blinding diseases.

The technique of implanting plastic lenses to cure cataracts, for example.

The discovery that the puppy dog worm, toxocara canis, was blinding young children.

The connection between excess oxygen at birth and the incidence of blindness in premature babies.

The invention of the first diode 'suitcase' laser.

Not to mention countless surgical procedures now being used at Moorfields.

As you read this, they're on the verge of even more important breakthroughs.

But sadly, that's where they'll stay, unless we can raise £42 million quickly.

The building on Judd Street is now too small, too badly equipped and too far away from Moorfields. Although the Institute attracts the world's top eye specialists, there's nowhere to put them.

Some are working in corridors, most are using obsolete equipment and none have adequate laboratory and workshop facilities.

Worst of all, they're separated from the people they're trying to help by three miles of busy London traffic.

The solution is simple, but expensive.

Move the Institute to a new building smack next to Moorfields, where there'll be plenty of room for all the offices, labs, libraries and lecture rooms.

Fill it with the latest equipment.

Staff it with enough trained technicians.

Found new Chairs in Molecular Genetics, Cell Biology, Developmental Neurobiology and Inherited Retinal Disorders. (That'll please Michelle.)

Then let the researchers get on with it.

The result will be a centre of excellence into the prevention and cure of blinding diseases that will be the envy of the world.

Our patron, The Duke of York, has recently launched The Fight For Sight Appeal to make all this possible.

If you'd like to know how you can help, send us the coupon below.

If you'd like to contribute, send us your cash.

Or ring our Credit Card line on 071 383 0528 if you're an Access or Visa holder.

Thank you for listening.

If you'd like to know how you or your business can help The Fight For Sight (Special Appeal), please complete the coupon (or attach your business card) and send to the address below.

Name _____
Company _____
Address _____
_____
Postcode _____ Tel No _____
Send to: Fight For Sight (Special Appeal), Judd Street, London WC1H 9QS.
Telephone 071-383 0528.

THE FIGHT FOR SIGHT APPEAL

547

Imagine being locked in a rush hour tube carriage for 36 hours.

All around you people are collapsing from thirst, hunger and exhaustion. There'd be urine and faeces all over the floor.

Now imagine the train's travelling at 100 mph, but there's nowhere to sit and nothing to hold on to. You'd be thrown about, crushed and trampled. If you're frail or weak you might not survive.

Now imagine there are 600 people crammed in there with you. That's five times more than the worst rush hour crowd.

Aren't you glad you're not a lamb being transported across Europe?

PLEASE HELP THE RSPCA FIGHT THE NEEDLESS TRANSPORT OF LIVE ANIMALS. PHONE 0800 400 478.

548

# You might have put money on him in the past. Please do it again.

This ex-racing greyhound was found starving on the streets.

Because he was registered (all racing greyhounds are) we traced his owners and prosecuted them for neglect.

But they didn't pay to nurse him back to health.

We did.

Cruelty towards dogs is now at a record high.

Fighting it is becoming more and more expensive.

The RSPCA is not government funded. We rely entirely on your donations.

Please help us to back dogs like this.

549

---

# WHAT GOOD IS FIBER IN YOUR DIET IF THERE'S CANCER IN YOUR WATER?

Think about it.

How much sense does it make for you to eat a healthy diet when there are carcinogens and poisonous residues in your tap water?

But, with little more effort than it takes to pick out a box of oat bran or a dozen high-fiber cookies from the shelf, you can help ensure that we'll have a safe, clean water supply. Now and for years to come.

You can start by joining millions of other Americans on Earth Day, April 22, to send a clear message to Washington that we want a safe, healthy environment.

Check your local paper for the time and location of one of the Earth Day events near you.

If you know what's good for you, you'll be there.

**EARTH DAY**

550

---

# WHAT GOES UP MUST COME DOWN.

The real problem with air pollution is that nobody's doing anything about it. The air just keeps getting worse and worse. So let's get together and stop this abuse of our environment. Show up for Earth Day on April 22.

In fact, we urge you to bring your whole family to one of the thousands of Earth Day events happening across the country. So be sure to check your local newspaper for the time and location of an event near you. And then we can all breathe a little easier.

**EARTH DAY**

© Earth Day 1990

551

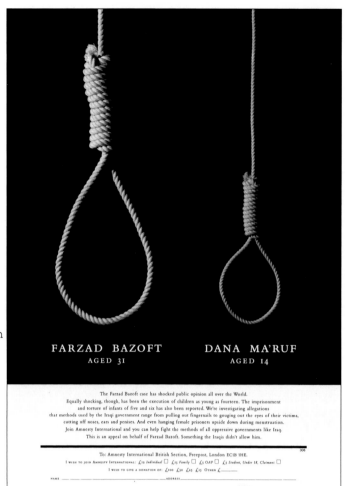

FARZAD BAZOFT
AGED 31

DANA MA'RUF
AGED 14

The Farzad Bazoft case has shocked public opinion all over the World.
Equally shocking, though, has been the execution of children as young as fourteen. The imprisonment
and torture of infants of five and six has also been reported. We're investigating allegations
that methods used by the Iraqi government range from pulling out fingernails to gouging out the eyes of their victims,
cutting off noses, ears and penises. And even hanging female prisoners upside down during menstruation.
Join Amnesty International and you can help fight the methods of all oppressive governments like Iraq.
This is an appeal on behalf of Farzad Bazoft. Something the Iraqis didn't allow him.

To: Amnesty International British Section, Freepost, London EC1B 1HE.

AMNESTY INTERNATIONAL

552

# ADMIT IT. A PART OF YOU WANTS TO PARTICIPATE.

Volunteer for this National Condom Preference Study funded by the U.S. Public Health Service and the data you provide
will be used in a non-profit survey to encourage safe sex. For more information call 1-800-336-1935, Mon-Fri, 9AM-3PM.
This confidential mail survey is conducted by NeuroCommunication Research Laboratories, Inc., Danbury, CT. ©1990.

## NATIONAL CONDOM PREFERENCE STUDY

553

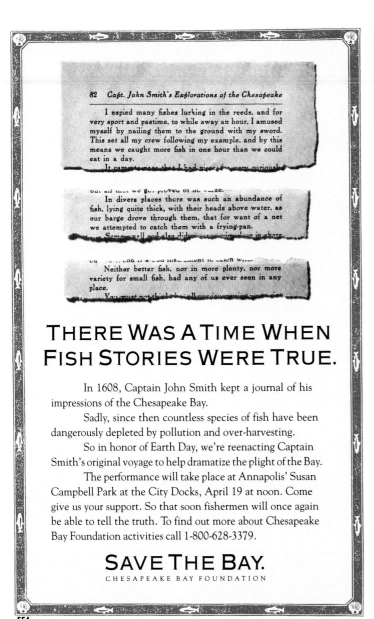

82  *Capt. John Smith's Explorations of the Chesapeake*

I espied many fishes lurking in the reeds, and for very sport and pastime, to while away an hour, I amused myself by nailing them to the ground with my sword. This set all my crew following my example, and by this means we caught more fish in one hour than we could eat in a day.

In divers places there was such an abundance of fish, lying quite thick, with their heads above water, as our barge drove through them, that for want of a net we attempted to catch them with a frying-pan.

Neither better fish, nor in more plenty, nor more variety for small fish, had any of us ever seen in any place.

# THERE WAS A TIME WHEN FISH STORIES WERE TRUE.

In 1608, Captain John Smith kept a journal of his impressions of the Chesapeake Bay.

Sadly, since then countless species of fish have been dangerously depleted by pollution and over-harvesting.

So in honor of Earth Day, we're reenacting Captain Smith's original voyage to help dramatize the plight of the Bay.

The performance will take place at Annapolis' Susan Campbell Park at the City Docks, April 19 at noon. Come give us your support. So that soon fishermen will once again be able to tell the truth. To find out more about Chesapeake Bay Foundation activities call 1-800-628-3379.

## SAVE THE BAY.
CHESAPEAKE BAY FOUNDATION

554

**IF SOCIETY CAN PROVIDE HOUSING FOR A MAN LIKE THIS, CAN'T WE DO MORE FOR THE HOMELESS?**

In the United States, we take better care of convicted killers than we do innocent homeless people. Help us correct this injustice. Call the Mayor's Voluntary Action Center at 212-566-5950.

555

**IF CHILDREN COULD VOTE, MAYBE POLITICIANS WOULDN'T IGNORE THEIR PROBLEMS.**

Elected officials respond to those with the power to elect them. So the needs of America's children, from child care, to immunization, to education, get little action. Children have no voice. Give them yours. **THE CHILDREN'S DEFENSE FUND**

556

GET A GIRL PREGNANT AND THIS IS WHERE YOUR FUTURE WILL GO.

557

# ISN'T IT IRONIC THAT JUST AS THE SOVIETS ARE BECOMING MORE LIKE US, WE'RE BECOMING MORE LIKE THEM?

For twenty-five years The National Endowment for the Arts has helped Minnesota arts organizations make the arts accessible and affordable for everyone. Everything from the Guthrie Theater and St. Paul Chamber Orchestra to rural school arts programs receive a substantial portion of their support from the Endowment.

But now, because of controversy over only a few grants, some extreme critics like television evangelist Pat Robertson and Senator Jesse Helms are calling for the total elimination of the Endowment. Considering that of the 80,000 grants the NEA has awarded over the years, only 20 have caused any controversy, it's a drastic measure.

Unfortunately, the money will not be replaced from other sources. Admission prices will go up. Museums, dance companies and community arts programs could disappear.

And it will happen if you don't do something right now. Call or write your senators and congressmen today.

Please, don't let our country take a giant step backwards just as the rest of the world is taking such a big step forward.

**SAVE THE NATIONAL ENDOWMENT FOR THE ARTS, OR THE ARTS WILL BECOME HISTORY.**

558

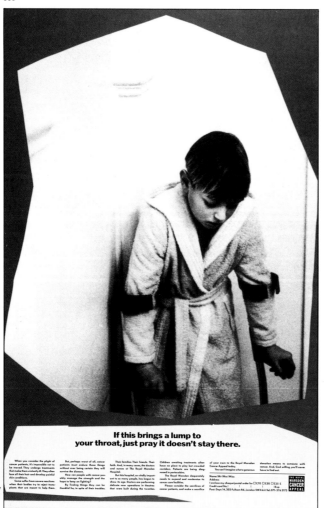

### If this brings a lump to your throat, just pray it doesn't stay there.

559

# Imagine hearing your six year old daughter is dead.
## Now imagine something far worse.

The words numb as instantly and surely as an anaesthetic.

'Your little girl is dead.'

As you grasp at the full meaning of the news, the sound of the words echo and swirl around you.

Can you imagine any situation worse than this for a parent? Perhaps only one.

When a young child goes missing, the human mind's capacity to imagine what the youngster is going through can be harder to cope with than the reality of death itself.

Where is she now? Who is she with? What is happening to her now? Now. This minute. This second. On and on it goes.

Why isn't everyone out looking for her? Twenty four hours a day? Seven days a week? Why is everyone carrying on as normal? The anguish is made worse by misplaced guilt. If only, if only.

If you have never been involved in a tragedy of this kind you may wonder how people cope.

The police, of course, do a stalwart job. So too do local GP's. Even the much-maligned media can provide an important outlet for the stress.

Obviously, none of these people, however dedicated, however expert, can possibly be expected to give all their time to one case.

So now an organisation has been formed to help the family and friends of anyone who is missing from their home.

The Suzy Lamplugh Trust was founded after Suzy went missing.

Her disappearance has provided the catalyst for a number of the most respected men and women in the country to bring attention to this growing problem.

Last year alone, over 160,000 adults and children were reported missing. 1000 of these were still unaccounted for at the end of the year.

Why they decide to walk away from their lives is not always known, even by those closest to them.

This often makes it difficult to find them. And makes the job of helping the people left behind more complex.

Sometimes an attentive, interested voice on the end of a phone can ease the pain and relieve the sheer sense of panic that occurs.

So the Suzy Lamplugh Trust has set up a Missing Persons Helpline on 081-392 2000. (Regrettably, it is only one line at the moment, so please keep trying if it's engaged.)

The aim of the Helpline is simply to offer advice and counselling on what to do when someone close goes missing.

It's not just a sympathetic ear, however.

Distraught callers often do not know where or who to turn to. We can put them in touch with the police, or other agencies. We can also help them deal with the media.

If the missing person is a teenager then our 'street' contacts could be invaluable in suggesting things to do or even places they might be.

The Trust is also working for better liaison between the various bodies involved as well as improved police procedures.

We want a Missing Persons Bureau that would ensure that all police forces have access to vital information.

After all, people who go missing rarely stay in the immediate vicinity of their home.

Of course, not all these people go missing of their own free will.

So to help make daily and working life safer the Trust has commissioned a number of research projects into aggression and violence in society.

What exactly are the risks involved in travelling in a mini-cab at night? Can persistent sex offenders be helped with new treatments?

We want to know. More importantly, we hope you want to know too.

If the Suzy Lamplugh Trust can help explain why people go missing or what makes others abduct children or if it simply helps those left behind to endure the seemingly unendurable, then some good will have come from Suzy's disappearance.

Please write or call for copies of our books, leaflets, videos or to purchase a shriek alarm.

Better still, help the Trust's charitable work by becoming a Friend of the Trust through covenants, or a personal or corporate donation.

The Suzy Lamplugh Trust, 14 East Sheen Avenue, London SW14 8AS. Phone: 081-392 1839.

**The Suzy Lamplugh Trust**

560

---

## This is what America pays for the Sunday paper.

This Sunday, two hundred million Americans are going to settle back and enjoy reading the newspaper. It takes an entire forest...over 500,000 trees to supply that paper. Every week.

Making new paper from old paper uses 30% to 50% less energy than making paper from trees; and it reduces air pollution by 95%.

So, the next time you have a nose for news, separate the paper from the garbage. Stack your newspapers and recycle them. Look in the Yellow Pages under recycling to find the center nearest you.

If everyone in the U.S. recycled even 1/10 of their newspapers, we would save 25 million trees a year. That's a lot of forest for the trees.

In addition to recycling, your contribution to The Environmental Challenge Fund will help establish scholarships for environmental education.
Please send your check to The Environmental Challenge Fund, Radio City Station, P.O. Box 1138, NY, NY 10101-1138. Advertisement created by HDM Los Angeles, photograph by Bill Ross/Westlight.

562

---

# IF THE EARTH ISN'T WORTH SAVING, CONSIDER THE ALTERNATIVES.

Saturn: Raindrops are liquified methane gas.

Uranus: Blanketed in radioactive smog.

Mercury: The temperature here reaches 780°F.

Pluto: Frozen solid.

Venus: The clouds drip pure sulphuric acid.

Neptune: One hemisphere won't see sunshine until 2030 A.D.

Mars: The atmosphere is like car exhaust.

Jupiter: Sulphur and phosphorus make it one giant match head.

Earth: Perhaps we should take better care of it.

One way to take better care of our planet is to contribute to The Environmental Challenge Fund, sponsored by Time Magazine. All funds will be distributed as scholarships, enabling students to acquire the skills and training needed to protect the environment. To make a contribution, or to get more information, write: The Environmental Challenge Fund, Radio City Station, P.O. Box 1138, New York, New York 10101-1138. **THE ENVIRONMENTAL CHALLENGE FUND.**

This advertisement was prepared for the Time Environmental Challenge as a public service by Lord Einstein O'Neill & Partners.

Printed on recycled paper.

561

---

# NOT ALL NAZIS ARE LIVING IN SOUTH AMERICA.

They're living in places like Hayden Lake, Idaho, where an organization called the Aryan Nations maintains its 20-acre, whites-only compound.

A compound that is the site of an annual national congress for hate groups from around the country, and that has a church where the "minister" preaches that Jews are "children of Satan."

They're in places like Fallbrook, California, where an organization called the White Aryan Resistance is headquartered.

Headed by a former Grand Dragon of the Ku Klux Klan, the organization recruits high school students to become neo-Nazi "skinheads" and publishes a newspaper which recently ran this headline: "Happy Birthday Uncle Adolf!"

And they're in places like Costa Mesa, California, where an organization called the Institute for Historical Review is dedicated to promoting the incredible notion that the Holocaust never occurred.

It hosts conventions, and publishes articles and books which claim, for example, that The Diary of Anne Frank is a hoax, and that the photographs of concentration camps have been falsified.

Fortunately, there is an organization dedicated to working against these groups: The Anti-Defamation League.

The ADL tracks the activities of these groups. Works with lawmakers to enact legislation which makes it harder for them to operate. And with law enforcement officials to apprehend them when they break those laws.

Please give us your support. Hundreds of thousands of Americans lost their lives fighting the Nazis in World War II. Is this what they had in mind?

Anti-Defamation League
823 United Nations Plaza, New York, New York 10017

Yes, I want to help the ADL fight neo-Nazi violence. I have enclosed my tax deductible contribution of:
___ $25 ___ $50 ___ $100 ___ $250 ___ (other)
Name
Address

ADL

For regularly updated information about current neo-Nazi activities and ADL's fight against them, call 1-900-820-3225. There is a charge of $3 per minute per call, and a portion of the charges will be used to support and strengthen the work of the ADL. Average call is 4 minutes.

563

**PUBLIC SERVICE**
**NEWSPAPER OR MAGAZINE:**
**SINGLE**

**564**
**ART DIRECTOR**
Cathi Mooney
**WRITER**
Ken Mandelbaum
**PHOTOGRAPHER**
Pavlina Eccless
**CLIENT**
Anti-Defamation League
**AGENCY**
Mandelbaum Mooney Ashley/
San Francisco

**565**
**ART DIRECTOR**
Cliff Sorah
**WRITER**
Liz Paradise
**CLIENT**
Richmond Metropolitan
Blood Service
**AGENCY**
The Martin Agency/Richmond

**566**
**ART DIRECTOR**
Margaret McGovern
**WRITER**
Paul Silverman
**PHOTOGRAPHER**
Stock
**CLIENT**
Manchester League of
Women Voters
**AGENCY**
Mullen/Wenham

**567**
**ART DIRECTOR**
Tom Lichtenheld
**WRITERS**
Pete Smith, Bill Hillsman
**CLIENT**
Wellstone for U.S. Senate
**AGENCY**
North Woods Advertising/
Minneapolis

**568**
**ART DIRECTOR**
Mark Giambrone
**WRITERS**
Gary Sloboda, Melanie Marnich
**PHOTOGRAPHER**
Sierra Club
**CLIENT**
Sierra Club
**AGENCY**
Sive Associates/Cincinnati

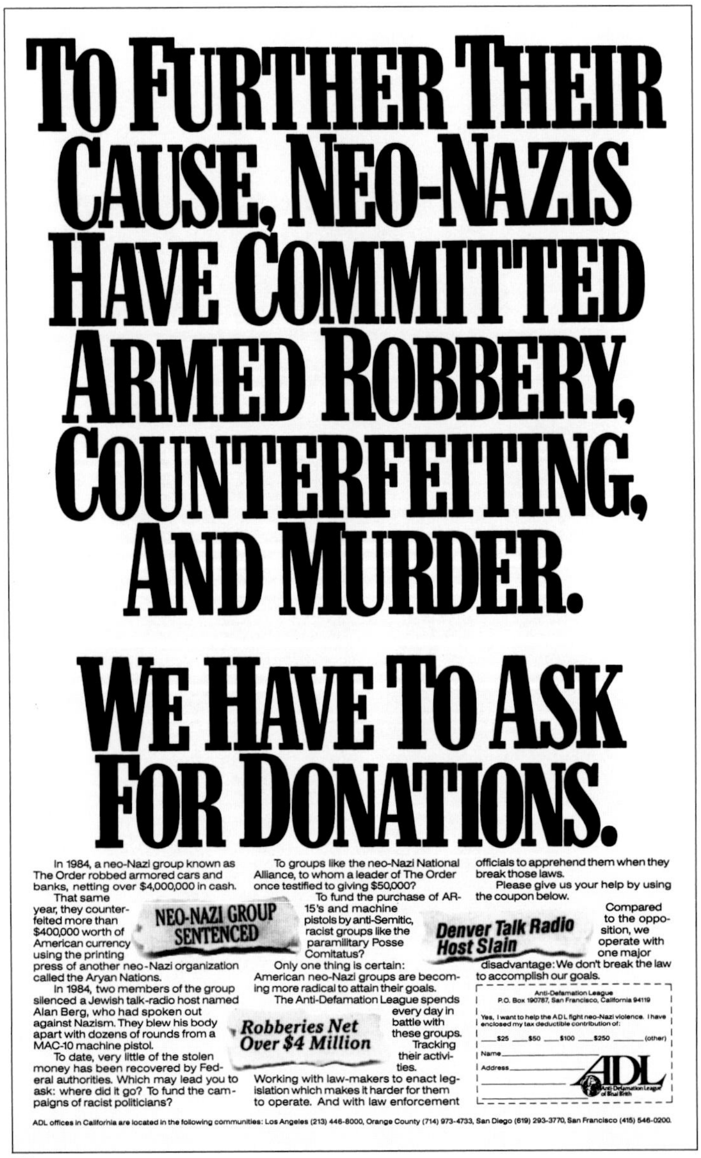

564

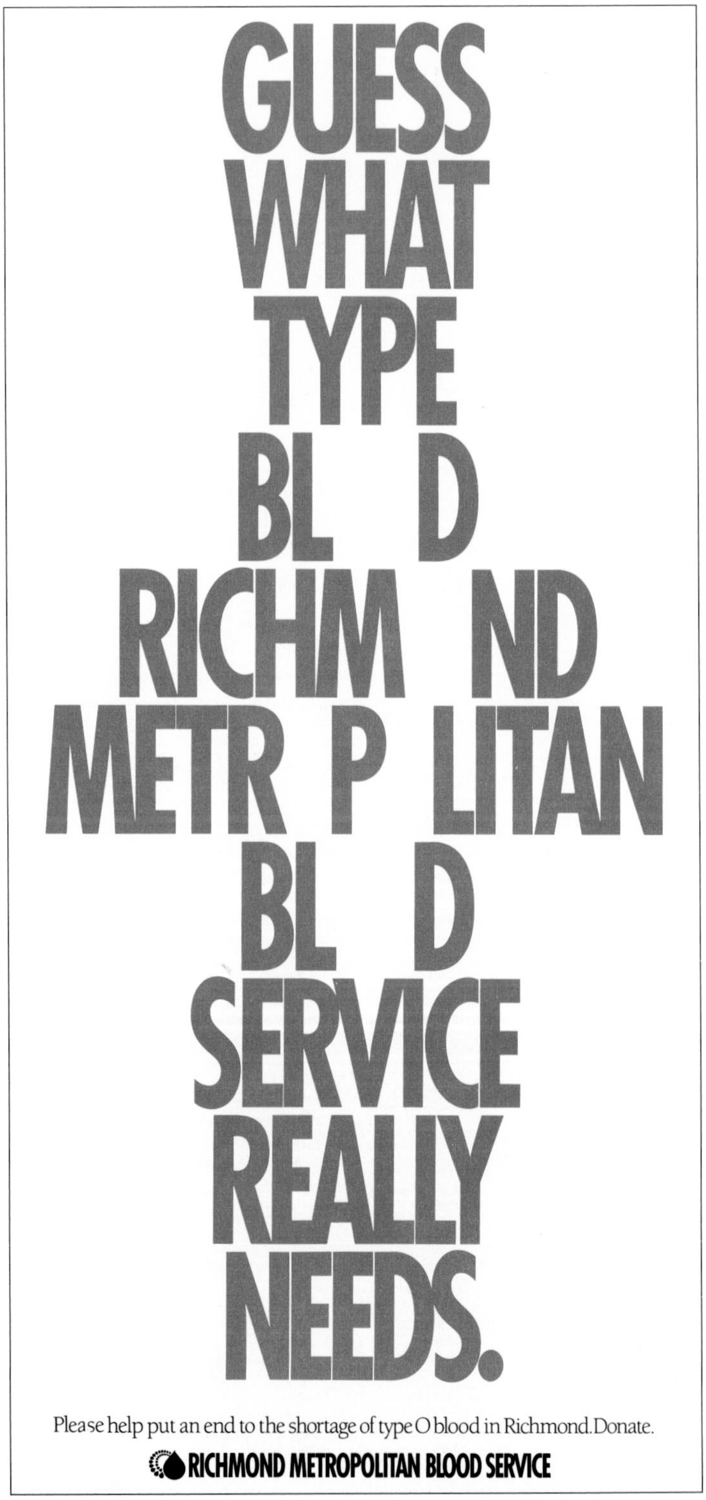

565

# Dead leaves should be buried, not cremated.

Leaves and grass left out for the trash pickup go to a public incinerator, adding to the pollution index as well as your tax bill. Simple backyard composting can solve both problems. Find out more May 5 at Earth Care Fair, the Memorial School, 8:30 AM to 12:30 PM. Sponsored by the Manchester League of Women Voters and the Solid Waste Committee.

**EARTH CARE FAIR, MAY 5.**
GARDENING. COMPOSTING. RECYCLING.

566

---

## WHAT RUDY BOSCHWITZ DID FOR YOU.

**June 17, 1985** Sponsors a concurrent resolution welcoming the President of Tunisia on his official visit to the United States.

**October 2, 1986** Sponsors a joint resolution to designate the week of September 7-13, 1986, as "National Independent Grocer Week."

**February 26, 1987** Cosponsors legislation designating March 11, 1987, as "Operation Prom/Graduation Kickoff."

**July 6, 1988** Cosponsors Senate Joint Resolution 296 to establish an "Outdoor Power Tool Safety Month."

## WHAT RUDY BOSCHWITZ DID TO YOU.

**May 1, 1985** Votes against retaining existing Social Security cost-of-living adjustments.

**May 8, 1985** Votes against altering the budget to reduce the rate of growth for defense spending.

**May 9, 1985** Votes against restoring funding for Medicare and Medicaid programs for fiscal years 1986-88.

**October 21, 1985** Votes to end the Work Incentive Program (WIN) a program that provides jobs and training services for recipients of Aid to Families with Dependent Children.

**November 12, 1985** Votes against allowing Medicaid reimbursement for respirator-dependent individuals. Votes against Medicaid reimbursement for foster children. Votes against Medicaid reimbursement for demonstration projects on home-care alternatives for the elderly.

**November 14, 1985** Votes against Medicare coverage for "reasonable and necessary" liver transplants.

**April 24, 1986** Votes against increased funding for the supplemental food program for needy women, infants and children. Votes against increased funding for the maternal and child health block program, the child immunization program and the community health centers program.

**April 30, 1986** Votes against increased funding for education and training programs. Votes against restoring funds to provide job training and placement assistance to welfare recipients.

**October 3, 1986** Votes against expanding donations of U.S. surplus food commodities to the poor.

**March 31, 1987** Votes against a rate reduction for elderly tenants covered by the Department of Housing and Urban Development Section 8 rental subsidy program.

**April 14, 1988** Votes against increased spending for childhood immunization, geriatric training for nurses and other health programs.

**October 7, 1988** Votes against requiring businesses to provide unpaid, job-protected leave to parents of newborn or sick children. Votes against funding federal standards for child-care service. Votes against funds to crack down on child pornography and adult obscenity.

**June 22, 1989** Votes against authorizing subsidies to parents and day care providers. Votes against requiring states to set standards for child care. Votes against increasing tax credits for dependent care. Votes against a health insurance premium tax credit for families with children.

**March 8, 1990** Votes to table an amendment to reduce toxic emissions from motor vehicles.

**March 27, 1990** Votes to handcuff the Environmental Protection Agency's ability to enforce the Clean Air Act.

**October 18, 1990** Votes against raising the tax rate on the wealthy. Votes in favor of a capital gains tax cut.

**October 18, 1990** Votes against imposing a windfall profits tax on the 30 largest oil companies.

**October 19, 1990** Votes against federally funded abortions for poor women who are the victims of rape and incest.

For the past 12 years, Rudy Boschwitz has represented you in the United States Senate. In that time, he has sponsored hundreds of bills. Only 8 of them have become law—and only one was a significant piece of legislation.

It takes more than a plaid shirt and a folksy image to effectively represent the people of Minnesota in the U.S. Senate. As we move into the 1990s, we need a senator more in touch with the feelings and hopes and dreams of most Minnesotans. We need Paul Wellstone. **WELLSTONE FOR U.S. SENATE**

Paid for by Wellstone for Senate

567

---

## IF WE DROPPED THIS MANY TOXIC CHEMICALS ON ANOTHER COUNTRY, IT WOULD BE CALLED WAR.

Latest statistics show 7 billion pounds of toxic chemicals are being released on our country each year—into our soil, our water, our air. These chemicals are known carcinogens, known killers. You can change this. Wage your own war. A war of words. To find out how, contact Sierra Club, Dept. S2, 730 Polk Street, San Francisco, CA 94109, (415) 776-2211.  SIERRA CLUB

568

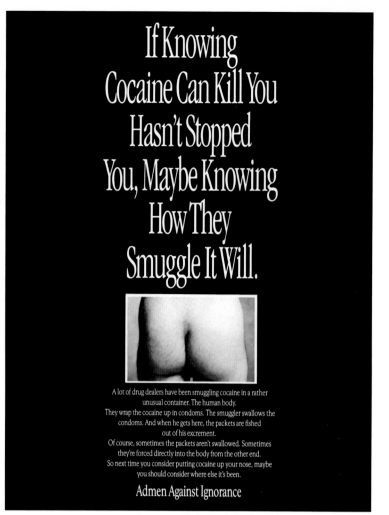

# "How would you like your lamb, sir?"

Would you like it crushed in the back of a lorry with five hundred other lambs?

Would you like it starved of food and water for its entire journey across Europe?

Would you like it covered in the faeces and urine of the lambs that are packed in around it?

Would you like it collapsing from exhaustion, battered and bruised, legs broken from manhandling?

It could even be suffocated.

Or would you like to help the RSPCA stop the barbaric transport of live animals across Europe?

For more information about the RSPCA's live transport campaign, call us free, anytime on 0800 400 478,
Or write to us at RSPCA (Dept. NL), Causeway, Horsham, West Sussex RH12 1HG.

---

Imagine being locked in a rush hour tube carriage for 36 hours.

All around you people are collapsing from thirst, hunger and exhaustion. There'd be urine and faeces all over the floor.

Now imagine the train's travelling at 100 mph, but there's nowhere to sit and nothing to hold on to. You'd be thrown about, crushed and trampled. If you're frail or weak you might not survive.

Now imagine there are 600 people crammed in there with you. That's five times more than the worst rush hour crowd.

Aren't you glad you're not a lamb being transported across Europe?

PLEASE HELP THE RSPCA FIGHT THE NEEDLESS TRANSPORT OF LIVE ANIMALS PHONE 0800 400 478

---

# The continentals love freshly butchered horsemeat. When are we going to supply it?

Sadly, we're going to supply it after 1992.

Because in 1992, it will once again become legal to transport live British horses to the continent for slaughter. (A practice that was effectively banned here over 30 years ago on the grounds of extreme cruelty.)

If the trauma that some other animals suffer during live transport is anything to go by, the slaughterhouse could provide our horses with a merciful relief.

Our horses could be herded in the transporters with electric cattle prods. They could be locked in the transporters to kick and trample each other for up to 24 hours.

By the time they reach the slaughterhouse, they could be bruised, battered and bleeding. Some could be collapsing from exhaustion. Some could have broken legs. Some could even be dead.

And all because the continentals like their horsemeat freshly slaughtered.

Please, telephone the RSPCA on 0800 400 478. We'll tell you how you can help fight live animal transport.

We can't control the continentals' appetite for horsemeat. But we must control the transport of live British horses.

PLEASE HELP THE RSPCA FIGHT THE NEEDLESS TRANSPORT OF LIVE ANIMALS PHONE 0800 400 478

PUBLIC SERVICE
NEWSPAPER OR MAGAZINE:
CAMPAIGN

**572**
**ART DIRECTOR**
David Wojdyla
**WRITERS**
Michael Wilson,
Leland Rosemond
**PHOTOGRAPHER**
Barry Seidman
**CLIENT**
NeuroCommunication
Research Laboratories
**AGENCY**
Bozell/New York

**573**
**ART DIRECTOR**
Ron Anderson
**WRITER**
Mike LaMonica
**ILLUSTRATOR**
Rick Meyrowitz
**CLIENT**
Partnership for a Drug-Free
America
**AGENCY**
Bozell/New York

# WE'RE NOT ASKING YOU TO DO ANYTHING WE WOULDN'T DO OURSELVES.

Volunteer for this National Condom Preference Study funded by the U.S. Public Health Service and the data you provide will be used in a non-profit survey to encourage safe sex. For more information call 1-800-336-1935, Mon-Fri, 9AM-3PM.
This confidential mail survey is conducted by NeuroCommunication Research Laboratories, Inc., Danbury, CT. ©1990.

**NATIONAL CONDOM PREFERENCE STUDY**

# STAND UP AND BE COUNTED.

Volunteer for this National Condom Preference Study funded by the U.S. Public Health Service and the data you provide will be used in a non-profit survey to encourage safe sex. For more information call 1-800-336-1935, Mon-Fri, 9AM-3PM.
This confidential mail survey is conducted by NeuroCommunication Research Laboratories, Inc., Danbury, CT. ©1990.

**NATIONAL CONDOM PREFERENCE STUDY**

# A VOLUNTEER PROJECT YOU CAN PUT MORE THAN JUST YOUR HEART INTO.

Volunteer for this National Condom Preference Study funded by the U.S. Public Health Service and the data you provide will be used in a non-profit survey to encourage safe sex. For more information call 1-800-336-1935, Mon-Fri, 9AM-3PM.
This confidential mail survey is conducted by NeuroCommunication Research Laboratories, Inc., Danbury, CT. ©1990.

**NATIONAL CONDOM PREFERENCE STUDY**

# ISN'T IT IRONIC THAT JUST AS THE SOVIETS ARE BECOMING MORE LIKE US, WE'RE BECOMING MORE LIKE THEM?

For twenty-five years The National Endowment for the Arts has helped Minnesota arts organizations make the arts accessible and affordable for everyone. Everything from the Guthrie Theater and St. Paul Chamber Orchestra to rural school arts programs receive a substantial portion of their support from the Endowment.

But now, because of controversy over only a few grants, some extreme critics like television evangelist Pat Robertson and Senator Jesse Helms are calling for the total elimination of the Endowment. Considering that of the 80,000 grants the NEA has awarded over the years, only 20 have caused any controversy, it's a drastic measure.

Unfortunately, the money will not be replaced from other sources. Admission prices will go up. Museums, dance companies and community arts programs could disappear.

And it will happen if you don't do something right now. Call or write your senators and congressmen today.

Please, don't let our country take a giant step backwards just as the rest of the world is taking such a big step forward.

**SAVE THE NATIONAL ENDOWMENT FOR THE ARTS, OR THE ARTS WILL BECOME HISTORY.**

---

## SENATOR JESSE HELMS SUPPORTS YOUR RIGHT TO BEAR ARMS. IT'S PAINTBRUSHES, CAMERAS AND PENS THAT HE'S AFRAID OF.

For twenty-five years The National Endowment for the Arts has helped Minnesota arts organizations make the arts accessible and affordable for everyone. Everything from the Guthrie Theatre and St. Paul Chamber Orchestra to rural school arts programs receive a substantial portion of their support from the Endowment.

But now, because of controversy over only a few grants, some extreme critics like television evangelist Pat Robertson and Senator Jesse Helms are calling for the total elimination of the Endowment. Considering that of the 80,000 grants the NEA has awarded over the years, only 20 have caused any controversy, it's a drastic measure.

Unfortunately, the money won't be replaced from other sources. Admission prices will go up. Museums, dance companies and community arts programs could disappear.

And it will happen if you don't do something right now. Fill out the attached card and leave it with your usher or in boxes provided in the lobby. We'll see that it gets to your congressman or senator.

Thankfully, writing a letter is one right no one can take away from us.

Dear Legislator,
The arts in Minnesota are important to me. I believe in keeping them accessible and affordable for all. Please vote for the reauthorization of the National Endowment for the Arts and freedom of artistic expression.

Signature _____
Address _____
City _____ State _____ Zip _____

**SAVE THE NATIONAL ENDOWMENT FOR THE ARTS, OR THE ARTS WILL BECOME HISTORY.**

---

## WHAT'S WRONG WITH LETTING THESE TALENTED ACTORS DECIDE WHICH PLAYS WE CAN SEE?

For twenty-five years The National Endowment for the Arts has helped Minnesota arts organizations make the arts accessible and affordable for everyone. Everything from the Guthrie Theater and St. Paul Chamber Orchestra to rural school arts programs receive a substantial portion of their support from the Endowment.

But now, because of controversy over only a few grants, some extreme critics like television evangelist Pat Robertson and Senator Jesse Helms are calling for the total elimination of the Endowment. Considering that of the 80,000 grants the NEA has awarded over the years, only 20 have caused any controversy, it's a drastic measure.

Unfortunately, the money won't be replaced from other sources. Admission prices will go up. Museums, dance companies and community arts programs could disappear.

And it will happen if you don't do something right now. Fill out the attached card and leave it with your usher or in boxes provided in the lobby. We'll see that it gets to your congressman or senator.

Only with your help can we be sure this drama will have a happy ending.

Dear Legislator,
The arts in Minnesota are important to me. I believe in keeping them accessible and affordable for all. Please vote for the reauthorization of the National Endowment for the Arts and freedom of artistic expression.

Signature _____
Address _____
City _____ State _____ Zip _____

**SAVE THE NATIONAL ENDOWMENT FOR THE ARTS, OR THE ARTS WILL BECOME HISTORY.**

## AFTER COOKING THE DINNER I PLANNED TO MURDER MY HUSBAND.

was going to divorce me. Cut me off without a penny, just because he'd caught me with Tyrone, his chauffeur. What did he expect? Me nineteen and him...well...nearly forty. "There's nothing for it," I told Tyrone. "We have to kill him." Easier said than done, of course. Murder's so . . . messy. But he did it. He'd have got away with it too, if I hadn't rung the police. Honestly! You can't go round killing people and expect

147

Imagination. It's what kids don't use when they're watching TV. It's why kids who can't read aren't in the race. Which is what International Literacy Year is all about. Get your kids reading. Because it's hard to imagine life without it.

## I PUT THE KIDS TO BED AND WENT RIDING WITH A MOTOR CYCLE GANG.

to an old diner at the end of the New Jersey Turnpike. The bikes were lined up outside, gleaming. Chromed Harleys in Flamingo . . . Candy Apple Red . . . Orange Sunburst. No place for a dirty black Norton. But I walked inside anyway, shrugging out of my old leather jacket. "Coffee," I said. Silence fell. And twenty Hell's Angels watched as the one armed short order cook placed a cup in front of me and filled it. Never spilled

127

Imagination. It's what kids don't use when they're watching TV. It's why kids who can't read aren't in the race. Which is what International Literacy Year is all about. Get your kids reading. Because it's hard to imagine life without it.

## I KISSED MY WIFE GOODNIGHT AND FOUND MYSELF TRAPPED ON THE NORTH FACE.

blizzard for about three days. Trapped on a tiny crack high above the Hinterstoisser Traverse, our position was looking decidedly precarious. We had no food and only enough fuel for one more brew of tea. Young Jones had been flung to his death by the violent avalanche which had swept down from Death Bivouac that morning. Frobisher and I were amusing ourselves with some interesting chess variations when suddenly

139

Imagination. It's what kids don't use when they're watching TV. It's why kids who can't read aren't in the race. Which is what International Literacy Year is all about. Get your kids reading. Because it's hard to imagine life without it.

575

**PUBLIC SERVICE
NEWSPAPER OR MAGAZINE:
CAMPAIGN**

**576**
**ART DIRECTOR**
Anne Baylor
**WRITER**
Steve Bautista
**PHOTOGRAPHER**
Gene Dwiggins
**CLIENT**
The United Way of Southeastern
New England
**AGENCY**
Pagano Schenck &
Kay/Providence

**577**
**ART DIRECTOR**
Gary Greenberg
**WRITERS**
Peter Seronick, Court Crandall
**ILLUSTRATOR**
John Burgoyne
**PHOTOGRAPHER**
Carol Kaplan
**CLIENT**
Anti-Defamation League
**AGENCY**
Rossin Greenberg Seronick/
Boston

# Some chemicals are so strong, they can dissolve entire families.

Substance abuse is a force so powerful that it threatens to erode the very foundation of society – the family. With the United Way Donor Option Program, you can give to any of the member organizations that are fighting the critical problems which contribute to family breakdown. Call 521-9000 to find out how.

UNITED WAY
It brings out the best in all of us.™

# To an illiterate adult, these are stumbling blocks.

Illiteracy is more than not reading and writing. It's not realizing life's dreams and aspirations. With the United Way Donor Option Program you can give to the specific issues, like illiteracy, that you care about most. Call 521-9000 today and find out how you can help.

UNITED WAY
It brings out the best in all of us.™

# The saddest part isn't that this photo exists, but that we had 1,500 more to choose from.

It is estimated that there are some 2.5 million homeless people in America. And that over 25% are children. With the United Way Donor Option Program, you can give to the specific issues, like homelessness, that you care about most. Call 521-9000 to find out how.

UNITED WAY
It brings out the best in all of us.™

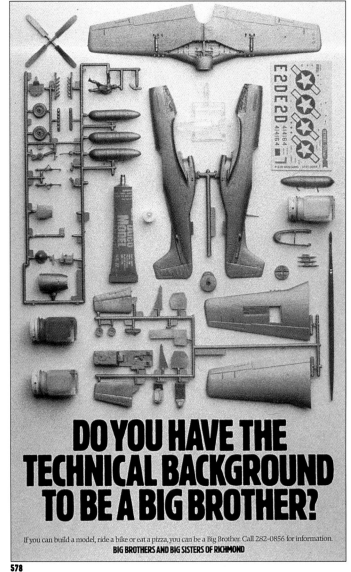

578

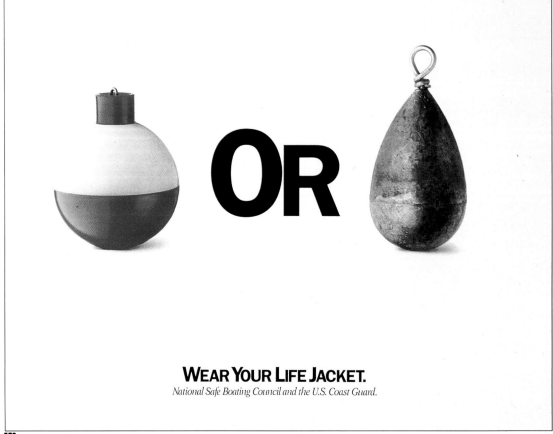

579

# IT'LL BE AS GOOD FOR YOU AS IT WILL BE FOR US.

Volunteer for this National Condom Preference Study funded by the U.S. Public Health Service and the data you provide will be used in a non-profit survey to encourage safe sex. For more information call 1-800-336-1935, Mon-Fri, 9AM-3PM.
*This confidential mail survey is conducted by NeuroCommunication Research Laboratories, Inc., Danbury, CT c1990.*

## NATIONAL CONDOM PREFERENCE STUDY

580

# YOU CAN PUT AS MUCH OR AS LITTLE INTO THIS AS YOU WANT TO.

Volunteer for this National Condom Preference Study funded by the U.S. Public Health Service and the data you provide will be used in a non-profit survey to encourage safe sex. For more information call 1-800-336-1935, Mon-Fri, 9AM-3PM.
*This confidential mail survey is conducted by NeuroCommunication Research Laboratories, Inc., Danbury, CT c1990.*

## NATIONAL CONDOM PREFERENCE STUDY

581

YOU SHOULD HAVE SEEN THE PEDESTRIAN.

STOP AT CROSSWALKS.

NOW IT'S THE LAW.
KING COUNTY PUBLIC WORKS

582

## PUBLIC SERVICE OUTDOOR

**583**
**ART DIRECTORS**
Robert Stanton, Ken Kirschner,
Jonathan Lee
**WRITERS**
Robert Stanton, Ken Kirschner,
Jonathan Lee
**CLIENT**
United Way
**AGENCY**
DDB Needham Worldwide/
New York

**584**
**ART DIRECTOR**
Peter Cohen
**WRITER**
Peter Cohen
**CLIENT**
Coalition for the Homeless
**AGENCY**
Chiat/Day/Mojo,
New York

**585**
**ART DIRECTOR**
Kenny Sink
**WRITER**
Daniel Russ
**PHOTOGRAPHER**
Matthew Brady
**CLIENT**
Brandy Station
**AGENCY**
Earle Palmer
Brown/Bethesda

**586**
**ART DIRECTOR**
Kenny Sink
**WRITER**
Daniel Russ
**PHOTOGRAPHER**
Matthew Brady
**CLIENT**
Brandy Station
**AGENCY**
Earle Palmer Brown/
Bethesda

**587**
**ART DIRECTOR**
Jac Coverdale
**WRITER**
Joe Alexander
**CLIENT**
Mothers Against Drunk
Driving/Minnesota Chapter
**AGENCY**
Clarity Coverdale Rueff/
Minneapolis

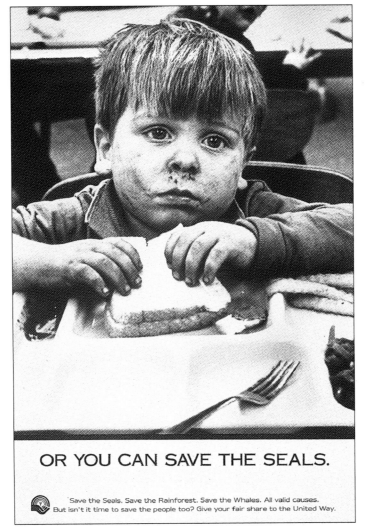

OR YOU CAN SAVE THE SEALS.

Save the Seals. Save the Rainforest. Save the Whales. All valid causes.
But isn't it time to save the people too? Give your fair share to the United Way.

583

**HOW CAN YOU WORSHIP
A HOMELESS MAN ON SUNDAY AND
IGNORE ONE ON MONDAY?**

They could use your prayers. More importantly, they could use your help. Call the Coalition For The Homeless at 460-8110 to find out how.

584

Pity the poor citizens of Culpeper County. Every so often, they seem to be invaded.

First outsiders armed with muskets roared into these verdant rolling hills. Now they're coming armed with rezoning proposals.

One hundred and twenty seven years ago, more cavalrymen fought here than all the cavalry that Hannibal used during his 17 year siege of Rome. More than all the cavalrymen under Napoleon and Wellington at Waterloo, combined.

Around May of 1863, rumor had it the Confederates were about to invade the North again. General J.E.B. Stuart was staging showy dress parades in Central Virginia. His men were throwing taunts at the Federal cavalry.

General Alfred Pleasonton responded by crossing the banks of the Rappahannock with a 10,000 man cavalry force, hungry for blood and ready to prove they could fight.

When all was said and done, plenty of Americans had bled to save a country. The battlefield was littered with dead riders and their mounts, many of whom were buried on the spot.

But soon, all this history will be paved over. It will be known as Elkwood Downs—1475 acres of warehouses, laboratories, and manufacturing plants. And though it is not being planned as a

## IF YOU ENJOY BROWSING AT CEMETERIES, YOU'RE GOING TO LOVE THE NEW SHOPPING CENTER AT BRANDY STATION.

shopping center, shopping centers and strip malls are allowed in the rezoning charter and are an inevitable consequence of thousands of people needing places to eat, or take their laundry or get their car fixed, etcetera.

If you think that the consequent tax increases will fill county coffers, keep in mind that every red cent of it will be needed to pay for new schools, teacher's salaries, fire and rescue squads, police, and so on ad infinitum.

And when all is said and done at Brandy Station, only one man will claim victory during the last battle. The developer.

But he doesn't live here.

He won't have to wake up to bulldozers for the next 20 years while it's being built. He won't have to smell the stench of the polluted Rappahannock, and he won't suffer depleted wells and groundwater.

You will, however. Unless you act now.

Call your Congressman. Better yet, call the Culpeper Board of Supervisors. They are: Jack E. Fincham, (H) (703) 825-6958, (W) (703) 825-6958, William C. Chase, (H) 399-1218 (W) (703) 825-3644, Ruth B. Updike, (W) (703) 547-1700, Vincent Beasley, (H) (703) 825-9292, Kim A. Williams, (703) 547-2431, Marvin L. Bates, (703) 825-4944, Bradley C. Rosenberger, (703) 937-4928.

**SAVE THE BATTLEFIELD AT BRANDY STATION.**

585

---

From the land that brought you tofu, spirit channeling and crystal energy healing, now comes another idea we hope will go nowhere: the commercial development of one of the most beautiful and historic places on this Earth.

Real estate tycoon Lee Sammis, from Irvine, California has designs on Brandy Station in Central Virginia. Designs which include a 1,500 acre light industrial park, the widening of Route 29/15 into a six lane super-highway and eventually 3,500 acres of residential housing.

He calls the "planned community" Elkwood Downs. He says it will bring jobs and millions of dollars in tax revenue.

What he doesn't tell you is what else Elkwood Downs will bring to Culpeper County. Like traffic estimated at hundreds

## BRANDY STATION NOW FACES AN ENEMY FAR WORSE THAN THE UNION CAVALRY: A DEVELOPER FROM CALIFORNIA.

of thousands of vehicle trips into, out of and around Brandy Station per day. He doesn't say much about the 600,000 gallons of noxious industrial wastes from newly built manufacturing plants that will pour into the Rappahannock, not to mention the sewage from this future community development.

Land speculators with dollar signs in their eyes don't realize that every red cent of tax revenue that Elkwood Downs generates will be spent managing and governing Elkwood Downs, or the schools, fire and rescue and police personnel that will spring up in this "planned community." The cancerous overdevelopment of Central Virginia notwithstanding, few seem to value the sheer weight of history of this land.

Brandy Station is a place where the largest single cavalry engagement in the Western Hemisphere took place. It is a place where Americans, some little more than boys, died while trying to mend a broken nation.

In 1863, a two-pronged Federal cavalry force, 10,000 strong, crossed the Rappahannock in the early hours on June 9th. They clashed in a bloody melee with a Confederate force of equal size. When the sun set on Brandy Station, both sides limped back to their territory, shorn of life and limb. The Union cavalry had proven itself to the stunned Confederates, but the land still rested in control of Robert E. Lee's forces. All of this at a cost of hundreds of lives and hundreds more wounded.

Now it is time to fight again.

Only this time, if you lose, you can never regain your territory. If you allow warehouses and parking decks and neon hamburger joints to litter this landscape, you'll pay every time you look out your window.

If you care to preserve a gorgeous parcel of land, and an important piece of American history, or if you can't bear a painful 20-year-long buildup, then call your elected officials on the Culpeper County Board of Supervisors. Jack E. Fincham, (H) (703) 825-6958, (W) (703) 825-6958, Ruth B. Updike, (H) (703) 547-1700, (W) (703) 825-1550, William C. Chase, (703) 399-1218, Vincent Beasley, (703) 825-9292, Kim A. Williams, (703) 547-2431, Bradley C. Rosenberger, (703) 937-4928, Marvin L. Bates, (703) 825-4944.

**SAVE THE BATTLEFIELD AT BRANDY STATION.**

586

---

## SOMETIMES IT TAKES A FAMILY OF FOUR TO STOP A DRUNK DRIVER.

MADD

587

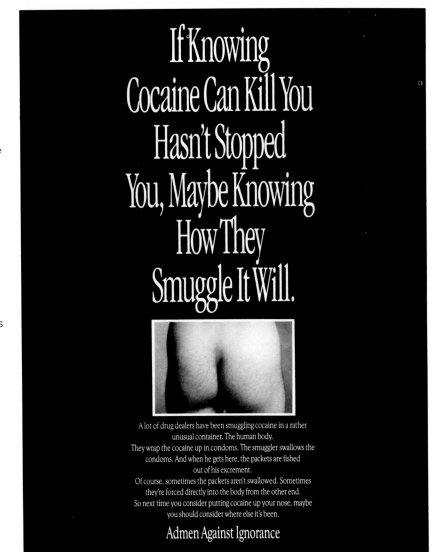

588

589

590

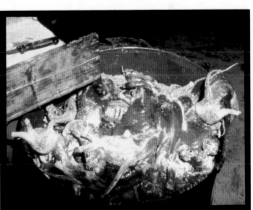

**592**
**ART DIRECTOR**
Wendy Hansen
**WRITER**
Lyle Wedemeyer
**PHOTOGRAPHER**
Rick Dublin
**CLIENT**
Minnesota Department of Health
**AGENCY**
Martin/Williams, Minneapolis

**593**
**ART DIRECTOR**
Richard Ostroff
**WRITER**
Amy Borkowsky
**PHOTOGRAPHER**
Cailor/Resnick
**CLIENT**
Ad Council
**AGENCY**
Levine Huntley Vick &
Beaver/New York

**594**
**ART DIRECTOR**
Bill Schwartz
**WRITER**
Joyce Spetrino
**ILLUSTRATOR**
Dave Fitch
**CLIENT**
Clean-Land, Ohio
**AGENCY**
Meldrum and Fewsmith/
Cleveland

**595**
**ART DIRECTOR**
Rob Dalton
**WRITER**
Jim Newcombe
**PHOTOGRAPHER**
Kerry Peterson
**CLIENT**
The Episcopal Ad Project
**AGENCY**
Young & Rubicam/
Minneapolis

**596**
**ART DIRECTOR**
Jeff Martin
**WRITER**
Pete Pohl
**CLIENT**
Kalamazoo Humane Society
**AGENCY**
Lawler Ballard/Kalamazoo

It Looks Just As Stupid When You Do It.

Minnesota Department of Health

592

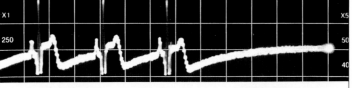

# UNFORTUNATELY, THE WAY TO A MAN'S HEART REALLY IS THROUGH HIS STOMACH.

While your cooking was supposed to help you win someone's heart, it may also help you destroy it.
Because a diet that's too high in fat may increase the risk of heart disease as well as certain kinds of cancer.

Fortunately, you can help reduce your risk simply by eating a low-fat diet containing lots of fruits and vegetables, whole grain foods, lean meats, fish, poultry and low-fat dairy products.
For a free booklet on how to reduce the fat in your diet,

call 1-800-EAT-LEAN.
Don't let yourself be counted among the thousands of people every year who literally eat their hearts out.

**1-800-EAT-LEAN**

A public service message from The Henry J. Kaiser Family Foundation

593

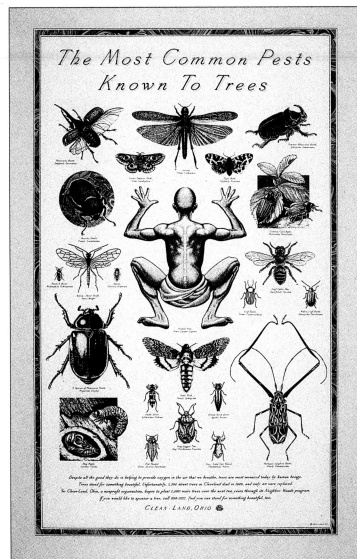

594

595

Is this
where you pray on
Sunday morning?

The Episcopal Church

596

ADAMS

Here kitty, kitty, kitty, kitty, kitty, kitty, kitty, kitty, kitty, kitty, kitty, kitty, kitty, kitty, kitty, kitty, kitty, kitty, kitty, kitty, kitty, kitty, kitty, kitty, kitty, kitty, kitty, kitty, kitty, kitty, kitty, kitty, kitty, kitty, kitty, kitty, kitty, kitty, kitty, kitty, **HAVE YOUR PET SPAYED/NEUTERED.**

KALAMAZOO
HUMANE
SOCIETY

**RADIO FINALISTS**

## CONSUMER RADIO: SINGLE

### 597
**WRITERS**
Will Awdry, Martin Galton
**AGENCY PRODUCER**
Susan Baldwin
**PRODUCTION COMPANY**
Angell Sound
**CLIENT**
Swinton Insurance
**AGENCY**
Bartle Bogle Hegarty/London

### 598
**WRITERS**
Kim Papworth, Tony Davidson
**AGENCY PRODUCER**
Gay O'Rourke
**PRODUCTION COMPANY**
Mandy Wheeler Sound
Productions
**CLIENT**
Crookes Healthcare
**AGENCY**
BMP DDB Needham/London

### 599
**WRITER**
David Shane
**AGENCY PRODUCER**
Vicki Blucher
**CLIENT**
NYNEX Information Resources
**AGENCY**
Chiat/Day/Mojo, New York

### 600
**WRITER**
David Shane
**AGENCY PRODUCER**
Vicki Blucher
**CLIENT**
NYNEX Information Resources
**AGENCY**
Chiat/Day/Mojo, New York

### 597
MAN: So I got into bed with a hot water bottle and a packet of cheese and onion, and settled for an early night with the wife. I was just puffing up my pillow, when she suddenly said, "Do you know that Swinton Car Insurance has more than 650 branches nationwide, so there's always one nearby to help out?" I offered her a crisp to break the silence. She then drops a bombshell. She said, "I'm having an affair." I said, "Who with pet?" She said, "You don't know him." I said, "It's not the man from Swinton?", putting two and two together. She said, "As a matter of fact it is and I've said he can move in on Tuesday." Typical, I thought, over 650 places he can conduct his affairs in and he picks mine.

ANNCR: Check local directories for your nearest branch of Swinton. We always give the motorist priority.

### 598
DESMOND: Ow! Ooh! Aggh!
WALLACE: Something wrong?
DESMOND: He just started rubbing me again.
WALLACE: Well, it's one of the hazards of being an eye, of course, having a rub occasionally.
DESMOND: I happen to know the hazards of being an eye. Being an eye, obviously.
WALLACE: Besides, he's probably tired and weary. Working all hours. He works ever so hard.
DESMOND: Who's side are you on?
WALLACE: On the left side.
DESMOND: No! Whatchoo crawlin' round him for, all of a sudden.
WALLACE: I'm not.
DESMOND: You are. Just cos you think you'll get more Optrex drops!
WALLACE: Well I might!
DESMOND: Don't be ridiculous! He doesn't favouritise one over the other, does he?
WALLACE: Look! Look! Here it comes little blue and white bottle! Ah!!!
(SFX: JOYFUL CHORAL MUSIC)
WALLACE: So how many did you get?
DESMOND: One.
WALLACE: Huh.
DESMOND: So how many did you get?
WALLACE: Two.
DESMOND: That is no proof what so...
WALLACE: See! If you're a kind and understanding eye...
DESMOND: Sheer coincidence.
WALLACE: It's not actually!
DESMOND: It is, in fact!
ANNCR: Optrex Drops. Are your eyes trying to tell you something?

**599**

(SFX: OFFICE SOUNDS)

MIKE: It's true, you can find anything in the NYNEX Yellow Pages, and today I found Marc Shane, the president of Confidence Builders, Inc.

MARC: Hi there Michael. How you doing?

MIKE: I'm doing fine, Marc.

MARC: That's great, that's great.

MIKE: I'm fascinated by your company here. What exactly is it that you do?

MARC: Basically I lose, Mike.

MIKE: You lose.

MARC: Yes. Some rich guy will hire me to come over to his home and lose to his kids at some video games. Maybe I'll go to his club, lose a couple of quick sets of tennis, squash, whatever.

MIKE: So, somebody might hire you to come over and fall off a bike too . . .

MARC: Entirely possible. When a young child is learning how to ride a bike, I might just get on one myself and run it right into a brick wall.

MIKE: I see.

MARC: Course, compared to your job it's just a day in the park for me.

MIKE: Oh really? You really think so . . .

MARC: Absolutely, I could never do what you do.

MIKE: Oh, seriously?

MARC: You're tremendous.

MIKE: Sometimes I have my doubts.

MARC: How you think of those questions is wonderful.

MIKE: Oh, thanks a lot.

MARC: You know, I'm just kidding, Mike. Forget everything I just said, of course. Just giving you a little taste, a little sample of what I do every day in my job.

MIKE: Yeah, thanks a lot. Well, there you have it. Further proof that if it's out there, it's in the NYNEX Yellow Pages.

MARC: Nicely done.

MIKE: Mmmmm, why would anyone need another.

**600**

MIKE: They say you can find anything in the NYNEX Yellow Pages. Well, today under Portrait Artists, I found Edwin Laguerre, an artist who specializes in . . .

EDWIN: Abstract doggie portraits, portraiture.

MIKE: Right. What, exactly, do you mean by "abstract" dog portraits?

EDWIN: Well, basically Mike, I don't try to draw doggie per se, you know. Rather, I interpret doggie through the kaleidoscope of my mind's eye.

MIKE: Uhuh.

EDWIN: I tell all of my customers, if you want to see what doggie looks like, take a snapshot. If you want to see what doggie means, well, I'm the guy.

MIKE: So what kind of dog have you painted here?

EDWIN: Well, what do you see?

MIKE: I see a black canvas.

EDWIN: Well, doggie was very troubled here. Maybe new kittie on the street, in the house, I don't know.

MIKE: Right.

EDWIN: I can paint a picture of a doggie very happy, smiley, but it's a lie. As an artist I can't do it.

MIKE: Well, all your portraits seem kinda dark and gloomy.

EDWIN: That's because all doggies are troubled. It's what makes them doggies. And what makes me want to paint them.

MIKE: Uh.

EDWIN: I can paint a picture of your doggie without ever seeing him.

(SFX: CHARCOAL PENCIL ON PAD)

EDWIN: Lots of dark clouds, shapes of misery . . .

MIKE: Well, there you have it. Further proof that . . .

EDWIN: Pain, anger.

MIKE: If it's out there, it's in the NYNEX Yellow Pages.

EDWIN: Angst . . .

MIKE: . . . I, uh, I don't have a dog. Why would anyone need another?

EDWIN: Every man has a dog somewhere.

MIKE: No, it's in my lease.

(SFX: RUSTLING PAPER)

EDWIN: Look, this is your dog. His name is Popo. He's calling out to you : Pet me, pet me.

**601**
(MUSIC: THROUGHOUT)
ANNCR: Put that down. You don't know where it's been. Never wear good underwear to the doctor or your bill will be higher. Wait til your father gets home. Always tell the truth, even if you have to lie to do it. The most important thing to get is a good bra. Turn out the lights. We don't own stock in the electric company. What will the neighbors think? You'll never get a boyfriend if you don't learn to play bridge. You're gonna poke somebody's eye out with that thing. Go back and this time use soap. You're not going out like that, are you? If he tries to kiss you, call me. Don't sit so close to the television, it'll ruin your eyes. If you fall out of that tree and break your leg, don't come running to me. You'll thank me for this someday. Mom . . . how could you forget her? Mother's Day is this Sunday. See's Famous Old Time Candies.

**602**
TOM: Well, we're here at a Red Roof Inn and we're talking now with .
MIKE: Mike Hyde.
TOM: Mike, how tall are you?
MIKE: Six foot nine.
TOM: Six foot nine. Did you get a good night sleep last night?
MIKE: Yes, I did.
TOM: Did your feet hang over the end of the bed?
MIKE: No, they didn't.
TOM: You know why they didn't?
MIKE: No.
TOM: That's because at Red Roof Inns the beds are six inches longer than standard.
MIKE: Very good.
TOM: So your feet were nice and toasty warm?
MIKE: Yes, they were.
TOM: How big are your feet?
MIKE: Well, they're a size fifteen.
TOM: So if those babies get cold it could drop the whole temperature of the world by one or two degrees, right?
MIKE: Maybe two or three.
TOM: You could wreck the summer growing season for a lot of farmers.
MIKE: Yeah, the fruit people would be after me.
TOM: So thank goodness you stayed at Red Roof Inns.
MIKE: Thank you.
TOM: Well, there you have it folks, we have Red Roof Inns to thank for a longer growing season. So if you're out on the road and want to stay at a nice, clean, comfortable, quiet room with longer beds, hit the roof, Red Roof Inns. Call 1-800-THE ROOF. Now, with size fifteen feet, you're not the elusive bigfoot are you?
MIKE: No, I'm not.
TOM: Because I noticed on your jacket it says, "Hello, my name is Sasquach".

DESMOND: I'm fed up with being an eye!

WALLACE: Why's that then particularly then?

DESMOND: Because here we are swimming, it's a fabulous day and he's forgotten his goggles.

WALLACE: It wouldn't be so bad if he at least remembered to buy some Optrex drops.

DESMOND: I've got a good . . .

WALLACE: After three quarters of an hour worth of water bashing against us!

DESMOND: Yeah, I've got a good . . .

WALLACE: Buffeting and crashing and lashing against us . . .

DESMOND: Absolutely. I've got a good . . .

WALLACE: Battering and mauling and thrashing and . . .

DESMOND: Thank you.

WALLACE: Okay.

DESMOND: Ooh we're going for a dive now. I've a good mind to suddenly shut just as he takes off.

WALLACE: He might bump his head then.

DESMOND: Precisely.

WALLACE: That'd jog his memory a bit.

DESMOND: Memory! He's got no more memory than I've got . . .

WALLACE: Any Optrex drops.

DESMOND: Exactly.

WALLACE: So that's why you're fed up being an eye?

DESMOND: Yeah.

WALLACE: I get it.

ANNCR: Optrex Drops. Are your eyes trying to tell you something?

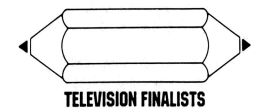

TELEVISION FINALISTS

**CONSUMER TELEVISION
OVER :30 (:45/ :60/ :90)
SINGLE**

**604**
**ART DIRECTOR**
Mark Roalfe
**WRITER**
Robert Campbell
**AGENCY PRODUCER**
Frank Lieberman
**PRODUCTION COMPANY**
Abbott Mead Vickers. BBDO/
Stock Footage
**CLIENT**
Volvo
**AGENCY**
Abbott Mead Vickers.
BBDO/London

**605**
**ART DIRECTOR**
Bruce Hurwit
**WRITER**
Susan Credle
**AGENCY PRODUCERS**
Bob Emerson, Steve Friedman
**PRODUCTION COMPANY**
Gibson Lefevre Gartner
**DIRECTOR**
Jim Gartner
**CLIENT**
Pizza Hut
**AGENCY**
BBDO/New York

**606**
**ART DIRECTOR**
Susan Westre
**WRITER**
Chris Wall
**AGENCY PRODUCERS**
Bob Belton, Patrick Walsh
**PRODUCTION COMPANY**
HKM/Los Angeles
**DIRECTOR**
Michael Karbelnikoff
**CLIENT**
Apple Computers/Macintosh
**AGENCY**
BBDO/New York

**607**
**ART DIRECTOR**
John Webster
**WRITER**
John Webster
**AGENCY PRODUCER**
Howard Spivey
**PRODUCTION COMPANY**
BFCS
**DIRECTOR**
Michael Seresin
**CLIENT**
V.A.G. (UK)
**AGENCY**
BMP DDB Needham/London

**604**
(SFX: CARS SPEEDING PAST, CAR HORNS AND TIRES SQUEALING)
(SFX: CAR CRASH)
SUPER: CAGES SAVE LIVES.
SUPER: VOLVO.

**605**
WESLEY: Bring the ball home Daryl.
DARYL: Well it's all come down to this. Sixty million trillion fans are waiting for this one last play. You know it's going to Daryl Jenkins. He moves left, he moves right, he's double-teamed, triple-teamed, the whole-team-teamed, whoa. Now, the only thing between him and the basket is his big ugly brother Wesley. He gives him the old shake and bake. His mom and dad are jumpin' up and down. Boy is his brother jealous. He looks at the clock, four seconds, three, two. . . he leaps, he shoots, and . . . he was fouled!
ANNCR: For all of you who ever dreamed of playing big time basketball, Pizza Hut and the NCAA would like to say thanks for "Makin' it great!"

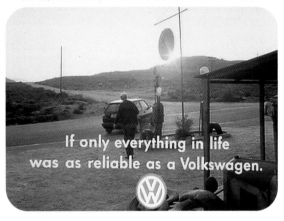

**606**

PROFESSOR: We are entering a whole new era . . . the decade of positive change. Around the world, organizations have realized. . .that you cannot intimidate human beings into productivity. The key is to let people do what they do best, whatever way works best for them. At the same time, fundamental principles of mass production give ordinary people access to powerful technology. That which was affordable to the few becomes available to the many. Mass production becomes mass productivity. The Industrial Revolution meets the Age of Enlightenment. The walls have come down! Opportunity has gone up! And your only limits will be the size of your ideas and the degree of your dedication! People, this is an exciting time to be alive.

SUPER: INTRODUCING THE MOST AFFORDABLE MACINTOSH COMPUTERS EVER.

SUPER: APPLE. THE POWER TO BE YOUR BEST.

**607**

(SFX: SQUEAK, SQUEAK THROUGHOUT)

GAS ATTENDANT: Ha, ha.

(SFX: OIL CAN, SQUEAKING STOPS)

SUPER: IF ONLY EVERYTHING IN LIFE WAS AS RELIABLE AS A VOLKSWAGEN.

**CONSUMER TELEVISION
OVER :30 (:45/ :60/ :90)
SINGLE**

**608
ART DIRECTOR**
Tom Notman
**WRITER**
Alistair Wood
**AGENCY PRODUCER**
Karen Hughes
**PRODUCTION COMPANY**
Tony Kaye Films
**DIRECTOR**
Tony Kaye
**CLIENT**
Woolworths
**AGENCY**
BSB Dorland/London

**609
ART DIRECTOR**
Jonathan Teo
**WRITERS**
Michael Linke, David Rollins
**AGENCY PRODUCER**
David Judge
**PRODUCTION COMPANY**
Film Graphics
**DIRECTOR**
David Denneen
**CLIENT**
CCA Snack Foods
**AGENCY**
The Campaign
Palace/Darlinghurst, NSW

**610
ART DIRECTOR**
Paul Szary
**WRITER**
Gary Topolewski
**AGENCY PRODUCER**
Craig Mungons
**PRODUCTION COMPANY**
Plum Productions
**DIRECTOR**
Eric Saarinen
**CLIENT**
Chrysler
**AGENCY**
Campbell-Mithun-Esty/
Southfield

**611
ART DIRECTOR**
Mike Moser
**WRITER**
Jeff Billig
**AGENCY PRODUCER**
Trish Reeves
**PRODUCTION COMPANY**
Plum Productions
**DIRECTOR**
Eric Saarinen
**CLIENT**
Reebok
**AGENCY**
Chiat/Day/Mojo, New York

**608**
(MUSIC: "BOYS AND GIRLS COME OUT TO PLAY" THROUGHOUT)
SUPER: FROM LADYBIRD.
SUPER: EXCLUSIVE THAT IS TO CHILDREN.
SUPER: AND TO WOOLWORTHS.  LADYBIRD.

**609**
JOCKEY: WOAH!!
HORSE: Neigh.
MAN: You okay?
JOCKEY: Sure. Just thought I'd drop in.  I hope
you don't mind.
MAN: No, not at all.  Would you like a drink?
JOCKEY: You bet.
WOMAN: I know . . . Let's have some fun.  Let's
nibble Nobby's Nuts.
HORSE: Neigh.
(MUSIC: THIRTIES-STYLE PARTY)
SURFER: WOAH!!
(SFX: SURF CRASHING)
(SFX: PARTY NOISES)
SUPER: NIBBLE NOBBY'S NUTS.

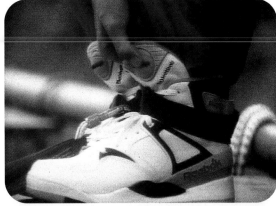

**610**

(SFX: WOODPECKER AND JACKHAMMER, TIMBERWOLF AND SIREN, GEESE AND CAR HORNS, BEAVERS AND TUGBOAT WHISTLES. . .)

ANNCR: Jeep Cherokee. The ultimate vehicle for the hustle and bustle of everyday life.

PILOT VOICE: Rush hour seems to be winding down. Traffic is moving at posted speeds. . .

SUPER: PENTASTAR 7/70. THERE'S ONLY ONE JEEP . . . ADVANTAGE: CHRYSLER.

**611**

(SIGN: DO NOT THROW MATERIAL FROM BRIDGE)

(SFX: AMBIENT WIND AND RIVER SOUNDS)

ANNCR: The Pump from Reebok. It fits a little better than your ordinary athletic shoe.

(SFX: HEART BEAT AND WIND)

SUPER: REEBOK.

**612**

(MUSIC: BLUES CUTS IN AND OUT)
SUPER: WHY IKEA DOESN'T HAVE DELIVERYMEN.
MAN 1: We like to take breaks.
MAN 2: Ya know, there's always tomorrow. We'll get it there.
SUPER: WE DON'T WANT TO PAY FOR THESE GUYS.
MAN 2: We make about $15.50 an hour.
MAN 1: Sometimes we drop things.
SUPER: DROP THINGS?
MAN 3: Occasionally we drop a piece of glass and it just . . .
SUPER: DOESN'T GET DELIVERED?
MAN 3: Sometimes we miss a delivery but you can only do so much in eight hours.
SUPER: WHAT IF YOU WANT IT TODAY?
MAN 4: The furniture that we're going to be delivering today has been in the warehouse for about a couple of weeks.
SUPER: A COUPLE OF WEEKS?
MAN 5: . . . But if it's not in stock, it takes anywhere from two to four weeks.
SUPER: FOUR WEEKS?
MAN 6: Some pieces, they wait for years for these pieces to get in.
SUPER: YEARS?!
MAN 7: Delivering furniture's a tough job.
SUPER: IT'S EASY.
SUPER: JUST TAKE IT HOME TODAY.
SUPER: IT'S A BIG COUNTRY. SOMEONE'S GOT TO FURNISH IT. IKEA.

**613**

(MUSIC: ROCK MUSIC CUTS IN AND OUT)
SUPER: WHY IKEA DOESN'T HAVE SALESMEN.
MAN 1: What would you like? You like something firm but comfortable, right?
MAN 2: You like this style but you don't like this color, you can pick out any of these.
SUPER: WE DON'T WANT TO PAY FOR THESE GUYS.
MAN 3: No other crib on the market, that I know of, turns into a full size double bed.
MAN 4: 'Cause we're throwing in the seashells and the starfish and who knows what some of these things are.
SUPER: SO YOU DON'T HAVE TO PAY FOR THESE GUYS.
MAN 5: . . . to make it a little bit unique, as we have right here. A little bit different.
WOMAN: Besides having wicker and rattan, we do have some life-like animals.
SUPER: DO YOU EVEN NEED THESE GUYS?
MAN 6: . . . satin black lacquer finish, with a Parcathian Elm Burl.
SUPER: PARCATHIAN ELM BURL?
SUPER: YOU KNOW WHAT YOU WANT.
SUPER: GO AHEAD. PICK IT OUT YOURSELF.
SUPER: IT'S A BIG COUNTRY. SOMEONE'S GOT TO FURNISH IT. IKEA.

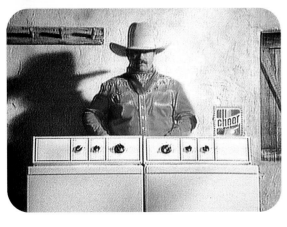

**614**

(MUSIC: WESTERN STYLE THROUGHOUT)

SUPER: ARE YOUR COLORS FADING?

SUPER: FIVE WASHES.

SUPER: TEN WASHES.

SUPER: TWENTY WASHES.

SUPER: TWENTY-FIVE WASHES LATER.

SUPER: A LEADING POWDER. CHEER WITH COLOR GUARD.

ANNCR: Cheer with color guard. Dirt goes. Color stays.

**615**

(MUSIC: THROUGHOUT)

SUPER: A WOMAN WHO WASHES HER HAIR EVERYDAY NEEDS A MILD AND GENTLE SHAMPOO. AND WHAT COULD BE MORE GENTLE THAN A SHAMPOO YOU'D USE ON A BABY.

SUPER: JOHNSON'S NO MORE TEARS BABY SHAMPOO. START USING IT AGAIN AND AGAIN AND AGAIN.

**CONSUMER TELEVISION
OVER :30 (:45/ :60/ :90)
SINGLE**

**616
ART DIRECTOR**
David Jenkins
**WRITER**
Jim Riswold
**AGENCY PRODUCER**
Bill Davenport
**PRODUCTION COMPANY**
Pytka Productions
**DIRECTOR**
Joe Pytka
**CLIENT**
Nike
**AGENCY**
Wieden & Kennedy/Portland

**CONSUMER TELEVISION
OVER :30 (:45/ :60/ :90)
CAMPAIGN**

**617
ART DIRECTORS**
Don Schneider, Kevin Donovan,
Scott Schindler
**WRITERS**
Lee Garfinkel, Jonathan Mandell,
Todd Godwin, Jennifer Noble
**AGENCY PRODUCERS**
Regina Ebel, Sandi Bachom,
Hyatt Choate, Bob Kirschen
**PRODUCTION COMPANIES**
Pytka Productions, Steve Horn,
Inc., The Partners
**DIRECTORS**
Joe Pytka, Steve Horn, Barry
Young
**CLIENT**
Pepsi Cola
**AGENCY**
BBDO/New York

**618
ART DIRECTORS**
Randy Spear, Ernie Cox
**WRITERS**
Jennifer LeMay, Gerry Miller
**AGENCY PRODUCER**
Bob Davis
**PRODUCTION COMPANY**
Koetz & Company
**DIRECTOR**
Leroy Koetz
**CLIENT**
Procter & Gamble/Cheer
**AGENCY**
Leo Burnett Company/Chicago

**CONSUMER TELEVISION
:30 SINGLE**

**619
ART DIRECTOR**
Steven Mitsch
**WRITER**
Rosalind Greene
**AGENCY PRODUCER**
Mary Ellen Verrusio
**DIRECTOR**
Steve Horn
**CLIENT**
Claiborne for Men
**AGENCY**
Altschiller Reitzfeld/
Tracy-Locke, New York

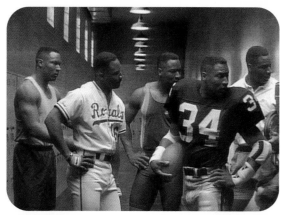

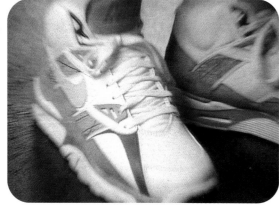
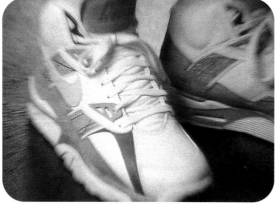

**616**
BO FOOTBALL: Don't I know you?
(MUSIC: THROUGHOUT)
BO BASKETBALL: Nice shoes!
BO TENNIS: Yo, tennis anyone?
BO FOOTBALL: Are you sure we haven't met before?
(SFX: SCREECHING TIRES)
BO CYCLIST: Where's the Tour de France thing?
VO BO: Nice Shoes!
BO CYCLIST: I know I should have taken that right
 turn at Albuquerque.
BO FOOTBALL: You ever been to L.A.?
ALL BOS IN UNISON: Bo don't surf!
BO SURFER: That's what you think, dudes.
(SFX: CAR ENGINE REVVING)
BO CRICKET: Might you all join me in a spot of tea?
BO FOOTBALL: Where'd you play college ball?
(MUSIC: "I GOT YOU BABE")
BO BASKETBALL: What is he doing here?
SONNY BONO: I thought this was another "Bo
 Knows" commercial.
BO GOLFER: Fore!
BO GOLFER: Has anyone seen Bo's ball?
BO FOOTBALL: I know, Kansas City?
(SFX: TRUMPET FANFARE)
VO BO: Nice shoes!
(SFX: SPEEDING CAR)
VO BO: Nice shoes!
BO FOOTBALL: Have you ever played with Bo
 Diddley?
(SFX: BIKE BELL AND HORSE NEIGHING)
BO DIRECTOR: Cut!
ALL BOS IN UNISON: HUH!

**617**
(MUSIC: UPBEAT)
OLD WOMAN 1: Rock and roll is okay but I prefer
 rap.
OLD MAN 1: Hey Joe.
OLD WOMAN 2: Right on.
OLD MAN 2: Hot, hey, hey.
OLD MAN 3: Awesome.
OLD MAN 1: This music is good but nobody can
 touch Hendrix.
OLD MAN 3: Awesome.
DELIVERY MAN 1: Wait a second. Shady Acres was
 supposed to get the Coke and the frat house
 was supposed to get the Pepsi.
DELIVERY MAN 2: Coke, Pepsi, what's the difference?
(MUSIC: CLASSICAL)
FRAT BOY: I-24.
(MUSIC: UPBEAT)
OLD WOMAN 3: Do you like slam dancing?
OLD MAN 1: Love it.
OLD MAN 3: This is radical.
SUPER: PEPSI. THE CHOICE OF A NEW
 GENERATION.

**618**

(MUSIC: THROUGHOUT)

ANNCR: Cheer with color guard.  Dirt goes.
  Color stays.

**619**

MAN: I see this woman.  She's perfect.  She's
  alone.  She's looking at me, she's smiling.  But
  wait, is she smiling at me?  Or laughing at
  me?  Or looking at someone else . . .

ANNCR: Man is not so simple, after all.
  Claiborne.  The fragrance for men.

**CONSUMER TELEVISION
:30 SINGLE**

**620**
**ART DIRECTOR**
Ted Shaine
**WRITER**
Kevin McKeon
**AGENCY PRODUCER**
Susan Shipman
**PRODUCTION COMPANY**
BFCS International
**DIRECTOR**
Bob Brooks
**CLIENT**
Cadbury/Schweppes
**AGENCY**
Ammirati & Puris/New York

**621**
**ART DIRECTOR**
Paul Blade
**WRITER**
Tom Thomas
**AGENCY PRODUCER**
Fran Cosentino
**PRODUCTION COMPANY**
Johns & Gorman Films
**DIRECTOR**
Gary Johns
**CLIENT**
Saab Cars USA
**AGENCY**
Angotti Thomas Hedge/
New York

**622**
**ART DIRECTOR**
Jeff Layton
**WRITER**
Boris Damast
**AGENCY PRODUCER**
Gordon Stanway
**PRODUCTION COMPANY**
The Partners
**DIRECTOR**
Gillean Proctor
**CLIENT**
Black & Decker Canada
**AGENCY**
Baker Lovick/BBDO, Toronto

**623**
**ART DIRECTORS**
Norman Alcuri, Neil French
**WRITERS**
Andy Lish, Neil French
**AGENCY PRODUCER**
Sara Uduwela
**PRODUCTION COMPANY**
The Picture Farm
**DIRECTOR**
Neil French
**CLIENT**
The Pan Pacific Hotel,
Singapore
**AGENCY**
The Ball Partnership/Singapore

**620**
CLEESE: It's becoming ever more difficult to
surround one's self with absolute,
uncompromising quality.
(SFX: PFTTT!)
CLEESE: Which is why I take such extraordinary
pleasure in telling you about Schweppes.
(SFX: CLANGGG!)
CLEESE: With its unique Schweppervescence, and
distinctively refreshing taste, it may be the
last oasis of true excellence in an otherwise
vast desert of compromise.
(SFX: CRASH!)
CLEESE: Cheers!
ANNCR: Schweppes. The uncompromising line of
classic soft drinks.

**621**
ANNCR: For all those who love cars, a car that
loved someone back. A 9000 series Saab: Its
front end crumpled from the force of collision
. . its driver's-side air bag deployed . . . and
passenger safety cage intact. A car that
surrendered its own life to save its owner's.
The insurance company called this Saab a
total loss. Its owner totally disagrees.
SUPER: SAAB. WE DON'T MAKE COMPROMISES.
WE MAKE SAABS.

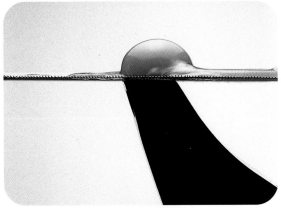

**622**

SUPER: BLACK & DECKER PRESENTS THE NEW, CORDLESS POWER PRO.

SUPER: DEMONSTRATION 1.

SUPER: DEMONSTRATION 2.

SUPER: DEMONSTRATION 3.

ANNCR: Power Pro. The most powerful dustbuster yet.

SUPER: BLACK & DECKER.

**623**

(MUSIC: "GONE FISHIN" THROUGHOUT)

SUPER: THE FRESHEST FISH ARE AT THE SEAFOOD PLACE AT THE PAN PACIFIC HOTEL.

**624**
**ART DIRECTOR**
Walter Campbell
**WRITER**
Tom Carty
**AGENCY PRODUCERS**
Sarah Jacobs, Jenny O'Connell
**PRODUCTION COMPANY**
Tony Kaye Films
**DIRECTOR**
Patricia Murphy
**CLIENT**
KISS FM
**AGENCY**
BBDO/London

**625**
**ART DIRECTOR**
Don Schneider
**WRITER**
Lee Garfinkel
**AGENCY PRODUCERS**
Sandi Bachom, Bob Kirschen
**PRODUCTION COMPANY**
Steve Horn, Inc.
**DIRECTOR**
Steve Horn
**CLIENT**
Pepsi Cola
**AGENCY**
BBDO/New York

**626**
**ART DIRECTOR**
Don Schneider
**WRITERS**
Lee Garfinkel, Jonathan Mandell
**AGENCY PRODUCERS**
Regina Ebel, Bob Kirschen
**PRODUCTION COMPANY**
Pytka Productions
**DIRECTOR**
Joe Pytka
**CLIENT**
Pepsi Cola
**AGENCY**
BBDO/New York

**627**
**ART DIRECTOR**
Joseph Cianciotti
**WRITER**
Joseph Cianciotti
**AGENCY PRODUCER**
Joseph Cianciotti
**PRODUCTION COMPANY**
Epoch Films
**DIRECTOR**
Jeff Preiss
**CLIENT**
Metropolitan Transportation Authority
**AGENCY**
Bergelt Litchfield Raboy & Tsao/New York

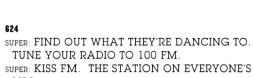

**624**
SUPER: FIND OUT WHAT THEY'RE DANCING TO. TUNE YOUR RADIO TO 100 FM.
SUPER: KISS FM. THE STATION ON EVERYONE'S LIPS.

**625**
BAND: Let's get it started.
ANNCR: MC Hammer, rap star and Pepsi drinker. Well, today, we secretly replaced his Pepsi with Coke.
ANNCR: Let's see what happens.
MC HAMMER: (SINGING) *Feelings, nothing more than feelings.*
YOUNG GUY: Hammer!
MC HAMMER: Proper!
SUPER: PEPSI. THE CHOICE OF A NEW GENERATION.

THE SUBWAY

**626**

(MUSIC: UPBEAT)

OLD WOMAN 1: Rock and roll is okay but I prefer rap.

OLD MAN 2: Awesome.

DELIVERY MAN 1: Wait a second. Shady Acres was supposed to get the Coke and the frat house was supposed to get thePepsi.

DELIVERY MAN 2: Coke, Pepsi, what's the difference?

(MUSIC: CLASSICAL)

FRAT BOY: I-24.

(MUSIC: UPBEAT)

OLD MAN 2: This is radical.

SUPER: PEPSI. THE CHOICE OF A NEW GENERATION.

**627**

CLARA: We see them working.

PHYLLIS: It's evident. We see it.

CLARA: We see them working.

PHYLLIS: We see it.

(SFX: MACHINE NOISE)

CLARA: They're fixing the tracks here.

PHYLLIS: Well, they're fixing the tracks, the trains.

CLARA: They put in a new escalator downstairs. They fixed this whole station beautifully.

PHYLLIS: They repaired. . .

CLARA: They're working very hard.

PHYLLIS: They repaired the tracks.

(SFX: MACHINE NOISE)

PHYLLIS: We're not there yet.

CLARA: They're trying to finish up.

PHYLLIS: When it'll be finished. . .

CLARA: It'll be lovely.

PHYLLIS: It'll be better.

(SFX: TRAIN RUNNING THROUGH TUNNEL)

PHYLLIS: You have to be patient.

CLARA: Let. . .

PHYLLIS: These things take time.

CLARA: Yes. I agree with her.

(SFX: TRAIN ON ELEVATED TRACKS)

SUPER: THE SUBWAY. WE'RE COMING BACK. SO YOU COME BACK.

Are your
eye's
trying
EYE L
to tell
you
something?

**628**

(SFX: RAIN AND WIPERS WITH CARS PASSING OCCASIONALLY)
WALLACE: Can't wait to get home.
DESMOND: Not long now.
WALLACE: Dive straight into a lovely splishy wishy
  Optrex bath.
DESMOND: Absolutely.
WALLACE: I'm amazed he can find his way home
  in this.
DESMOND: Yeah.
WALLACE: Oh look, there's that ten miles to
  Uxbridge sign again.
DESMOND: Yeah.
WALLACE: And there's that funny old church
  again.
DESMOND: Ho ho yeah.
WALLACE: Can't wait to get home.
DESMOND: Not long now.
ANNCR: Optrex Drops.  Are your eyes trying to tell
  you something?

**629**

(SFX: EXPLODING VOLCANO)
(MUSIC: PEACEFUL, CALM AND SOOTHING)
SUPER: ASILONE, YOUR SOLUTION TO
  INDIGESTION.  CROOKES HEALTHCARE.

**630**

(MUSIC: OPERA THROUGHOUT)

SUPER: GAETANO DONIZETTI,
COMPOSER. (1797 - 1848)

ANNCR: Gaetano Donizetti stunned Europe with
his wildly fantastic operas . . . leaving
audiences everywhere wondering how he
could possibly conjure up such beautiful
madness. . . Eventually, everyone stopped
wondering.

SUPER: COMMITTED TO LOCAL ASYLUM, 1844.

ANNCR: The opera.

SUPER: PORTLAND OPERA. ANYTHING
BUT STUFFY.

**631**

(MUSIC: ORCHESTRAL THROUGHOUT)

SUPER: ALESSANDRO MORESCHI,
CASRATO. (1858 - 1922)

ANNCR: In order to preserve his beautifully high-
pitched voice . . . Alessandro Moreschi
embraced the operatic tradition of the
"castrati" . . . and had himself castrated.
And to think all we're asking you to give the
opera. . . is a listen.

ANNCR: The opera.

SUPER: PORTLAND OPERA. ANYTHING
BUT STUFFY.

## CONSUMER TELEVISION
## :30 SINGLE

**632**
**ART DIRECTOR**
Terry Schneider
**WRITER**
Greg Eiden
**AGENCY PRODUCERS**
Josh Reynolds, Laura Simpson
**PRODUCTION COMPANY**
James Productions
**DIRECTOR**
Denny Carlson
**CLIENT**
Portland General Electric
**AGENCY**
Borders Perrin & Norrander/
Portland

**633**
**ART DIRECTORS**
Bryan Buckley, Frank Todaro,
Taras Wayner
**WRITERS**
Bryan Buckley, Frank Todaro,
Hank Perlman
**AGENCY PRODUCER**
Valerie Edwards
**PRODUCTION COMPANY**
Sandbank Films
**DIRECTOR**
David Simpson
**CLIENT**
New York Restaurant Group/
Smith & Wollensky
**AGENCY**
Buckley DeCerchio Cavalier/
New York

**634**
**ART DIRECTOR**
Frank Haggerty
**WRITER**
Kerry Casey
**AGENCY PRODUCER**
Jack Steinman
**PRODUCTION COMPANY**
Glen Lau Production
**DIRECTOR**
Glen Lau
**CLIENT**
Normark
**AGENCY**
Carmichael Lynch/
Minneapolis

**635**
**ART DIRECTORS**
John Staffen, Gary McKendry
**WRITERS**
Marty Cooke, Matt Sherring
**AGENCY PRODUCER**
Andrew Chinich
**PRODUCTION COMPANY**
Medialab
**DIRECTOR**
Kevin Godley
**CLIENT**
NYNEX Information Resources
**AGENCY**
Chiat/Day/Mojo, New York

PGE
Portland General Electric

**632**
(MUSIC: MOODY, WIND INSTRUMENTS)
ANNCR: The frightening thing about downed
    powerlines is that it's impossible to tell if
    they're dangerous or not. Just like it's hard to
    tell a harmless bull snake from a deadly
    cottonmouth. Now, would you pick one
    up. . .hoping it's the harmless snake? If you
    see a downed powerline, don't touch it. Call
    PGE. We'll handle it.
SUPER: PORTLAND GENERAL ELECTRIC.

**633**
WAITER 1: Alas poor Yorick.
WAITER 2: You are nothing but a two bit punk in a
    three piece suit.
WAITER 3: Badges. We don't need no stinkin'
    badges here.
WAITER 4: Deny thy Father, . . .
WAITER 5: To be or not to be. That is the question.
WAITER 6: Adrian.
WAITER 7: Hey Stella. Stella.
WAITER 8: You talking to me?
WAITER 9: You dirty rat.
ANNCR: No one's ever discovered a great actor at
    Smith & Wollensky. Only great steak.
SUPER: SMITH & WOLLENSKY.
    "THE QUINTESSENTIAL NEW YORK
    STEAKHOUSE." - GOURMET MAGAZINE.
SUPER: SMITH & WOLLENSKY. 49TH & 3RD NEW
    YORK CITY.

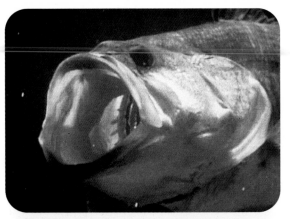

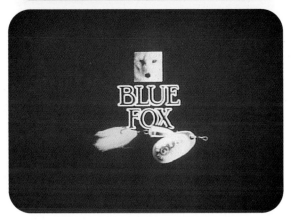

**634**

(SFX: HUMAN YAWNS)

ANNCR: Some days, you just have to wake 'em up. The Super Vibrax. It creates bell vibrations that get fish. . . up and at 'em.

SUPER: BLUE FOX.

**635**

COACH: To bunt or not to bunt . . . that is the question. Whether 'tis nobler to lay one down the line or to swing for the fences, to play per chance to win. And by a win to say we end this dreadful streak. A hit, a hit, my kingdom for a hit.

NYNEX TITLE: THEATRICAL COACHES.

ANNCR: If it's out there, it's in here. The NYNEX Yellow Pages. Why would anyone need another?

**CONSUMER TELEVISION
:30 SINGLE**

**636**
**ART DIRECTOR**
Ian Potter
**WRITER**
Steve Rabosky
**AGENCY PRODUCER**
Helen Erb
**PRODUCTION COMPANY**
Limelight
**DIRECTOR**
Alex Proyas
**CLIENT**
Taylor Made Golf Company
**AGENCY**
Chiat/Day/Mojo, Venice

**637**
**ART DIRECTOR**
Craig Tanimoto
**WRITER**
Joe Alexander
**AGENCY PRODUCER**
Kate O'Toole
**PRODUCTION COMPANY**
Departure Films
**DIRECTOR**
Ali Selim
**CLIENT**
YMCA of Minneapolis
**AGENCY**
Clarity Coverdale
Rueff/Minneapolis

**638**
**ART DIRECTORS**
Donna Weinheim,
John Colquhoun
**WRITERS**
Cliff Freeman, Rick LeMoine
**AGENCY PRODUCER**
Anne Kurtzman
**PRODUCTION COMPANY**
Robins & Associates
**DIRECTOR**
Bill Mason
**CLIENT**
Hills Department Stores
**AGENCY**
Cliff Freeman & Partners/
New York

**639**
**ART DIRECTOR**
Donna Weinheim
**WRITER**
Cliff Freeman
**AGENCY PRODUCER**
Anne Kurtzman
**PRODUCTION COMPANY**
Story Piccolo Guliner
**DIRECTOR**
Mark Story
**CLIENT**
Hills Department Stores
**AGENCY**
Cliff Freeman & Partners/
New York

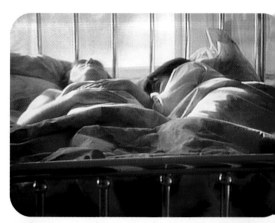

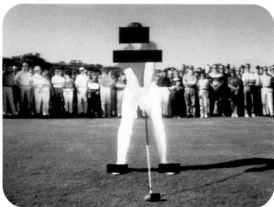

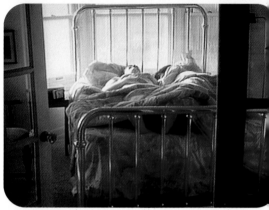

**636**
ANNCR: We can't show you this professional
golfer's shoes, because he's under contract
with another company to wear them. We
can't show you his ball for the same reason.
Or his shirt. Or even his visor. The only thing
we can show you is his driver. Because
nobody had to pay him to use it. Taylor
Made metalwoods. Played by more pros than
any other wood.
SUPER: TAYLOR MADE. DON'T HOLD BACK.

**637**
(SFX: BIRDS CHIRPING, MAN SNORING, CLOCK TICKING CONTINUES
  THROUGHOUT)
ANNCR: Remember what life was like . . . before
you had kids?
SUPER: YMCA SUMMER CAMP.
MINNEAPOLIS, ST. PAUL.

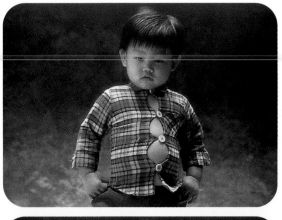

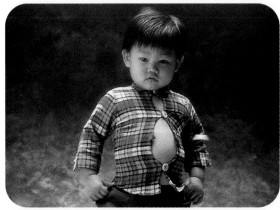

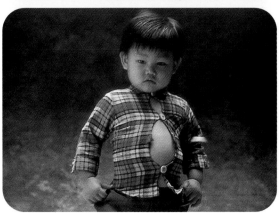

**638**

ANNCR: Why come to Hills Baby Fair?  Well, kids do grow out of things.

(SFX: RUBBER STRETCHING, SUSPENDERS SNAPPING, BUTTONS POPPING)

ANNCR: Hills Baby Fair.  Just in the nick of time.  Hills.  We're the store for great family values.

SUPER: HILLS DEPARTMENT STORES.

**639**

WOMAN: So, you think I did good with the Christmas presents?

MAN: Yes, but how could we afford all of this?

WOMAN: Well, I cut a few corners.

MAN: This could work.

WOMAN: Yes, the key thing is keeping everything on this side of the room.

MAN: Which you've done nicely.

RELATIVE: More egg nog please.  More egg nog please.

(SFX: FAMILY SINGING IN BACKGROUND)

ANNCR: No cutting corners when you shop at Hills.  With the best brands and prices, we're the store for great family values.

SUPER: HILLS DEPARTMENT STORES.

**640**
**ART DIRECTORS**
Donna Weinheim, John Colquhoun
**WRITER**
Cliff Freeman
**AGENCY PRODUCER**
Anne Kurtzman
**PRODUCTION COMPANY**
Story Piccolo Guliner
**DIRECTOR**
Mark Story
**CLIENT**
Little Caesar's Enterprises
**AGENCY**
Cliff Freeman & Partners/
New York

**641**
**ART DIRECTOR**
Shony Rivnay
**WRITER**
Johanna Quinn Templeton
**AGENCY PRODUCER**
Joe Scibetta
**PRODUCTION COMPANY**
Berkofsky Barrett Productions
**DIRECTOR**
Julian Cottrell
**CLIENT**
Mobil International
**AGENCY**
DDB Needham Worldwide,
New York

**642**
**ART DIRECTOR**
Dennis Stevens
**WRITER**
Johanna Quinn Templeton
**AGENCY PRODUCER**
Debbie Lawrence
**PRODUCTION COMPANY**
Petersen Communications
**DIRECTOR**
John St. Clair
**CLIENT**
Bermuda Department of
Tourism
**AGENCY**
DDB Needham Worldwide,
New York

**643**
**ART DIRECTOR**
Max Jerome
**WRITER**
Stacy Wall
**AGENCY PRODUCER**
Tricia Caruso
**PRODUCTION COMPANY**
Jones Films
**DIRECTOR**
Phil Morrison
**CLIENT**
NBA Hoop Cards
**AGENCY**
Deutsch/New York

**640**
MAN 1: Two pizzas with ten toppings for $9.99?
  That's impossible.
MAN 2: Are you kidding?  Anything's possible . . .
  look at this . . . Sistine Chapel on the head of
  a pin.
WOMAN: Two pizzas with ten toppings for $9.99?
  That's impossible!
MAN: Anything's possible.  I taught my dog to
  say I love you.
DOG: I wuv you.  I wuv you.
ANNCR:  Little Caesars has done the impossible.
  Two pizzas with ten toppings for $9.99.
LITTLE CAESAR: Pizza!  Pizza!

**641**
ANNCR: Take a conventional motor oil.  Take
  Mobil 1.  Start them at 35 below.
(SFX: CAR RACE THROUGHOUT)
ANNCR: Then push them to extremes . . . where
  temperatures inside your engine can
  reach 570.
(SFX: BRAKES SCREECHING)
ANNCR: Now which one would you choose?
SUPER: MOBIL 1.
ANNCR: Mobil 1.  Isn't your car worth the extra
  protection?

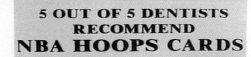

**642**

SUPER: BERMUDA. SHORTS.

ANNCR: Sweeping views, late-night blues, stirring sound, paradise found.

SUPER: BERMUDA. A SHORT TRIP TO THE PERFECT HOLIDAY.

**643**

VO DENTIST 1: NBA Hoops Cards.

SUPER: 5 OUT OF 5 DENTISTS RECOMMEND NBA HOOPS CARDS.

DENTIST 1: These cards have my full support.

DENTIST 2: Great source of basketball information.

DENTIST 3: Action photos . . .

VO DENTIST 3: . . . career stats . . .

DENTIST 3: . . .height, weight . . .

DENTIST 1: Earvin Magic Jackson; he's famous.

DENTIST 3: . . . where they were born.

DENTIST 4: Collect them all.

DENTIST 2: NBA Hoops Cards, great pictures.

HYGIENIST: Cool stats.

DENTIST 5: No Gum.

DENTIST 4: No Gum.

SUPER: GREAT PICTURES. COOL STATS. NO GUM.

VO DENTIST 1: As a group, I would say they have some of the best teeth I have ever seen.

DENTIST 5: Ah, you can spit now.

## CONSUMER TELEVISION :30 SINGLE

**644**
**ART DIRECTOR**
Barbara Scardino
**WRITER**
Dean Buckhorn
**AGENCY PRODUCER**
Bruce Wellington
**PRODUCTION COMPANY**
Holtzman Productions
**DIRECTOR**
Wayne Gibson
**CLIENT**
Bob's Big Boy
**AGENCY**
Earle Palmer Brown/Bethesda

**645**
**ART DIRECTOR**
Wayne Gibson
**WRITER**
Dean Buckhorn
**AGENCY PRODUCER**
Bruce Wellington
**PRODUCTION COMPANY**
Holtzman Productions
**DIRECTOR**
Wayne Gibson
**CLIENT**
Roy Rogers
**AGENCY**
Earle Palmer Brown/Bethesda

**646**
**ART DIRECTOR**
Jeff Tresidder
**WRITER**
Jan Pettit
**AGENCY PRODUCER**
Frank Soukup
**PRODUCTION COMPANY**
Big City Films
**CLIENT**
Sovran Bank
**AGENCY**
Earle Palmer Brown/Norfolk

**647**
**ART DIRECTOR**
Peter Holmes
**WRITER**
Peter Holmes
**AGENCY PRODUCER**
David Eades
**PRODUCTION COMPANY**
Rawi Sherman Films
**DIRECTOR**
Richard Radke
**CLIENT**
Rubinet
**AGENCY**
Franklin Dallas Kundinger/
North York, Ontario

**644**
OLD MAN: The wife and I have been coming to Bob's Big Boy for over 40 years. Every Wednesday. And every Wednesday, we order the Original Big Boy Burger . . . french fries . . . and a salad. Then I heard they dropped the price to just $3.49 . . . so I figured I'd come to Bob's more often. So here I am. And you know what . . . It's only Tuesday. And you know what else . . . this ain't my wife.
SUPER: BOB'S BIG BOY COMBO $3.49.
ANNCR: The Original Big Boy Combo, just $3.49. Any day of the week.

**645**
FISH 1: Hey . . . hey . . . she's home.
FISH 2: Alright . . . chowtime.
FISH 1: Oh man . . . flakes! I hate flakes.
FISH 2: Hey, what's she got?
FISH 1: Oh man . . . it's Roy Roger's Big Chicken Club.
FISH 2: Holy Moly . . . look at all that chicken . . . and bacon . . .
FISH 1: Oh man . . . and toppings.
FISH 2: C'mon, c'mon . . . let's get it.
FISH 1: Alright. Hit the music.
(SFX: SHARK MUSIC BEGINS)
(SFX: THUD OF FISH HITTING GLASS. SQUEAK OF SLIDING)
FISH 1: Oh man . . . the glass . . . I forgot the glass.
SUPER: ROY ROGERS. NEW BIG CHICKEN CLUB.
ANNCR: Roy's Big Chicken Club. Only for a limited time.
FISH 1: Limited time! Hit the music.
(SFX: SHARK MUSIC BEGINS)

**646**

(SFX: GARBLED TALKING)

CHILD: Daddy!

ANNCR: Last week, the Hendersons bought a new video camera. It has all the latest features . . including a zoom lens and low light capabilities.

CHILD: I made the camera go splash.

ANNCR: In fact, that camera does just about everything, except float.

FATHER: You what?!

ANNCR: Fortunately, the Hendersons paid for their new video camera with a check from their Sovran Select account, which has built-in Buyer's Coverage.

FATHER: Helen!!

ANNCR: So even though they sunk some money into it . . .

(SFX: BZZT OF PICTURE GOING OUT)

ANNCR: . . . they'll have no trouble getting it all back.

SUPER: INTRODUCING SOVRAN SELECT.
SOVRAN BANK.

**647**

ANNCR: This is Gino. Gino is studying to be a plumber. He's looking forward to a simple life of fixing leaky faucets . . . corroded faucets that don't work. But Rubinet faucets have changed all that. They're guaranteed not to leak. Guaranteed not to corrode. They're guaranteed for five years. So what's a guy like Gino supposed to do?

GINO: Drywall.

ANNCR: Rubinet. The faucet most plumbers don't recommend.

**648**
ART DIRECTOR
Russell Wailes
WRITER
Rupert Sutton
AGENCY PRODUCER
Erika Issitt
PRODUCTION COMPANY
Limelight
DIRECTOR
John Lloyd
CLIENT
Fuji Camera
AGENCY
Generator Partnership/London

**649**
ART DIRECTOR
Rich Silverstein
WRITER
Jeffrey Goodby
AGENCY PRODUCER
Debbie King
PRODUCTION COMPANY
Bassett Productions
CLIENT
Heinz Pet Products/
Skippy Premium Dog Food
AGENCY
Goodby Berlin & Silverstein/
San Francisco

**650**
ART DIRECTOR
David Page
WRITER
Dave O'Hare
PHOTOGRAPHER
Barney Colangelo
AGENCY PRODUCER
Cindy Fluitt
PRODUCTION COMPANY
Fleet Street Pictures
DIRECTOR
Jeffrey Goodby
CLIENT
Northern California Honda
Dealers
AGENCY
Goodby Berlin & Silverstein/
San Francisco

**651**
ART DIRECTOR
Michael Vitiello
WRITER
Rochelle Klein
AGENCY PRODUCER
Rachel Novak
PRODUCTION COMPANY
Coppos Films
DIRECTOR
Mark Coppos
CLIENT
Maidenform
AGENCY
Levine Huntley Vick &
Beaver/New York

**648**

(MUSIC: HAPPY THROUGHOUT)
SUPER:  IF ONLY I HAD A QUICKSNAP.
ANNCR: The Fuji Quicksnap . . .the camera and
   film . . . rolled into one!

**649**

INTERVIEWER: I just want to ask you a couple of
   quick questions.
TENNIS LADY: We're playing a tournament.  I'm
   sorry, we can't . . .
INTERVIEWER: Can I ask you, just really quickly?
TENNIS LADY: Alright.
INTERVIEWER: Which of these two leading dog
   foods looks the best to you?
LAWNBOWLER: Heh, heh, heh.
WOMAN 1: This one.
WOMAN 2: That one.
TENNIS LADY: This.
INTERVIEWER: That's Skippy Premium.  It just plain
   looks better, doesn't it.
SUPER: IT JUST PLAIN LOOKS BETTER.
JOCK: This is conceptual art, right?
LAWNBOWLER: Heh, heh, heh.
DRIVER: I'm not a dog by the way.  Why don't
   you ask a dog?
INTERVIEWER: Woody, what's it going to take to get
   you to stop eating that Skippy Premium?  How
   about a one hundred dollar bill?

**650**

SUPER: SANTA CLARA, CALIFORNIA.

GUY: All I did was build a computer. Next thing you know, I own this company, it goes public, the stock splits, I got a ton of money. I guess along the way I turned into a real jerk. I just want to simplify things, you know? Get my values back. That's why I'm here.

INTERCOM: Parts, line three. Parts, line three.

SALESMAN: I think you're doing the right thing.

SUPER: IS HONDA THE PERFECT CAR FOR NORTHERN CALIFORNIA, OR WHAT?

SUPER: THE PROOF'S AT YOUR NORTHERN CALIFORNIA HONDA DEALER.

SALESMAN: Now, based on those feelings, are we talkin' two doors or four?

**651**

(MUSIC: "DID YOU EVER SEE A LASSIE?")

ANNCR: Isn't it nice to live in a time when women aren't being pushed around so much anymore?

CONSUMER TELEVISION
:30 SINGLE

**652**
**ART DIRECTOR**
David Ayriss
**WRITER**
Scott Vincent
**AGENCY PRODUCER**
Shelley Winfrey
**PRODUCTION COMPANY**
Livingston & Company
**CLIENT**
Seattle Mariners
**AGENCY**
Livingston & Company/Seattle

**653**
**ART DIRECTOR**
Benjamin BenSimon
**WRITER**
David Innis
**AGENCY PRODUCER**
Sandy Cole
**PRODUCTION COMPANY**
Calibre Digital Design
**DIRECTOR**
Chris Armstrong
**CLIENT**
Ciba-Geigy/Otrivin Nasal Spray
**AGENCY**
MacLaren: Lintas/Toronto

**654**
**ART DIRECTOR**
Steve Montgomery
**WRITER**
Joe Lovering
**AGENCY PRODUCER**
Carol Singer
**PRODUCTION COMPANY**
Griner/Questa & Schrom
**DIRECTOR**
Mike Schrom
**CLIENT**
Volvo
**AGENCY**
Scali McCabe Sloves/New York

**655**
**ART DIRECTOR**
Tim Teegarden
**WRITER**
Mark Simon
**AGENCY PRODUCER**
Heikki Kuld
**PRODUCTION COMPANY**
The Partners
**DIRECTOR**
Doug Moshian
**CLIENT**
Leon's
**AGENCY**
W. B. Doner & Company/
Southfield

**652**
(SFX: CARTOONISH SOUNDS OF PEOPLE GETTING CLOBBERED ON THE HEAD)
ANNCR: Just a reminder. Next Saturday is Helmet Night. Free to kids fourteen and under.
SUPER: HELMET NIGHT. SATURDAY, JULY 14. THE NEW MARINERS.

**653**
(SFX: QUIET RESTAURANT SOUNDS, CONGESTED BREATHING)
SUPER: DER I WAS WID DIS LOBELY LADY. MY NOSE TOTALLY BLOGGED. SHE LOOKED DEEB INDO MY EYES. I GASPED FOR BREAD. TOLD HER I COULDN'T BREED. SHE SLABBED ME. I DEED PROFESSIONAL HELB.
SUPER: THE NAZAL SPRAY BOST REGOMMENDED BY DOGDORS.
(SFX: SQUIRT, SQUIRT)
(SFX: SIGH OF RELIEF)
SUPER: THE NASAL SPRAY MOST RECOMMENDED BY DOCTORS.
SUPER: OTRIVIN DECONGESTANT NASAL SPRAY.

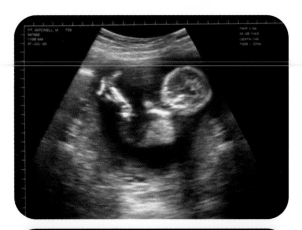

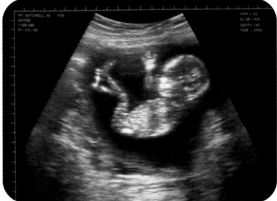

**654**

(SFX: HEARTBEAT)

ANNCR: Is something inside telling you to buy a Volvo?

SUPER: VOLVO. A CAR YOU CAN BELIEVE IN.

**655**

MAN 1: The only way to describe it . . . is to call it a miracle.

ANNCR: Leon's No Money Miracle.

MAN 2: It gave me the power to turn water into ice.

ANNCR: Everything you want for your home with no money down. No interest. And no payment till next year.

WOMAN: You want proof? This dinette set was not here two days ago.

ANNCR: Come to Leon's now and witness the miracle for yourself.

MAN 1: I can sit! I can sit!!

**CONSUMER TELEVISION
:30 SINGLE**

**656**
**ART DIRECTOR**
Rick McQuiston
**WRITER**
Jerry Cronin
**AGENCY PRODUCER**
Will McDonald
**PRODUCTION COMPANY**
Pytka Productions
**DIRECTOR**
Joe Pytka
**CLIENT**
Nike
**AGENCY**
Wieden & Kennedy/Portland

**657**
**ART DIRECTOR**
Craig Tanimoto
**WRITER**
Bob Moore
**AGENCY PRODUCER**
Liza Leeds
**PRODUCTION COMPANY**
Pittman/Hensley
**DIRECTOR**
Donna Pittman
**CLIENT**
Nike
**AGENCY**
Wieden & Kennedy/Portland

**658**
**ART DIRECTOR**
Michael Prieve
**WRITER**
Jim Riswold
**AGENCY PRODUCER**
Bill Davenport
**PRODUCTION COMPANY**
Propaganda
**DIRECTOR**
David Fincher
**CLIENT**
Nike
**AGENCY**
Wieden & Kennedy/Portland

**659**
**ART DIRECTOR**
Michael Prieve
**WRITER**
Jim Riswold
**AGENCY PRODUCER**
Bill Davenport
**PRODUCTION COMPANY**
40 Acres & A Mule
**DIRECTOR**
Spike Lee
**CLIENT**
Nike
**AGENCY**
Wieden & Kennedy/Portland

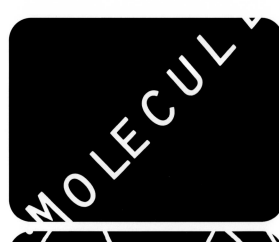

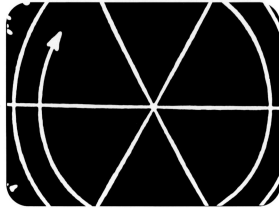

**656**
(SFX: OCEAN AND SEAGULLS)
SUPER: THE CONDENSED LIFE STORY OF THE SAN ONOFRE SENIOR SURFERS.
SUPER: SLEEP
(MUSIC: SURF MUSIC THROUGHOUT)
SUPER: SLEEP.
SUPER: SURF.
SUPER: SLEEP.
SUPER: SURF.
SUPER: SLEEP.
SUPER: SURF.
SUPER: SLEEP.
SUPER: GO TO HEAVEN.
SUPERS: SURF, SURF, SURF, SURF, SURF, SURF.
SUPER: JUST DO IT. NIKE.

**657**
(SFX: THROUGHOUT)
SUPER: MAGNIFIED 10 TRILLION TIMES.
ANNCR: The smallest particle known to man is the . . .Quark. Quarks throw a party and form . . .
SUPER: ELECTRON.
ANNCR: . . . an electron. Electrons form . . .
SUPER: MOLECULES.
ANNCR: . . . molecules . . . and molecules form things like . . .
SUPER: FIG. 1. SPATULA.
ANNCR: . . . spatulas. . .
SUPER: FIG. 2. PLATYPUS.
ANNCR: . . .and platypuses. Sometimes the fastest and lightest molecules get together and form a . .
SUPER: FIG. 3. CHEETAH.
ANNCR: . . . cheetah . . . or a . . .
SUPER: (A.) ROCKET.
ANNCR: . . . rocket . . .or . . .
SUPER: FIG. 5. JERRY.
ANNCR: . . . Jerry Rice. Under ideal conditions they form the Nike . . . Air Trainer TW Lite. The lightest . . . fastest . . . Nike cross-training shoe . . . in the world. So you can wait . . .12 billion years for these . . . to occur randomly in nature . . . or buy a pair preassembled today. Isn't science wonderful?
SUPER: NIKE. JUST DO IT.

**658**

(MUSIC: THROUGHOUT)

ROBINSON: This season, Mister Robinson averaged twenty-four points a game, twelve boards, four blocked shots, shot over fifty percent from the floor, made the All-star team, and led his team to the play-offs . . .with a really good record. Can you say, Contract Renegotiations? Mister Robinson can.

SUPER: THE FORCE SERIES. FORCE BY NIKE.

**659**

MARS: Yo, Mars Blackmon here with my main man, Michael Jordan . . . and Professor Douglas Kirkpatrick of the American Institute of Aeronautics and Astronautics. Yo Professor, how does Mike defy gravity, do you know, do you know, do you know, do you know?

PROFESSOR: Michael Jordan overcomes the acceleration of gravity by the application of his muscle power in the vertical plane thus producing a low altitude earth orbit.

MARS: A what?

PROFESSOR: Do you know what I mean? Do you know, do you know, do you know?

SUPER: AIR JORDAN FROM NIKE.

MARS: Money, check him out!

**CONSUMER TELEVISION
:30 SINGLE**

**660**
**ART DIRECTOR**
Michael Prieve
**WRITER**
Jim Riswold
**AGENCY PRODUCER**
Bill Davenport
**PRODUCTION COMPANY**
Propaganda
**DIRECTOR**
David Fincher
**CLIENT**
Nike
**AGENCY**
Wieden & Kennedy/Portland

**661**
**ART DIRECTOR**
Michael Prieve
**WRITER**
Jim Riswold
**AGENCY PRODUCER**
Bill Davenport
**PRODUCTION COMPANY**
40 Acres & A Mule
**DIRECTOR**
Spike Lee
**CLIENT**
Nike
**AGENCY**
Wieden & Kennedy/Portland

**662**
**ART DIRECTOR**
Kevin McCarty
**WRITERS**
Chuck Withrow,
Tom Woodward
**AGENCY PRODUCER**
Michael Chaney
**PRODUCTION COMPANY**
James Productions
**DIRECTOR**
Jim Lund
**CLIENT**
True Temper
**AGENCY**
Wyse Advertising/Cleveland

**663**
**ART DIRECTOR**
Jill Bohannan
**WRITER**
Scott Burns
**AGENCY PRODUCER**
Lee Goldberg
**PRODUCTION COMPANY**
Red Dog Films
**DIRECTOR**
Marc Chiat
**CLIENT**
Hartmarx Specialty Stores
**AGENCY**
Young & Rubicam/Chicago

**660**
(SFX: KNOCKING AT DOOR)
ROBINSON: Who could that be? It's Coach Brown, with today's word.
BROWN: Today's word is, transition game.
ROBINSON: Oooooo, transition game. Can you say transition game?
BROWN: This is exactly what I'm talkin' about. You've gotta pass the ball to the guard. We've gotta break. We've gotta run, run, rebound, rebound, rebound. Running is when you move your legs. Quickly, David, you think you're . . .
ROBINSON: I don't think we're gonna have Coach Brown on the show anymore.
BROWN: If you don't do that I'm going to have to yell at you again.
SUPER: THE FORCE SERIES. BY NIKE.

**661**
MARS: Yo, Mars Blackmon here with my main man, Michael Jordan. Yo Mike, what makes you the best player in the universe? Is it the vicious dunks?
JORDAN: No, Mars.
MARS: Is it the haircut?
JORDAN: No, Mars.
MARS: Is it the shoes?
JORDAN: No, Mars.
MARS: Is it the extra-long shorts?
JORDAN: No, Mars.
MARS: It's the shoes then, right?
JORDAN: Naw.
MARS: Is it the short socks?
JORDAN: No, Mars.
MARS: The shoes. The shoes. Shoes. The shoes. You're sure it's not the shoes?
JORDAN: I'm sure, Mars.
SUPER: MR. JORDAN'S OPINIONS DO NOT NECESSARILY REFLECT THOSE OF NIKE, INC.
MARS: What about the shoes?
JORDAN: No, Mars.
SUPER: NIKE.

BASKIN WARDROBE SALE

**662**

(MUSIC: DAWN OF MAN MUSIC)

(SFX: "THWACK", CONVERSATIONAL GRUNTS)

SUBTITLE: HE TRIED TO KILL IT.

(SFX: "THWACK", CONVERSATIONAL GRUNTS, SUBTLE PUT DOWNS, TWITTERS)

SUBTITLE: NICE SHOT, ALICE.

(SFX: CONFIDENT GRUNT)

ANNCR: Introducing Black Gold, shafts from True Temper.

(SFX: BIG "THWACK", OOOHS AND AHHS)

SUBTITLE: OOOH.

ANNCR: If you're not using our shafts . . . .you're just carrying clubs.

(SFX: GRUNT)

SUPER: TRUE TEMPER SPORTS. A BLACK & DECKER COMPANY.

**663**

ANNCR: At the Baskin Spring Wardrobe Sale almost every suit and tailored outfit in the store is under $400 when you buy two. Not two from last year. Not two that nobody else wanted. And not two that only come in two sizes. So, now you're probably asking yourself do I really need two suits? Everybody needs two suits.

SUPER: BASKIN WARDROBE SALE.

**CONSUMER TELEVISION
:30  CAMPAIGN**

**664**
**ART DIRECTOR**
Tony Davidson
**WRITER**
Kim Papworth
**AGENCY PRODUCER**
Sarah Pollitt
**PRODUCTION COMPANY**
Hutchins Film Company
**DIRECTORS**
Martin Brierly, Steve Lowe
**CLIENT**
Crookes Healthcare
**AGENCY**
BMP DDB Needham/London

**CONSUMER TELEVISION
:24 AND UNDER
SINGLE**

**665**
**ART DIRECTOR**
Dolores Marcoux
**WRITER**
Jim Aaby
**AGENCY PRODUCERS**
Steve Ropplo, Chuck Kinsinger
**PRODUCTION COMPANY**
Charlex
**CLIENT**
Webster Industries/Renew
Trash Bags
**AGENCY**
Backer Spielvogel Bates/
New York

**666**
**ART DIRECTOR**
Eddie Greenwood
**WRITER**
Marianne Little
**AGENCY PRODUCER**
Maggie Blundell
**PRODUCTION COMPANY**
John Swannell Films
**DIRECTOR**
Peter Chelsom
**CLIENT**
National Dairy Council
**AGENCY**
BMP DDB Needham/London

**667**
**ART DIRECTOR**
Jerry Gentile
**WRITER**
Rob Feakins
**AGENCY PRODUCER**
Jennifer Golub
**PRODUCTION COMPANY**
Coppos Films
**DIRECTOR**
Brent Thomas
**CLIENT**
Eveready Battery
**AGENCY**
Chiat/Day/Mojo, Venice

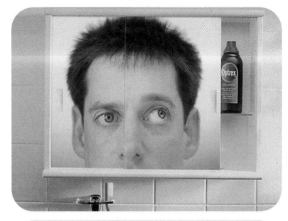

**664**
WALLACE: I spy with my little self something
    beginning with . . .O.
DESMOND: Optrex.
WALLACE: How did you know?
DESMOND: We've just had ten hours staring at a
    VDU screen.  And he is hoverin' over the
    medicine cabinet.  It was hardly going to be
    orangutan was it.
WALLACE: I'm only trying to raise morale till we
    get our Optrex.
DESMOND: Go on then.
WALLACE: It's your turn.
DESMOND: I spy with my little self something
    beginning with T.
WALLACE: Turnip?
DESMOND: No.
WALLACE: Train?
DESMOND: No.
WALLACE: Tadpole?
ANNCR: Are your eyes trying to tell you
    something?

**665**
DUBBED VOICE: By recycling this commercial, we
    saved a bundle.  That's the idea behind
    Renew . . . the first trash bag made almost
    entirely of recycled plastic.  We saved, so you
    save.  Everyone saves when you
    recycle and Renew.

**666**

GIRL: Want to come in for coffee? Haven't got any milk, though.

BOY: Alright then, see you.

SUPER: ARE YOU GETTING ENOUGH?

**667**

DIRECTOR: Cut, great take!

COWBOY: Maybe for you but my hemorrhoids are killing me.

ANNCR: Try Sitagin for fast relief . . .

(SFX: BOOM . . .BOOM . . .BOOM . . .)

ENERGIZER ANNCR: Still going. Nothing outlasts the Energizer. They keep going . . . .and going and . . .

CONSUMER TELEVISION
:24 AND UNDER
SINGLE

**668**
ART DIRECTOR
Mark Johnson
WRITER
Luke Sullivan
AGENCY PRODUCER
Judy Carter-Brink
PRODUCTION COMPANY
Sandbank Films
DIRECTOR
Henry Sandbank
CLIENT
Ralston Purina
AGENCY
Fallon McElligott/Minneapolis

**669**
ART DIRECTOR
Rich Silverstein
WRITER
Jeffrey Goodby
PHOTOGRAPHER
Rick Wise
AGENCY PRODUCER
Debbie King
PRODUCTION COMPANY
Bassett Productions
DIRECTORS
Jeffrey Goodby, Rich Silverstein
CLIENT
Heinz Pet Products/Skippy
Premium Dog Food
AGENCY
Goodby Berlin & Silverstein/
San Francisco

**670**
ART DIRECTOR
Dennis Soohoo
WRITERS
Andy Spade, Jennifer Noble
AGENCY PRODUCER
Amy Saunders
PRODUCTION COMPANY
Johns & Gorman Films
DIRECTOR
Gary Johns
CLIENT
Huffman Koos
AGENCY
Kirshenbaum & Bond/
New York

**671**
ART DIRECTOR
Dennis Soohoo
WRITERS
Andy Spade, Jennifer Noble
AGENCY PRODUCER
Amy Saunders
PRODUCTION COMPANY
Johns & Gorman Films
DIRECTOR
Gary Johns
CLIENT
Huffman Koos
AGENCY
Kirshenbaum & Bond/New York

**668**
ANNCR: If every dog in the world were a puppy, all we'd make is Puppy Chow. But they're not. That's why Purina makes a complete line of nutritious dog foods. Pet-tested. Veterinarian-recommended.
SUPER: PET-TESTED.  VETERINARIAN-RECOMMENDED.

**669**
INTERVIEWER: Which of these looks the best to you?
LAWNBOWLER: Heh, heh, heh.
WOMAN 1: This one.
WOMAN 2: That one.
TENNIS LADY: This.
INTERVIEWER: That's Skippy Premium.  It just plain looks better, doesn't it.
SUPER: IT JUST PLAIN LOOKS BETTER.
INTERVIEWER: Woody, what's it going to take to get you to stop eating that Skippy Premium?  How about a one hundred dollar bill, huh?

**670**

(MUSIC: "THE HUSTLE")
ANNCR: Twenty years ago, you could have bought this classic dining room from Huffman Koos and it would still be in style today. How many things can you say that about? Huffman Koos. Where you'll never think "What was I thinking?".
SUPER: HUFFMAN KOOS.

**671**

ANNCR: Twenty years ago, you could have bought this classic love seat from Huffman Koos and it would still be in style today. How many things can you say that about? Huffman Koos. Where you'll never think "What was I thinking?".
SUPER: HUFFMAN KOOS.

**672**
ART DIRECTOR
Mark Hughes
WRITER
Tom Cunniff
AGENCY PRODUCER
Charlie Curran
PRODUCTION COMPANY
Brad Christian Films
DIRECTOR
Brad Christian
CLIENT
Lea & Perrins
AGENCY
Lord Dentsu & Partners/
New York

**673**
ART DIRECTOR
Mark Hughes
WRITER
Tom Cunniff
AGENCY PRODUCER
Charlie Curran
PRODUCTION COMPANY
Brad Christian Films
DIRECTOR
Brad Christian
CLIENT
Lea & Perrins
AGENCY
Lord Dentsu & Partners/
New York

CONSUMER TELEVISION
:24 AND UNDER CAMPAIGN

**674**
ART DIRECTORS
Jerry Gentile, Steve Rabosky
WRITER
Rob Feakins
AGENCY PRODUCER
Jennifer Golub
PRODUCTION COMPANY
Coppos Films
DIRECTOR
Brent Thomas
CLIENT
Eveready Battery
AGENCY
Chiat/Day/Mojo, Venice

**675**
ART DIRECTOR
Bill Oberlander
WRITER
David Buckingham
AGENCY PRODUCER
Amy Saunders
PRODUCTION COMPANY
Glenn Ribble
DIRECTOR
Glenn Ribble
CLIENT
New York Post
AGENCY
Kirshenbaum & Bond/New York

**672**
(SFX: CHAINSAW REVVING)
(SFX: BILLBOARD FALLS)
(SFX: COWS CHEER, REVVING CHAINSAW)
ANNCR: Lea & Perrins Steak Sauce. The steak
 sauce only a cow could hate.

**673**
(SFX: GUNSHOT 1)
(SFX: GUNSHOT 2)
(SFX: COWS MOAN IN DISAPPOINTMENT)
ANNCR: Lea & Perrins Steak Sauce. The steak
 sauce only a cow could hate.

**674**

H.I.P.S. ANNCR: New on the Adventure Channel . . . They're tough . . . They're brave . . . And they're all women. They're H.I.P.S. You've never . . .

(SFX: . . . BOOM . . . BOOM . . .BOOM . . .)

ENERGIZER ANNCR: Still going. Nothing outlasts the Energizer. They keep going . . . And going . . .

**675**

(MUSIC: THROUGHOUT)

SUPER: THE THREE BIGGEST LIES IN NEW YORK.

SUPER: I LOVE BEING SINGLE.

SUPER: I DON'T HAVE ANY SPARE CHANGE.

SUPER: I NEVER READ THE POST.

SUPER: NEW YORK POST.

ANNCR: The New York Post. You know you love it.

THREATEN

PREACH

1-800-475-HOPE

National Citizens Commission on Alcoholism. (NCCA)
National Council on Alcoholism and Drug Dependence. (NCADD)

**676**
(MUSIC: THROUGHOUT)
WOMAN: What a disgrace. Getting drunk like that at your sister's graduation party. You should be ashamed of yourself.
ANNCR: You can preach.
WOMAN: A drinking problem. He's only fourteen, he doesn't have a drinking problem. It's a phase.
ANNCR: You can deny.
WOMAN: If you come home drunk again mister, you are gone. Out of my house! And don't think I won't do it. Do you hear me?!
ANNCR: Threaten . . .
WOMAN: You've got to stop. I'm begging you, please . .
ANNCR: Beg. . .
WOMAN: You're a drunk. Just look at you. Look at you! A drunk! A drunk!
ANNCR: Or yell. But if your son or daughter has a drinking problem, the best thing you can do is call. We're the National Council on Alcoholism and Drug Dependence.
We help thousands of people,every year. Call us at 1-800-475-HOPE. That's 1-800-475-HOPE. Get through to us and we'll help you get through to them. Just don't give up.

**677**
ANNCR: When Alzheimers disease strikes, the first thing it takes is your memory. Then it takes your ability to read, or even to speak. You forget how to do the simplest tasks, like cooking and washing. The brain degenerates until you forget what you look like and even your own image becomes terrifying. It robs you of all faculties until all that's left is an empty shell. Finally, you forget how to breathe. Alzheimers disease has no known cause, and no known cure. We desperately need money to care for those who've been robbed of everything they've got.

**Sometimes breaking the rules means staying in school**

BURGER KING

**678**

(MUSIC: "NEARER MY GOD TO THEE" BY SAM COOKE)

SUPER: THE JACKSONS. WASHINGTON, D.C.

JOHN: This is the White House. And this is where President George Bush lives at. The White House is very much bigger than my house.

MOTHER: (SINGING) *In a voice that was loud and clear.*

JOHN: This is the nation's Capitol where all the congressmen and senators pass the new laws and bills such as a, like a, taxation bill. They be arguing. I'm standing on the grounds at the Lincoln Memorial and on the inside they have a giant statue of Abraham Lincoln sitting down in the chair. I've lived in Washington, D.C. my whole life and this is my first time being at the Lincoln Memorial.

MOTHER: (SINGING) *Nearer my God to thee. . .*

JOHN: This is the Washington Monument. And this is a sight for the tourists to come and see, and as you go inside, go up the flight of stairs, look out the window. See down at the people. Little people look like little ants. Now we stands on the playground for the Chesapeake Tourist Complex. When they first put it up, the playground looked very nice. Now it don't look like nothing.

MOTHER: (SINGING) *Nearer my God to thee.*

JOHN: That doesn't mean much like the White House, the Capitol, the Monument, the Jefferson Memorial, the Lincoln Memorial. All that. The people don't like to come around here and check out the sights cause there's nothing really to look at. I don't really know, I think I might have a chance one day. I'm not hanging around in the wrong environment. Get a chance to get my GED or something.

SUPER: 40% OF THE STUDENTS IN OUR NATION'S CAPITAL DROPPED OUT OF HIGH SCHOOL IN 1989.

SUPER: SOMETIMES BREAKING THE RULES MEANS STAYING IN SCHOOL.

## PUBLIC SERVICE TELEVISION SINGLE

**679**
**ART DIRECTOR**
Stuart Byfield
**WRITER**
Greg Harper
**AGENCY PRODUCER**
Greg Harper
**PRODUCTION COMPANY**
Great Southern Films
**DIRECTOR**
Peta Schmidt
**CLIENT**
Transport Accident
Commission
**AGENCY**
Grey Advertising/Melbourne

**680**
**ART DIRECTOR**
Simon Morris
**WRITER**
Simon Carbery
**AGENCY PRODUCER**
Sarah Horry
**PRODUCTION COMPANY**
Rose Hackney Productions
**DIRECTOR**
David MacDonald
**CLIENT**
The Faith Foundation
**AGENCY**
Lowe Howard-Spink/London

**681**
**ART DIRECTOR**
Bob Meagher
**WRITER**
Steve Bassett
**AGENCY PRODUCERS**
Morty Baran, Randy Shreve
**PRODUCTION COMPANY**
BES Teleproductions
**CLIENT**
Partnership for a Drug-Free
America
**AGENCY**
The Martin Agency/Richmond

**682**
**ART DIRECTOR**
Kevin Thomas
**WRITER**
John Silver
**AGENCY PRODUCER**
Jeff Stickler
**PRODUCTION COMPANY**
Tony Kaye Films
**DIRECTOR**
Tony Kaye
**CLIENT**
Telethon-Homeless
**AGENCY**
Lowe Howard-Spink/London

**679**
FEMALE DRIVER: Where's Tracy?
AMBULANCEMAN: She's in the car at the moment.
FEMALE DRIVER: I'm alright. It's not very bad.
POLICEWOMAN: Can you remember at all how the accident occurred?
FEMALE DRIVER: I was changing a tape . . . we were in a bit of a hurry.
POLICEWOMAN: How fast were you going?
FEMALE DRIVER: Maybe we were going 85, 90 or someth . .
POLICEWOMAN: Do you realise what speed zone it is along here?
FEMALE DRIVER: Oh, my mum, can you call my mum.
POLICEWOMAN: I'll call her.
FEMALE DRIVER: Can I go and see her?
AMBULANCEMAN / POLICEWOMAN: No. It's best to stay here.
FEMALE DRIVER: No, I really want to see her.
AMBULANCEMAN: Alison, I'll come down.
FEMALE DRIVER: Oh gee. . . Where is she . . . I can't even see her. She, she . . . she's not going to die?
AMBULANCEMAN: I don't know.
FEMALE DRIVER: Tracy. I'm sorry Tracy. What if she dies on the way? She's my best friend and I've killed her.

**680**
SUPER: THIS IS THE NUMBER OF BULLETS NEEDED TO WIPE OUT THE REMAINING BLACK RHINOS IN TANZANIA.
(SFX: 200 BULLETS FIRED IN SECONDS)
SUPER: SO YOU CAN SEE WHY WE DON'T HAVE MUCH TIME.
SUPER: WE NEED FUNDS AND EQUIPMENT. PLEASE WRITE TO THE FAITH FOUNDATION, FREEPOST 28, LONDON W1E 3AT.

Turn off your TV

and talk to your kids.

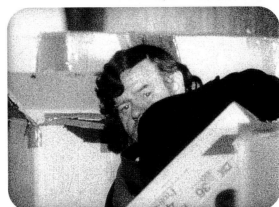

Partnership for a Drug-Free America

**681**
SUPER: NO TV COMMERCIAL IN THE WORLD . . .
SUPER: CAN KEEP YOUR KIDS OFF DRUGS.
SUPER: BUT YOU CAN. . .
SUPER: TURN OFF YOUR TV. . .
SUPER: AND TALK TO YOUR KIDS.
SUPER: PARTNERSHIP FOR A DRUG-FREE
   AMERICA.

**682**
SUPER: THERE ARE 300,000 HOMELESS IN BRITAIN.
(MUSIC: "THREE BABIES" BY SINEAD O'CONNOR)
SUPER: SOMETIMES THE NUMBER GOES DOWN.

**683**
WRITER
David Fowler
AGENCY PRODUCER
Dick Clark
CLIENT
Thomson Consumer Electronics
(RCA)
AGENCY
Ammirati & Puris/New York

**What the hell do we do with the dog?**

**683**
ANNCR: The following is a confidential assessment of one of the most pressing issues confronting RCA.
INTERVIEWER: Excuse me, do you recognize this animal?
ANNCR: By popular demand, Nipper has returned. And he's not alone. He's come back with a little attitude.
SUPER: RCA.

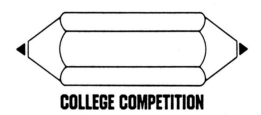

COLLEGE COMPETITION

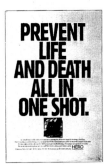

# And You Thought Advertising Could Only Save The Life Of A Product.

Thanks to advertising there are more people around to read this ad. From campaigns against substance abuse to promoting AIDS awareness, it has saved thousands of lives and prevented countless others from being destroyed.

Surprisingly, few people ever think of advertising as a useful means of communication. The popular misconception is that it's merely a method of selling things.

The next time you think of advertising keep in mind; it can't save the life of a bad product but it can save yours.

**ADVERTISING**
ONE OF THE MOST EFFECTIVE MEANS OF COMMUNICATION
American Association of Advertising Agencies

684

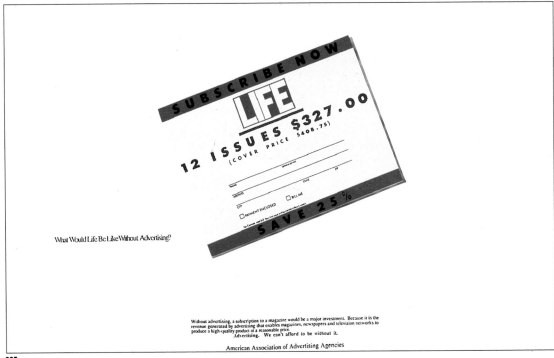

What Would Life Be Like Without Advertising?

Without advertising, a subscription to a magazine would be a major investment. Because it is the revenue generated by advertising that enables magazines, newspapers and television networks to produce a high-quality product at a reasonable price.
Advertising. We can't afford to be without it.

American Association of Advertising Agencies

685

# LIFE WITHOUT ADVERTISING WOULD BE A LOT SIMPLER.

In America, we take variety for granted. But if it weren't for advertising, there'd be a lot less to choose from.

It works like this. Advertising stimulates competition, producing new and better products at reasonable prices. And informs you about the products available, so you can compare them.

The United States has only 6% of the world's population, but 57% of the advertising. Which is why the average American supermarket offers more than 12,000 products. That's twice the number in any other country and 6 times the world average. Nearly 60% of all the new products introduced to the world in the last decade were developed in the United States.

Advertising does more than provide Americans with more products. It creates a mass market, bringing down costs for everyone. It puts money directly into our national economy. And it helps support our free press.

Without TV commercials, you'd pay for every TV show. And without ads, even this magazine could cost you up to $25.

The American way of life would be much simpler without advertising.

Because every ad you see represents another choice you have.

**ADVERTISING**
ANOTHER WORD FOR FREEDOM OF CHOICE.
American Association of Advertising Agencies

Who needs advertising anyway?

Through the years, advertising has not only raised important funds for some of our most needed public service organizations, it has raised public awareness and understanding as well. In other words, advertising has helped sell more than potato chips. It has helped sell people on the idea of making life a little better for everyone.

American Association of Advertising Agencies

**COLLEGE COMPETITION**
**ASSIGNMENT: AMERICAN ASSOCIATION OF ADVERTISING AGENCIES**

**688**
**ART DIRECTOR**
Eric Houseknecht
**WRITER**
Tom Miller
**COLLEGE**
University of Texas at Austin/Austin

**689**
**ART DIRECTOR/WRITER**
Paul Hirsch
**COLLEGE**
The Portfolio Center/Atlanta

**690**
**ART DIRECTOR**
John Barnard
**WRITER**
Scott Wild
**COLLEGE**
The Portfolio Center/Atlanta

CHILD ABUSE
DRUNK DRIVING
INCEST
ALCOHOLISM
RAPE
DRUG ABUSE
HUNGER

**JUST A FEW OF THE AMERICAN TRADITIONS ADVERTISING HELPED UNDERMINE LAST YEAR.**

Last year American advertisers spent millions of dollars attacking the above American traditions.

Who says advertising has no social value?

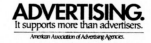

**ADVERTISING.**
It supports more than advertisers.
American Association of Advertising Agencies.

688

# WE DO A LOT OF ADVERTISING FOR THINGS NOBODY WANTS.

Last year over 350,000 people died of heart attacks.

While over 2 million people stood around and watched.

Learn CPR.

**HEART DISEASE**
*Young-Liggett-Stashower, Cleveland*

IF YOU'RE EMBARRASSED BY A PIMPLE TRY EXPLAINING THIS.

THE CHILDREN'S DEFENSE FUND

**TEENAGE PREGNANCY**
*Fallon McElligott, Minneapolis*

THE ONLY ALTERNATIVE IS NO SEX AT ALL.

*Carrying a condom with you, and using it properly, is one of the best defenses against AIDS. For more information, call the Minnesota AIDSLine at 870-0700.*

Anyone Can Get AIDS
Everyone Can Prevent It.

**AIDS**
*Grant Communications, Minneapolis*

This little piggy has arthritis.

United Way/CHAD
Community Campaign

**ARTHRITIS**
*Phillips-Ramsey, San Diego*

Each year advertising agencies contribute significant time and money to develop awareness campaigns for a variety of not-for-profit organizations. These advertisements may not save you money - but they may prevent you from getting something you don't want.

**ADVERTISING**
ANOTHER WORD FOR FREEDOM OF CHOICE

---

# Advertising has been putting ideas into people's heads for years.

"Before I'll ride with a drunk, I'll drive myself." *Stevie Wonder*

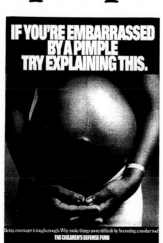

IF YOU'RE EMBARRASSED BY A PIMPLE TRY EXPLAINING THIS.

THE CHILDREN'S DEFENSE FUND

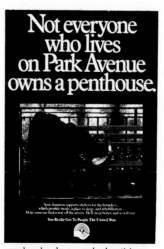

Not everyone who lives on Park Avenue owns a penthouse.

*Your donation supports shelters for the homeless, which provide meals, a place to sleep, and rehabilitation. Help someone find a way off the streets. He'll sleep better, and so will you.*

You Really Get To People The United Way

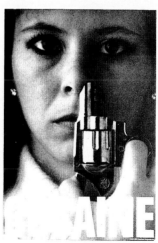

Advertising has put drunk drivers behind bars.
It's encouraged safe sex, convinced people to stop taking drugs, and generated millions of dollars for charity causes.
Every year thousands of public service ads are made for free by the same people who do general advertising.
These ads have contributed to the success of many great causes and have improved the lives of many people.
It's not only businesses that profit from advertising. It's everyone. **Advertising**
American Association of Advertising Agencies

INDEX

## WRITERS

## ILLUSTRATORS

## PHOTOGRAPHERS

## COLLEGES